W9-BTJ-934

HUMANS
BEING

B2430
534
M27

HUMANS BEING

BEING

The World of

JEAN-PAUL SARTRE

JOSEPH H. McMAHON

THE UNIVERSITY OF CHICAGO PRESS
Chicago and London

FEB 1 8 1974

180371

International Standard Book Number: 0-226-56100-3
Library of Congress Catalog Card Number: 74-127606

THE UNIVERSITY OF CHICAGO PRESS, CHICAGO 60637
THE UNIVERSITY OF CHICAGO PRESS, LTD., LONDON

© 1971 by Joseph H. McMahon
All rights reserved
Published 1971
Printed in the United States of America

For the Students
of Pierson College, 1961–1966.
And in memory of
Quincy Porter
who made my work with them
possible.

Contents

Because there are empty spaces,

we are able to use them.

— Lao-Tse

No one of us can save himself

alone; we must either be lost together

or get along together.

Take your choice.

— Huis-clos

Preface

I have attempted to present a text as unimpeded as possible by footnotes. Where they appear, they are intended to enlarge the immediate context of the discussion or to point to another work in which Sartre has offered a somewhat different perspective. Each chapter is followed by a note indicating, first, background information and observations which could not be easily fitted into the body of the text; second, other works which in my estimation may be usefully consulted by a reader seeking more detailed discussion of particular concepts or works; and, third, general indications of related discussions in other books by Sartre or Simone de Beauvoir.

Quotations have presented a problem, not simply because so much of Sartre's work has been translated into English, but also because there are multiple editions of his works in both languages. In the absence of a standard edition, I have had to make judgments and choices which may appear arbitrary; they result generally from the immediate availability of the text used. Quotations from the novels, plays, and the *Situations* volumes are all from the Gallimard editions of these works; the translations are mine. Because the renderings in Hazel Barnes' translation of *L'Etre et le Néant* and Bernard Frechtman's translation of *Saint-Genet, comédien et martyr* have supplied the English terms for Sartre's philosophical vocabulary, I have used quotations from these sources. I have also used the English translations of *La Transcendance de l'Ego* and the *Esquisse d'une théorie des émotions* because of their ready availability. In the case of other works, I have quoted and translated from the French edition which was most immediately accessible to the public at the time of the writing of this book. To avoid any confusion, the particular edition quoted is indicated by an asterisk in the bibliography.

The writing of this book was made possible by a year's leave of absence from Yale University during which I was the beneficiary of a Morse Fellowship. I wish to express gratitude to that program, which releases junior faculty members from their usual responsibilities and also provides the material and intellectual conditions which allow for reflection and the kind of work one hopes the reflection will produce. A research grant from Wesleyan University was of great help in defraying the costs of preparing the final manuscript.

I am also grateful to the late Mme Henri Petsche for the genial hospitality she offered me in Paris, and to Mrs. Hillard Hommel of the Haines Falls Free Library whose good cheer and efficient service made it possible for me to obtain books not in her library from other sources; her cooperation spared me all need to interrupt the peace of several summers in order to go in search of books.

Some acknowledgement is due to many members of my summer community. In moments when I was tending to become skeptical of Sartre's pessimistic discoveries and to believe he was given more to exaggeration than to exactitude, they faithfully demonstrated, by their fears and prejudices, their hobbles and hatreds, that the realities of which he writes often exist very close to my door.

J. H. McM.

Abbreviations

Materials cited frequently in the text are abbreviated in references as follows.

AR	*L'Age de raison*
BN	*Being and Nothingness*
CRD	*Critique de la raison dialectique*
Ego	*The Transcendence of the Ego*
Emotions	*The Emotions: Outline of a Theory*
FA	Simone de Beauvoir's *La Force de l'âge*
FC	Simone de Beauvoir's *La Force des choses*
Litt.	*Qu'est-ce que la littérature?*
Mort	*La Mort dans l'âme*
NRF	*Nouvelle Revue Française*
Sit.	*Situations I-VII*
TM	*Les Temps Modernes*
YFS	*Yale French Studies*

Unless otherwise indicated, words and sentences which appear in italics in quoted material reproduce emphases in the original texts.

HUMANS BEING

Our capacity for happiness depends on

a certain balance between what childhood denied us

and what it allowed us.

— "Merleau-Ponty"

1 *A Growing Hatred*

The shifting moods of Jean-Paul Sartre's autobiography, *Les Mots* (1964), persuade a critic that this work can serve better than any other as an introduction to the writer's world. The tone of the book is alternately irate, ironic, witty, cruel, reflective, and resigned as it conveys its author's belief that the child who is turned out by French bourgeois society becomes, more often than not, a grotesque man. Like all of Sartre's work, this book is a map; more particularly, it is a small segment from a vaster map, isolated in order to place the terrain in high relief with the hope of abetting the total reformation of society. In a significant way, the autobiographical fragment is also the capstone to his other works. Here he comes home again, equipped with all the techniques and the substantial wisdom he has acquired during long years of hard thinking, in order to tell us that the horrors of some homes deserve to be condemned except as sources for cautionary lessons.

Long before writing *Les Mots*, Sartre made it clear how little affection he held for the child he had been. His studies of Baudelaire, Genet, Tintoretto, and the long work he is writing on Flaubert had at least one thing in common. Each was concerned with the impact of the child's formation on what he eventually became and with the child's conscious awareness of the importance of those formative years to his later endeavors. From these studies, certain elements emerge. Sartre apparently agrees that the child has a basic predisposition to adhere to the norms of the surrounding society or, more specifically, and in some cases ruinously, to the governing class with which he is associated or to whose influence he is subjugated. The class is concurrently motivated by a desire to elicit the child's total allegiance to its mores and beliefs, however mutually contradictory they may be. The child's predisposition and the motivation of the class most often run afoul of each other and drive the child aground because the class does not have enough elasticity to allow for the specific differences the child may eventually discover between his inclinations and the class's institutionalized values.

But there is another element which is almost as important. What the class will tolerate may fail to make allowance, not only for irregular and possibly dangerous behavior, but also for the individual's normal and natural interest in his own growth and the changes it may produce. The governing class looks upon such spontaneity as a menace to its own solidity and durability. The class's predominant interest, then, defines a pattern of instruction that invites true allegiance by offering enticing rewards. Against the seductive but mysterious allure of rebellion, it offers the rewards paid for adhesion;

against active rebellion, it promises punishment.[1] In his biographical essays, Sartre has been concerned with individuals for whom the rewards did not quite work, or else he has chosen cases where the punishments meted out eventually boomeranged on the society.

More often than not the child either accedes to the greater wisdom of the class or capitulates to its solid power. Only those instances showing tension and some kind of eruption seem to interest Sartre; what concerns him most is the way in which the subsequent hostility of the governing class has been compensated for by the *révoltés* and the excluded. With Baudelaire—about whose life Sartre does not say much that is flattering; Baudelaire's art is another question—we have the example of an individual who discovers his liberty in a society where everything appears to have been labeled and then inserted into its destined slot. To profit from the liberty he has discovered, the young poet would have to set forth and explore new lands; that is an adventurous enterprise which, according to Sartre, the poet has no real will to undertake. His mission subsequently becomes the complicated and contradictory one of trying to establish his independence within the context of his class. He will become "the most irreplaceable being" (*Baudelaire*, p. 34). Instead of setting out on fresh explorations, he will decry the stale society in which he lives; but he will expect, as his reward for elegant insult, to be "consecrated" by the class. In other words, he ultimately will allow the class to win by allowing it to recognize and thereby justify the function he has exercised. Tintoretto offers us the example of an artist torn between his desire to be the favorite child of his native Venice and his realization that his particular genius is not likely to please the Venetians. Shrewdly, he finds a way out—a "way out" meaning a method of bridging the divide between him and them—by painting the subjects which please them, all the while using a painterly method which expresses the truth of his vision (see below, pp. 176–79). Flaubert is a similar and

---

1. Sartre's reaction to the events of May, 1968, in France, when generally bourgeois youth took to the streets and occupied public buildings in order to demonstrate their disillusion with their education and also their hope of forging an alliance with the working class, was predictable but also perplexing. He quickly associated himself with their cause and made sympathetic and admiring comments to and about Daniel Cohn-Bendit. What is perplexing is that Sartre did not exercise the same cautious hesitations about the real significance of those events as did other forces and individuals on the Left. Their caution stemmed from two beliefs: (1) that the workers were not about to associate their fortunes with the complaints of a group of *fils de papa*; (2) that the students, if they were sure of anything they were seeking, were only looking for the installation in the university of the ease and comfort they knew at home. The motives behind the outburst had more complicated and elusive elements, to be sure. One guesses that Sartre's initial enthusiasm was born from his hope that France was on the verge of one of those moments of high historical temperature which can change the destiny and direction of a people. One notes with interest Claude Lévi-Strauss's evaluation of the result of those heated weeks: "Since May, 1968, all objectivity has been repudiated. The position of the youth corresponded to that . . . of Sartre" (*New York Times*, 31 December 1969).

yet different case; he is the man who sought in his writing to give an honest and thereby bleak and unflattering picture of his class. Yet, when the chips were down—they fell, in Sartre's view, during the Commune—he took refuge in his class. The esthete, having squandered his class's values in his "sordid" books, abruptly followed the prodigal son's path home, there to seek forgiveness. The class, having earlier been vexed to the point of condemning one of his books, had the pleasure of winning in the end, though it may not have been conscious of its victory.[2]

In the case of the young Genet, the class identified the child as a thief, remanded him to corrective discipline in a reformatory, and, as a result, turned him into a criminal. Here the authority of the class wins out, too—at least initially. The child, hearing himself defined as a thief, decides or agrees that that is what he must be. Only through a long process, a process never fully independent of what he has learned from the class which condemned him, does Genet break away from this iron collar and achieve an existence authentically his own. In the process, he becomes a lesson to all of us (see below, pp. 289–304).

What occurred in the lives of these men underscores a tension no one of them resolved easily, because the tension was between two contradictory forces. One force was the effort of a class to achieve that solidity I have already alluded to—a solidity which fights against disturbers out of fear that they may become earthshakers who will topple carefully engineered structures. To stave off such shattering events, the class fights to preserve its immobility through a process of conversion which does not fully accord with the lived experience of the individual. For, whatever may be the attractions of immobility, the calm unworried massiveness of objects, *man* is no object. The class will tempt him to become one by discouraging him from any enterprise which may raise doubts about the class's right to be satisfied with its norms and ways. In short—and here I am simplifying—the class will seek to divert him from the dynamism of existing as a subject and into the safe security of generally passive being; in classical terms, it will try to make him all act and no potency, in the hope that he whose sole act is to be one with the class will be too busy with that capital task to engage in any dis-

---

2. Sartre sees Flaubert as a man so thoroughly imprisoned in his class as to be almost incapable of escaping from it. A crucial element in this imprisonment is Flaubert's confused and unhappy relationship to his parents who rejected him, not by an outright act, but by paying greater attention to his older brother whom they then proposed as the model Gustave should imitate. Gustave's project became that of escaping from this situation by seeking to become another kind of model: the man who knows the truth and announces it steadily despite (or perhaps because of) its dreariness. The trouble with the project was that, based on individualism, it was thwarted by social developments—the slow and limited rise of the working class, for example—which unsettled him considerably more than had the inattentions of his parents or the banalities of his own class; it thus drove him to his prison because the prison, more solid than the emerging forces, was the only bastion of resistance available to him.

tracting and possibly destructive activities. The class, in its godliness, seeks
to discourage all upstarts who want to place other gods before it.

In its effort the class is collectively reacting to the worst individual experience all members of the broader class, man, have undergone. The class is
trying to come to terms with another inherently contradictory force: human
freedom and the fear unleashed by that freedom in the individual and in
the class. Through its institutions the class tries to control and influence
man's discovery that he is free and therefore haunted with a sense of purpose in a universe which seems purposeless. That universe utters no wisdom;
it issues no pronouncements as it follows out its as yet unfathomable ways.
What Sartre claims in *Les Mots*, and had claimed in all his writings prior
to the *Critique de la raison dialectique*, is that such individual conversions to
the ways of the middle class are not made simply because the attractive
force is irresistible. The conversions are made because the individual
chooses to make them. He makes them for a number of reasons, the most
important of which is that he chooses to abdicate his liberty in order to
associate with the solidity offered him by the structures and values of the
class. He may do this either by invoking the invincible power of the class
or by acknowledging the sweet reasonableness of its position. In either case,
he fails to escape from the burden Sartre places on all men:

> Who shall decide whether that mystic crisis in my fifteenth year
> "was" a pure accident of puberty or, on the contrary, the first sign
> of a future conversion? I myself, according to whether I shall
> decide—at twenty years of age, at thirty years—to be converted.
> The project of conversion by a single stroke confers on the adoles-
> cent crisis the value of a premonition which I had not taken seri-
> ously. Who shall decide whether the period I spent in prison after
> a theft was fruitful or deplorable? I—according to whether I give
> up stealing or become hardened (*BN*, p. 498).

Examining crises and conversions which took place long before adolescence
set in, Sartre shows in *Les Mots* that such vital decisions are indeed made
with full awareness of the goals to be achieved; they are made either by
moving beyond or choosing to ignore contrary and equally authoritative
information. The book also seeks to give further fulfilment to the promise
Sartre had made in *Qu'est-ce que la littérature?* In the part of that long
essay entitled "Pour qui écrit-on?" he had recognized that radical affirmations
of total human freedom, no matter how rigorously they correlated with
objective truth, could only at their peril ignore the deep-reaching influences
of educational patterns and class persuasions. "The writer," he said, "knows
that he speaks in the name of free men who have been engulfed, muffled,
and shunted aside; he knows, too, that his own freedom is not all that pure;

it needs to be brushed up; he writes in order to brush it up" (*Sit. II*, p. 116).

Les Mots is his personal recital of a common experience. It was not written for reasons of nostalgia, to weep over a better world which has been lost, to seek to recreate past joys from the midst of present tears. It was written to express and to condemn the way in which Sartre was formed. The autobiography thus serves as evidence for a process Sartre has defined in *Being and Nothingness*: ". . . the Past is my contingent and gratuitous bond with the world and with myself inasmuch as I consistently live it as a total renunciation" (p. 141). The extensions of that statement are clear: the past, and the terms it has established for my existence, *could* be lived as my contract with the world, a contract to whose terms I must be faithful as a man of honor; but that is not what the past *is* nor does it represent any meaningful statement about the present. The past is a threat; the past is a siren voice which calls me back from the nearby reefs I must negotiate if I wish to be, not an honorable man, but an honest one. The underlying irony is that, though I may derive pleasure from hearing the siren's song, I cannot answer it. I still must cross those reefs because they are the surfaces of the future.

Bourgeois man—and that label has deep and precise meaning for Sartre—does not believe this. For him, the remote past was a time of troubles subsequently vanquished and annihilated by his forebears in the near past; Sartre's grandfather used to sum up the past by assuring the boy that since the kings had been driven away everything was all right. Since everything was now all right, the past which the present was in the process of creating should not be subjected to any turbulence at all; for the past, from the time everything had begun to be all right, must be preserved. Why should any enlightened youth want to drill holes in well-made, stabilized ships and expose the voyagers to needless dangers? The bourgeoisie's interests demand that the child accept complacency instead of challenge, rights instead of requests, privileges instead of freedom; everything is already properly arranged, the structure is in good order. The bourgeoisie aims at producing *l'homme moyen sensuel*, the man of measure who will join the company of the right-thinking and who will limit his disorders to respectable sins. What it succeeds in producing is a monster. The monster, however, is not one of colossal dimensions; he does not bestride and therefore tower over the world. Rather, as one of the characters in *La Mort dans l'âme* says, he is an abortion, a grotesque version of what he might have been had he been allowed to grow fully and honestly. The bourgeoisie, according to Sartre, has not only cheerfully vowed itself to the production of monsters, it has also become a monster itself. "An anti-communist is a dog; that is what I hold; that is what I will always hold" (*Sit. IV*, p. 248). "I vowed a hatred of the bourgeoisie which will end only with me" (p. 249).

When considered in conjunction with the essay on Merleau-Ponty from which I have just quoted, *Les Mots* becomes an even more appropriate starting point for an investigation of Sartre's career. It is his version of how he moved from a fairly normal, generally happy middle-class childhood into the troubled and shifting ideological battleground he has frequented as an adult. It is also a statement of what his career as a writer means and has meant to him; and it is an examination of the way in which the governing forces he had described in the lives of his fictional characters sought to work their will on him during his formative years. Despite its gentle ironies and many charms, it is frequently an angry book whose anger has been tempered, not by age, but by the long habit of obduracy in observation and analysis which led to Sartre's declaration of undeviating hatred for his class.

Sartre's one specific effort at explaining his free growth in a constricting environment is based on his claim that, as a half-orphan, he had no super-ego. (His father died in 1907 when Sartre was two years old.) A reader is not quite sure how seriously to take this, primarily because Sartre has only recently allotted any unarguable importance to Freud; in the past he had frequently dismissed the whole Freudian effort because of the critical place it gives to the operations of the subconscious as a determining force within the individual. Yet, seen against other works, *Les Mots* reveals a number of crucial forces which, once set free to operate, conveyed Sartre to the philosophical and ideological positions he now holds.

The method he uses in the book is one he identified in *Saint Genet* and the *Critique de la raison dialectique* as a combination of Marxist and existentialist outlooks. The Marxist point of view sees every individual situated in a dialectical relationship with himself and his environment. In his day-to-day existence he is aware of broad social forces which influence and shape him. An inevitable abrasiveness results from the individual's confrontations with himself and his environment. Since every individual experiences such encounters, Marxism offers the only available method capable of analyzing the experience in a universal context, for it insists that all individual human behavior must be seen against the background of the movement of history. The existentialist point of view projects the elements of individual experience against the narrower background of the use the individual has made of his specific faculties. Existentialist biographical methods are based on a concern with the individual as a particular being, shaped in a particular context; the individual's total makeup is best explained by thorough examination of that context. This is a perspective Marxism does not supply, because it sees men *sub specie aeternitatis*—eternity in the Marxist vocabulary being, not heaven, but history or, more essentially, the march of economic forces. What *Les Mots* does in explaining Sartre's social childhood, the Merleau-Ponty essay does in explaining what we might call his political infancy. Together, the two form a reliable portrait of the man.

With the departing kings went all the problems. What remained was a tidy social order which echoed harmoniously the music of distant but amiable spheres, turning gracefully with them in a dance designed to please the God who, in the next world, gave the just whatever rewards they had missed in this one. Providence would eventually compensate the discontented for the few moments of terrestrial cacaphony they had endured. The just possessed this earth; if they managed it well, if they preserved its schematic order, and if they periodically indulged in generosity, they would possess the kingdom of heaven, too. The postmonarchical world was not only the best of possible worlds, it was the best world imaginable; no sane person would wish to change it fundamentally. Progress was its guiding force. Everything would get better in due time if the managers, who were aware of what was needed, were allowed the time and means to produce further achievement. They would heal old wounds and, if no one interfered with them, they would create no new ones. These were the ideas Sartre imbibed as a child.

They are also ideas which have been part of the Western tradition for over two thousand years. A whole vocabulary, mythology, and system of ethics had evolved along with these ideas to give them an impressive cohesiveness. The cohesiveness explains why a class of men should want to hold tenaciously to such ideas: the world view they established was useful, and usefulness should not be mindlessly derogated. The world view also explained away mysteries or else incorporated them into higher designs; it shaped the universe into sense; it offered enticing promises to the man who accepted its terms and, more or less, respected its restrictions in order to have its structures. It was based on the belief that this world is either a manifestation, shadowy and not easily apprehended, or an emanation, orderly and purposeful, created by a Being whose feelings towards men were basically friendly. Man's role was the relatively simple one of integrating himself into the process by recognizing its truth. Furthermore, by agreeing to become part of the process, he spared himself the pain of having to devise one of his own. In a world created benevolently and explained sensibly, his only task was to exist as a cooperative subject.

What Sartre, very much under the influence of Heidegger, finds wrong with this world view is its manufactured inauthenticity. It has been fabricated over the centuries, not on the basis of direct observation of the world or as the result of attention to individual psychological experience, but rather by spinning out and complicating a number of a priori ideas. What that long experience has produced is a detailed description of the mechanisms of the universe elaborated within the context of an ontology which has more to do with metaphysical systems and their preservation than with accurate descriptions of what men really and repeatedly experience. It is a world view whose presupposition is that one can readily apply methods used for the scientific description of the universe's operations to descriptions of human reality. From this has come the notion that human reality has a similarly stable context. But stability has very little to do with human reality, especially with human reality as it is encountered by individual men. It may also have very little to do with the universe.

Pascal had seen this and given a vivid description of man's consequent panic. And yet Pascal was and remains a pertinent example of what is wrong with this world view, for Pascal, even though he accepted the idea of an ordered world, sustained by a benevolent and communicative deity, experienced the terror which the lonely man feels once he realizes how immense and apparently purposeful the world is. His initial reaction is to decide that it is no friend of his because, in its grandeur, it is vastly more impressive than he in his misery. In brief, what many Western philosophers have usually argued for is a systematized description of the universe; they have not, in Sartre's view, paid adequate attention to man's disquiet when he is confronted, at first, with the direct experience of the universe and, later, with those systematic descriptions. Neither one consoles him because neither one—especially when the latter has lost its affinity with a credible theology—seems to allow him a sufficiently important and reassuring place. Obviously, any system which does not pay proper and major attention to this reaction is a system which is describing an operation quite different from human reality. The major thrust of Western philosophy has been part of an attempt to direct man away from his own immediate evidence—for terror before the universe is a common experience—in order to encourage him to live within a system which is at best inadequate and at worst deliberately dishonest. But obviously, too, the fact that the explanation has been accepted with some frequency indicates that, true or false, honest or dishonest, it has one major advantage. Like the tidy world of the bourgeoisie, it solaces man even though it may not completely absorb all of his terror.

Kindness may indeed be the virtue which inspires men to help other men turn away from the sources of terror; but the kindness exacts a steep price— the sacrifice of truth. The terror, rather than the compensatory system, remains the locus of truth. To turn from the terror in order to seek refuge in the system is to turn away from the truth with no guarantee that the terror will not recur. (Systems are made with words and, as we shall see, words must reflect reality before they can aspire to change it.) Heidegger, arguing for ultimately greater rewards, will suggest, and Sartre, arguing the need for honesty, will demand that the confrontation take place, not because it is necessarily a happy experience but because it is an inevitable one. The philosophical activity of both men will, in great measure, be the effort to convince other men that a frank living-out of the encounter is in their own best interests.

The German philosopher takes a fundamentally cheerful view which latterly has been expressed in meditations on poets as exemplars of man's conversation with Being and the world. Poetry has become a major prop for Heidegger's belief that man should see the world as a light which is given to him so that he may understand; language is the tool by which he tries to understand. What man has to understand is that existence is fundamentally this: his presence in the world, his possession of language, and the consequent possibility that by using language he can establish a true and productive lifelong encounter with the world.

With more rigor, less poetry, and fewer promises of comfort, Sartre generally agrees with this basic description, at least to the extent that the description defines human reality as man's presence in and to the world. Heidegger, contemplating the world and anticipating the light it will emit, is not unlike Shakespeare's Antony contemplating Egypt's queen; with enthusiasm he can say, here is my space. Sartre does not at all deny that the world is man's space. What he questions is the possibility of being enthusiastic about a potentially tragic fact. Man's disquietude before the universe, if it does not always preclude his enthusiasm, gravely weakens that enthusiasm because his experience of the universe is one of objects external to and possibly hostile towards him. This discovery leads him to the recognition that the apparent serenity of objects is thoroughly distinct from the troubled reaction that serenity creates within his consciousness. For consciousness is not an object; consciousness is no fixed star. Consciousness relentlessly interrogates a universe which, if it holds any answers to human dilemmas, is keeping them to itself. Heidegger recurrently insists that this discovery does not by its nature have to be a troubling one; rather it should be looked upon as an exciting experience.

There was a moment, in his essay on Husserl (1939), when Sartre shared this sense of excitement; his later experience, while it has not cooled his excitement at the prospect of change, has made him realize that whatever banquet the invitation has convoked him to has not yet had a date fixed for its celebration. Here we see what has probably become the fundamental distinction between Heidegger and Sartre. Heidegger has spent his philosophical career meditating on the fundamental relationship between man and the world; his later works have been examinations of literary texts in which he sees this fundamental experience either incarnated or described. Sartre's career has been more and more concerned with the obstacles that stand in man's way, obstacles that are as numerous as they are weighty, obstacles which might be described as social reality's effort to keep human reality from working out the consequences of its freedom. And so the two men have gone separate ways, Heidegger condemning what Sartre has done to his basic thought, Sartre more and more ignoring Heidegger; Heidegger going deeper and deeper into the exposition of his philosophy of letting go to the world, Sartre moving further and further into his unshakeable conviction of the need to have a firmer and franker hold on the world so that men can make it respond to their needs. They dare not let go, he believes, before they have a sharper idea of what they are holding on to or, more significantly, what has been holding on to them with the undeclared intention of holding them back.

Seen within the framework of these considerations, *Les Mots* is the history of a consciousness coming to life in the world; it is also an attempt to show the obstacles, engineered by a specific social reality, that consciousness has encountered. Precisely because it was drawing unawares to its end, *la belle époque*, Sartre suggests, was a bad period in which to be born. Bad, not in the sense that the end was near, but rather in the sense that the period was at the apogee of its self-contentment and thus could easily persuade a youngster of the rectitude of its ways. Its pampered and privileged denizens saw the world through rose-colored glasses, unsuspecting of how quickly that tint would turn to red. The governing class was happy, well-fed, and safe in the assurance that the world was going swimmingly; the horizon remained bright, and therefore the luminous future of their children was assured. But theirs was a false world; their political optimism was soon to be destroyed by war and their moral optimism eroded by the aftermath of that disillusioning conflict.

In the case of Sartre, the erosion began with his awareness of the irrelevance of such ideas to the real world. If the ideas gave off any light, they did so in order to blind a youngster to deeper, more stubborn realities. His family had fine sentiments and used language prodigally to talk about those sentiments. But their language was unfaithful to the basic function of language because they used it, not to speak truth, but to express *their* truth; they confidently assumed that there was no other. They assumed this because their language was meant to justify and praise a social system which automatically presupposed that there could be no better one. As a result this language was a dead loss, because it lacked precision and was not supported by a will to describe the true situation of the world. The richness of the language lay in its ability to wrap the real world in a doomed optimism. Though his family and his peers never realized this, their language was a defensive system created to sustain bourgeois values and, fatally, to hide the threats being organized against those values.[3]

3. Sartre has repeatedly asserted that their attitudes led the bourgeoisie to the conviction that the French language, as they used it, was their especial property and at the same time the French language expressed at its purest level. That conviction has an authoritative appeal for the children of the class since its assures them that the novelties they are discovering have been approved: "In effect everything is a novelty for the child; but this novelty has already been seen, named, and classified by others; every object

The language offered such protection at a dangerous price; it described a reality, a field of being, which did not correspond to the whole field of being. It offered a comforting system whose comfort could only be seen as long as one did not remove the rose-tinted spectacles. More dangerously, it offered a final supporting explanation in which its users no longer believed:

> Decent society believed in God in order not to have to talk about Him. . . . In our milieu, and in my family, the Faith was a slogan word for mellow French freedom; like so many others I had been baptized in order that my independence might be preserved. If they had refused to baptize me, they would have feared doing violence to my soul; as a registered Catholic, I was free, I was normal. . . . I was driven to nonbelief, not by any conflict with dogma, but by my grandparents' indifference (*Les Mots*, pp. 80, 81–82).

What we see here is a double loss—the loss of concern with fundamental reality and the loss of meaningful involvement with the myth of a friendly God. In the beginning there is God; and in the end, too, when against the ravages of death men need reassurance. In the middle, there is the bourgeoisie deciding what it will sanction and what it will condemn.

One of the major concerns of the bourgeoisie is the education of its children. They must be made to appreciate the reality into which they have been born so that they will continue it. They must be made to see that the world is grateful that they have come into it and asks only that the children return the gratitude. On its own terms, this is a perfectly reasonable exchange, but the economy which supports it is twice defective: first, because it is only a section of the total economy; secondly, because, as a partial economy, it does not spare the child the disquieting experiences which are the lot of all men. The bourgeoisie is a monad which will not look out on other monads. It has closed all the windows; unfortunately, it has forgotten or been unable to bolt them. As a result, the curious child one day pushes up one or several of them and is terrified by what he sees:

> I lived in terror, undergoing a genuine neurosis. If I search out the reasons for it, it comes to this: because I was a spoiled child and Providence's gift, my profound uselessness was all the more manifest to me when I realized that family ritual had constantly to be hammered out. I felt I was surplus and thus I had to disappear. I was a dull brightness perpetually subject to being abolished. In

he encounters already bears a label; it is magnificently reassuring and sacred because the eyes of grown-ups still linger on it. Far from exploring unknown regions, the child thumbs through an album, he browses through an herb book; he is the owner making a tour of his property" (*Baudelaire*, p. 64).

other words, I was condemned; from one second to the next, the sentence might be carried out. Still I rejected it with all my power, not because my existence meant a great deal to me but, on the contrary, because I did not hold very much to it: as life becomes more absurd, death becomes less bearable.

God would have pulled me out of such pain. I would have been a signed masterpiece; assured of having a part in the universal concert, I would have waited patiently for Him to reveal His design and my necessity. I sounded out religion, placed hopes in it: it was the remedy. Had it been denied me, I would have invented it on my own. But it wasn't denied to me: raised as a Catholic, I learned that the Almighty had created me for His glory: that was more than I had dared dream. But later, in the fashionable God I had been taught about, I no longer recognized the being who was waiting for my soul. I needed a Creator and was given a Big Boss; the two were identical, but I didn't know that. I was serving with fervor the False God and the official doctrine took away my taste for looking for my own faith (*Les Mots*, pp. 78–79).

This is the reaction the existentialists call *geworfen*, the feeling of having been dropped into a world in which one is surplus being or, in Sartre's own term, *de trop*. It unleashes a chain reaction whose three major links are shame before the world, the unsettling recognition of the Other, and subsequent alienation from the Other and from the world. "Shame is the feeling of an original fall . . . that I have 'fallen' into the world in the midst of things and that I need the mediation of the Other in order to be what I am" (*BN*, pp. 288–89). The Other is the person or the group which is already functioning in the world when I discover it. In order to pick oneself up from the original fall, one turns to the Other because the Other appears to be the only available mediator, the only way back to a sense of integrality. Yet the Other, though his mediation may be accepted for a while, and in some cases permanently, frustrates my freedom. (We shall see presently an example of this in the young Sartre's awareness that he was only as free as his family wished him to be.) I discover a world that is "already looked-at, furrowed, explored, worked over in all its meanings, and whose very contexture is already defined by these investigations" (*BN*, p. 520).

The worked-over world only emphasizes my gratuitousness. I am not needed. The fact of my freedom, though it does not tell me I am needed, does tell me that "to be free is not to choose the historic world in which one arises—which would have no meaning—but to choose [myself] in the world whatever this may be" (*BN*, p. 521). I have a dilemma. What should I make of myself in a world that does not need me? I also have a task: to respond to the pulses and impulses of my freedom. The degree to which the dilemma paralyzes me is the degree to which I capitulate or fight. This experience of discovery may involve something as commonplace as the child's realization that others do not wish to play with him; something with such various effects as the awareness that there is no God who will eventually reward us for our sufferings; something as immobilizing as the uneasy sense that there is nothing at all. Reactions to these experiences may run the range from becoming a bully, to replacing God, to committing suicide.[4]

This basic experience, as Sartre describes it in his autobiography, followed on a period during which he looked upon himself as the Gift kindly presented to his family and affably received by them. The question of who had given the gift was not one to be examined too closely as long as the young Sartre was aware that he was not only the Gift but also the Giver who carefully selected the acts and gestures which would prolong his family's pleasure in his existence. The passage of time and closer observation of his family's ways slowly showed him, however, that he was able to be the Gift and the Giver only because of his family's willingness to indulge his belief. Instead of being esssential and self-justifying, he was an impostor who depended on his family's approbation in order to be assured of his merits. And he could win that approbation on a permanent basis only by accepting the stability of their world. That was the price demanded before they would allow him title to the rights which would define precisely the nature of his presence in the world.

His insecure status, Sartre claims, was further accentuated by the fact that his father died when Sartre was an infant. The result of this was that he had no paternal legacy to cope with, no property to inherit, no counsels to heed, no future goods which would properly fall to him, and, as we have noted, no domestic representative of the superego. He could not claim, as might the son of the local tavern-keeper, "When my father's not here, I'm the boss" (*Les Mots*, p. 70). Though he did not suffer particularly from this condition, he remained withdrawn from its implications. "The goods the property owner possesses reflect what he is; they taught me what I wasn't. *I was not* all of a piece or permanent; *I was not* destined to carry on my

4. If shame is the fall, pride is what may come after it as the most efficacious response to the experience of shame. That pride is efficacious does not mean that it is desirable strategy even though its dynamism may be a better starting point towards something other than the static passivity of shame. Sartre writes: "Pride does not exclude original shame. In fact, it is on the ground of fundamental shame or shame of being that pride is built. It is an ambiguous feeling. In pride, I recognize the Other as the subject through whom my being gets its object-state, but I recognize as well that I myself am also responsible for my object-ness. I emphasize my responsibility and I assume it. In one sense therefore pride is at first resignation; in order to be proud of *being that*, I must of necessity first resign myself to *being only that*" (*BN*, p. 290).

father's work; *I was not* necessary to steel production. In a word, I had no soul" (p. 71).[5]

Religion might have served as a buffer against that final discovery by assuring the child that he did indeed own a soul. But we have seen how his family's indifference to religion deprived him of that consolation. His task consequently became that of finding some way of fighting against the powerful sense of being condemned which possessed him; his struggle became that of trying to find some reason to want to live. Had he been able to believe in eternal life, he would have found a way forward and a reason to keep moving ahead. But that possibility had already evaporated under the slow but steady heat of indifference. The only other way left open was to find some device by which he could make himself indispensable to the universe. The books he read, and in which he had discovered the rich fertility of imagination, made him believe words could succeed where actions had failed.

He would become a creator. In his imagination he would recast the fairy tales he had read in such a way as to find a place for himself in them; he would thereby impose himself on the whole creation. His presence would become so vital that, were he not present at the ceremonies conducted in that surrogate world, his absence would quickly be noticed. Once someone said "Sartre isn't here," it would be obvious to the others that the unoccupied space was Sartre's, his rightful patch of the universe. He would be justified. This tactic ceased to be efficacious once the child realized that, by *imposing* himself on the creation he had discovered in others' books, he was clearly showing that he was not its creator; the literary creation predated him quite as much as the cosmological and with the same consequences. He was not "justified" as were the heroes of Jules Verne's books from the very moment they appeared in the story. It was not enough to have pushed his way into this already existing world. Pushing his way in did not make him elect; rather it was only additional evidence of the fact that he was *not* one of the elect. He had already become an impostor in the world of his family where he lived with the hope of giving constant pleasure; he was now also an impostor in the world of his own imagination which he had

5. Subsequently, in his introduction to Georges Michel's *La Promenade du dimanche* (1967), Sartre reinforces the suggestion that this is a valuable, because productive, experience: "The only character in the play who still knows the anguish of being born, who questions himself a bit about the meaning of his existence is the child; he has not had the time to learn his lesson; his parents, already trained animals, do what they can to help him forget himself. They are already making inroads; not the least of our uneasiness is the spectacle of this young kid, still debating with himself, falling prey to commonplaces. If it is God who has loaned him a life, then he will become like the adults—the passive prop to those impersonal and negative relations of everyone with everyone. At each moment, a particular event takes hold of and disturbs him; at each moment, his father or his mother teaches him how to go along with it by supplying a proverb or a fine stereotyped banality" (p. 8).

created as his haven from a hostile social world. In both worlds, he was using lies in order to come to grips with his lack of justification.

Since he could not become Michel Strogoff—because Strogoff emerged already justified in Jules Verne's already created fictional world—he chose to become a writer, creating through his words a world in which he would figure prominently. But his early writing also turned on a lie. Through it, he sought to transmit an idea from his mind to the page, where it was supposed to create reality: "I was pretending to be an actor who was pretending to be a hero" (*Les Mots*, p. 117). In short, he was using words as though they contained the quintessence of reality. He found some justification for this in plagiarism; by stealing others' words, he had the impression that he was giving a true report because he was not inventing anything. But he was neither using words as they should be used nor reporting truths of any merit. Rather he was manipulating words and contemplating a writer's career as means of repelling truth. Literature would allow him to escape; it would be his refuge from life. But it would also allow him to live: if he were read, he would be needed, he would have his place; if he were not read, he would be the writer-martyr, stoutly pursuing his work, bolstered only by the certain knowledge that, in time, celebrity would come either to him or to his books. In writing he would find the mandate and the place he lacked. He would save the world through literature.[6] His class had hoped to save it through other, possibly equally fictional, devices.

Some readers may find a needless solemnity in Sartre's way of recollecting experiences which, when set off properly against the world of childhood, are charming before they are catastrophic. Most children live for a time with imaginary friends; they dream of rescuing the distressed and of achieving a celebrity cut to the measure of their exaggerated ambitions. Recollections like *Les Mots*, which place such commonplace experiences under a sinister light, appear to make much ado about nothing very consequential. Sartre disagrees, and his disagreement is not that of the sexagenarian who wants to recast his life so that it will be all of a piece. His disagreement has to do with his belief that such experiences, no matter how ordinary and even fetching they may be, eventually become a way of seeing the world. The child gradually learns either that there are no damsels in distress or else that any damsel needing help will probably be suspicious before she is thankful

6. Sartre describes Flaubert's similar project: "For the young author, poetry is a mental attitude; it is a process for getting away from reality . . . which usually manifests itself as a defensive reaction: pursued by reality, the child escapes into the imaginary. The undertaking is like a mystical levitation. And Gustave made no mistake about it, as his description of mysticism shows: 'I would willingly be a mystic; there must be fine voluptuous sensations produced by believing in paradise, by drowning oneself in waves of incense, by annihilating oneself at the foot of the Cross, by taking refuge under the wings of the dove. . . . I would like to die a martyr's death there' " ("Flaubert: du poète à l'Artiste," *TM* 22 [1966]: 211).

for the kind of aid he might proffer. He learns, too, that dreams of childhood have little to do with the duties of maturity; learning this, he does not necessarily abandon the perceptual habits he has picked up from his original encounters with the world.

In his autobiography, Sartre is not making any late-in-life effort to adjust the facts of his childhood to the theories of his maturity. From the point of view of ideas and theories, there is nothing new in *Les Mots*; what is novel is the specific application of these ideas to the details of Sartre's early life. All the major observations and categories of interpretation can be found elsewhere in his writings. In this sense, *Les Mots*, especially when compared to the Flaubert study, adds nothing to Sartre's philosophy; it does, however, reveal certain critical experiences in his life that produced the conditions from which the philosopher and his philosophy developed. The book's title alludes to the tools Sartre has used throughout his life, both in reading and writing. It also contains implicit questions. What do we *mean* by words? What place do they play in our discovery of the world? What do we do with them once we have discovered what we believe is the real world? The subdivisions of the book—"Lire" and "Ecrire"—isolate two ways in which we live with and use words. The concept underlying the choice of the book's title and subtitles is Sartre's observation that "having discovered the world through language, [I] assumed for a long time that language was the world" (p. 151).

This is where a fundamental but tempting misapprehension, both of the function of language and the nature of the world, begins. If the language through which one discovers the world is defective, and if the systems devised through use of that language are incomplete or ultimately impertinent, then both the language and the systems—philosophical as well as social systems—will be defective and will produce additional unfortunate consequences. The primary and secondary consequences will always be perilous. Where words themselves are concerned, there is the immediate danger of assuming that they, as individual units of speech, identify a meaningful reality and, in that sense, *are* reality. Sartre will insist—and claim the support of unidentified psychologists—that the word is no more than a proposition, a proposition whose terms are not clear until it is placed in a sentence. But the sentence does not confer any specific reality on any single word since the sentence does not enable the word to identify a fixed and thereby immutable reality. The sentence serves to identify a context which explains what is meant by the word; it thus enables the word to function. Whether a corresponding reality comes into operation as a result is a question demanding further analysis.

Words are not necessarily interchangeable with the things or issues they refer to; certainly, they are not those things and issues. Despite this, there remains a persistent tendency among men to make such a confusion and to believe that in manipulating words they are manipulating reality. While that is a possibility, and in some places a program, it is not a necessary one. The desire to consider it inevitable is born from the use men wish to make of language. Sartre writes: "To understand the word in the light of the sentence *is very exactly* to understand any given in the light of the situation and to understand the situation in the light of the original ends" (*BN*, p. 515). What this means is that we cannot apprehend the intention of language as it is used by an individual or a class unless concurrently we understand the aims and goals of that individual or class. The use of language by the individual or the class is a free use behind which is a definite if not openly articulated intention. But the individual or the class may want, for reasons which are usually explained by self-interest, to believe that "speech is *a language which speaks all by itself*" (*BN*, p. 516). The reason for wanting to do this is clear. If language speaks itself, then what I say is what has to be said. By investing language with independent authority, by implying that what is said is true because it has been said, I am making an appeal to language, as the higher authority, to validate my utterance and the project it asserts or dissimulates.

Language, as a series of sounds I am able to emit and eventually to adjust to the sounds others make, has no invariable meaning, certainly no innate authority. Nor does the class in its utterances. Language achieves meaning only when I want to organize the sounds in order to convey something. Yet what I want to convey is not necessarily contained in the sounds; it is also contained in my intention, that is, in the signs I wish to create from my use of the sounds. And my intention may be hidden, degraded, and contaminated. The intention is fundamentally conditioned by two concurrent influences. The one is my discovery of the world as a space, inhabited by others who use a language that seems to obey laws, which does not necessarily allow room for me. The other is the discovery of two basic ways of dealing with that world. Sartre has at different times labeled these two methods in varying ways. In *L'Esquisse d'une théorie des émotions* (1939), they were called the emotional and the instrumental. In his later book, *L'Imaginaire* (1940), they were called the imaginary and the perceptual. The intentional situation each refers to has not been altered. The emotional/imaginary way is compensatory: the use of magic, of forms of withdrawal or spurious self-imposition, in order to deal with the world in my terms rather than its. The instrumental/perceptual way is the recognition that my perception of the world is a fact and that the fact, at the very moment that I discover the world, reveals certain instrumental techniques I can employ in dealing with the world. Gradually, if not immediately, I discover that one of those techniques is the emotional: the possibility of withdrawing from direct perceptual contact with the world by electing to apprehend it through the imagination. An extreme example of this process would be that of the paranoiac who, seeing me smile warmly at him, concludes *from my smile*, that I wish to do him harm.

This kind of faulty interpretation is the danger that comes with reading. Not only do books represent a portrait of the world at second remove, they also tend to blunt the individual's understanding of the need to encounter the world directly. In this sense a social class can be considered an equally faulty text. The act of reading, especially in the case of the child, is passive; having absorbed what he has read, the child tends to identify it with reality. He is not thereby removed from reality, since the daily needs of his existence bring him into constant contact with it. But if the greater challenges of that contact displease him, he can escape from them by using a technique learned from reading—the technique adopted by the young Sartre when, retreating from his lived reality, he attempted to insert himself into the imaginary world he had discovered in books. This is a more comfortable because a more supple world. "From his bed, the very young child works on the world through commands and prayers. Objects obey these commands of his consciousness, they appear" (*L'Imaginaire*, p. 239). They appear, however, as the result of an incantatory process which is employed precisely because its initiator is unwilling, for one reason or another, to come to terms with the difficulties he encounters in his direct perception of the world. The process, if it readily produces the effect sought, can easily replace the perceptual process, or place such a low compensatory value on that process, as to make its operations appear less effective than those of the imagination or the emotions.

When it does not achieve such easy success, imaginative functioning will be obliged to come to terms with its failure. One way of doing this would be to recognize the inadequacy of the imaginary as a means of achieving a significant grasp of the world; another would be to go even further in exploiting the imagination. In short, when disappointment with immersion in the world of already created words develops, one tries to create one's own world. The latter was the way chosen by the young Sartre. Once he became aware of the difficulties of making himself part of the world of Jules Verne, he decided to create his own world with borrowed words. The world he manufactured was at three removes from the real world because the bases on which it was created were those discovered in the books he had read and not in the world in which he was living. It is evident, of course, that the real world remained the catalyst for both compensatory efforts.

What Sartre is showing is that the movement from reading to writing was a movement from one level of passivity to another. By "passivity" I am alluding to a secondary activity designed to replace that primary activity which accompanies an open and knowing confrontation with the world. The intention—the desire to be justified *somehow*—is indeed active; but the realization of the intention depends upon withdrawal. The child subtracts himself from the world using whatever means are available to him.[7] This withdrawal is something freely done and with a specific purpose in mind. Though its inspiration is emotional, it remains an instrumental use of language and clearly shows the poverty of all claims that seek to give language an independent authority. Language, for Sartre, is nothing but what we make of it; and what we make of it—that is, *the uses we put it to*—shows why it cannot reliably be said to express human reality. What can be said more reliably is that it expresses individual or class attitudes towards that reality. Language is technique before it is truth; because it is technique, it may never be truth.

I have outlined above how much it was technique and how little it was truth for the young Sartre; he was using it as a rapier with which to fend off a known truth he chose not to deal with on terms other than his own. The technique, language, can be used to express truth; but it can also be used as the vehicle by which I reach my own ends. In Sartre's case, this was the creation of a world in which he would be important. Yet, once truth is subjected to such usage, it loses its meaning for all men or even for a group of men; it becomes a process of self-assertion which operates with the intention of deluding others. In making language my own, I do not incorporate myself into it; rather I make language obey me precisely by refusing to examine the ramifications of the reasons why I use it as I do.

Sartre's earliest intention was to make a world in which he would matter and then present that world to others so that they would discover and appreciate the universe in which he mattered. In a way, the intention was parallel to and modeled on that of the class which produced him; it, too, had a language of its own, elaborated in order to show the rectitude of its view of the world. What Sartre intended to offer the world, as his claim to justification, was no more than an altered reflection of what he had perceived in his own class.

Neither the shrewd use of words nor his class's fatuous belief in its own unthreatened permanence could forestall the arrival of World War I. The imagination could not dispel either the constant friction of school life or the incidental but not inconsequential cruelties which crop up in children's

7. Sartre has always actively defended a theory of consciousness which describes two modes of operation within consciousness. One is spontaneous and unreflective—the direct encounter between the individual and experience; this can, of course, be so imbued with firmly held attitudes as to color the encounter in hues which degrade reality—for example, the bigot's reaction to the group he scorns. The other is reflective—the moment of thinking back or meditation on already encountered experience. While the latter mode can produce good results—for example, Descartes' *cogito*, which can only emerge as theory after the experience has been had and analyzed—it can also be used to defend the kind of withdrawal into literature that Sartre is discussing here. To write false books, one must be resolutely active; still, the desire to expend one's energies in order to write false books results from fear of reality and produces a method—not unlike Flaubert's—whose activity is undertaken in order to preserve the passivity that has grown up in the aftermath of the original fear.

games. The passage of time relentlessly stripped away literary pretensions to show that literature was neither a means of salvation nor the privileged unaffected locus of metaphysical happenings which were to be admired in direct proportion to their inability to change anything. The world, Sartre learned, was not prepared to move to or even to hear truths enunciated by writers. These encounters and discoveries gradually brought him to another idea of writing which he details towards the end of the book.

The discoveries gave him what he considers a humbler, more sober, and therefore more realistic notion of writing's real value. Against his original notion of imposing himself on the world through literature, he now sees the act of writing as one term in a dialectical process, the other term of which is the act of reading. Intelligent reading is not passive; quite as much as writing, it is an act. Literature has no meaning unless it involves a dialectical give-and-take between the writer and the reader, each of whom has as his referent the world that he can perceive, the *real* world which literature does not ever convey either purely or totally. In his book the writer struggles to establish a perspective on that world which the reader then accepts or rejects or modifies. The reader's attitude must be based, of course, not on whether he likes that world, but on whether he is convinced that it is the world he, too, has perceived. There are many promontories from which to see the world. Literature is only one of them, and its worth depends on whether the world it sees is the real world or an imaginary one.[8] We have seen what profit the child drew from gaining a whole imaginary world as compensation against the discovery that he had no soul and therefore no distinct and defined purpose.

What happens when that compensatory world is lost and when the imagination is exposed to the shakiness of the structures it has erected is the story of Sartre's career. He has not sought to regain possession of the soul he lost; he has tried to live in a physical world which strikes him as being indifferent to individual men and in a social world which is frequently hostile to some men and, in some situations, to most men. Important stages of his adult career are described in the essay, "Merleau-Ponty" (*Sit. IV*, pp. 189–286), that Sartre wrote for the memorial issue (1961) *Les Temps Modernes* published in honor of the deceased philosopher. When read in connection with *Les Mots*, this moving and searching essay demonstrates that the experience of *geworfen*—the individual's sense of having been tossed into a world which has no acceptable function to assign him—is crucial to life because it recurs with unpredictable frequency. One does not overcome it once and for all. The experience keeps coming back or the individual keeps encountering it or finding its traces; with each recurrence

8. In *Litt.* Sartre writes: "Bourgeois art will stick to the mean or simply will not be; it will forbid itself to touch at principles for fear that they will crumble and to sound too deep into the human heart for fear of finding disorder" (p. 157).

the meaning of an individual life is brought once more into question. The world shows little interest in letting us be what we want to be; privileged social classes share that apparent indifference to individual wishes but for quite different reasons. What is important in both instances is that each reminds the individual with varying frequency that, if he is not totally alienated from his environment, neither is he totally integrated into it.

This recurrent phenomenon of a sense of difference, intimately accompanied by a sense of possible union, is well explained in a passage from Merleau-Ponty's *Phénoménologie de la perception*: "I am the absolute source. My existence is not derived from my antecedents, from my physical and social environment, but reaches out and sustains them, since it is I who give being for myself (being in the only sense which this word can have for me) to the tradition I choose to carry on on the horizon whose distance from me would collapse were I not there to view it, since distance is not a property of that horizon." [9] Merleau-Ponty is here describing an encounter which is central to his thought: the individual brings an organization to perceived events and realities—genuine or surrogate—in the sense that he describes them or reacts to them. But his description or reaction is also the result of a personal organization or orientation which he has assumed. The individual does not escape from the event; but, in a way, the event does not escape from the individual either.

In his early career, Sartre, very much under the influence of Husserl's phenomenology and his own belief in the *total* freedom of the individual at every moment, had tended to describe man as a force capable of abstracting himself from events. Man looked at events; he chose his reaction to them; he compared this reaction with the available referents; then he acted. In each of these steps he showed that he was a free agent rather than an incapacitated victim. The event, and especially the sweep of events, was rarely examined in all its force, grandeur, and horror. The event, no matter how apparently overwhelming, was always looked upon by Sartre as a challenge which could be met freely. *Les Mots* offers a good example of this by showing us how a child, reacting in a variety of ways to a multiplicity of events, finally came to see honestly what his potential was in and against the world. Until its final ruminating pages, the autobiography traces out a process of development which stressed the individual's power to avoid being overwhelmed; he could choose either to capitulate to the stronger social class or to seek refuge in dishonest solutions.

What Sartre observed in the later years which are not fully covered in *Les Mots* was this: though the individual might save himself (in the sense of living authentically with the psychological entity he is), he in no way guaranteed that social reality would also be saved. In saving himself, the

---

9. *Phénoménologie de la perception* (Paris, 1945), pp. ii–iii. I am using the translation of Joseph P. Fell in his *Emotion in the Thought of Sartre*, p. 6.

individual risked losing the world because his salvation took place outside
the world's history and with little or no concern for the world's destiny. By
this I mean that an individual could exist [10] his life without affecting any
course of events broader than that influenced by his own existence. Having
done so, he could congratulate himself on the purity of his motives and the
success of his efforts; but he could not congratulate himself for having
changed anything.

Sartre and Merleau-Ponty encountered World War II carrying similar
baggage from the past. Both had had essentially the same kind of happy,
secure childhood. (Merleau-Ponty never ceased to appreciate his and to
look upon it as exemplary of a certain agreeable mode of existence.) Both
had been educated in the same system and had studied at the prestigious
Ecole Normale Supérieure; both had been professors of philosophy whose
primary orientation was the outlook they had derived from the phenomenological method; both had stood outside history and the passage of
events, not in order to escape from them, but in order to see them better
and thereby define with greater precision man's role in meeting them.

Sartre, as I have said, apparently gave little thought to the possibility that
events had independent and determinant power. Merleau-Ponty had long
been concerned with the event's autonomous force. The war gave him an
immediate and undeniable example of the event's independence from the
influence of individual men. As a result, he was better prepared to meet it
than was Sartre. With the outbreak of hostilities Sartre discovered that
immediacy and that power of history which had long been among Merleau-
Ponty's central preoccupations. The war surrounded Sartre as a phenomenon from which he could not get away; abstract evaluations of its
meaning were no more than bitter manifestations of the broad gap between
language and reality. An event had occurred which flooded consciousness
so fully that consciousness could survive only by coming to terms with the
onrush. What he discovered was an element which had been unacknowl-
edged during a childhood colored heavily with a firm belief in the inevitability of progress and the certainty of further enlightenment. That missing
element was the reality of violence employed on a massive scale in order
to attain ends which had nothing at all to do with *his* progress. Convinced
that their comfort was solid and unassailable, his mentors had taught him
that he and they would never need to elect the strategies of violence.
Violence would come from *other* quarters and, by virtue of its alien origins,
would be unmistakably evil. It would therefore be promptly defeated. In

10. Sartre uses *exist* as a transitive verb, a usage his various translators have, with
good reason, respected. One exists one's life, one does not simply endure it, for, in
enduring it, one chooses that form of resignation as the mode of one's existence. Later
in his career, Sartre admits that there are at work on the individual powerful conditioning influences whose force may be so great as to be insurmountable. Those influences explain why a man may erroneously believe that he is not free.

the meantime, the knowing would keep the motors of progress whirring; individuals would learn that their ideals were sure armor against the assault of isolated events; during the infrequent periods of trouble they would put on the comforting mantle of the stoic.

Sartre's encounter with violence provoked the realization that some events must be met directly, sometimes with brutality. Man's freedom, at crucial moments, depended on his willingness to fight dubious battles with no assurance of victory. Sartre was discovering an abyss between his philosophy and social reality which reproduced the abyss he had discovered as a child between his aspirations and the real world's operations. "There is a sweep of events," the mature Sartre wrote, "which cracks the dam of individualism" (*Sit. IV*, p. 217).

He had come across the situation described in the passage quoted above from Merleau-Ponty and had discovered *praxis*. Praxis, in the simplest description, is the reaction produced by the encounter between an individual and an event; in Sartre's thinking it is, however—and this is essential—a reaction which looks to the future. "The event," he wrote, "makes us by becoming an action; that action undoes us because, by our intervention, it becomes an event. This is what we call . . . *praxis*" (*Sit. IV*, p. 217).[11] This dual involvement—where the event influences men and produces a reaction by which a man prolongs and becomes directly involved in the event—seriously reduces the reality of *total* individual freedom. Sartre's previous reflections had underscored the ways in which a man reacted to what had been done to him. Implicitly, Sartre suggested that a man's reactions and exterior events were ultimately discontinuous; the ocean wave which sweeps over me withdraws, if I resist it properly, without carrying me away. It influences but does not determine my behavior, especially if I have prepared myself for encounters with waves by learning how to swim or, less actively, to float. But there are waves more powerful than any I had anticipated, as there are situations which defy my talent at using words; they pick me up and involve me in moments I cannot ignore and am unable to describe adequately. I emerge from them fundamentally changed and frequently redirected. The event, by humbling me, reshapes me.

The apparently unending waves of conflict—the struggles between

11. Praxis is closely related to Sartre's idea of consciousness as intentional. The intentionality of consciousness means, in crude terms, that consciousness is always up to something; frequently what it is up to is related to patterns of self-deception, self-congratulation, or self-protection; when these concerns are the motor forces, consciousness seeks to escape from genuine praxis by invoking determining influences it cannot overcome or by nourishing projects created in bad faith. We shall see numerous examples of such inauthentic projects during the course of this book; and we shall also see, in chapter 11, how praxis, honestly undertaken and carefully nurtured, can still produce events whose massive consequences seem to give those events an existence of their own and a force which far surpasses man's ability to cope with them.

nations as well as those between individuals and classes—made Sartre realize that there were philosophical shores more perilous than those he had been roaming. Discrete changes become visible in his models. His basic concern, however, is more modified than changed. Henceforth, he will be concerned not only with how a man reacts to what he is; he will be equally concerned with how he reacts to what he himself has done. A man can break with the bourgeoisie by saying that he will not capitulate to their demands in order to have their rewards, that he will not undo what he is for the small privileges they offer. He cannot *subsequently* refuse to live with the consequences of this decision and still hope to be considered a rational or even a consistent being. If a man freely decides to have children, he must come to terms with the reduction in his freedom brought about by the responsibilities he should assume for their care and upbringing.

In the years before the war Sartre had lived far from this kind of concern because he had lived with the notion that the direction of his life and the movement of political and social reality were on two different planes. During and after the war the dam of his individualism was more than cracked; it was threatened with total destruction. Some of the resultant rubble and even more of his new vision went into constructing the new dam which was to be *Les Temps Modernes*, the distinguished journal of provocative opinion he founded with Merleau-Ponty and others. Its establishment was the visible sign of Sartre's conviction that the man of letters must be involved in politics since politics is directly related to and expressive of the sweep of events which is the movement of social reality. Its establishment represented a new outlook or, more exactly, the refinement of a former outlook; its articles would be the loci where language and reality encountered each other unabashedly. Its publication over the years has sharply reflected a subsequent dilemma—Sartre prefers to call it an ambiguity—that arises in the confrontation between individual and event: can there be a victor? Must there be a victim?

The most important element in the refinement of the original outlook was the realization that there are times when a man cannot react effectively simply by removing himself from his class and rising above it; he must revolt, not necessarily against his class, but also against whatever other class may keep him or others in bondage. Unlike individualism, revolution is not, Sartre writes, a state of the soul. It is a daily exercise whose working out shows that there are events which have an existence quite their own. They grow and develop and thus appear to shape history. In coming to grips with the revolutionary mood of the postwar period in Europe, Sartre was deflecting his existentialist methods from descriptions of the mechanisms and possibilities of individual existence towards the area of what he calls human collectivities. It would no longer be a question in his thought of *human beings* who have only to be made aware of the autonomy of their consciousness and of their total possession of freedom of action in order to live authentically; it would henceforth be a question of *humans being*, in the midst of a social reality where they are buffetted and sometimes beaten by the sweep of events which they have to dominate if they are not to be defeated and, in that bad bargain, deprived of being at all.

The establishment of *Les Temps Modernes* was Sartre's plunge into the waters of history; it produced eddies of irony and ambiguity. He had been encouraged to take the plunge by what he had learned from Merleau-Ponty; once in the water, he had to watch as Merleau-Ponty withdrew to the shore because of his growing conviction that involvement blurred vision: the intellectual *needed* to stay out of the current in order that there might be some observer who could try to maintain the balance between initial passion and consequent achievement. Sartre was not unaware that he himself was moving farther and farther away from detachment, sacrificing the pleasures of "objectivity" to the imperious necessity of being where the struggle was. He has not—as I hope the later chapters of this book will show—been blind to the tensions and the difficulties in the struggle or to the uncertainty of the outcome. In a moving description of the reasons why Merleau-Ponty withdrew from involvement, he shows us how acute his own awareness is: "[History] wears out the men she uses and kills them under her as though they were horses. She chooses the actors and transforms them, right to the marrow of their bones, by the role she imposes on them; then, at the slightest change, she dismisses them and takes on others who are completely fresh" (*Sit. IV*, p. 242).

Sartre accepted the risk, inspired no doubt by that stout and resilient optimism he possesses—or by which he is possessed. He decided to "live the adventure out, to accept the sentence under which we live, to execute it, to institute it" (ibid, p. 253). The irony and the ambiguity embodied in the relations between him and Merleau-Ponty have persisted, however; the individual and the event, dialectically involved, are not, because of that intimacy, necessarily at ease with each other. Merleau-Ponty, who began by emphasizing the event, ended by emphasizing the individual set off against but not necessarily opposing history; Sartre, beginning with an emphasis on individual freedom, ends by accentuating the event, the single moment carried along in the all-embracing tides of history. He does not thereby undo his original emphasis; rather he carries it ahead to the point where individual freedom must be seen as it is conditioned by history and as it conditions history. It is indeed an adventure; but, as we shall see, it produces more anguish than euphoria. History wears men out, not only by riding them too hard but also by forcing them frequently to their knees before she dismisses them. One of Sartre's most admirable traits is that he has risen from each fall more hardened than hurt.

RELATED THEMES AND WORKS

Neither Sartre nor Simone de Beauvoir, though each was an educator for many years, discusses the educational process as it is carried on in schools and universities. In her memoirs, Mme de Beauvoir describes her and Sartre's attitudes towards their teaching: they liked it, they enjoyed the association with young people, they tried to upset the preconceived attitudes and prefixed values of their students without expecting or meeting much success. They thus struggled against class attitudes brought into the schools from the youngsters' homes; they apparently did not fight against the undemocratic structure of the French educational system or agitate for any curricular reform. Mme de Beauvoir was fired from a Paris lycée late in the war on a trumped-up charge of corrupting youth, presumably by trying to teach them to think. Sartre resigned from a similar position before the end of the war because of the demands of his other careers. In several of his socio-political essays he has discussed the need for educating the working class; the education he refers to has little to do, however, with school education and very much to do with processes designed to make the worker an active and therefore effective member of the proletariat. There are, as a result, inconsistencies in his attitude, for he seems to spare the workers two experiences others do not escape so easily from. One exception appears to be somewhat gratuitous: the worker does not appear to be as psychologically ruined by his class as is the product of the bourgeoisie; he is, of course, most often paralyzed by his economic servility. The other is perplexing: the worker does not seem to be allowed any mobility as a result of education; Sartre will not allow him to become a doctor or a professor—only a militant. That may be the result of the closed structures of French education; it may also result from the fact that Sartre cannot see individual workers because his gaze is fixed on the proletariat solely as a unit which can ultimately be forged into a weapon.

Sartre describes his childhood in his interview with Madeleine Chapsal (*Les Ecrivains en personne*, 1960, pp. 205–33) and in a more recent interview in the issue of *Livres de France*, devoted to him (17:1 [1966]) in fairly much the same terms as those used in *Les Mots*. The same period is briefly discussed by Colette Audry, a personal friend, in her excellent "Connaissance de Sartre" (1955) and by Beigbeder in his *L'Homme Sartre* (1947) where Beigbeder sifts some of Sartre's fundamental attitudes through a Freudian sieve. His childhood is more lengthily discussed in close connection with his major themes and in relation to his fictional characters in Francis Jeanson's brilliant and beautifully argued *Sartre par lui-même* (1955, rev. ed. 1961). Jeanson's book is probably the most faithful and the most complete short work which deals with Sartre's thought as an expression of deep personal experience. A further perspective on this kind of approach can be obtained from D. W. Winnicott's *The Maturational Processes and the Facilitating Environment* (see especially the chapter, "Ego Distortion in Terms of True and False Self") (New York, 1965) which, though not devoted expressly to Sartre, does treat the question of family influence on the child who shows or develops creative promise. Sartre's essay on Giacometti, "La Recherche de l'absolu" (*Sit. III*, p. 289–305) applies his ideas on *geworfen* to a different and more mature situation and comes up with conclusions similar to those in *Les Mots* and "Merleau-Ponty."

His biographical studies of Baudelaire, Tintoretto, Genet, and Flaubert are listed in the general bibliography. The manuscript of a fairly substantial fragment of a work on Mallarmé was lost; the preface to the Mallarmé poems (*Poésies*, 1966) is no replacement. His preoccupation with Mallarmé recurs in scattered fashion throughout his work. The most elaborate statement of his biographical method is presented in the *CRD* (pp. 89–103) where the disorganized periodic remarks on technique found in *SG* are shaped into a system. Roger Blin in an intelligently argued article in *Fontaine* (April 1949, pp. 3–17; May 1949, pp. 200–16) opposed Sartre's treatment of Baudelaire as being based on Sartre's terms rather than on Baudelaire's reality.

In the philosophic works published prior to *BN*, Sartre makes frequent references to Husserl. At first these references are full of admiration; later they are shadowed with hesitations and objections and corrections. Heidegger's name and his vocabulary stud *BN*, but in later works, when Heidegger is mentioned, the citations are usually for purposes of disagreement or rejection. Mme de Beauvoir discusses Sartre's opinion of Heidegger in *FA*, p. 364.

Sartre's views on language can be separated into several phases. The first is reflected in his early critical essays, collected in *Sit. I*, where he is concerned with the uses and abuses of language and where he gives vent to his conviction that his generation of French writers inherited an especially corrupt language and thus a fundamental problem in attempting to talk meaningfully about their experience of reality. The second phase is his analytic discussion of language in *BN* (pp. 514–31) as one of the techniques men must freely acquire for their own use and also as the faculty which conditions their relations with other men. The third phase follows from the other two and is concerned with the social functioning and purpose of literature. This phase receives passionate and eloquent expression in *Litt*. The final and current phase is a three-pronged pitchfork and serves somewhat the same purpose. It is offensive: Sartre attacks an emergent mode of literature, the antinovel, of which he immediately disapproves because it is indifferent to the most immediate problems of men (see the Chapsal interview and Beauvoir, *FC*, pp. 52–54, 291 [on Nathalie Sarraute], 648–49 [on the nouveau roman]). It is defensive: Sartre is explaining himself against critics like Lévi-Strauss, Foucault, and Lacan. It is probing and analytic: Sartre is adjusting his ideas on language to the terms of the *CRD*.

The defensive and analytic operations are conducted in two complementary interviews: "L'Ecrivain et sa langue" (*Revue de l'Esthétique*, 3–4 [1965]: 306–334) and "Jean-Paul Sartre répond" (*L'Arc, 30* [1966]: 87–96). In the first interview he discusses his own various uses of language—literary, philosophical, and polemical—and language as a possible manifestation of a dynamic principle gone stagnant which he calls the "practico-inert"; in the second he continues the preoccupations of the first but places more stress on his theory as opposed to others'. In the same issue of *L'Arc* (pp. 65–70), Jean-Jacques Brochier offers a lucid explanation of Sartre's theory and defends it reasonably against a bright, argumentative, and not very careful attack, Jean-Pierre Faye's "Sartre et les Huns" (*Lettres Françaises*, 1122: 10 March 1966). Faye develops his arguments further in "Sartre, entend-il Sartre?" (*Tel Quel*, 27 [1966]: 72–81).

Sartre's studies of literary figures are replete with language theory and reflect, according to the date of their original publications, the current stage of his thought. Frederic Jameson's *Sartre: The Origins of a Style* (1961) is an intelligent and provocative examination of Sartre's own use of language conducted from the general point of view of Roland Barthes's method. A reliable and clear presentation of Merleau-Ponty's thought on perception and its relationship to language can be found in Philip E. Lewis' "Merleau-Ponty and the Phenomenology of Language" (*YFS* 36–37 [1966]: 19–40). Georges Darien's *La Belle France* (written in 1900; reprinted by J.-J. Pauvert, 1966) is a remarkable reinforcement from another period and from a different point of view of Sartre's description and evaluation both of *la belle époque* and the bourgeoisie.

Every book aims at a concrete liberation

from a specific alienation.

— Qu'est-ce que la littérature?

2 Choices of Being

In his 1939 essay on Husserl's notion of intentionality, Sartre wrote enthusiastically: "It is not by any kind of withdrawal that we will discover ourselves; rather it is on the road, in the city, in the midst of the crowd—a thing among things, a man among men" (*Sit. I*, pp. 34–35). Those sentiments were expressed a year after the publication of *La Nausée;* their mood, with its suggestion of a great reservoir of energetic commitment which would serve to sustain involvement with others, is quite different from the sentiments we find in the novel which first brought Sartre the promise of fame and lasting misunderstanding of his purposes. By its very title, which was suggested by the publisher, *La Nausée* was likely to create confusion and the caricature which is one of confusion's readier by-products. It is the kind of title which sticks in the mind and becomes like flypaper, attracting all of Sartre's other ideas and miring them. Among journalists and that part of the public which needs only one idea in order to organize elusive complexity into ready nonsense, the title has become the central discription of Sartre's thought: his is a philosophy of sickness, and, as a convenient consequence to those who like convenience, it is a sick philosophy.

This is a fundamental error, for to consider *La Nausée* as Sartre's fixed statement on the meaning of life is to misunderstand thoroughly the intention of the work. There is no doubt that the book is the result of a personal experience, though there is every doubt that the experience was precisely the same for Sartre as it is for Roquentin, the novel's protagonist. Sartre's colleague on *Les Temps Modernes*, Colette Audry, tells us that "he lived out *La Nausée* in Le Havre [where he was teaching philosophy] before writing the book. He had lived it out really, in anguish, as though suffering from an illness . . ." (*Connaissance de Sartre*, p. 13). Sartre himself in *Les Mots* tells us that Antoine Roquentin was an expression of what he, Sartre, was at the time of writing the novel. And Francis Jeanson quotes Sartre as saying: "For a long time I searched after the Absolute—right up to the time when I wrote *La Nausée*" (*Sartre par lui-même*, p. 175).

Sartre, however, had felt other influences and lived through other experiences which find no place in *La Nausée* and which thus justify my claim that the total experience of Roquentin is not the total experience of his creator. The novel was a major preoccupation during the late 1930s. Those were the years in which Sartre was discovering Husserl and Heidegger, during which he was teaching and traveling and mulling over the concepts that were to find expression in the several essays he published prior to *Being and Nothingness*. They were years of intellectual ferment, years given over to troubled and troublesome thought. *La Nausée*, however, is not the record of victory over those troubles. Though the novel does not record a triumph for its protagonist, it does represent a kind of liberation for Sartre.

The 1930s, finally, were the years in which Sartre was reading and commenting on the novels of Dos Passos and Faulkner, works which were to exercise a major influence on his own literary techniques. What he found original and admirable in Dos Passos' work was a method which went beyond the omniscient techniques of the traditional psychological novel. In Dos Passos' novels, the writer was not the great overseer and manipulator who pulled the strings which made his characters move and then explained both why they had moved that way and the consequences which would result from their motions. In Dos Passos' books "the game is not already up; the fictional character is free. The game takes place right under our eyes; our impatience, our ignorance, our expectation are the hero's. . . . Time in Dos Passos is the author's creation . . . or, better, it is the time of History" (*Sit. I*, p. 16). The most striking result of this technique for Sartre was that it demanded the reader's involvement: "This consciousness which speaks in the novel comes into existence only through me; without me there would only be black marks on white pages. But even as I *am* that collective consciousness, I want to tear myself away from it, look upon it with the viewpoint of a judge; in other words, I want to tear myself away from myself. This is what explains that shame and that uneasiness which Dos Passos imposes so shrewdly on his reader . . ." (p. 22).

Sartre will seek the same effect in *La Nausée*; he will resist being the omniscient overseer, preferring to let the experience described in the book come to life as both the experience of Roquentin and the experience of the reader. The novel will be a blossoming flower which conceals an exploding bomb. If it is seen as the flower, the reader will probably have a reaction; if it is experienced as the bomb, the reader necessarily will have a reaction. Sartre adroitly seeks a method which will put the reader to work at the task of understanding the full meaning of the experience being related. The latter's consciousness will have to apprehend what is happening and, having apprehended it, come to terms with whatever is discovered or demolished. The author's aim is to impose his book on the reader, not as an argument designed to persuade him, but as part of a dialogue in which the reader, if he is intelligent and knows what he is doing when he reads, must participate. In the case of *La Nausée*, that participation is inevitable if the reader has the slightest amount of human curiosity, for the book begins and ends with puzzles.

Sartre presents the novel as a journal found among Roquentin's papers, thereby suggesting that the protagonist is either dead or resolutely mute. The latter is not very probable since at the end of his journal, Roquentin announces that he intends to write a book which will "be as beautiful and as hard as steel and which will make people ashamed of their existence"

(p. 222). That book was intended to be his response to the crises he had been through; since it is not written—need it be, since the journal exists?—the reader is left with the task of deciding what such a book might be like and whether any book could provide either solution or response to the questions raised by Roquentin's crisis. The journal, then, has to do with some form of death. Though we do not know all the details, we do know the general nature of the death: it is a suicide, not in the sense that the protagonist has put a pistol to his head, but, more pertinently, in the sense that he has put some questions to his mind and been forced to decide that the person he was or had tried to be must now take into account the vast force of reality. It is precisely because *La Nausée* is an invitation to a form of suicide that it must be seen as the beginning of Sartre's thought and not its home port; it is the point of departure which, with the passage of time, has been left so far behind as to make a return journey difficult. The book is about the death of a certain kind of consciousness.

Though its author was at the time unknown to the public, the novel was an unexpected success with critics and readers. One wonders why, since it is not the kind of book which cheers the reader up; its lack of happy messages has more often than not been interpreted as the sure sign that no happy messages can ever come from Sartre. I suspect the initial admiration for it was the result of appreciation of its style and confusion about its meaning. As sympathetic a reader as Camus thought it was ultimately a failure because its underlying theory betrayed life by presupposing that "because life is miserable it is tragic"; with keen instinct for future fulfillment of present promise, Camus looked forward to the author's later works which he was sure would build more solid structures on this wobbly foundation.[1] The confusion may well have stemmed partially from the confusion of the times; Roquentin's initial belief in a universe of swarming masses whose movement only showed its indifference and hostility to men may have had unconscious appeal to a French public menaced by war. The confusion may also have stemmed from the kind of superficial reading which produces wrong conclusions. A reader could feel sorry for Roquentin, that poor mixed-up chap who, rejecting all the sure values of life, was bound to find himself in such a state; or the reader could assert, as some distinguished critics have done, that Roquentin's story is interesting as the portrayal of an individual crisis but that it has little to do with common experience and less to do with the operations of common sense. Sartre's claim, I think, is the contrary; not only does the book have to do with common experience, it also has to do with a common and fatally wrong mode of consciousness. If the story holds no

1. Camus's review of *La Nausée* was published in the newspaper *L'Alger Républicain*, 20 October 1938. Camus observed: "To take note of the absurdity of life cannot be an end but only a beginning."

immediate appeal for common sense that is probably because common sense, though it has eyes to open, does not have the will to keep them open at all times, in all situations.

Such attitudes echo ironically the quotation from Céline chosen as the epigraph for the novel: "He's a lad without collective importance and barely an individual." The epigraph is dense with allusions. It appears to define Roquentin's social situation accurately, for he is in the process of separating himself from social reality even as he wonders what it means to be an individual. Taken more broadly, the epigraph also refers to the significance of this situation. Apparently what it means for Sartre is that this individual, who has no importance to social reality and only slightly more to himself, is not the exception, but the rule; he is the commonplace rather than the rare individual. In another one of his essays, Sartre quotes the same phrase again and claims that it refers to "natural man, i.e., to the isolated man, the individual . . ." (*Sit. I*, pp. 131–32). He further claims that any litera-ture which wishes to be concerned with reality must be concerned with this man because he or, more accurately, his situation of doubt and questioning exposes us to the whole disturbing question of what man is for. Is he for himself? Or is he for the collectivity? And what happens to him if, in order to have any sense of being at all, he must be for either the collectivity of people or the collectivity of things and thus, by implication, must exist against himself? *La Nausée* will not answer these questions completely; it is, however, written against the background they furnish and it aims at clearing away just enough debris to allow us to see what it means to discover oneself as an individual.

The title helps us to understand much of the complex interaction in the book. In Latin the word referred to seasickness, to an indisposition pro-voked by movement and to the resulting discomfort, which lasted as long as the movement continued. The indisposition, though felt only by the individual, comes to him from an outside force. And it is important to remember that the feeling of nausea may or may not produce actual vomit-ing. The threat of having to vomit produces a heavy sense of disgust and squeamishness which is caused by a number of factors. Though it comes from us, vomit repels us. It stinks. Its disagreeable mixture of solid and liquid elements is unsettling; the vomit does not seem to know what it wants to be. That indecision suggests a comment upon us and an explanation of why we have vomited or of why we fear that we shall have to vomit: there are elements in the world we cannot safely consume, movements we cannot endure. Though we expel what we cannot digest, we are still left with the obligation of cleaning up the resultant odorous mess. When nausea is in-duced within us by an outside force like the sea, it gives us a disquieting experience with the limits of our freedom. The sea surrounds us and con-trols us right to the depths of our guts. It will not tell us when it will let us go. Because of this uncertainty, the experience of nausea also creates fear. Once it has occurred, the nausea can recur and may accompany us either frequently or constantly throughout the voyage; while it is with us, we will not be free agents, benefiting from the full use of our faculties.[2]

Antoine Roquentin's journal is the logbook of such a voyage; it is begun only after the feeling of nausea is upon him, with the result that we see his past under the light projected by his present experience. He is a young man of independent but limited means who has come to Bouville in order to write the biography of a supposed early nineteenth-century nobleman, M. de Rollebon, whose papers are in the local library. He lives in almost total solitude, communicating only with Ogier P.—identified throughout the book as the Autodidact—and the *patronne* of the local bistro. The first contact is involuntary, for the Autodidact practically imposes himself on the young scholar; the second results from a sexual necessity which is convenienced by the *patronne's* preference for daily variety in bedmates. Roquentin has only his work with which to occupy his mind, and, as the book opens, he is beginning to be bored with it: "I have the impression of doing work which is purely imaginary" (p. 27). There is some irony in his statement since his personal speculations are, for the most part, purely imaginary, too, and raise the question of what connection there is between reality and his modes of thinking.

He initially experiences the nausea as something which comes to him from outside, slowly insinuates itself into him, and then takes possession of him. It is a quality he first espies in things and whose presence compels him to look away from them.[3] It is impossible, however, to avoid things; he is in constant contact with them and comes to believe that they make him take hold of them in a way *they* determine. Nausea slips away from the things in order to stick to him: "[That sickly sweet disgust] came from the pebble, I'm sure of that, it came into my hands from the pebble. Yes, that's it, that's certainly it: a kind of nausea in the hands" (p. 23).[4] This confirms his earlier impression that he is no longer free and that the curtailment of his freedom is

2. In *BN* Sartre writes: "The perpetual apprehension on the part of my for-itself of an *insipid* taste which I cannot place, which accompanies me even in my efforts to get away from it, and which is my taste—this is what we have described elsewhere under the name of *Nausea*. A dull and inescapable nausea perpetually reveals my body to my consciousness" (p. 338).

3. Cf. *BN*: "The thing, before all comparison, before all construction, is that which is present to consciousness as not *being* consciousness" (p. 174). "It is in fact in terms of the being which is not that a being *can make known to itself* what it is not" (p. 176). ". . . the upsurge of the For-itself is not only the absolute event for the For-itself; it is also *something which happens to the In-itself*, the only possible adventure of the In-itself" (p. 316). ". . . affirmation *happens* to the In-itself; it is the adventure of the In-itself to be affirmed" (p. 317).

4. Cf. *SG*: ". . . what is disgust? Quite simply an incipient vomiting. And what you vomit must in some way have been inside of you. How Genet laughed at M. Mauriac's

the result of the rule of things. These various observations provoke his first crisis of nausea which is mainly characterized by his effort to fight against what would be a disempowering idea: that the nausea is not something which comes from outside but rather is a phenomenon within him which he projects onto the things; he prefers to think of it as a kind of filth into which he has been plunged. For the moment, he is successful: "The Nausea isn't in me. I feel it *there* on the wall, on my braces, everywhere around me. It is all of a piece with the café; *I'm* in it" (p. 34).[5]

The sense of having been rescued from the worst possibility seems confirmed by the music—"Some of these Days"—he subsequently hears. At first the melody is no more than a little bit of happiness in the midst of the nausea; then it becomes almost a kind of antinausea which also comes from without, which makes demands on him, but which promises more desirable rewards. From having been in the nausea, he passes to being in the music. The music is something which has happened; it is an adventure that has come to him and, after having heard it, he can roam the streets again, convinced that he has left the nausea behind. Yet even as he assures himself about this with one part of his mind, another part is accumulating further fatal information. It keeps logging the special qualities of things; it decides, as Roquentin shows photographs of his travels to the Autodidact, that there are no adventures because adventures don't really change anything. The nausea, though it may once have been an exterior threat, has not been left behind. Roquentin is no longer alone: "There is that idea, in front of me, waiting. It's wrapped itself up into a ball; it sits there like a fat cat" (p. 54).

Roquentin is the victim of what Sartre has elsewhere called the "fascinated consciousness" which "no longer enjoys the freedom of the moment and forms an absurd synthesis by conferring on the new image a *sense* which allows the universe of reasoning to be preserved. . . . this consciousness is not the captive of objects; it is the captive of itself" (*L'Imaginaire*, p. 92).[6] It is not simply the sight of the objects that has fascinated Roquentin, it is rather the horror engendered in him by his encounter with the objects. Once he has admitted that such a horror can exist in the present, he is giving it the right to exist in the future, too. In the *Outline of a Theory*

---

painful effort to vomit him out . . ." (p. 502). Mauriac had written a scathing critique of Genet in which he allowed some small redemptive value to Genet as the incarnation of evil.

5. Cf. *BN*: "Freedom gives itself things as adverse (i.e., it confers on them a meaning which makes them things), but it is by assuming the very given which will be meaningful; that is, freedom assumes its exile in the midst of an indifferent in-itself in order to surpass this exile. . . . at the same time that freedom is a surpassing of *this given*, it chooses itself as *this* surpassing of the given . . ." (p. 508).

6. Cf. *BN*: "In fascination . . . the knower is absolutely nothing . . . he *is not*. The only qualification which he can support is that he *is not* the fascinating object" (p. 177).

of the Emotions (1939), Sartre had written, almost as though commenting in retrospect on his novel: "The horrible is now within the thing, at the heart of the thing; it is the affective texture; it is constitutive of it. . . . The horrible is not only the present state of the thing; it is threatened for the. future; it spreads itself over the whole future and darkens it; it is a revelation of the meaning of the world" (pp. 80–81).

The notion that has taken hold of Roquentin's mind and transfixed it with horror is that the grimmer of two opposed forces has won the upper hand. In the past he had had an outlook: his belief in a series of adventures one could count on. He had also had an expectation: from those adventures he could make something "rare and precious" of his life. His life would then have the drama and the organization, the sense of being *for* something, that is conveyed in most novels. In the background of such expectations was the realization that if there were to be the good moments identified as adventures there would be other moments, too. Those other moments, the periods of ennui, had automatically been characterized as lesser moments. What Roquentin discovers in the first quarter of *La Nausée* is that the lesser are the more reliable moments; their return is more certain and undeniably more frequent than the arrival of adventures.

His state at this point is not that of those who enter Dante's hell, for he has not yet abandoned all hope. He has one explicit hope: that there is a way out. Another does not become explicit until later in the book: his hope that the nausea is an exterior force; if that is true, he has a right to believe that he is its victim. That he speaks with irony and even disdain about his hope does nothing to diminish it; even as he accumulates information about the experience of nausea, he is considering possible remedies. The collision of his hopes with his surroundings could not be less promising. He decides to read *Eugénie Grandet*, not because he particularly wants to peruse that merciless description of provincial avarice, but because he has to do something. The book and Bouville comment on each other in drab fashion, especially because he reads Balzac's novel on a Sunday when nothing in the activities of the townspeople strikes him as being either rare or valuable. Against the thought of finding a way out by loving humanity, there is the grim evidence of the townspeople coming to terms with ennui by surrendering fully and completely to its gummy embrace.[7]

His afternoon, oddly enough, ends on the fringe of optimism because, as he looks back upon it, he joins the company of many protagonists in contemporary fiction who discover that they have knowledge denied to or

7. Sartre's estimate of the meaning and boredom of Sunday has not changed over almost three decades. In his Introduction to Georges Michel's *La Promenade du dimanche* (1967) he writes: "Loved, hated, looked forward to, always a letdown, Sunday is a collective ceremony. Michel makes a myth of it: it is human life. Not life's symbol. But life itself, summarized by one of its particular moments, as the whole is entirely present in each of its parts" (p. 10).

refused by others. If he cannot save himself by being with them, possibly he can save himself—break through the night is the expression he uses—by knowing why he is not with them. "Behind me, in the city, on those broad straight streets, under the cold light of the street lamps, an extraordinary event was suffering its death: Sunday was drawing to an end" (p. 77). That judgment is only one element in his ensuing feeling of happiness; the other is his conviction that the only real adventure is the passage of time and the discovery of how instants in time are linked together. The only adventure is to know that time is irreversible.

If you hoist yourself to the pinnacle of private wisdom, the beauty or ugliness displayed before you is irrelevant: you are above it. The questions that haunt others, leading them to create solutions in which they and the questions can hide, do not bother you. You can see that their talk about experience, and the knowledge and maturity it brings, is no more than an effort to impose on the past a distinction the past doesn't merit; it is their attempt to fight against chance and its unpredictable behavior by disciplining chance in a purely verbal way. Yet, despite the height of your pinnacle and the splendid reassuring uniqueness of your thought, once you start meditating on time you find that it is not only irreversible but also that it has an end. For you. Wisdom may be a great individuating principle, but death remains the great leveler that brings an end both to your time-span and to whatever individuation private wisdom momentarily afforded you.

At first Roquentin is above even this knowledge. He does not flee from it; on the contrary, he believes he is looking at it with unblinking eyes while the others are hiding from it. He is tempted to smile at the aging doctor he sees from time to time in a café in order to show that he has seen through the ruses that the old man, and all other men, organize against the inevitability of death. But on the following day Roquentin seems to understand what leads to such ruses when he writes and underscores in his journal a single entry: "*I must not be afraid*" (p. 94). The sentence may be intended as no more than a declaration of stoic intention. It resounds as a cry of discovery, for fear is the great enervating emotion which bares our weakness and implies someone else's power. And fear begins to take hold of Roquentin despite his efforts to extricate himself from the human condition and assume the role of an observer at a spectacle which doesn't concern him; his fear, precisely and ironically, is his dread of death.

This dread is expressed in a bizarre way. As he takes his breakfast in a café, he notices that the owner, M. Fasquelle, is not there. The idea that the owner is dead grips his mind and ruins his day. He sees signs of death all about him, he cannot work, he is haunted by the idea that anything can happen and that nothing is predictable. He admits openly to himself that all this is closely connected to the possibility that the owner is dead: "I must go back [to the café], see if M. Fasquelle is alive and if need be touch his beard or his hands. Perhaps then I'll be set free" (p. 102). Roquentin, of course, is in the mood for such thoughts because he has been meditating on death. His sudden, almost hysterical, concern with M. Fasquelle's demise is explained only by observations made in the early pages of the book where Roquentin had spoken of Fasquelle as a man who faced life calmly, who was spared solitude because, when "he is alone, he goes to sleep" (p. 18). Though he does not admit it openly, Roquentin needs Fasquelle because he needs the stability which Fasquelle represents for him, the stability of an outlook on experience which can keep a man from feeling dismay at what he sees.

More precisely, what affects him at this point is the realization that whatever stability any individual possesses is not immune to mortality. The doubt about Fasquelle becomes part of a greater, never exactly defined menace which hangs over the city and which is partially expressed by an exhibitionist Roquentin sees in the city park. The menace is probably best expressed as a threatening incapacity to go on—with one's work, with one's walk through the park, with one's assault upon another, with life. It is reflected in the hesitation of the readers in the library, where Roquentin is working, to leave at closing time and face the night. A young man precedes Roquentin out into the misty evening; Roquentin follows him, his eyes closed; then he hears the young man whistling as he hurries off. The combination of his own "courage" in plunging into the night and the exhilaration the young man's whistling conveys leads Roquentin to want to cry to the other reluctant readers that the menace is gone. Movement has begun again. The next day he finds out that Fasquelle is suffering from a heavy cold only. Once more Roquentin has been delivered; he can return to his pinnacle.

He returns to it with more information; still, knowledge, with its unpredictable consequences, keeps seeping unwanted into his mind. As he watched the young girl become prey to the exhibitionist, Roquentin had the impression that desire had welded the girl and the exhibitionist together until, without touching each other physically, they formed a couple. A somewhat similar welding takes place when, on the next Sunday, Roquentin visits the portrait gallery of the Bouville museum. And it takes place for much the same reason: Roquentin, like the young girl and the exhibitionist, simultaneously wants and rejects what he sees in the portraits. What he rejects is the bourgeois smugness which emanates from them, a smugness produced by the burghers' sense of their own solidity, of their right to govern because of the responsibilities governing implies, of their just claim to flaunt their weight and privileges in a world which would not have been made quite as it is were it not for the pattern of their work and the changes it produced. They have shaped the city and the surrounding area; they have intervened in nature and altered it; they have earned the right to live on as objects, calmly and complacently contemplating the city they have built. That city, in its guidebook, and in its museum, gratefully gives them the thanks they sought.

Roquentin rejects all this because of his own smugness, his conviction that he sees through all of it. What he cannot reject and what therefore has appeal to him is the sense that, through their compromises, these burghers have nonetheless discovered—and in comfort—what he cannot obtain: an untroubled mode of existence. As portraits, they bother him in much the same way that his encounter with the objects has been bothering him; but the portraits are even more irksome. Though they are objects, they refer to a way of life or a mode of consciousness which he does not possess.

Two things are happening to Roquentin at this moment. One has been described by Sartre in his book on the emotions in a passage concerned with what happens when we look at paintings: "I am . . . plunged into a world of objects; it is they which constitute the unity of my consciousness; it is they which present themselves with values, with attractive and repellent qualities—but *me*, I have disappeared; I have annihilated myself. There is no place for *me* on this level" (*Emotions*, p. 49). Yet this is an illusion, for, as Sartre explains in discussing the same subject in *L'Imaginaire*, the portraits would not exist for me unless I looked at them: "Those lips [which I see in a portrait of Charles VIII] have two simultaneous functions: on the one hand they refer to real lips, which have long since been dust, and find their meaning only in that; but on the other hand, they work directly on my sensibility because they are a *trompe-l'oeil*, because the colored markings of the portrait are given to my eyes as a forehead or as lips" (pp. 51–52). In other words, the portraits assume only the meaning I allow them to assume. And they do so because my emotions provoke my imagination into establishing the meaning I wish to see.

In this sense, Roquentin's reaction to the portraits tells us as much about him as he wants to tell about them. Though he looks at them with scorn—a scorn which splendidly reflects Sartre's own evaluation of the bourgeoisie—they still get at him, not by encouraging him to be what they were, but rather to be what they are: immobile and untroubled. He takes his leave of them with a short, scathing adieu: "Farewell. You shits" (p. 123). But the next day he shows one of the unpredictable results of unwillingly imbibed knowledge when he asks himself: "What am I going to make of my life?" (p. 123). Though he professes to hate the burghers whose portraits he has seen, his question might very well have been theirs, especially if we interpret the verb "make" as referring to the creation of something which would be very much like an object.[8] We can almost hear the worried father addressing the son who has been sowing wild oats too long. If we pursue the analogy, we can speak of Roquentin as being both worried father

8. Sartre uses, of course, the French verb *faire*, which permits the combined idea that all making implies doing and all doing leads to the making of something.

and oatsowing son; father to the extent that he places a value on a fixed way of life, son to the extent that random activity, while it may not have everlasting appeal for him, reflects a real urge which he cannot ignore.

The confusion of father and son, of the settled and unsettled, of sower and reaper, is a clear reflection of the confusion of Roquentin's mind at this point. He is fighting an impossible battle: he wants immobility, the settled; but such wants, by their very existence, tell him of the impossibility of achieving immobility. The paintings, and his emotions, represent, in Henry James's phrase, only "too inadequately the idea, and it was the idea that won the race, that in the long run came in first." The idea, of course, is that life cannot be immobile; the burghers were at once more and less than what is delineated in the portraits. One is always more and less than what one wanted to be.

However elusive the realization of the idea may be, Roquentin pursues it. He gives up his work on the Rollebon biography, admitting that it had nothing to do with the subject but only with his idea of the subject; he had depended on Rollebon, a figure plucked from a dead and meaningless past, to provide him with a raison d'être and also with a model to follow. What he had most admired in Rollebon was the diplomat's detachment, his removal from the hurly-burly about him, and his artistocratic disdain. Roquentin's admiration turns to anger once he realizes that, from beyond the grave, Rollebon's discretion, disdain, and evasiveness extend even to his biographer. Still, having given up his work, he does not leave the library for fear of once again meeting "that" outside—"that" being the things and, of course, the nausea they induce in him. But "that," he soon discovers, does not respect either physical or psychological doors. He persists in his effort to keep all the doors barred: " 'not to think . . . I don't want to think . . . I must not think that I don't want to think. Because that's a thought, too'. Isn't there ever an end to it?" (p. 129; the ellipsis points are Sartre's own.) Though the notion of thought as the incomparably faithful companion of existence strikes horror in him, he realizes that nothing will come to stop the horror on this side of the grave. He immediately makes a faint gesture at suicide, stabbing his hand and producing only a superficial wound which provokes only a superficial reaction.

Headlines in an evening newspaper tell him that the raped and murdered body of a young girl—Lucienne—has been found. This *fait divers* and Roquentin's reaction to it are something of a puzzle. No Lucienne has been mentioned before in the novel; a close reading allows for two guesses about her identity. The fact that the reader must piece the evidence together by himself points to a minor technical inconsistency in the book; since it is offered as an edited text, the editor, who has elsewhere supplied notes, could have supplied one here. That omission appears to be done deliberately so that further light can be shed on Roquentin's frame of mind. His

reaction to the murder is purely abstract; though he mulls over its significance for him, he does not see the connection between the murder and
certain experiences he has recently had. Another man would have thought
about those experiences immediately upon seeing the headlines.

First, there is the possibility that Lucienne might have been the victim
of the man in the capecoat whom Roquentin had seen at several different
times on the same day, sitting on a park bench, and whom he had later
caught in an exhibitionist gesture towards a young girl. Roquentin, fascinated by their fascination with each other, had made no deliberate effort
to protect the girl, though his gaze, once the exhibitionist became aware
of it, had disquieted the latter and given the girl a chance to scurry off. That
the exhibitionist might have sought other prey and chosen Lucienne is a
notion that never occurs to Roquentin. Nor does he consider the possibility
that M. Achille, the short nervous man, "slightly off his rocker" as the local
doctor says, who had come to Chez Camille, looking fearful and muttering
about "the poor girl," might have some relevance to the case. External
reality does not exist for Roquentin as a field where actions which have a
significance and result of their own take place. External reality is a display
case from which he selects incidents and impressions to corroborate his own
attitudes. Fascinated, he finds importance only in the fascination he sees
between the exhibitionist and the girl; fearful, he detects only the fear visible in M. Achille's behavior. Fear also conditions his reaction to the murder.
The dead child has meaning only because her death confirms an old observation and provokes a new one. Lucienne no longer *exists*; there *is* a dead
body. The implications of the italicized verbs are clear, and they lead us
beyond Sartre's usual distinction between man and things by indicating that
Lucienne has become a thing as the result of another's violent intervention.
The base of fear is immeasurably broadened to show that the understanding
Roquentin has been priding himself on, or the involvement in a community's
destiny that had been the lifework of the Bouville burghers, do not eliminate
the threats that creep up from behind to take hold of a man and possibly
to destroy him. The unpredictable may not be sure; it is always possible.
To disconcerted minds, that is enough.

Roquentin is now moving towards discoveries for which he does not have
an adequate vocabulary. He is moving in that direction because he has
moved away from what Sartre calls the unreflective consciousness and into
the reflective consciousness. In other words, he is moving away from the
moment in which he receives his experience and into the moment when he
begins to think about the experience he has received. His vocabulary, as
a result, produces confusions which catch appropriately the midpoint of
uncertainty and dismay where he finds himself. The old points of reference,
with their promise of fixity, are falling away; new points have not yet come
either to replace the old or to explain what they really mean. His statement

that "my thought is me" is a confession of an inability to take into account
the meaning of that part of the world which is not yet incorporated into his
thought; it is also a confusion since it shows that he has been thinking of
the me as an ego which has substance and which represents some firm core
of being which is particularly his. But the mobility of consciousness, its
constant attention to the spectacle of the world—a crucial Sartrean idea—
denies the possibility of any fixed ego upon which an individual can
honestly fall back when the going or the thinking gets tough.

As an extension of his idea of the ego as a fixed quantity, Roquentin had
held the idea of the outside world as an equally fixed quantity but a quantity which, in the earlier pages of the book, was trying to get hold of his ego
in order to demean it. In a reverse process Roquentin has been trying to get
hold of the world in order to demean it. Sartre calls such fixed quantities
"totalities" and stresses throughout his writings, but especially in the
Critique de la raison dialectique, that such totalities are themselves always
in the process of change. The ego, to the degree that it is meant to have
something to do with consciousness, is not a fixed totality because the ego
is always in process; a class or a society is not a fixed totality either because
it, too, is always in process. "Nature," as Roquentin sees it, is a totality
which, by its very being, detotalizes him; it is a steady quantity whose very
steadiness undoes him and leaves him with a vigorous fact: "Rien. Existé.
[Nothing. Existed.]" (p. 133).

Those two words comprise the entire entry for one day. They comprise,
too, a mystery, since grammatically they convey no precise meaning,
though as sounds rather than signs, they allow for a number of interpretations. "Rien existait [Nothing existed]," would express the unsettling discovery Roquentin has made; it also imposes the question of what the nothing is which exists. The two words can also be heard as an equation: "rien =
exister" [nothing = to exist]. Or a reader can supply the missing auxiliary
and reformulate the phrase to read: "Rien est existé" [nothing is existed].
The last two readings conform to a fundamental Sartrean idea which I shall
examine later in this book and which has to do with the notion that man
introduces nothingness into the world; nothingness is existed by him.

The fact of existence which Roquentin has discovered now creates the
task of finding out how to exist. Having given up his projected biography
of Rollebon, he is thrown back onto the world with nothing particular to
do save contemplate and evaluate the "solutions" others have found.
Roquentin's mood reflects all the confusions I have written of; it also reflects an unwillingness on his part to meet the rigorous fact he has encountered with equally rigorous thinking. As he lunches with the Autodidact
and watches the young couple seated at the neighboring table, he still has
the sense of possessing a privileged understanding they cannot claim. He
is denying them the sense of flux and change which is his and looks upon

their ways as the paths of dishonesty; he does not stop to reflect on the dishonesty or partiality that underpins his own reactions. Because he is envious of them, he condemns those immediately surrounding him for their humanism and their belief in love; and he lies in replying to the Autodidact's assertion that it is hard to be a man. "Excuse me for saying—but then I'm not quite sure of being a man—that I never found that very difficult. It's seemed to me that you only had to go along" (p. 154). As he looks at the chicken sitting in its gravy, he thinks with clear disgust: "I have to eat that" (p. 145). The Autodidact's plate has already been emptied.

Where Roquentin's imagination was earlier fascinated by his observation of the natural world, it is now transfixed by the sight of the food. There is nothing in the chicken which of itself explains the nauseous hesitation about having to eat "that." But "that" is not the chicken so much as it is everything: the talk of the nearby couple, the Autodidact's humanism, life's flow, the omnipresent risk of slipping into or being caught in a bog. What Roquentin wants is to live with his nausea, to use his nausea as his way of life. Were he to eat "that," he might vomit, the nausea might disappear, something might happen. But, precisely because it is his nausea, Roquentin does not want to renounce it; the nausea has become identical with what I have been calling his special knowledge.

That knowledge has to do with the apprehension of a world—aptly symbolized by the chicken imprisoned in the gravy as Roquentin is imprisoned in his discovery—he has himself created. The natural world was the one which wanted to grab hold of him; now it is the social world which wants to stake claims on him as the liquid gravy seems to have taken hold of the solid chicken. Roquentin wants the basic experience of being grabbed; he does not want to be grabbed by others, much preferring to be grabbed by himself. In other words, at this moment he is using the information accumulated by his unreflective consciousness to imprison the operations of his reflective consciousness. The unreflective consciousness has allowed him to believe that he is a victim of exterior forces. That is what he wants to believe; that is what appeals to him for a reason Sartre explains in a later work: ". . . the original bond between the slimy and myself is that I form the project of being the foundation of its being" (*BN*, p. 606).[9]

9. In *L'Imaginaire* Sartre had already insisted that every act, no matter what other convenient explanations might be available and usable, was an intentional act. With particular regard to the feeling of nausea, he wrote: "Vomiting . . . cannot simply slip willy-nilly into the general image-making attitude and pass unperceived. But it should be noted at the moment when vomiting becomes the real object of our consciousness, the unreal object of consciousness has passed into the state of memory. The stages of consciousness succeed each other in the following order: the consciousness of a repugnant unreal object; the consciousness of genuine vomiting given in connection with the mnemonic consciousness of the repugnant object. Naturally that means that the unreal object has been given in the awareness of vomiting as the real author of the real vomiting" (p. 266).

Roquentin is not lucidly aware of having done this; he still tends to believe that the terms of any project he might choose have been imposed from outside. Since his reflective consciousness continues to operate, he cannot avoid moving further into understanding of his discovery. In his next encounter with the nausea, he learns that it does not result from his being ensnared by any outside force, whether object or person; the nausea comes from his realization that he is surplus being in an indifferent physical world whose relations are in no way affected by what he, or any other man, might want to say about them. He learns that the nausea is nothing other than his discovery of the contingency of his *existence* when measured against the immobility of the physical world's *being*. He senses that he is transcended by a world he must transcend.

Roquentin does not correspondingly sense that he has either the optimism or the will to carry out the operation. The physical world *is*. fixed and undisturbed; he *exists*, undefined and dismayed: " . . . I understood the Nausea. I possessed it. . . . contingency is what is essential. What I mean is that, by definition, existence is not necessity. To exist is simply *to be there*" (p. 166). Where one is, is in a world where fixed unconscious being tempts one with the example of its movement and its immobility—the tree bows to the wind but is basically stable. Above all the tree asks itself no questions and therefore tells itself no lies; it inhabits a world where unthinking being, by its contentment with itself, tempts humans being to become instead human beings, to slip into immobility. This is the basic human temptation—the desire to give in, to put responsibility elsewhere, to believe in currents of influence or determination which dominate us; it is, as Sartre says in *Being and Nothingness*, being's revenge on existence.

If the things, the fixed beings, tell themselves no tales, they are not without meaning for the man who contemplates them. They have what Roquentin calls "un drôle de petit sens" (p. 171) which necessarily exists only for men and not for the things themselves. We have seen that the most crucial aspect of that meaning is their lack of consciousness and the consequent absence of any need on their part to wonder what they should make of themselves They are made; they are "like thoughts that got stopped on the way, that forgot about themselves and about what they had wanted to think" (p. 171); but they are also everywhere, filling the world from horizon to horizon, from nearest earth to farthest sky. And their mute call is as fetching as the sirens' song; the temptation is to join them, to become a thought formed and unconscious of where else it might have wanted to go. Roquentin cannot give into the temptation, precisely because he is aware that he would be giving in and, more vaguely, because he knows that a steady, sustained effort of consciousness would be necessary in order to emulate the things. Though he cannot give into the temptation—and it is crucial to note that the temptation is one of conducting an impossible undertaking—he must find a response to it. The swarm of things disgusts him; his own existence disgusts him. The earth is no man's land and every man's home.

The first response he chooses leads him back to a former love, Anny. This is, at least, paradoxical since Anny is a moment from that past whose existence he has denied; what he has not denied is the value of that past, and it is to its nostalgic worth rather than to its existence that he refers. Anny is about to reenter his life physically. During their separation she has been a presence in his mind and, during his worst crises with the nausea, she has been a memory of better times, of "perfect moments" they had spent together during their relationship; clearly, his addiction to the song, "Some of these Days," is an unconscious indication of what Anny represents for him. Those perfect moments were not adventitious, as the nausea has been. They were carefully planned and diligently enacted by Anny, and their total effect was to abstract him from the movement of time and, by so doing, to make him happy. In remembering Anny at desperate moments during his observation of the flux around him, he is remembering a known stability, an experienced happiness. He is also remembering an Anny who is fixed in time, and therefore he is not making adequate allowance for what might have happened to her and, in the undefinable bargain of time, to him, too.

In *L'Imaginaire* Sartre discusses what is going on in such a situation and, not quite by coincidence, centers his discussion about what a young man expects from an absent "Annie." Anny has become an unreal object for Roquentin which he summons back to his imagination in order to retrieve a past feeling. It is not the unreal object contemplated in the imagination which brings back the feeling; rather it is his need which summons forth the object so that need and object, meeting in his mind, will produce the memory of the past tenderness. The result of this process is that the real Anny, the one who is living in another city, doing other things, has nothing necessarily to do with the Anny who lives on in his imagination—the Anny who, at the call of his will, answers his solicitations as he wants them answered. An eventual encounter between Anny and Roquentin can, as a consequence, be a disaster.

It is; but more than that it is immensely sad. For the places where Anny has been and the things she has seen have produced in her an experience which is almost parallel to the experience Roquentin has detailed in his journal. They meet in total intentional confusion, Roquentin hoping to find those "perfect moments," Anny hoping to find an unchanged Roquentin who will serve as the measure of the progress she has made away from the "perfect moments." She has discovered that the perfect moments were no more than images created from images, since she had found the inspiration for them in an illustrated edition of Michelet. It is significant that the illustrations, which had suggested a process whereby events were abstracted from time in order to be inserted in a timeless universe of distinct but established hierarchies, were never found near the text they were meant to illustrate. So had it been with her own perfect moments; in creating them for Roquentin, she was trying to pretend that there was no text. Those perfect moments were illustrations of a life that could not occur in the normal sequence of time; they were abstractions created in the imagination; their elements were assembled from nothing more real than human frustrations in order to fight against the possibility that in reality there might be nothing at all.[10]

Certainly this was how they had worked for Roquentin; and certainly, in meeting Anny, he is hoping to retrieve the escape they offered. But it is equally certain that once he discovers that Anny's experience during the years of their separation has been the same as his, he is willing to start from where they are. Where they are is practically nowhere: newborn babes, not very eager because they have been wizened by the wisdom accumulated during their previous incarnation as a couple. Anny will have none of any of his claims that he understands what she is talking about. As Roquentin at a certain moment needed to believe that he possessed a wisdom superior to that of the citizens of Bouville, so she now needs to assert a comprehension of life significantly superior to his. She knows what he does not know and will neither hear nor believe that he is at the same point. Permeating their conversation is the whole worrisome world of the Other, which I will discuss in a later chapter but which is already visible in Roquentin's reaction to Lucienne's murder. In their past relations this world of reciprocated hostility and fear had not been too visible because he and Anny were using each other for an exercise in mutual deception: neither one sought the other as a person but only as an element in the creation of a mood and style which answered immediate but different needs. Anny had been the active partner in the relationship, defining and creating and explaining the situations; Roquentin had been the indispensable passive actor who moved into the situations she created and who responded to them as she wished.

Now that they are beyond the point where a global deception will justify individual deceptions, they cannot find a meeting place. To Roquentin's expression of pleasure that she has achieved the same knowledge as he, Anny answers sharply: "It pretty much displeases me to know that someone

10. Much later, in his essay "Portrait de l'aventurier" (*Sit. VI*, p. 15), Sartre will claim that the desire for perfect moments is a peculiarly bourgeois phenomenon wherein the bourgeois seeks to effect on this earth an image of a universe with which he is in fundamental harmony. It is not fanciful to say that the bourgeois Sunday, as Sartre evaluates it, is an effort at creating a perfect moment where the family joins together to profit from the day of rest established on the model of God's rest after the creation. If it turned out that God was as much bored with his day off as his creatures subsequently were with theirs, Sartre would probably claim that God had got his just desserts.

has thought the same things as I. And anyway you're probably deceiving yourself" (p. 189). Anny's repeated claim is that she is living beyond herself, by which she, and more particularly Sartre, means that she is living beyond both her past and her former notion that she was a fixed quantity.[11] But clearly Anny's position is contradictory or insufficiently examined by her; for if she has profitably learned about the unreliability of the ego, she should be willing and perhaps obliged to accept Roquentin's claims that he, too, has survived beyond that deception. But, as I have pointed out, she needs him in order to measure her achievement; if she admits that he, too, has made the same discovery and is at the same point, she loses the individuation she so relentlessly seeks to protect.

Having arrived at an honest understanding of what the individual's place in the world is—that of a spectator in a hostile universe of uncommunicative things and alien others—she reacts dishonestly. And she knows it, for she says to Roquentin as he takes his leave: "Poor fellow! No luck at all. For the first time you're willing to play your role well, and no one's going to thank you for it . . ." (p. 194). In so saying she confirms Roquentin's earlier observation that she, like himself, is alone.[12] Each returns to his solitude. We learn nothing further of Anny; we remain for a brief spell longer with Roquentin, who still must seek a response, not only to his discovery of the things' indifference, but also to his discovery of Anny's refusal to cooperate.

He accepts Anny's term and decides that he, too, will survive beyond his ego; in other words, he will acknowledge that there is no fixed value which can be labeled "Roquentin" and whose ingredients and uses can be exhaustively listed. But immediately he decides that he will also live like the trees and the puddles of water, letting events happen, imitating the objects' resignation. He knows, however, that this is no way out, no usable response. Events will continue to change him; he will continue to exist in a mode quite different from that of the trees. He will still know fear, and it is against the fear that he now exerts his consciousness.

The event that occurs immediately does not happen to him but to the Autodidact, who is the book's chief propagandist of enlightened bourgeois humanism. Roquentin sits as a paralyzed observer in the town library,

11. The verbal play in the phrase she uses is clear because Sartre writes *je me survis*, thereby indicating that what is surviving is the "I" as the inevitably active present principle; what is dying or has died is the ego (in French, *le moi*) as a reliable reservoir to which one can return with the assurance that it will be as well-stocked as ever.

12. There is not a little vanity in Anny's attitude and an immeasurable amount in Roquentin's. Cf. *BN*: ". . . vanity impels me to get hold of the Other and to constitute him as an object in order to burrow into the heart of this object to discover there my own object-state. But this is to kill the hen that lays the golden eggs. By constituting the Other as object, I constitute myself as an image at the heart of the Other-as-object; hence the disillusion of vanity" (p. 291).

watching as the Autodidact discreetly makes indelicate advances to two
young boys. Humanism can be a mask to disguise many things. Roquentin
also watches the librarian watching the Autodidact; the librarian is waiting
for the appropriate moment to pounce on the Autodidact, accuse him of
pederasty, and banish him from the library which has played such an
essential role in his existence. Roquentin does nothing until the event has
come to an end; then he punches the librarian in a brief moment of rage
whose short duration he cannot explain. His action is in thorough contradis-
tinction to what he would have done in the past—a past that must predate
this book since he had done nothing to defend the young girl from the
exhibitionist. He then tries to say something to the Autodidact, who turns
away. Where Roquentin wishes to function, he can do nothing; where he
wishes not to function, he cannot escape.

He has abandoned almost everything and has been abandoned; he has
no certainty that anyone will even remember him. He still feels the temptation to think of himself as an ego. He is after all Antoine Roquentin; and
Antoine Roquentin ought to be something. To be something, he would have
to do something, and he knows that the experience he has traced in the
pages of his journal is one primarily characterized by the futility of action.
Action activates not only unreflective or automatic consciousness, it also
activates thinking about thinking; and whenever he has thought about his
thoughts the results have been dismal when not disastrous. The old temptation, though put to critical question, has not been dismissed. He still wants
to be—to leave some fixed quantity behind which would be his accomplishment, the weight he has willed to the earth as the memorial to his passage.

The music he listens to as he prepares to leave Bouville—the jazz song
heard many times before—provides him with an example, for he looks upon
the music as a kind of antinausea, a response to the nausea which emulates
the nausea's terms and even its operations. Like the nausea, the music cannot be destroyed; like the nausea, it returns and can make people ashamed
of their existence because it soars where they do not, because it has the measure they lack. Against the nausea, one must establish an antinausea. Setting
off for Paris, Roquentin decides that he will write a book "that must be as
beautiful and as hard as steel and which will make people ashamed of their
existence" (p. 222).[13] It will also allow him to look back on himself without
repugnance, for the book will be the exercise by which he will seek to live

13. Sartre finds a similar intention in Flaubert. He quotes from Flaubert's *Souvenirs*
(1841) a sentence where Flaubert says that humanity has only one end: to suffer.
Sartre then comments: "By infecting humanity with his own suffering, Flaubert, one
might say, brings his readers closer to him, makes them more lucid, more authentic,
more courageous; isn't he, after all, rendering them a service by de-moralizing them,
that is, by delivering them from a conventional moral code which is flowing away
in every direction? Not at all. All that would be true if Flaubert did not first of all
hate his public, that is, his class. He does not think any book, however sublime it

as the music lives, suffering in measured ways. He has found a response to his double alienation from the physical and social worlds.

What he has not found is a solution to the alienation, for it is clear that what he is seeking at the end is a haven for the ego, a fortress against the exterior flux. Though he apparently will not live in imitation of the trees, he will live and write in order to create an object which will have some of the qualities of trees—their hardness and beauty.[14] He has a project, consciously formed—in later Sartrean terms this is a good thing—and a point of departure. And his experience at Bouville, if it has not given him collective importance—he will seek that through the book—has at least made him fully the individual who wishes to write that book. He becomes collectively important through the book which establishes his individuality; he does not thereby become part of the collectivity. If he has not come to terms properly with existence, he has not turned his back fully on it either, as has the protagonist of Sartre's short story, "La Chambre" (1939).

The greatest fear of Pascal's prototypical man was to be forced to remain alone for half an hour in a room; some greater fear has driven Sartre's protagonist in that story to enclose himself in a room for the rest of his days, there to commune with strange, hallucinatory visitors who come to dominate him. His room is clearly not the place where he meditates on his solitude; but just as clearly it is the closed space which cuts him off from the diversions and distractions in which Pascal's man lost himself in the hope of avoiding confrontations with the greater perplexities of the universe. The room is to Pierre what the desire to write a book is to Roquentin: a response. But like that projected book, the room is also an artifice, a space set aside by human intervention and furnished according to the tastes or needs of

---

might be, could detach bourgeois men from the bourgeoisie. They will continue to do what they are doing because that is their lot" ("Flaubert: du poète à l'Artiste," *TM* 22 [1966]: 616).

14. In his essay on the ego Sartre had already indicated the futility of Roquentin's undertaking. This does not at all mean that, at the time of writing the concluding pages of *La Nausée*, he was being faithful to his own earlier estimate. He wrote: "What matters to us is that an indissoluble synthetic totality which could support itself would have no need of a supporting X, provided of course that it were really and concretely unanalyzable. If we take a melody for example, it is useless to presuppose an I which would serve as a support for the different notes. The unity here comes from the absolute indissolubility of the elements, which cannot be conceived as separated, save by abstraction. The subject of the predicate here will be the concrete totality, and the predicate will be a quality abstractly separated from the totality, a quality which has its full meaning only if one connects it again to the totality" (*Ego*, pp. 73–74). In these terms, Roquentin's projected book, while it might convey a fairly accurate and unified description of something, would do nothing lasting for him since, once it was done, or even while he was doing it, he would be back in the same intentional stew where he found himself once disillusion with his biography of M. de Rollebon had set in.

the individual who inhabits it. In the absence of trustworthy real furniture, it can be filled with fleeting images, enlivened with strange fantasies. It is the personal space to which Pierre has retired purposefully.

He has not sequestered himself in order to be alone but rather in order to have the kind of company he wants. That it is strange company—hostile, offensive, and troubling—does not detract from the fact that it serves a clearly intended function. It severs his relationship with another world, best represented by his mother-in-law, Mme Darbédat. She, too, is sequestered in her room where she eats Turkish delight and turns the pages of books. There is an apparent difference, since Mme Darbédat's room is not a port of call for strange spirits; it is the recognizable space—not very lovely, to be sure, but not terribly disturbing either—of the bourgeois woman who is pampering herself with unidentified and not very dangerous illnesses.

There are, then, different kinds of closed-off space. Some, like Mme Darbédat's, are only small samples cut from broader cloth; others, like Pierre's, are whole cloth of a different pattern, for his room, unlike his mother-in-law's, has been created in opposition to hers and as an answer to it. His space is an antiworld created in order that he "may escape from every constraint of the world . . . from the condition of *being in the world*" (*L'Imaginaire,* p. 261). His and Mme Darbédat's are not, however, the only spaces described in the story. All told there are four.

First of all, there is the space created by the story itself. This, like the space of *La Nausée,* is open space in the sense that the ceiling is missing; the reader can look into the grouping of walled-off spaces and decide either which space he prefers or else that no one of the spaces is satisfactory. The latter choice amounts to a decision to live consciously with the problematic and undefined aspects of existence. The second space is the sealed-off area of Mme Darbédat's room; it perfectly reproduces the closed reality of the moral world in which she lives. It is the space of genteel paralysis in which all the major issues have been weighed on fraudulent scales and their value decided. The only disquiet ever aroused in this space is expressed in fleeting concern with those who do not share the principles which have been applied in its construction. The concern is fleeting because it presumes that the surrounding structure is impregnable against any assault.

The third space is a variation on the second, but a variation which intends to bury the theme. This, too, is closed space, but it has been sealed off by someone who, unable to accept the presuppositions of a secure world, has, in opposition to that world, invited into his space hostile forces, emissaries from a world in flux whose purpose is to overwhelm. In a certain way, Pierre's hallucinations are radical reductions of the forces of the bourgeois world in which he has refused to live. In this sense his space has its roots in that other world, for it was in that other world that he must have developed the idea of "things"—social customs and practices, moral principles and persuasions—as forces plotting to take possession of him. Against those manufactured "things" he sets off more basic things: the brute facts of existence which we have seen in Roquentin's encounter with the nausea. In doing so, he is seeking to show that his mother-in-law's world is an effort to refine those brute facts into softer realities whose hold on the individual is in no essential way changed for having been padded. By enclosing himself in his room he has acted freely against one world and has freely accepted another. The paradox, of course, is that his free movement has been towards an abdication of his freedom; what justifies the abdication in his mind is his conviction that he has given himself over to real rather than to fabricated forces. Madness consciously entertained as madness has more honesty than madness embraced as though it were sanity.[15]

The fourth space is also enclosed. It is a midway space where emissaries from the other two closed spaces meet. It has two doors. One leads to Pierre's world and is used by his wife, Eve; the other leads towards Mme Darbédat's world and is used by her husband. Each of the emissaries has commitments. M. Darbédat, though touched by love for his daughter, sees the world only through the lenses of his class's values; such lenses necessarily distort his daughter's desire to live and have sexual relations with a mad husband. Such a desire is "unhealthy." But the values of the class periodically create missions: one does not, without protest, allow one's daughter to live in the vicinity of folly. She is, after all, one's daughter, a member of the same class; her obstinacy threatens family, class, and all other values by suggesting that a madman is indeed a tolerable companion.

Eve is uncomfortable in this midway space. It is a room for "normal people" who never "glance behind them," who readily push aside any obstacle they enounter ("La Chambre," p. 59). Though it is part of her apartment, this room does not reflect, as does Pierre's room, the essence of her life—her love for a madman. It is the hinterland of her world, neutral but uncomfortable, the territory she enters in order to meet her father. It is his hinterland, too, and he will not go beyond it into the openly declared enemy lands. Here they meet as negotiators of a settlement Eve is not willing to make. Here, too, each one loses something: M. Darbédat some of his assurance, though none of his certainty; Eve something of her special world, but none of her conviction. They cannot negotiate, because neither one seeks a compromise. Neither one wants to give an inch and so each loses a whole world.

This is why the fourth space, while it resembles the first, is in the final analysis quite different: it allows for no solution other than those found in

15. Cf. *SG*: "It must be understood that to *prove* is also a function of the imagination. The imagination *represents* objects to us in such a way as to incline our judgment in the direction we wish. The drawings of a madman do not simply *express* his terrors; they aim at maintaining them and confining him within them" (p. 463, n.).

the second and third spaces, each of which represents a particular kind of surrender. Mme Darbédat lives under the government of her bourgeois mores, Pierre under the tyranny of his hallucinations. Their rooms have been used as ultimately irrelevant solutions to the experience that had been traced in *La Nausée*—irrelevant because in one way or another the temptation to be a fixed quantity, governed by exterior forces, has won out. Both Pierre and Mme Darbédat have elected to refuse to live as free human beings because of their fear of freedom or, more accurately, their fear of its consequences.

It seems obvious that, in any choice between the two attitudes, the author's preference would go to Pierre's and Eve's response. Pierre's room at least contains a more exact awareness of the true universe and allows a more direct encounter with its issues. Their decision is also a conscious act by which they seek to respond to the social situation that would also have imprisoned them had they remained with it. In an introductory letter to R. D. Laing's and D. G. Cooper's *Reason and Violence* (1964), Sartre writes: "I consider . . . mental illness as the way out which the free organism, in its total unity, invents in order to be able to live an intolerable situation" (p. 7). The solution, if it has understandable causes, is none the less unacceptable to Sartre for the very simple reason that it involves acting freely in order that freedom may no longer exist, acting in order to eliminate the possibility of future decisions. The edge that Pierre and Eve have, in the author's mind, over her parents is that, at least once, they have performed a free and conscious act.

By contrast, the Darbédats earn the author's scorn because their passivity pretends not to know its own passive nature. As much as Pierre and Eve, they have let go, inserting themselves into a prefabricated world and living automatically according to its ways. They have asked no questions, discovered no truths; though they belong to a certain collectivity, they are hardly individuals at all. They have used their class as a buffer against the basic questions; their class has driven Pierre to the basic questions, there to choose madness. He has moved from one enemy to another, but in his movement he has at least gone to the lair of the true, the fundamental, enemy. Each side, the Darbédats and Pierre, has surrendered to some form of the viscous, by which I mean that each has elected a solution whose aim is passivity, resistance to change, and refusal of external influence. It is against this kind of passivity and its close relationship to belief in a core-self, which must be protected at almost any cost, that Sartre is fighting. A proverb like, "if you can't fight them, join them," is nonsense in Sartre's thought because the if-clause makes no sense: since you have discovered that "they"—the things, the social mores, all real or pretended fixed quantities—are principles you cannot accept, the only choice is to fight them or to capitulate to them.

This is the situation in which Eve finds herself. She has fought against one—the world of her family—in order to accept the other—the folly of her husband, his immersion in a world of forces she can only pretend to see through his eyes. Rather than fight against her husband's world, she sustains it, all the while knowing it is a manufactured world. " 'A game' she thought with remorse; 'this is nothing but a game and never for an instant have I sincerely believed in it' " (pp. 70–71). She thereby becomes the living contradiction her two names indicate. In the world of reality, she is Eve, the free woman who must come to terms with her fall and meet the questions of an angry god; in the world of her husband, she is Agathe, the martyr whose reaction to challenge is to permit her own destruction. Her attitude suggests a conviction on her part that she can neither save the world nor change it. But her day-to-day activity mocks her conviction because she actually spends her time saving her husband's world, acting to preserve the space he has created for his immobilized freedom. And she will have to continue acting if that space is to maintain its function up to the end. Against the possibility of her husband's eventual incarceration in an institution—the final demonstration of the surrounding society's greater wisdom and coercive power—she has only one response: "I'll kill you first" (p. 73).[16]

Pascalian man, confronted with a universe which terrified him, turned to the creation of another which eventually set up the same terrors. Pascal's task then became that of showing man where the solution lay. Sartrean man, confronting an equally terrifying universe, seeks consciously to find a mode of existence deliberately patterned on that world; the greatest terror it holds for him is its visible lack of his concerns. If only he can become like it, he surely will share its calm. The need for a solution to such human dismay is not new; Lucretius had felt the need and written *De rerum natura*. But, with Lucretius, as later with Pascal, the persuasiveness of the proposed solution depended on reference to a third term which validated it. In the Sartrean world the third term most often turns out to be the original discovery disguised and presumably tamed. Roquentin's is music; Mme Darbédat's, her class; Pierre's, capitulation to illusory forces; Eve's, capitulation to Pierre. Confronted with the dilemma posited by apprehension of the viscous, they all give into some remedy modeled on the viscous.

16. There is in Eve something of a phenomenon Sartre discusses in *SG*. There he sees Genet making an effort to associate himself with the world of others by using *his* imagination, first to see their world, then to see himself as existing at its core. In a note Sartre writes, making specific reference to Genet in whom he believes he sees the characteristics of "feminine passivity": "This perhaps parallels a distinction between the 'feminine' imagination (which reinforces in the woman—when she is her master's accomplice—the illusion of being at the center of a beautiful order) and the 'manly' explosive imagination (which contains and transcends anguish by means of the images it forms)" (p. 468).

I have not yet defined this term—the viscous—to which I possibly give a broader meaning than Sartre intends. We apprehend the viscous as a solution to our observation of a contradictory situation. What we see in the world is a stability of which we are not a part. Though that stability is in flux, we realize—even as we become aware of it—that its flux only further defines the degree of difference between it and us.[17] The flux suggests movement and change, and yet what is in flux remains. It passes back and forth through states—the stone is rained upon and worn down—without losing a certain apparent constancy. Relations exist between its various elements— a group of trees stirred by the wind has something in common; sugar melts and is absorbed into the coffee; it does not disappear. The natural world seems to move back and forth from mobility to immobility, from liquid to solid, without paying any price; matter becomes energy, energy matter; the law of conservation refers to a kind of variability which is saved by another kind of irreducibility.

Men, too, are in flux, but no law (Pascal and Lucretius offered, not laws, but invisible realities) guarantees their conservation. Certain Western thinkers, by establishing a body which disappears and a soul which remains, have of course sought to establish such a law. The contrast between men and the natural world becomes bitter when men realize that they are mauled and damaged as the natural world is not. It survives its changes and goes on; men survive their changes as Roquentin had survived the loss of his ego. But, like Roquentin, they are aware of something lost. And perhaps the bitterest spice in their realization—it drove Sade to madness and dazzlingly insane theories—is the knowledge that in the end they shall become part of the natural world, nutriment for some of its soil. It is no consolation to be told that, created from dust, men shall return to dust since all that men learn from that gray refrain is this: everything gained is everything lost.

This kind of dismal description depends, of course, on a world in which there is no God, no immortality, no reward for the individual whose good life on earth earns him somewhere else what he has missed here: permanence and bliss. When the idea of God is gone—and, according to Sartre, it had to go because it is a creation of man; it is another form of letting go in the face of all the contrary evidence—men are on their own, staring at a natural world which does not know their fear or at a social world which instills other forms of fear in them. Wherever men look, they find evidence of their fundamental weakness in the face of exterior threats. The

17. Cf. *BN*: ". . . the slimy when perceived is a 'slimy to be possessed' . . . the original bond between the slimy and myself is that I form the project of being the foundation of its being" (p. 606). ". . . the slimy appears as already the outline of a fusion of the world with myself" (p. 606). ". . . slime is the revenge of the In-itself" (p. 609). Professor Barnes in her translation uses the word "slime" or "slimy" for *visqueux*. I have preferred to use "viscous" because I believe that Sartre has imposed it on both the French and English languages as a meaningful term.

first and greatest temptation in this situation is to blame exterior forces—
these late eclipses in the sun and moon—and to claim that they determine
human modes of action. Thus Roquentin at first wants to believe that the
external world is seizing hold of him, insinuating its nausea into him; thus
Pierre gives way to madness in response to the pressures his class wishes
to exert upon him. Indecisiveness riddles man; it resembles that indecisiveness between solid and liquid states which can be observed in the natural
world, but it threatens man as it does not threaten the natural world.

The reason for this is quickly discovered: the natural world does not
think. From this discovery comes man's second temptation: to pattern his
life on the natural world, to allow himself to be carried along, to give himself
over to an already established way of life where other forces will determine
what he does. In short, he feels a strong urge to model himself on the world
of natural being. Such an urge ignores one essential point: while descriptions of the natural world may allow for a concept of the viscous, any attribute or virtue accorded to the viscous does not come from objective phenomena but from projections men make. Men can only reasonably describe
what the flux looks like; they cannot describe what its feelings are since it
has none, not even those men assign to it. In brief, the viscous never knows
nausea, though it may seem to store it up; it never experiences the desire
to take refuge in madness, though its own meanderings may seem insane.
As a result, men's desire to let go either to the natural world—which
Roquentin at one moment saw as marmalade from which he could not
escape—or to the mores of a class or to the reign of madness is the election
of an impossible solution: men are using the freedom of their existence to
escape from that freedom.

Sartre's point in La Nausée, as in "La Chambre," is to show the in-
efficacy of such solutions because each of them represents no more than
the replacement of one form of the viscous with another. The solutions come
from a sense of defeat and the sense of defeat results from man's recognition
of the fact that he cannot annihilate the world of being in which he finds
himself plunged; this explains why he is tempted to subordinate himself
to it by considering it an evil he cannot eliminate. Eliminate it, he cannot;
but he can modify it. "He must be able to put himself outside of being and
by the sames stroke weaken the structure of the being of being" (BN,
p. 433). But, in so doing, he must be willing to take the consequences and
to live openly with them rather than seek to sublimate them in one form
or another.

In his brief essay on Husserl, Sartre had said that men will never discover
themselves by cherishing or relying on what they think they most intimately
are; they will only find themselves on the road, among other men, confronted with the things. In his short story, "Intimité"—which develops ideas

expressed in the Husserl essay as well as in the book on the ego—Sartre seeks to show that what men are intimately is a composite of their reactions to the sweep of the universe and the threat of others considered as part of that sweep.

The story line of "Intimité" (1939) is uncomplicated. Lulu, whose husband is impotent, is tempted to run off with another man. Her friend, Rirette, encourages her to do so because, love and happiness being scarce in this world, Lulu should take advantage of whatever quantities of them are available to her. Roquentin's sudden repulsion when confronted with the chicken he had ordered for lunch has shown us why the act of consuming one's share can become unpleasant: the consequences are unpredictable. In Lulu's case, it is obvious what the consequences risk being: a dilution of her intimacy (that is, of her ego), and an invasion of that part of the world she has reserved for herself.

Lulu's basic fear is the one that children early learn in a nursery story: if you don't watch out, something will get hold of you. It will get hold of Lulu because, no matter what precautions she takes, she suffers from a basic defect which she shares with the race: she has no eyes in the back of her head. Things, forces, and threats can come at her from behind no matter how careful she may try to be. And if forces can come at you from behind, then your intimacy—the preservation of what you are—is threatened. She takes a number of prophylactic steps: to meet the threat of sexual possession she has married an impotent husband and concurrently convinced herself that only in masturbation can she find release; to answer those eyes that look desiringly on her, she has girdled her buttocks voluptuously, probably as part of a shrewd strategy derived from the hunch that if she makes herself fetching enough from the rear "they" are bound to come around and look her seductively in the eye.[18] In her contradictory behavior, Lulu is a manifestation of the contradictions Sartre sees in the idea of the ego.

The ego is thought to be an inner fortress, equipped to help the individual regularize the demands of the id and to negotiate encounters with the outer world. But precisely because those encounters take place, the ego can only remain a fortress by cheating: it pretends that its bastions have not been weakened, that its walls have not been damaged; yet in the moment of battle it loses its definition and becomes indistinct. Only when the battle is over or when a strategic retreat has been effected does it rediscover itself. By that time, of course, it has been modified and is no longer the bastion it was. This does not mean that it is any weaker as an organizating principle; it means only that the ego is indeed an organization, a concept. It is not a

18. Cf. *SG*: "Many women loathe their backside, that blind and public mass which belongs to everyone before belonging to them. When they are grazed from behind, their excitement and their shame will mount together. The same holds for Genet. Having been caught stealing from *behind*, his back opens when he steals, it is with his back that he awaits human gazes and catastrophes" (p. 80).

steady or even reliably unwavering force, and this is not because of the victorious emergence of the id; it is because of the world. The fortress men repair at the end of the battle is not the fortress they had when the battle began.

Lulu's intimacy is threatened by two armies. One is the ill-defined force of life: "Life was a great wave which was going to break on Lulu and carry her away from Henri's arms" (p. 138). Life is a network of confusions which seizes hold of her, spins her about, and then sends her back either to nothing or to herself. The other threat comes from others who try, like life, to get hold of her. Lulu realizes that in any direct confrontation with these two forces she cannot do much, primarily because she does not wish to cooperate with either of them. Instead she wants to use them for her ends, and when her intentions and theirs are at cross-purposes she withdraws to lick her wounds and survey the terrain. There is a fine scene where physical action conveys the struggle that is going on within her. She really wants to remain with her husband; nonetheless she feels a need—perhaps the periodic desire to give dramatic proof that she is capable of independent action, perhaps anger at snubs received from her husband's family—to go off with her lover. But when the moment of decision comes, she acts like soggy linen being fought over by competing washerwomen (p. 129). Her husband pulls at one arm; her friend, Rirette, at the other. Lulu can then readily believe that she has been neutralized, that no action is available to her because she is caught between two forces determined to tear her asunder. In such moments, when actions that may transform her life are happening, she withdraws, not into the fortress of her ego, but into inactivity. As Rirette says: " . . . the facility with which she could decompose herself was frightening" (p. 131). The self must decompose under the impact of events because the self cannot exert any suasion that will necessarily modify those events. It decomposes and waits; it pleads exterior influences; then it retreats back into the fortress for the needed repair work. It can only assert its existence when removed from the stream of life or, more accurately, it can only act exclusively in its own interests when it is out of the fray; in the fray it may not be able to decide what its interests are.[19]

Lulu's dilemma is that there is no way of remaining permanently away

19. In the *CRD*, Sartre accuses the German philosopher Karl Jaspers of performing a similar operation in the interests of preserving his individualism from the collective involvement of a movement like Marxism and thereby of absenting himself from history. "Jaspers is moving in a backward direction from the historical movement— which is the real movement of the *praxis*—towards an abstract subjectivity whose unique goal is to attain a certain intimate *quality*." In a note, Sartre adds: "This is that quality, at once immanent (since it extends across our lived subjectivity) and transcendent (since it remains without our grasp) which Jaspers calls existence" (p. 22). We shall see later the way in which Sartre has gone about trying to maintain his own individuality within the general framework of Marxism.

from the stream; nor is there any way of being immersed in the stream without being dirtied, without having some of the silt stirred up by others who have waded in it stick to you or at least flow across you. Lulu has no particular revulsion about her own dirt; in limited quantities, it becomes part of her intimate being. What she detests is the dirt that comes from others, the flakes from their intimacy which speckle and change her and which suggest that there is room for them on or in her.

We see how she rebuilds her ego in the aftermath of intercourse with her lover. The sperm he has left on her belly is the filth he has transferred amidst joyous murmurs; his conviction is that he has given her pleasure. Her thoughts turn to compensation and lies: she will get rid of his filth, turn her imagination to thinking about pure forms of love, insist that she did not cry out her own pleasure at the moment of orgasm. And anyway the doctor has assured her that she cannot have an orgasm unless it is self-induced. She returns to her husband; because he is impotent, she can play with his penis without fearing any change; and she can convince herself that she doesn't need other people:

> What it comes down to is that you really can't ever take it in your hands, if only it could stay quiet, it scares me when it's hard and standing straight in the air, it's brutal; love, what a lot of dirt it is. I love Henri because his little affair never gets hard, never raises its head, I laughed, I kissed it sometimes, it didn't scare me any more than a child's; at night I used to take his sweet little thing between my fingers . . . it behaved well in my hand. . . . Then I used to stretch on my back and think about priests, about pure things, and I used to begin by stroking my belly, my beautiful flat belly, I moved further down and had pleasure; the pleasure no one else knows how to give me (pp. 105–6).

Yet she does need others for her pleasure. She needs her husband because he is her captive; she needs him because she can then tell herself that she stays with him out of a sense of responsibility; she needs Rirette because Rirette's existence supplies material for her sexual fantasies; she needs the world in order to nourish the ego that is paralyzed every time she encounters that world. The existence she has chosen is a long, patient, futile exercise in contradiction; she lives in the world as an active force whose one goal is to retain her ability to act in the defense of her ego; yet she persistently claims that her ego is the victim of the world to a point where she is not free. She does not act to change the world; she acts to compensate for whatever change actions may bring about within her.[20] What the book was to Roquentin and the room to Pierre, her ego becomes to her: a concrete answer to a

20. Sartre sees Flaubert involved in a similar task which Sartre characterizes as "impossible." He writes: "He will have to maintain contact with our species by means

particular problem. Whether the answer is a liberation or represents a step ahead remains another question. Each response that we have seen so far allows us to make only one observation: the act by which an individual shows that he is free does not necessarily lead to a series of acts which shows that he wishes to *remain* free.

RELATED THEMES AND WORKS

Sartre's judgments on William Faulkner and John Dos Passos are reprinted in *Sit. I*: "*Sartoris* par W. Faulkner," pp. 7–13, and "A propos de John Dos Passos et de *1919*," pp. 14–25. For contrasting judgments which help to give a fuller idea of what Sartre then believed literature should seek to be, see his unflattering essays on François Mauriac ("François Mauriac et la liberté," pp. 36–57) and on Vladimir Nabokov ("Vladimir Nabokov: *La Méprise*," pp. 58–62). Mauriac is severely taken to task for depriving his characters of their freedom by inserting them in a universe where they are determined in their behavior and subjected to the judgments which ultimately will be made on that behavior. Nabokov is in effect dismissed because the world of his novel has little to do with the real world and much to do with the cultivation of its author's ego. A denser and less defendable essay in the same volume is: "M. Jean Giraudox et la philosophie d'Aristote. A propos de *Choix des élues*," pp. 82–98. It merits attention because its subject keeps evading Sartre's desire to pinpoint and categorize him.

Sartre's theories of consciousness, emotion, and imagination are all interlinked, the latter two depending on the structures of conscious behavior outlined in the first. His early book *L'Imagination* (1936) is a survey which rejects most traditional views of the imagination because they suggest that the image is something held within consciousness as a kind of permanent possession. Sartre claims that the image is only a mode of consciousness, a mode consciousness expressly chooses because it best suits the intention consciousness most wishes to satisfy. In the background of this survey is his conviction that the phenomenological approach is the most accurate; the book ends with a panegyric to Husserl. *L'Imaginaire* (1940) extends the earlier survey by discussing and analyzing situations in which the imagination is employed on a sustained basis; the attempt is to show the differences between imaginative apprehension and perception. The conclusion of the book argues that imagination, though fraught with dangers, is a necessary and useful process since it sets up points of view and isolates possibilities that might not necessarily or automatically be available to direct perception.

The essential distinction between the two fundamental modes of con-

---

of the facticity which has immersed him in it and at the same time uncover it as a foreign species which he scorns as much in himself as he scorns himself for being part of it" ("Flaubert: du poète à l'Artiste," *TM* 22 [1966]: 479).

sciousness are discussed in the text. Sartre has remained faithful to these elemental distinctions though he has latterly recognized the very strong impact of formation and external influences on the original shape and direction given to the consciousness of the young. The failure to take adequate account of this significant adjustment in Sartre's theory is the only defect which mars Joseph Fell's otherwise excellent discussion, *Emotion in the Thought of Sartre*. Fell presents lucid charts of the different functions of consciousness on pages 43 and 90. His discussion of the content and context of Sartre's idea of consciousness (pp. 149–75) is most helpful both in presenting the background of that thought and in describing its essential intention. Fell's major criticism of Sartre's theory of consciousness is a most telling one, for he sees Sartre setting up a division between the reflective and unreflective modes of consciousness which is too neat, too clear-cut. Fell argues that consciousness moves much more fluidly, fluently, and fleetly from one mode of operation to the other.

One of the reasons why Sartre has been able to remain faithful to a theory which sets up such strangely rigid divisions is because Marxism seems to validate the division and thus appears to be a naturally justified system since some of its terms are the terms Sartre himself had used before he had any ready fluency in Marxist theory. Marx's belief that the human world manifested three interacting aspects—a spontaneous element, a reflective one, and an illusory one—corresponds to Sartre's description of consciousness as something which is spontaneous, capable of reflecting on its spontaneity, and also tempted to lose itself, when blocked, in imaginary or magical (emotional) solutions. Since Marx also claimed that the reflective element of consciousness was allowed for and directed by communist theory (or reality), it is not surprising that Sartre has been able to feel at home with Marxism. Others may feel very much less at home with his theories of imagination and emotions.

Fell's book presents cogent objections to the latter theory. Guenther Anders-Stern's essay, "Emotion and Reality" (*Philosophy and Phenomenological Research* 10 [1950]: 553–62), is a very fine brief discussion of the serious defects in Sartre's theory, based primarily on the author's conviction that Sartre has not in any way paid adequate attention to the positive, non-magical role that emotions play in human apprehension, not only of the world, but also of other human beings. The body of contrary theory on the imagination is so vast as to defy comprehensive citation; it would have to include studies like (1) Liam Hudson's *Contrary Imaginations* (London, 1966) which shows that the way in which an imagination has been trained may play a major part in the formation of particular kinds and levels of intelligence, (2) recent researches into dreams which seem to show that the imagination plays an irreplaceable part in the maintenance of psychic stability, (3) studies like Lévi-Strauss's series, *Mythologies*, and (4) André

Virel's *Histoire de notre image* (Paris, 1966) where, from different points of view, it becomes clear that it can be argued that man would understand nothing about himself and find no solutions for his dilemmas without the existence of his imaginative faculty.

A very solid, valuably footnoted edition of Sartre's *La Transcendance de l'Ego* has been done by Sylvie Le Bon (1966; original publication, 1936). Sartre's work-in-progress on Flaubert shows further that he has remained faithful to this theory, though it, too, has been modified to recognize the enormous appeal the ego offers to the individual as a value to be protected against all kinds of assault and thus as a value one is most unwilling to do away with or even modify. It seems, however, to be the weakest part of Sartre's theory of consciousness, especially in the light of Bruno Bettelheim's *The Empty Fortress* (Glencoe, Ill., 1967), where the discussion of autistic children is powerful proof that, if the ego is not automatically a good thing, its absence is throughly disempowering. Anna Freud's work on disturbed children is more nuanced than Sartre's abstract theory and thus raises serious questions about the pertinence of his theory. Professor Freud shows that, without an ego, the child cannot meet anxiety in any adequate way and thus seeks compensatory behavior which produces consequences worse than any encountered by those characters in Sartre's work who spend their time maintaining the status quo of their "ego."

Some readers may wish to consult the following: *L'Imaginaire*, pp. 273–85, for a discussion of the meaning of a young man's waiting for a young lady named Annie; *BN*, pp. 600–615 ("Quality as a Revelation of Being"), for Sartre's discussion of the viscous and the statement of his agreements and disagreements with Gaston Bachelard. (All of part four of *BN*, "Being, Doing, and Having," is useful for understanding the options available to men and the reasons which inspire their specific choices.) Pp. 84–96 of *Emotions* for the ego theory which most aptly applies to Lulu. Thody's *Jean-Paul Sartre* presents a less sympathetic view of *La Nausée* than the one I have offered; Magny's essay in *Les Sandales d'Empédocle* discusses the novel in close relationship to *BN*. Sartre's early essay, "L'Homme et les choses," (*Sit. I*, pp. 245–93) is related to the kind of experience Roquentin is having but sees it from a different and more detached point of view; the later essay on Giacometti, "La Recherche de l'absolu" (*Sit. III*, pp. 289–305), supports the assertion that Sartre does not approve of Roquentin's project of finding a response through the composition of a book. *L'Imaginaire*, pp. 299–303, contains a precise description of the elements and intentions Sartre feels are expressed in hallucination. George Howard Bauer's *Sartre and the Artist* (University of Chicago Press, 1969) contains an excellent discussion of *La Nausée* ("Melancholy of the Artist," pp. 13–44) which disagrees in significant and challenging ways with my interpretation.

We are sorcerers for ourselves

each time we view our me. . . .

— La Transcendance de l'Ego

3 Beings of Choice

What we have seen so far are either moments preliminary to a life of action or else modes of being developed and sustained in order to keep their initiators as far away as possible from such a life. Each moment or mode has been chosen in order to forestall certain observed consequences. *Les Mots* described the influences and stated the goals which had produced dishonest maps of perilous terrains; the bourgeois cartographers sought to forget the real geography of the world by disguising it. Subsequently, Sartre had discovered that less pleasant landscape and had set himself to the task of making better maps. In *La Nausée* Roquentin took us on a journey to and through the things. That journey turned out to be absurd because it brought us only to the perspective with which we should have started and left us with the question of what to do about the new outlook. The answer it had provided—Roquentin's proposed book—conceivably outlined more problems than it solved. Something had been accomplished on that trip, however, since the threat of self-imposed paralysis which comes with the discovery of the contingency of human existence in an apparently noncontingent universe was kept at bay. Roquentin had found a strategy, if not an answer. Still, there was no firm assurance that he intended to draw a really reliable map.

The world we have been observing so far is a world set apart—bracketed, as the phenomenologists would say—by individuals who want to live apart from it. Their goal has been clear: Lulu, like the young Sartre of *Les Mots*, wants to have a world in which she will be both the creator and the created; she is willing to go through whatever mental somersaults are necessary in order to be the chief if not the sole cartographer of her existence. Pierre and Eve have turned away from an empty but threatening social structure, not in order to create a truer structure, but rather in order to create an antistructure which will surround them as the shell surrounds the oyster—and with the same results; encased in a shell, they cannot see beyond their elected space. The space they occupy consoles them for their dissatisfaction with society, even as it comments on the bourgeois world they have abandoned in honest despair. A vaguely common goal is shared by all these characters. Each seeks a static way of life which will eliminate the abrasive effect of living with others; each has either sought or chosen a mode of life which assigns blame to an external force; each has experienced the temptation to limit the number of questions he is willing to raise.

In "Erostrate" and *Huis-clos* we move beyond that preliminary world where individuals either have not encountered the social world or else have refused or transmuted it. In these two short works, we are in the world

where men meet and work together, and where they cannot avoid conflict because their own free acts have created the terms of the conflict.
The characters in these works are thus quite conscious of the conflict and
quite actively inspired with a desire to overcome it to their advantage. They
have rejected immobility; they have not retreated into some apparently safe
sanctuary but rather have set up projects for themselves and mapped out
paths of action. They know what they want. The decision to act has not,
however, removed them from the threat of recurrent anguish since, in trying
to modify the world through their acts, they find that the world is resistant;
it sets up a coefficient of adversity—the measure of its resistance—which
either determines the nature of their subsequent acts or supplies the terms
of their self-defense.[1] They journey further and more venturesomely into
the world than have the others we have considerd; their trips, like those
of psychedelic enthusiasts, do not necessarily produce the hoped-for results.

Paul Hilbert, the narrator of "Erostrate" (1939), is far beyond concern
with the meaning or purpose of the natural universe; he is plunged into the
social world whose collective acts represent for him what the movement
of the things represented for Roquentin. The social world threatens him with
its massiveness; it invites him to slip into its ways and thereby to lose his
individuality. Against this threat, he seeks an act quite unlike the acts
chosen by Roquentin and Lulu. The act he seeks is one which, though it
will destroy him, will also twist the neck of the threatening world until it
howls in dismay. If the ego must go, with all it has suffered in the way of
unalleviated frustration and disappointment, at least it will go in the aftermath of the violence it will have enacted.

It would be easy enough to dismiss Hilbert as a banal individual, a dull
madman who does not even succeed in brightening up the world for an
instant with the disastrous realization of his project. But, as Hannah Arendt
has incidentally demonstrated in her book on Eichmann, banal men can
be the conveyors of important truths. The central truth about Paul Hilbert
is that, like so many colorless men, he does not want to be mediocre. In a
vast world, he wants his particular space. Since the world as he sees it is
not willing to parcel out space to imprecisely ambitious individuals, but
rather insists that they become incorporated into its ways, the world and
its mass of cooperating men become his enemy.

1. The term "coefficient of adversity" is one Sartre has borrowed from Gaston Bachelard and uses throughout his work, gradually attributing more and more importance
to adversity's influence in conditioning the individual's notion of just how much he
can do. His earlier emphasis is different since, when he speaks of the coefficient of
adversity, he is speaking of something to be overcome; later, Sartre will use the
term in speaking of obstacles surmountable only after the greatest expense of energy
and ingenuity. The meaning of the term will become immediately clearer when we
note that Hilbert, though he is equipped with tools adequate to the realization of his
project, cannot overcome the adverse forces he encounters or, more precisely, cannot
change the idea he has of those forces and their strength.

He does not believe that his hostility is cause for especial worry on his part; it has been with him from birth and has not been sublimated by the compensatory images the young Sartre exploited. The humanistic attitude of the milieu in which he lives has not convinced him to give up his hostility, for Hilbert has discovered that bourgeois humanism is a melody played loudly by a small group in an effort to drown out the real sounds coming from the surrounding world. Those real sounds are the faint cries of a horde of ants busily committed to doing the work of ants. He hopes for something better. Though Hilbert may be disagreeable—primarily because he keeps raising the kinds of fundamental questions bourgeois humanism is supposed to have answered for all time if not for all men—the problem he embodies is real. It has to do with the tensions between the individual and the group which every man has felt at some time and which have become the center of the major organized activities of the present generation of American university youth. Tucked into that fundamental problem are other questions. Is it reasonable to ask a man to live in society? What must a man give up in order to do so? How many compromises must he make with what he believes to be his essential self? What compensation does the society offer for the sacrifices it exacts?

Hilbert finds neither clear nor positive answers to these questions and therefore finds no way to enlist in the work and assent to the beliefs of the surrounding society. Since the questions remain, he must find an answer whose terms point to a mode of action. He decides upon the general goal of his project; he will perform an act which, even as it expresses his contempt for men, will also linger on in their minds as a sour warning. He will become like Erostratus who burned down the Temple of Diana at Ephesus in order to be remembered. Hilbert overlooks two relevant facts. Erostratus's act was performed on the birthday of Alexander the Great; few people remember Ephesus or Diana's temple and what happened to it. The paths of madness too often lead to the groves of anonymity.

The basis of his project is contradictory. That does not necessarily mean it is wrong, especially if we believe that man himself is a contradiction. Not only is Hilbert rejecting the community of men he has encountered, he is also rejecting man and, by reduction, himself. His condemnation of other men is derived from the sparse qualities he detects in them; yet his reaction to these squalid creatures is one of fear. Like Hugo in Sartre's *Les Mains sales*, and for somewhat similar reasons, he doesn't want to change the world; he wants to blow it up. He wants to eliminate other men from the scene of his inadequacies and simultaneously remove himself from his discomfort in their presence. There is a rigorous enough logic in his reactions since only two ways are open to him: either he passes beyond the state of anthood to become the chief ant or he removes himself from the possibility of being any kind of ant at all.

He cannot, for all the vitriol of his comments, cease being a man and therefore cease sharing in the appetites of the other workers on the anthill. He admits that he is ambitious; and he demonstrates in a memorable way that he has sexual appetites which, in his case, do not reflect a desire for sharing experience with women but rather a need of women in order to feed his onanistic fantasies. The need does not reduce his overall fear, since in order to satisfy his sexual hungers he must pay for the woman's presence. He justifies the hungers experienced and the money exchanged by humiliating those he employs. He does not seek a partner so much as a witness who must be reduced to a victim. Apparently he cannot bring himself to orgasm unless someone is watching; what the other is asked to watch is an elaborate form of image-provoked orgasm. In sexual release and in his other enterprises, Hilbert seeks to make the world behave according to his evaluation of it; it matters little to him that "certain layers of this world necessitate by their very nature a relation to others. This relation can be a mere quality of the world that I create and in no way obliges me to accept the real existence of the other *I*'s" (*Ego*, p. 104).

It matters very little until the moment when his projected action sets him up against the world he wishes to transcend; at that moment—when he discovers his desire to transcend the world—he admits the existence of that world and its coefficient of adversity. He admits, too, that other men have projects which he must confront before he can conduct his exercise in transcendence. He falls out of solipsism—out of *intimacy*—and into the world of interacting consciousnesses which is the world of men. In Lulu's case, the individual fell only for the time needed to reinforce her ego; then she retreated into that ego once again. Hilbert does not have this resilience. Once he falls into the world of men he finds himself imprisoned. The only way to escape from the prison is to escape from himself, leaving as his legacy an object which, like the Eiffel Tower or Erostratus's burned temple, will be beyond men's assaults.

Hilbert's ego cannot successfully manage its own project without making use of other men. His project is inspired by an act another man has already carried out and thus has no real originality; his tool—a gun which he intends to discharge randomly at passersby—is an object manufactured by other men. It is also an object which achieves a bizarre meaning for him since it, rather than his penis, is the device by which he will commune with others. Its discharge is meant to express on an even more colossal scale the contempt he has tried to convey in his use of prostitutes: it will humiliate his victims; it will fulfil him. What he is really after is the creation of a situation in which there will no longer be any need to act. By a single act he will cease to have to act again. But one act is not enough. Before he can bring himself to unleashing the holocaust, he must go through a whole series of actions which will serve as the interminably long prelude to the final act.

He loses his job through absenteeism; he spends all his money; he addresses a letter describing his coming crime to a select list of 102 writers; he progressively directs his freedom of action towards one act. He has transformed himself into an object about which he thinks in the third person: " 'He is cowering in a dark, shut-off room. For three days He has not eaten or slept. The doorbell rang and He didn't answer. In a while He is going down into the street and He'll kill' " (p. 93). The old fear remains, but it is now caused by this object he has made of himself and enthroned in his own imagination as a royal or divine person whose ferocity demands the capitalized pronoun.

The worst is never certain, Sartre writes frequently, borrowing the subtitle of Paul Claudel's *Le Soulier de satin*; in Hilbert's case it may not be certain, but it is what happens. His act ends in a mess. Reluctance to kill seeps into his mind; he explains it by saying that he is hesitant to kill people who are already dead. Finally, he fires at one man and presumably kills him. Then he flees, taking the wrong street, and hides in a toilet stall. Though he has kept one bullet for himself, he cannot bring himself to use it. He suggests that this is because he wishes to know whether he has really killed the man; but he also suggests that in the end he was paralyzed and could do nothing except give himself up.

The failure, however, is all of a piece with what he really sought. He has not wanted to take his leave of the world, nor has he wanted to blow the world up; he has wanted to draw attention to himself and to know that such attention is finally being paid. In the end, having laid out a battle-plan supposed to express his hostility towards men, he becomes their object: "If they take me they'll beat me up, smash my teeth, maybe put out one of my eyes" (p. 97). By implication, there will be a reward in this since, as an object in the hands of *them*, he will preserve his ego intact.[2]

The three characters in *Huis-clos* (1945) have gone even further than Hilbert in their involvement with action and with others. Though some critics have looked upon them as freaks who cannot be taken as representative of humanity, Inès, Garcin, and Estelle are sane people. What is not commonplace is the point in time and the place in space to which their sane lives have brought them. Each had had his idea of the "good" life; each had been forced to a form of radical action in order to maintain that good life; each is now in hell where the interaction of their consciousnesses can change nothing. They are fixed and presumably inalterable because their past, now

2. Cf. *Emotions*: "[Psychoanalytical psychology] . . . was the first to insist upon the fact that every state of consciousness is the equivalent of something other than itself. For example, the clumsy theft carried out by a person who is sexually obsessed is not simply a 'clumsy theft'. As soon as we consider it with the psychoanalysts as a phenomenon of self-punishment it sends us back to something other than itself. It sends us back to the first complex for which the sick person is trying to justify himself by punishing himself" (p. 43).

that it is over, has the quality of an object. Nothing that they say or do *now* can redefine, reform, or compensate for what they were *then*. They are locked up together to play a rueful endless game whose rules have been traced out from the patterns of their lives and whose outcome brings them fruitlessly back to the beginning.

It is no surprise that two of them are convinced that their game has been organized by someone else who lacked the good manners to ask whether it was the sort of game the participants would like to play for all eternity. They will play the game because, given the pattern of their lives, it is unavoidable; they will converse, try to touch each other, reject each other, fear each other, and hate each other. Then they will start again. There is no chance of friendship; there is no chance that two of the three will become lovers, because the third—it makes no particular difference which one is the third—will always be there, like an indefatigible god whose role is to watch and say no. But this witness is no god; he is another individual who will not allow any situation to develop which entails his exclusion.

The setting of the play is designed to present a fixed field of action which, because of its fixity, is unlike the field of the human world; this is not the real world, but it is like part of the real world in that its fixity corresponds to what its inhabitants had sought in the real world. In death they find what they could not have in life: an unchanging space. They negotiate it no better than they did the wide-open spaces of their existence. The setting, then, is a metaphor which has nothing to do with that hell defined by dogmatists and theologians as the place where the books of ethical accounting are finally put in order. This hell is created by the individual as his response to the Other who terrifies him. With the possible exception of Inès, the three characters learn that it is no more than an extension—or perhaps, and more accurately, a freezing over—of the hell in which they have always lived. There is only one difference: here they cannot hide either from themselves or from the dreaded Other. What they were in the world—a coward, a lesbian, and a nymphomaniac—does not matter as much as what those traits revealed of their more fundamental nature. Each is a narcissist, and a room populated with narcissists is bound to be transformed into a space considerably less comfortable than their earthly playgrounds. Here there is no exit; and here the spectator sees what happens when resistible forces meet movable objects and are deadlocked by their fears.

They had never before thought that their acts could have any consequences other than those they were willing to avow. The horror of this, for Sartre, is that they are perfectly right. The spillover from what they had enacted on earth never did engulf them because its impact, by their most careful planning, was deflected away from them; indeed they admit that there was spillover only when they find themselves blocked in hell with but two modes of action available to them: either they can try to get along with each other or they can contemplate in company with each other the object their past has become. In hell, they find an equilibrium of forces which, while stable, is also maddening; it contrasts grotesquely with the disequilibrium of their terrestrial existence. Though their lives had aims and goals, the aims and goals were never hedged or adjusted by any force other than their egotistic needs. In this sense, each one of them had an idea that was somewhat more "normal" than Hilbert's; each one lived with full awareness that life is a *series* of acts performed in order to achieve a certain end. But the objective goal of their acts was little different from the goal sought by Hilbert. Like him, they endeavored to make a world they could not afford dance to tunes they were unwilling to pay for. In hell, they will neither organize the dances they want nor pay for the jigs they have already enjoyed. In hell, they will make one another see what each refused to acknowledge on earth.

For one who does not believe in hell and therefore in a just force which eventually redresses the injustice of this world, the choice of a metaphor using hell is an indication of some desperation. It is an admission that the unjust and the cruel, the indifferent and the mindless, can live with their defects, and with the consequences those defects produce, without ever having to pay for the resulting damage. The recognition of this can lead to modes of behavior whose only limit is what you can get away with; one need only establish the social structures or political systems or ideological persuasions which will tolerate and also protect such behavior.[3] Precisely because there is no firm principle of justice, precisely because there is no supreme judge who will evaluate human acts, the earthly lives of these three people seem, if not justified, at least justifiable. Each has sought to satisfy the want he identified with happiness; each has recognized that man is quite on his own in the pursuit of happiness, at least in the sense that happiness will not be presented to him—he must labor for it. And each has been willing to strive, to negotiate, and, when all other ways were blocked, to cheat.

This makes the dilemma more complex and more desperate, for these three never let go entirely while alive; they never pleaded the sweep of forces they could not control. They met those forces and struggled with them; they did not try to absent themselves, like Roquentin, in order to write a book which would be an act of revenge and perhaps even scorn; they did not try, like Hilbert, to define one violent act which would revenge

3. As we shall see repeatedly throughout this book, the impossibility of justice and the recurrence of well-paying injustice is a scandal which haunts Sartre both because it has had such a long and healthy life and because no meaningful or durable means has been found to eradicate it. In his latest play, *Les Troyennes* (1965), the scandal is presented in its starkest terms. Though the play is lean, its time-span is long, since Sartre uses the Euripides text to comment on a present-day situation. The implication is clear: time moves on and civilization makes no progress in actualizing one of its foundations—justice.

them. Nor did they settle for the kind of carefully managed self-protection Lulu devised as her response, perhaps because they did not have a quiet victim, perhaps because their ambitions transcended hers. But the results were no better and, in certain terms of the comparison, were considerably worse, since they did measurably greater harm. If they had not been courageous, they had been strong, if they had not been moral, they had been mobile. They met the world in a whole series of confrontations and they tried to deal with it. It is not altogether frivolous to say that they met it as students who, having carefully read and not altogether digested *Being and Nothingness,* were determined that their actions would deliver them from the grimmer situations traced out by that long work.

The grimmest situation Sartre had described in that book was the area of intersubjective relations, where people meet in subtle lifelong battles, each person trying to protect himself against the possible tyranny of others. Hilbert had tried to solve the problem in a way which ultimately turned out to be contradictory: he wanted to show his contempt for others but could not do so without using those others; in the end his fear of them undid him and left them relatively undisturbed. One can imagine his act producing little more than some dinnertime excitement for the readers of *France-Soir.* The three characters in *Huis clos* met the world cautiously and shrewdly; their only excuse is perhaps that offered by Garcin: the lack of time to do all that was necessary in order to win. Yet it is not time which was short—as Inès tells Garcin, there is never enough time; it was understanding, perspective, a realization of what was possible which were scarce. Each one at some point had discovered that he had come naked into the world; what we are supposed to discover by the end of the play is that each had chosen the wrong wardrobe to clothe his vulnerability.

What is more pertinent than the possibility of their having read *Being and Nothingness* is the fact that they have lived out many of its terms. They have, for a variety of reasons, been forced to reject the available wardrobes because none of them properly suited their needs. The security of her class was not enough for Estelle since its norms did not make open allowance for her sexual needs nor, before the advent of the pill, had it found ways of controlling her fertility; the force of his idealism could not appropriately account for Garcin's cowardice; Inès was an outcast on at least two levels, for not only did she come from the lower classes, she was also, and by her own admission, *une femme damnée.* The religious conception of the world does not seem to have had a part in the lives of any of them. They all discovered the real world as a place where they encountered the anguish born from their discovery of their contingency: though they are this, they might just as easily have been that; they cannot as easily be what they want to be.[4]

4. Cf. *BN*: ". . . there is a full contingency of the being of consciousness. We wish only to show (1) that *nothing* is the cause of consciousness, (2) That consciousness

They have, in short, been through the fundamental existential experience; they have learned that consciousness is the faculty which directs their attention towards the world as the field where they *must* act. We have seen how that discovery leads man to confrontation with a world of objects which are radically different from him because they do not have to act; they are. Yet, in order to be, he must do something in their midst, either using them or fighting against them. We have seen, too, that in his observation of the world of natural being man espies the model which haunts him throughout his life with the temptation to become like it: placid, quiet, beyond reach. However strong that temptation, he knows at every moment that this is precisely what he cannot do: he cannot be. Surrounded by that which is contained completely in itself—Sartre calls this being-in-itself (*l'être-en-soi*)— he is aware that he lives in order to be. He is being-for-itself (*l'être-pour-soi*), that is, he is the being whose function it is to be ever and always in the process of becoming.[5] Part of his temptation is to let himself be carried along as he thinks being-in-itself is carried along; the notion that being-in-itself is carried along is, of course, a concept he creates.

Being-in-itself is massive and immobile; it does not consciously slip from one state to another under outside pressures. If the idea of slipping and sliding is being-in-itself's revenge on being-for-itself, this is because that idea provides men with a consoling explanation for wishy-washy conduct; it also encourages them to believe they are right in claiming, as Lulu did, that they are carried along by forces beyond their control. Man, in defining viscosity and in succumbing to it, is surrendering to an idea he has created; it is the denial he hurls back at a structure which apparently denies him. The initial discovery reflective consciousness makes is that, because it cannot be, it must exist. Sartre, as we have seen, uses the latter as a transitive verb: I exist my life; I exist my acts; that is, I bring them into the world, I act them out on or against the field of being. The process ends only with death.

Once the initial discovery is made, I become aware of consciousness as my presence not only *in* but more importantly *to* the world of things and people. One way or another I must have relations with them. They may not organize me, though surely they try; but they do organize the world in

is the cause of its own way of being" (p. lvi, n.). "What the for-itself lacks is the self—or itself as in-itself" (p. 89). ". . . this perpetually absent being which haunts the for-itself is itself fixed in the in-itself" (p. 90). ". . . without this being which it is in the form of not being it, consciousness would not be consciousness—i.e., lack. . . . This being . . . has no priority over consciousness, and consciousness has no priority over it. They *form a dyad*" (p. 91).

5. Cf. *BN* where Sartre writes of the for-itself: ". . . it is a being such that in its being, its being is in question. . . . *consciousness is a being such that in its being, its being is in question in so far as this being implies a being other than itself*" (p. lxii). ". . . the being of *for-itself* is defined . . . as being what it is not and not being what it is" (p. lxv). "The law of being of the *for-itself*, as the ontological foundation of consciousness, is to be itself in the form of presence to itself" (p. 77).

which I live and which I may try to organize or modify in some other way more fitting to my needs and ambitions. Indeed, I have to organize it in a way different from the way in which I first encounter it because I encounter it as an area in which I must operate in order to satisfy my needs and desires. I cannot know whether those needs and desires have been provided for. I discover myself as an individual who lacks what the world of objects possesses; I also discover myself as an individual who wants what the world of other people has. My consciousness leads me to a series of negative realizations: I am *not* being-in-itself; I am *not* Pierre but Jean-Paul; I do *not* have the food I need; I do *not* have the woman I desire. I am the creature who lacks everything except my consciousness of what I lack; as a result, I am essentially the man of unsatisfied desires.

The process by which I go about satisfying those desires is the process by which I am constantly manifesting nothingness in the world. I have discovered that I am a non-thing which amounts to no more than discovering that I am an emptiness to be filled. Once I have noticed this, I realize that I am totally free, not because I want to be free—no one has asked me my opinion about that. I am free because I alone can choose how I shall set about filling my emptiness. This is absurd; and this absurdity alienates me. But I can neither live with the absurdity nor celebrate my alienation unless I do so freely. Absurdity may be the halo I bring into the world with me; if it remains with me as my justification for living irresponsibly that is because I have chosen to keep it. I have no task except to make myself, and if I choose to live fascinated with my contingency—with seeming to be this rather than that—or under the domination of others, my choice is no less free. My greatest desire remains that of forming myself in such a way as to achieve the placidity of being-in-itself. This is impossible so long as the future stretches out its immeasurable space before me. I can only be when I am dead; and obviously at that point I have ceased to be what I was being: an emptiness to fill.

Nonbeing, then, exists in the world because of man. Each time he makes a choice he is saying yes to one thing and no to something else. Each time he is here, he is *not* there; he lives in solitude because he has *no* friends; he is starving because there is *no* food available; he is poor because he does *not* have money; if he abandons his family, he is *not* seeing to his responsibilities; if he lies, he is *not* telling the truth. Each one of these acts either defines a situation or describes a choice; and each one is a real category. Nonbeing is not that which is not; nonbeing is that which exists as nonbeing. It exists really and consequentially because it produces measurable effects.[6]

6. In *BN* Sartre discusses a situation where a man enters a café looking for his friend Pierre who, he finds, is not there. Sartre writes: "This example is sufficient to show that non-being does not come to things by a negative judgment; it is the negative judgment, on the contrary, which is conditioned and supported by non-being" (p. 11). Elsewhere in *BN*, he writes: "Nothingness is not. Nothingness 'is made-to-be'. Nothing-

To counteract the bleak evidence of this series of discoveries, men have been led to erect systems which, like their idea of the viscous, are no more than mental constructs which help them to get through life without having to look at its sterner issues.[7] The systems, again like the temptation of the viscous, frequently turn out to be no more than hiding places into which men retreat in order to avoid their own freedom. And when the various havens crumble and the diverse faiths fail, there is the final retreat into fatalism. I could not make myself as I wanted because vaster forces would not let me: time was against me; *they* were against me.

Huis-clos can only be understood against the background of this radical appraisal of human experience which rejects every ideological and philosophical ornament Western civilization has created in the effort to protect man from a direct confrontation with the barrenness of his initial situation. The systems, however, do not protect so much as they console, for at some point the individual cannot avoid the harrowing encounter with his fundamental reality. He can pull back from it; he can pretend it has not taken place. Though he cannot prevent the encounter, he can lie to himself about its significance.

I have already pointed out that the characters in this play have lived beyond the realm of things and in the midst of other people; I have also pointed out that they have acted and made choices and that, in this sense, they seem to conform to Sartre's basic insistence on the inevitability of action. But for all that—and this is Sartre's essential point—they have not lived any more honestly in the social world than had Lulu. On the contrary, the area each has chosen as the field of his acts, is a space carefully demarcated from the real world in an effort to pretend that that world does not exist. In its place each one of them has created a surrogate world.

They have done this, of course, in order to protect what they take to be their most essential self. They have performed no act which was not clearly designed and carried out to protect that essential self. But since there is no essential self already formed and packaged and needing protection, they

---

ness does not nihilate itself; Nothingness 'is nihilated'. It follows therefore that there must exist a Being (this cannot be the In-itself) of which the property is to nihilate Nothingness. . . . The Being by which Nothingness arrives in the world is a being such that in its Being, the Nothingness of its Being is in question. *The being by which Nothingness comes into the world must be its own Nothingness*" (pp. 22–23). That Being is the for-itself whose awareness that it is a void to be filled produces the concept of Nothingness and, in the immediately ensuing bargain, the possibility or the need of doing something about that Nothingness—denying it in the very act of trying to fill the void.

7. The viscous, as we have seen, is more than a mental construct; more accurately, it is a term which refers to a visible natural situation. The reality of that situation, however, does not justify human efforts to form projects on the basis of its operations since nature, in its moments of viscosity, is not *aware* of what it is doing.

have lived out their lives in a vain effort to effect an impossible result. They have acted in order to impede change; but in order to achieve this contradictory end, they have had to live with paradoxes. They have had to assert that the consequences of acts have no meaning; what counts is the intention behind the act. Garcin's pacifism, for example, is not changed because his acts seem to deny it; it still remains as a pure intention in his mind, and his mind is what he hopes to use as the organizing force of his life. They have also had to close their eyes to the intersubjective world even as they used that world to satisfy their wants. Estelle's infanticide must be seen in the light of the fact that she had never wanted the child; Inès's complicity in the death of a young man must be seen in the light of her wish to keep the woman she desired; Garcin's ill-treatment of his wife must be seen in the light of her willingness to put up with it.

Each has lived, then, actively engaged in an effort to be little more than a passive force with active needs; when things go wrong, the world is there to bear the blame. Each has needed others in order to achieve this kind of stasis, but each has denied any responsibility towards others. Each has lived in an intersubjective world, all the while engaging in acts which both deny the rights of the Other and suggest that one can live without the Other. The one defense which might have been available to them—that it's each man for himself in a cold competitive world—is one they cannot claim. No one of them has been able to be a hermetically contained in-itself-for-itself, because no one of them could have been himself if he had not made use of another. Each comes to hell sadly endowed with a lifetime's habits in order to find there an inflexible equilibrium of strategically necessary inaction. In hell, each has the same hopes and desires; but in hell each meets two others who are equally knowledgeable in the ways of egotism. Nothing short-circuits because nothing connects. They can do one another neither real good nor real harm because the only action which is left to them shows them the degree to which action is no longer meaningful: it can no longer produce results.

At first they seem to form a ladder of values, with Estelle on the lowest rung; she seems to have been the most inauthentic and dishonest of the three. She has lived with an airy conviction of her total innocence. Her marriage was an act of kindness towards an old man she didn't love; it was only reasonable that she should have entertained more potent lovers. The murder of her child was no different from getting rid of the garbage left behind by someone else. Everything unpleasant in life necessarily came from others, since her intentions patently had nothing to do with evil. But others have a much more important function in her life than that of being available to bear the brunt of her blunders; without others she is not sure that she exists, and the worst immediate punishment she must endure in hell is the deprivation of others. She cannot be sure she exists unless she can see herself, and in a mirrorless room she finally learns that the most important way in which she had always seen herself had been in the image she presented to others. Since she can no longer verify the image in mirrors, she must now rely on other eyes to reflect it. If the eyes refuse to look at her or, worse, if the eyes lie, she will no longer have the assurances she has always needed. Narcissism, like sexual fantasy, cannot do without another, whether the other be there truly or present only in the image returned from a reflecting pool.

Garcin, whose life has been spent amidst men and in the management of causes, seems immeasurably better than this self-indulgent daughter of a pampered class. He has pursued an ideal which ordinarily we do not question; he appears to have been a free agent. Yet, at each critical moment when he should have acted decisively, he failed to do so, removing himself either from the situation or from responsibility. In hell, his punishment is the removal of the possibilities of withdrawal: his eyes no longer blink and thus interruptions are no longer possible; the lights in the drawing room cannot be put out. But verbal play is still possible and Garcin retreats into it, talking either in the passive voice or else attributing his frustrations to *them*. When the door flies open, he does not leave; he needs to stay in order to convince Inès that he is not a coward.

Inès seems the least inauthentic of the three. She has faced her lesbianism openly and perhaps even courageously. But she has also used it as an excuse to explain her immersion in evil, and in this sense her decision has been free. She has decided to incarnate a certain kind of evil in order to be able to use it as a value.[8] Her punishment, in addition to being placed in the presence of an attractive woman she cannot possess, is to be in the presence of others whose equally free decisions rob her of her excuse. Her fear when the door opens is that the others will exclude her; her triumph is to learn that Garcin needs the approbation she will never give. But she also needs his complicity if she is to have Estelle.

In hell the three of them can no longer make excuses, just as they can no longer make adjustments designed to camouflage their actions. What they sought in life, an essence which would justify them, a fixed quantity which would be coeval with them, has now come to pass; they have joined the realm of being, not as a result of triumphant narcissism, but simply because their lived experience, their past, has now become an object. They cannot

8. "Value" in the Sartrean vocabulary does not allude to something meritorious. Cf. *BN*: "The ideal fusion of the lacking with the one which lacks what is lacking is an unrealizable totality which haunts the for-itself and constitutes its very being as a nothingness of being. This ideal we called the in-itself-for-itself or *value*" (p. 194). Colette Audry provides a helpful comment on this (*Jean-Paul Sartre*, p. 43): "The being of the Self, which is always aimed at and never achieved, is nothing other than value, that is, an unsurpassable absolute beyond which there is nothing more to achieve and which is silhouetted on the horizon of the For-itself as the being which the For-itself *has to be* and which gives the For-itself its meaning. . . ."

in any way—either by lies or acts or even the truth—change or adjust or become honest. Subjected to their egotism throughout life, they must now look back on what that egotism achieved: three wasted lives spent in flight from the Other who now controls them by controlling the interpretation of their past.

Death has created the objects they sought to be throughout their lives; it has brought them here where, helplessly, they can only look back on those objects which fade as the world forgets about them or moves in to exploit the void they have left. In hell, when it is too late, they not only discover the Other but they also discover how much their lives were worked out, well and ill, in terms of the Other. In life, they had tried to suppress the Other by refusing to admit that the Other had as much right to make claims on them as they on him; in death, where they still need the Other, they are confronted with a fixed situation where the Other, who can correspond to their needs (for Estelle is attracted to Garcin, Inès to Estelle, and Garcin to Inès) will not do so, not only because there is no way to do so but equally because there is no will to do so. They have learned nothing. Garcin will not have intercourse with Estelle, Estelle will not have intercourse with Inès, and Inès, unwilling to give up her scale in the equilibrium of forces, will not give Garcin the assurance he wants. Hell is a *ménage à trois* inhabited by potential couples who detest even the idea of any third participant, for they dread that the third participant is bound to be a witness and eventually a judge. Having been masters who sought to enslave others in life, they find in death that they are, all three, slaves hungering to remain masters. Mastery remains with the Other. In death they will continue to do *consciously* what they did throughout life; but there will be one essential difference—in death each has met his match.

The metaphor of hell moves in two directions; for, if the way they lived their lives has brought them to hell, that is only because the way in which they lived their lives was hell. They are not suddenly in hell; they are only suddenly conscious of the hell in which they have always existed. The drawing room where they find themselves is only a specification of the situation in which they found themselves throughout life.[9] By fleeing the hell they

9. In 1965, twenty years after the original publication of *Huis-clos*, Sartre wrote an introduction to a recorded version of the play. Referring to one of its most celebrated phrases—"hell is others"—Sartre commented: "There were those who believed that what I meant by that was that our relations with others are always poisoned and that such relations were always forbidden. What I meant was something else altogether. I mean . . . that others are, at bottom, what is most important in ourselves for our own knowledge of ourselves. When we think about ourselves, when we try to know ourselves, we end up by making use of the knowledge others already have about us. We judge ourselves with the means that others have and which they have given us so that we can judge ourselves.

"If my relations with others are bad, I place myself in total dependence on others and then, in effect, I am in hell. And there are a number of people in the world who

feared finding with the Other, they have placed themselves in the hell which exists without the Other. It is too late now to do anything about it; but it was always too late, since the fundamental project of each of their lives was to resist the Other without whom they could not have satisfied their wants. Freely, in each of their acts, they condemned themselves to a hell they did not wish to acknowledge. The hell of their lives, as the hell of their deaths, has been constructed from their fear of the Other.

RELATED THEMES AND WORKS

Sartre's comments on what he meant to mean by *Huis-clos* somewhat misconstrue the mood in which he wrote the play. That mood was primarily literary and not a little fascinated by the dramatic impact of providing as bleak a picture as possible; the same bleakness, which risks very much being onesided, also characterized *Being and Nothingness*. The play ran the danger of being misunderstood both because the metaphor of hell easily slipped into the Christian economy and was seen by many as an attempt to sophisticate and modernize the idea of hell by making it a psychological rather than a physical state and also because its three characters were so relentlessly depicted in their vanity as to run the risk of being wooden. Thody (pp. 83–4) suggests that those whom Sartre admires for their social involvement with the right causes would experience the dissatisfactions expressed in *Huis-clos* quite as much as its three characters; his implication was that Sartre was stacking the deck. Campbell (*Jean-Paul Sartre*, 1945, rev. ed. 1947) earlier raised the same question (p. 137) and concluded (p. 138) that Sartre had indeed stacked the deck by choosing individuals who would not offend the sensibilities of the Parisian public, which would understand that such people were bound to have such problems. Sartre's 1965 gloss, in his note to the recorded version, agrees in part with both commentators but suggests that all commentary must be made on the basis of the wider reaches and applications of his philosophy. A more recent and very fluent commentary on the place of *Huis-clos* in Sartre's theatre can be found in Gilles Sandier's "Socrate dramaturge" (*L'Arc* 30 [1966]: 77–86, see esp. pp. 80–81).

Ayer ("Novelist-Philosophers: V—Jean-Paul Sartre," *Horizon*, 12 [1945]: 12–20) provides a good summary of Sartre's description of the structure of being and the complementary operations of being, nothingness, and consciousness. Ayer's comments are disdainful and to be taken with more than a grain of skeptical thought for, while Ayer has read *BN* care-

are in hell because they depend too much on the judgment of others. But that in no way means that one can't have another kind of relation with others. What it indicates simply is the major importance of all others for each of us" (Quoted in *L'Express*, 11–17 October 1965).

fully, he has not read it sympathetically. As a result he falsifies its implications to suit his objections rather than suit his explications to Sartre's theories. A very angry—so angry that it is amusing—critique of Sartre's ideas on nothingness can be found in Kurt Reinhardt's *The Existentialist Revolt* (1952, rev. ed. 1960).

Huis-clos was originally entitled *Les Autres* and was first published in the review *L'Arbalète* (1944). It was dedicated to "an anonymous lady who once told Sartre that she would not want to be judged on the actions she had committed during her lifetime" (Thody, p. 80). The themes of the play are picked up in Sartre's scenario *Les Jeux sont faits* (1947), where they are displayed against a more complex background. Despite that complexity and despite the fact that the dead in *Les Jeux* are allowed to return to this earth, the result is no better: class differences are too great. The implication, early in Sartre's career, was that such differences needed deeper investigation and analysis than he was at the time willing to undertake, given his conviction that the bourgeoisie was so defective as to only deserve condemnation.

. . . the Other teaches me who I am.

— Being and Nothingness

4 The Other

Western thinkers have not, on the whole, been very much concerned with the problem of the Other as a source of fear. Most frequently, the Other has been considered as part of the category "man," and thus as a being who shares certain essential characteristics and potentialities with other members of his species. As a result, philosophers have preferred to study the question of the class's place in the universe, assuming that all members of the class would profit from such inquiry. The assumption is not in itself erroneous; what may be erroneous is the idea that all men react with the same degree of reassurance to the discoveries of the philosophers. Plato could thus be concerned with establishing harmony between individual men and higher hidden forms; he could also allow for cruel use of the others one discarded as one climbed the ladder of being. Aristotle could be preoccupied with making man part of the higher order by demonstrating that the organization man brought to his world entered into an overall pattern of movement in the universe; it was therefore part of the operations of the supreme mover who spent his time thinking about his own thought which in turn was concerned with thinking. The question of slavery was readily solved by making slaves lesser men.

The presupposition has often been that man, thinking about his own thought, would share the calm sense of majesty that was God's; Sartre's presupposition is quite the opposite, for Sartrean man when he thinks about his own thinking, that is, when he mulls over what he has observed, begins asking questions. The first explosive questions he raises—What am I doing here? Who am I?—leave him dismayed. This process introduces a radical change in thinking about man since it suggests that he is not happy simply with asking himself what he will do with the world which has been given him; he is not happy with the question because he cannot readily believe that the world, as he sees it, is his home. It is not his home, first, because it belongs to those who are already there, and, second, because he does not know what he, as a being distinguished from those others, will make of the space which appears to belong to them.

At earlier moments in Western thought, man was invited to put aside his dismay by associating himself with the goals vaguely or clearly defined in the higher purposes. He was invited and even exhorted to associate himself with the loftier destiny either of the nation or the race or the universe; hubris defined the limit of ethics beyond whose undemarcated threshold lay danger. In the Christian dispensation, he was told that he was only in temporary residence on a globe which, after Galileo, was no more than the spinning antechamber to the remote mansions of the Lord. Even among

An object is meaningful when,

through it, one perceives another object.

— "L'Artiste et sa conscience"

those who did not believe in a more satisfying haven after death, there was a tendency to make and apparently believe statements that began: "*All men. . . .*" It was not until the end of the seventeenth century that the assurance which went into such statements began to disappear. Descartes' common sense might have been the possession of all men, but what Montesquieu, Hobbes, and Sade saw was that that common faculty led to very contradictory and conflicting ambitions. If Hobbes encouraged men to yield to the governing force of the Leviathan, he did not for that believe that this was the sweetest surrender that could be effected. In a world where *homo homini lupus est*, there was little chance of survival unless you joined the most powerful pack.

The question of the Other manifests a disquietude that was detectable long before the seventeenth century and which has been reflected in literature when it has not found expression in philosophy.[1] Those who have thought about it have not necessarily denied that there is a class, man, nor have they automatically denied that the members of the class may possess common faculties and potentialities; they have raised the question of whether every member of the class seeks, or even should seek, the same goals. More fundamentally, they raise the question of whether every member of the class sees the world in the same way. As I have shown in the first chapter, Sartre, and with him other phenomenologists and existentialists, traces out a fundamental disparity between what the individual discovers and what surrounding influences encourage him to accept; the theory, or the ideal, does not always correspond to lived experience.

What the existentialists then seek to effect is a fresh description, claiming, as the scientists do, that the old description no longer corresponds to what man knows. It has lost its elegance, not only because it no longer has any appeal, but more crucially because in order to make it work too many adjustments have to be permitted. Former world views no longer apply because that world no longer exists, and there is no particular point in molding theories and elaborating reservations designed to give those views the apparatus of credibility. As the mechanical view of the universe had to give way to later discoveries, so the tidy teleological view of the universe and man must now give way to the volume of evidence which demonstrates their irrelevance. To believe in the twentieth century that all men love justice and seek the good is to believe, against the massive evidence of history, nonsense. It is also to pretend that words like justice

---

1. Two comparatively recent and admirable books of literary criticism treat this subject as it applies to two different periods. René Girard's *Mensonge romantique et vérité romanesque* (Paris, 1961), traces out the growth of the importance of the Other from the publication of *Don Quixote* to the work of Proust. Serge Doubrovsky's excellent *Corneille ou la dialectique du héros* (Paris, 1963) treats the same subject with reference to Corneille and the seventeenth century. In the conclusion of his book, Professor Doubrovsky writes explicitly about Sartre.

and the good have the same meaning for all men. Yet once such terms are given up, and the poles of the world seem to fall away, an ideological vacuum is created. There is no assurance that nature, supposedly hating vacuums, will hurry to fill this one; there is every assurance that man, fearing vacuums, will do his best.

His history in the West, and probably elsewhere, is the chronology of his efforts to fill in the blanks and the voids in order to reduce the tensions that become manifest once he starts to work out his existence. In the culture which emanates from his responses, he creates a force which presupposes that nature, if she is not the enemy, is not the indulgent friend either. The theory of original sin, for example, posits a fault that must be expiated; that fault is none other than man's decision that he and nature could or must go separate ways. Nature presumably knows her way; it is man's lot to find his. And there is something at once noble and desperate in his effort to construct theories which seek to elaborate a way and a destiny as fixed as nature's or in harmony with hers. There is also more than a little pathos in his early admission that the gap between him and nature is his fault; the appeal of the idea of preestablished harmonies which man has disrupted is not easily discarded.

One of the results of man's decision to go his own way, is that he constantly runs the risk of falling again. If he repeats the initial experience of the race, he will bite into the apple and declare, if not his independence of, at least his difference from nature. If he rejects the compensatory theories that others have worked out, he will separate himself, for a while or for a lifetime, from the majority. Sartre claims that every man has both experiences. In his confrontation with the natural world, the for-itself (individual man as consciousness) necessarily negates the in-itself, a negation which does not in any way mean that the for-itself ceases to envy the in-itself's lack of consciousness; and again, in his confrontation with the social world, the for-itself at some point must also, again for an indeterminate period, reject the Other. If there is indeed a class, man, it is a class whose members repeatedly discover the class as a potentially hostile grouping.

In the most primitive encounter, I discover the Other in function of what he tells me about my own existence. Though he is a man, and in that sense mirrors something of what I am, he is *another* man; because of that difference I have the certainty that he cannot be altogether like me.[2] He has a value for me—a value which one day can become negative or threatening—because he forces me to escape from what Sartre calls the

2. The violence to English syntax is done deliberately in an effort to use a grammatical form which will reproduce the subject-object relationship that I deal with subsequently and which is a keystone in Sartre's system.

"reef of solipsism." [3] In seeing him, I learn that, for him, I am not I, I am another. I am an object for him as he is an object for me. I am no longer exclusively the object I have been for myself, the object I call my ego and in whose interests I, as a subject, operate in the world. I am, additionally, the object I represent for him as he is the object he represents for me—an object which, beyond my description of it, is also a me being protected and defended by an I.

Hegel found positive value in this discovery for precisely the reason just explained; by a kind of magic my discovery of the Other as another who discovers me is also the verification of my discovery of myself. The Other serves to confirm the operation by which I have discovered myself. Sartre is less cheerful on this score, since he claims that in discovering the Other I have no justification whatsoever for presupposing that I know what he thinks of me, what he knows of me, and, most alarmingly, *what he wants from me*. The discovery is surrounded by mystery, and it is only by being fascinated by mystery or as a result of a long search that I can assent to Heidegger's notion that with the Other I share a field of being which it is our common task to plough and cultivate. That field— which Heidegger calls the *Mitsein*—is only a category which describes the presence of many men on the earth. We are here with others; that is a fact. The fact unfortunately tells us nothing about the quality of the others with whom we are here nor does it indicate a project we hold in common. It is quite conceivable that we are here together as beings who want no part of each other. Since I do not know what the Other wants from me, and may be instinctively hostile to him, it is advisable that I be cautious and that I not dismiss the possibility that he seeks to do me harm. As a result, confronted with him, I introduce the same negation I introduced in my encounter with the natural world: I recognize that he is neither I nor me, nor am I he or him. We confront each other in a union of nihilating reciprocity, seeing each other as obstacles to be met and eventually to be overturned. [4]

If the ego is the object that I, as a subject, create in order to defend both what I think it is and what it allows me to be, then the risk I face in confronting the Other is a dual one. He may totally ignore the body of knowledge and value-commitment which is the structure of my ego—and

3. Sartre discusses this concept in *BN*, pp. 223–32.

4. Cf. *BN*: "By proceding from Husserl to Hegel we have realized an immense prog-ress: first, the negation which constitutes the Other is direct, internal, and reciprocal; second, it calls each consciousness to account and pierces it to the deepest part of its being; the problem is posited on the level of inner being, of the universal and transcendental 'I'. Finally, in my essential being I depend on the essential being of the Other, and instead of holding that my being-for-myself is opposed to my being-for-others, I find that being-for-others appears as a necessary condition for my being-for-myself" (p. 238). Sartre discusses the theories of the Other put forward by Husserl, Hegel, and Heidegger on pp. 233–52.

I must repeat that, according to Sartre, the ego is no more than a mental image I have of myself—and he may try to destroy or harm the subject who cultivates that ego.[5] In short, he will transform me into an object of his creation. Clearly, I no longer have the mastery I either thought I had or else had sought to have. In my confrontation with the physical universe, there was dismay; in my confrontation of the Other, there is shame.[6] As he looks at me, he seems to look through me and into my feebleness because he makes me see that I am not only a being for myself, I am also a being for others. If he decides to treat me as he has had to treat being-in-itself—by negativising and possibly nihilating me—then I become an exploitable object for him.[7] Faced with the things, I may have wanted to capitulate by modeling my existence on theirs; in my initial meeting with the Other, I am not so easily tempted to capitulate, since I do not know what it is I shall be capitulating to. There is, then, a moment when I feel that my destiny is no longer in my hands but has been transferred to the Other's.

A primary reaction to this feeling is the conviction that I must get at the Other before he can get at me. If his look produces shame in me, I must use my eyes to induce shame in him. I must refuse him in order to nihilate the possible influence he may have on me. There are other reactions which I will deal with in other chapters. Here I am concerned with the primary reaction to what Sartre, in a memorable phrase, has described as the original fall I discover through the Other. He makes me fall, whether he explicitly wishes to or not, because he robs me of that sense of superiority I may have felt over the things; he adds to my insecurity and represents another battle I must fight. The horror in the situation lies in its reciprocity—I can, for strategic reasons, presuppose that his reaction parallels mine. If, like Roquentin, I have had to decide that I could not sensibly pretend that

5. Cf. *BN*: "The Other is not a *for-itself* as he appears to me; I do not appear to myself as I am *for-the-Other*. I am incapable of apprehending for myself the self which I am for the Other, just as I am incapable of apprehending on the basis of the Other-as-object which appears to me, what the Other is for himself" (p. 242).

6. Cf. *BN*: "Shame is the feeling of an *original fall*, not because of the fact that I may have committed this or that particular fault but simply that I have 'fallen' into the world in the midst of things and that I need the mediation of the Other in order to be what I am" (p. 288). See also above, chap. 1, n. 4, for the relationship between shame and pride.

7. There is a difference between the process of negativizing and that of nihilating, for the former does not necessarily produce the latter, though it is the latter the individual most fears when he confronts the Other. The Other, having decided that I am not he, may grow fearful that I will try to subjugate him in some way; out of this fear may grow his project of subjugating me first, that is, of nihilating me as a threat. Because the two verbs describe such a clearly sequential process I have chosen to use whichever of the two seemed to me most appropriate to situations I am discussing. The English verb *nihilate* is an ingenious invention of Professor Barnes's. She writes: "I think 'nihilate' is a closer equivalent to Sartre's *néantiser* than 'annihilate' because the fundamental meaning of the term is 'to make nothing' rather to 'to destroy or do away with'" (*BN*, p. 17 n.).

the things governed my existence, then, like the characters of *Huis-clos*, I can also decide that I shall not be governed by others either. But in making such a decision, I have also revealed that my place in the world is not one exclusively of my creation. By my birth, I have been located in space; by my discovery of the Other, I have been located in the social world. My reaction to both will necessarily be free since it will be chosen by me; but my freedom will be exercised in the particular circumstances which delimit my situation.

This is a fundamental element of Sartre's philosophical system; though it has been derived from Heidegger, it has been elaborated in a way that differs from the German philosopher's system mainly because Sartre has dealt with this element always in very precise, one might say local, terms. An individual's situation is conditioned by the discoveries we have already discussed; it is further conditioned by the undetermined future which stretches before him; it is also significantly influenced by his past, by particular restrictive details of his present, and by the possibilities of choice which are open to him. Man is somewhere; efforts have been made to make him into something. Those are only elements in his formation, however; they have no meaning until, by his free choice, he reacts to them either by accepting them or revolting against them.

He may have no choice about accepting his geographical location, for if he is poor, he cannot move from Paris to San Francisco. But he does necessarily have the choice of *how* he will accept his location. He may feel himself overwhelmed or incapable of dealing with what surrounds him and, as a result, decide to live passively in his situation. That changes nothing, for his decision is one that has been taken in that situation as an answer to the provocations of the situation. But if he subsequently claims that he has been a victim, he can sustain his claim only by lying to himself. He may even, in loftier moments of muddled coherence, assert that he is becoming one with the universe, casting his lot with that of human nature.

In Sartre's world such an attempt will get him precisely nowhere, for there is no human nature in the sense of something with a fixed and clearly defined purpose. There is a human condition that is always making something of itself, that is always becoming something it was not a moment or a century before. It is this condition—not a state, but a tendency; not a nature, but a possibility—which is common to men. It is therefore impossible to live under the canopy of an already fixed and clearly determined nature unless one lies to oneself or closes one's eyes to other aspects of the human condition.

Being and Nothingness is Sartre's abstract presentation of this situation; it is at once a phenomenology, an ontology, and a psychology of the *individual* in the world. In that sense, it is an initial work concerned with initial individual experience; in that sense, too, it is a partial work because the social world has a role in it only as an obstacle or barrier to the individual and his most fundamental aspirations. It is not until the *Critique de la raison dialectique* that Sartre will examine mobile social reality with the same thoroughness. As a result, *Being and Nothingness*, along with the other early works, gives a somewhat lopsided view of the world or, in starker terms, a despairing view of it. But this was inevitable, for Sartre could not talk of the world of men working together—what he will later call the collectivities—without first finding out what man is and what conditions shape and possibly govern his activities in the wider human reality which is the collectivity or the mass of collectivities. As the map of the world can only be formed from the maps of specific areas, so the geography of society can only be traced out from the geography of the individual consciousness. I have pointed out earlier that most men do not possess a spontaneous instinct to be good cartographers.

The social world, of course, is not absent from Sartre's early works. It is what stands off against the individual throughout *Being and Nothingness*; it is the challenge which Sartre repeatedly meets in the creative works that follow *La Nausée*. Yet in his creative works, we see the social world as the individual sees it. What we are seeing is the process by which the individual adjusts to the world; but we are at all times seeing this through the eyes of a mind which usually does not believe that the world, as it exists, is worth adjusting to. If the individual seems to emerge battered and not very lovable from Sartre's early works, this is because the individual has misused his freedom, abdicated to the mechanics of his situation, refused his condition and its possibilities. For all these sins, he cannot escape blame. He is the culprit Sartre would like to see reformed; he has an accomplice Sartre would like to see destroyed because the accomplice is beyond reform. The accomplice is bourgeois society, the glossy garbage bin in which all the fixed ideas of Western civilization have been slowly spoiling, unbeknown to the complacent keepers of the garbage. Since they have been sitting on the bin all along to keep it tightly covered, they are unaware of how sickening the stench has become.

For the most part Roquentin, preoccupied mainly with his encounter with the physical world, had bracketed the social world. In his judgment, the latter was beyond redemption because it had modeled its activities on those of the natural world; it was also beyond sympathetic consideration because it did not have the knowledge he had. But his choice of personal salvation was strangely akin to one of the usual bourgeois solutions: he would find his place in a work of art and thus leave behind an object which would not be altogether unlike the portraits in the Bouville museum. Pierre and Eve, Hilbert, and Lulu were all aware that their lives were acted out within the context of a surrounding society from which, for a variety of reasons, they wished to withdraw. In their cases, Sartre has shown us examples of individuals who, either hating or finding themselves uncomfortable with their freedom, have used that freedom in order to escape from it. *Huis-clos* was an exercise designed to bring us, and its characters, deeper into this contradictory situation. By using the device of hell, Sartre was able to show that each of his characters, though each made claims to the contrary, had been aware of the possibilities afforded by his situation and had freely reacted to those possibilities in the name of a personal project deliberately and therefore freely pursued. At the end of the play, each character was aware that he was where he was because he had willed to be there; he was also aware that it was too late.

In "L'Enfance d'un chef" (1939) Sartre gives us a full portrait of the development of a consciousness which clearly sees the world in which it is going to live before it chooses to live in that world. Lucien Fleurier, the young protagonist of the story, passes through most of the stages outlined by Sartre in *Being and Nothingness* before deciding to live inauthentically in a particular class. He makes his final decision because he recognizes that the class will allow him to fight against the forces which would impede him from possessing the world as a toy rightfully his. Lucien is a particularly apt bearer of a major Sartrean preoccupation: the choice of a specific situation in response to the threat of the Other.

There are six steps in Lucien's progress towards his final decision; at each step he discovers the Other in one form or another. Behind that Other there is always the wider world in which Lucien will have to live either with or against the Other. His first discovery is not unlike that Sartre described in *Les Mots*: as a child, he has the impression that the world isn't real; it is a mock-up of something else, presented to him so that he can play a role in it and thus join the theatrical club where everyone else is playing a role. He is not invited to choose a mode of life, but rather to accept the function that has been chosen for him. Since he does not yet know fear, and since the results of agreeing to accept the function are pleasant, there is no reason to protest; later he will be able to go hunting for the real world.

In the second stage of his movement towards maturity, he discovers the world of things: the tree kicked does not cry out in pain; the objects insulted do not insult back—their silence is perhaps the worst insult. The things, like the class in which he lives, don't really exist. The third step in the growth of his consciousness is his discovery of two modes of the Other, each of which is different from the friendly, indulgent, inviting Other represented by his family. There is the Other as seen in his father's employes: the Other neutralized, held in control, dependent for his existence on the work which Lucien's father supplies; he is the Other who greets you with respect and thus helps you to appreciate the security of your position or, more simply, the fact that you have a position. But there is another Other: those Lucien meets competitively at school, and about whom he does not have the information he possesses with regard to his family and the workers in his father's factory. The students are the Other as unpredictable mystery; they make Lucien uncomfortable because, among other things, they stare at him from behind and thus make him aware of his body "which was always existing on all sides at the same time without having asked his opinion" (p. 170).[8]

His response to this discomfort is to contemplate suicide. In killing himself he will, like Hilbert, send a message to the world telling the others that existence is an illusion. He is, of course, using self-deception as a replacement for an honest response to his curiosity about what the nature of existence is. He hopes by his act to show that existence is not; yet the act demonstrates, on the contrary, that existence, if it *is not*, still *happens.* Suicide would only be the negation of what he seeks to affirm. He is also deceiving himself by trying to transform those who bother him into nonexistents; if he removes himself from them, then they cannot nihilate him. He would also, in the bargain, remove himself from the task of having to nihilate them. The job of mitigating the temptation to destroy fear by destroying its victim falls to the school. There Lucien's mentors seek to imbue him with a sense of his function in sustaining the rule of the governing class. This assurance is not enough at this point—probably because, like the young of today and for similar reasons, he shares the notion that those over thirty are not to be trusted; nonetheless, the school's message supplies a residual raison d'être upon which he can fall back once he has discovered either his incapacity or his unwillingness to cope with later experience. On reaching thirty, he may find he has no other choice save to join those others who are not to be trusted.

The thirst for an individuation which is not derived from his class, coupled with the curiosity characteristic of his age, brings him into contact with Berliac, a young student who cherishes his alienation with the same devotion and even more enthusiasm than Roquentin had brought to cherishing his nausea. Through Berliac Lucien encounters Bergère, who has carried alienation into middle age, where he expresses it through a muddled but efficacious mixture of surrealism, hashish, and pederasty. Once seduced by Bergère, Lucien discovers that the wider horizons he has been seeking reveal panoramas he would rather not behold. The Other has got at him in a way as disturbing as it is humiliating; the buggered are not brave.

This brings him to the fifth stage of his development. He is living in an upsetting situation which cannot readily be dismissed since Bergère's seduction carried the implication of Lucien's willingness to be seduced, which

8. Cf. *BN*: "Fear is . . . the discovery of my being-as-object on the occasions of the appearance of another object in my perceptible field" (p. 288). "Fear is nothing but a magical conduct tending by incantation to suppress the frightening objects which we are unable to keep at a distance" (p. 295). We have already seen in our discussion of "Intimité" how Lulu reacted to the same discovery and to similar fears.

in turn implies that Lucien is also a homosexual. He asks himself that question once, then cowers and does not come confidently back to himself until he has translated the question into a declaration: "He took advantage of my disarray, but I'm not *really* a pederast" (p. 201). He is saved and, strong with the grace released by his salvation, he asks another apt question: What saved him? He gives an inapt answer when he claims that it was his moral good health; what has saved him is his fear of being made an object for a whole series of others: for Bergère, who, having had his pleasure with him, can henceforth consider him a homosexual; for his class, which cannot be expected to look with open favor upon such special tastes; for all the others who would have a ready label to paste on him—"a tall blond who likes men." Though these fears lead him to an answer that puts his soul to rest, the answer does not certify the real existence of the moral good health he claims to possess.[9]

Whatever the cause of his salvation, once saved he must decide what to do with the fund of probity he possesses. If his moral good health has saved him, he has only one further choice to make in order to round out his development: he must exercise the rights which moral salubrity confers upon him. Henceforth he will make use of the Other, of all the others. They will exist only as accessories to the role he now performs. He will accept his place in the governing class, and as a governor he will have the responsibility of directing the others for *their* good. He has quickly forgotten that his reason for wanting to direct them stemmed from his desire to avoid the possible empire they might seek to exercise over him. As a governor, *un chef*, he will have the right to rule because he will have accepted the responsibilities which come with that right.[10]

His apotheosis begins. With lordly generosity he thinks of seducing the family maid who is not only a born victim but who is also bound to feel blessed by a visitation from one of the household gods. He looks upon her as his "thing," but quickly remembers that she is a thing who, if not prop-

9. Lucien is here moving from fear into anguish. Cf. *BN*: ". . . anguish is distinguished from fear in that fear is fear of being in the world whereas anguish is anguish before myself . . . my being provokes anguish to the extent that I distrust myself and my own reactions in that situation" (p. 29). "I can in fact wish 'not to see' a certain aspect of my being only if I am acquainted with the aspect which I do not wish to see. . . . This means that anguish, the intentional aim of anguish and a flight from anguish towards reassuring myths must all be given in the unity of the same consciousness" (p. 43).

10. The essentials of Sartre's description of the formation of bourgeois youth have an inflexible hold on his mind. In his work-in-progress on Flaubert he writes: "In brief, he is a *young bourgeois*: that means that his social reality (supported by his father, he has no needs) and his deepest reality (structured by the particular and general structure of his family) are *latent*; on the surface, by contrast, he is everything and nothing. He thinks that he is the Spirit and, yawning all the while, plays with others' theories which he confuses with the movement of his own thought" ("Flaubert: du poète à l'Artiste," *TM* 22 [1966]: 246).

erly used, might produce other things, like children, who, in turn, would produce the need for explanations and the possibility of embarrassment. As a gesture towards civic responsibility, he joins the *Action Française* to which he commits himself so deeply as to feel free to enjoy himself frivolously on occasion. The road to apotheosis is not without its ruts, and frivolity can produce puzzling situations. In seducing another woman, Maude, Lucien is frightened by the mutuality he discovers in the sexual act, by the fusion between himself and the Other in which both he and the Other seem to disappear in order to form a unity.[11] He slowly resolves this difficulty by categorizing that disquieting Other whom he has penetrated. She exists to perform a function his class needs; since the governors cannot be expected to remain chaste before marriage, someone has to be there to satisfy their needs and protect the virtue of their future spouses.

These episodes alter his idea of the Other and make him realize that, if he cannot deny the Other's existence, he must learn how to neutralize the Other. The Other must be looked at as a constant menace against whom battle must be continuously waged because the Other represents a danger to all people of moral good health. Far from trying to forget that the Other is there, Lucien must keep the Other permanently before the gaze of his peers and his inferiors in order to have a ready victim who will absorb all the hostility he dreads and thus keep it from falling on him. This functional Other, in Lucien's case, is the Jew.

There is one last moment of honesty in his existence when, after having insulted a Jew in a mutual friend's house, Lucien experiences regret. But his gesture is validated by the other members of his class, who approve of what he has done; they acknowledge that, against all unpleasantness, one must defend his values. And so Lucien passes from the young man who thought the world of his class didn't exist into a young man who really doesn't want to exist: he wants to be. He is no longer alienated, he is no longer inquisitive, he is no longer dynamic in an authentic way. He is: "Lucien, that's me. Someone who can't stand Jews" (p. 272).[12] Translated,

---

11. Cf. *BN*: ". . . in the course of long acquaintance with a person there always comes an instant when all these disguises are thrown off and when I find myself in the presence of the pure *contingency of his presence*. In this case I achieve in the face or the other parts of a body the pure intuition of flesh. This intuition is not only knowledge: it is the affective apprehension of an absolute contingency and this apprehension is a particular kind of *nausea*" (pp. 343–44).

12. Cf. *BN*: ". . . hate presents itself as an absolute positing of the freedom of the for-itself before the Other. This is why hate does not abase the hated object, for it places the dispute on the true level. What I hate in the Other . . . is his existence in general as a transcendence transcended. This is why hate implies a recognition of the Other's freedom. . . .

"The second consequence of these observations is that hate is the hate of all Others in one Other. . . . The Other whom I hate actually represents all Others" (p. 411). "My project of suppressing him is a project of suppressing others in general, that is,

that means he is someone who, unable to abide the mystery of the Other, turns the Other into an abominable object which will serve to absorb all fear of the Other.[13] With the Other-as-menace carefully identified, Lucien can set himself to using the others he needs. He drops Maude, for she belongs to everyone; he looks forward to his marriage with a decent girl who is waiting chastely for him to come along; she will be his holocaust. To fight against the potential vulnerability of his youthful face, he decides to grow a moustache. He has decided to exist his class, to live out Roquentin's description: "The fine gentleman exists the Legion of Honor, exists his moustache; that's all. How satisfying it must be to be only a Legion of Honor and a moustache; no one sees the rest; he only sees the clipped ends of his moustache at either side of his nose. I don't think, therefore I am a moustache" (*La Nausée*, p. 131).

The moustache serves as the heraldic device for the circle Lucien has traced as his path towards maturity; it is the finishing touch on his coat of protective arms. But like many coats of arms, it hides more than it reveals and suggests an emblematic tradition more distinguished than the reality behind it. What Lucien is at the end (and the end of the story is only the beginning of his adult life) is more than an individual who will be appreciated by his elders because, having sown his wild oats, he has come back to his senses; he is more, too, than a caricature, for the moustachioed Lucien, though he comes from a particular class, is the embodiment of several central Sartrean theories.

The circle he has traced obviously is not a design offered for our admiration; rather than being perfect, it is vicious. Yet even the drawing of vicious circles requires some effort, and it is with this effort and the goal it envisions that Sartre is concerned.[14] At the end of the story, Lucien is back where he started from: safe at home with the values discovered in childhood. On his way to that capitulation—for we must remember that his first hesitations had to do with the reality of the world in which he lived—he has had to fight against a certain body of experience which would have confirmed his initial doubts. In other words, his circle has been drawn only by repeated decisions to ignore the force of experiences which might have made him draw something other than a circle. Each of these experiences—his discomfort in school, his encounter with the homosexual, his discovery of a growing

---

of recapturing my non-substantial freedom as for-itself. In hate there is given an understanding of the fact that my dimension of being-alienated is a *real* enslavement which comes to me through others" (p. 412).

13. Cf. *BN*: "The objectivation of the Other . . . is a defence on the part of my being which, precisely by conferring on the Other a being-for-me, frees me from my being-for the Other" (p. 268).

14. Cf. *La Nausée*: "A circle is not absurd, it is very well explained by the rotation of a straight segment around one of its extremities. . . . But the circle doesn't exist either" (p. 164).

sullenness in his father's workers, his confrontation by a Jew who fought back—was a prod from a wider reality urging him to keep his eyes open in order that he might see clearly. But each experience was also an invitation to an unknown, not only an unknown existing outside himself and in the future, but also an unknown within himself which he chose not to investigate.[15]

Because of these pressures and the realities they suggest, he has been exposed to a body of information he deliberately refuses to explore. Such a response, according to Sartre, is not rational; it is emotional. Lucien, who wanted at times to exert his individuality, renounces that individuality in order to hide, first in his conviction, and then in his class. His conviction is that he must be living in the benign company of the good because he knows where the wicked are. His class is the group which shares his conviction; it is thus a reality strong enough to disarm all insurgents. That it is a synthetic reality designed by him to combat the hard reality he has observed is no surprise, given his fear of the human reality he has encountered. Afraid, he gives in. But by giving in, he hides from his own fear; he considers his decision a positive gesture and an honest answer to the questions he has met. What he is doing, in effect, is replacing the real world which scares him with an unreal world in which he can scare others. This exalts him; in adopting his conviction and placing himself at the service of his class, he ceases to be an individual and becomes an embodied function. For Sartre, this is no answer at all, whether it is used by a bourgeois youth or by others. The real world goes on; circles joggle circles; and the circle which floats off into a private world is airily ignoring available information at the risk of its own destruction.[16]

15. There is a kind of classical clarity in Sartre's insistence on a bourgeois type who makes predictable decisions, like Lucien's, on the basis of a common heritage and in the name of shared goals. In *L'Imagination* he wrote, in a passage which is a needless interpolation in an otherwise technical discussion: "The conservative bourgeoisie, frightened by the Commune, turned towards Religion as it had already done in the first years of Louis-Philippe's reign. As a result, influential intellectuals had to combat in all areas the analytic tendency of the eighteenth century. Over and above the individual, it was necessary to postulate synthetic realities: the family, the nation, society. Over and above the individual image, it was necessary to reestablish the existence of concepts, of thought" (pp. 29–30). In the introduction to the first issue of *TM* he wrote: ". . . one makes himself a bourgeois by making a choice, once and for all, of a certain analytic vision of the world which one attempts to impose on all men and which excludes the perception of collective realities" (*Sit. II*, p. 19). Still later, in his discussion of the stranglehold French factory-owners exercised on the French economy and thus over the welfare of workers, he wrote: "The exercise of this right [of ownership] is an action; [the owner] gives orders; he makes the enterprise 'go'. When repeated, the action becomes a skill: 'He's the man we need; he has an iron fist'. Finally, everything is summarized in the pledge he makes to himself: 'I'll be a boss' " ("Les Communistes et la paix," *Sit. VI*, pp. 240–41).

16. A larger concept, which Sartre calls "hodological space" is involved here. He defines it as "the space which is originally revealed to me . . . it is furrowed with paths and highways; it is instrumental and it is the *location* of tools" (*BN*, p. 322).

The group that chooses to live enclosed in such a circle knows this; no matter how hard it tries to think that its belief in its circle is justified, no matter how much it encourages its junior members to believe that they can become as gods, it has nonetheless eaten of the tree of knowledge and heard the voice of an angry deity. If loneliness has led it to ask for a companion, if avidity and fear have led it to the tree in the company of that companion, and if the resulting knowledge has told it of dark possibilities, it has responded by putting on the fig leaf of its self-interest in order to protect its vulnerability. In so doing it has admitted that there is still both opposition and an angry god. The opposition, as we shall see, comes from the other classes; the god is history. The class moves in circles. History moves ahead; and it ignores no directional forces because its movement, like its convulsions, is the product of those forces.

The reason why the class moves in circles is explained by Lucien's decision to live, as a circle, within the circle of the class. In so choosing, he adheres to the philosophy of the class, to its belief that it is justified and, in the boldest terms, always has the right to act as it does. In discovering his moral good health, he believes that he has discovered something which the class has formed within him; but his discovery is really of another nature because it leads to gratitude towards the class and thus engages him in the task of supporting the class's goals and purposes. We have seen that as a reward for such allegiance the class tranquilizes Lucien's fear. The class, however, exacts a price for its services—Lucien can no longer be a free-floating force. It also offers an additional fringe benefit: in the safety of the class, Lucien is protected from the Other.

But in order that he may experience that protection there has to be another to whom he can feel superior; neither he nor the class can feel justified unless both can measure their election against the damnation of

---

The trouble is that "there are barriers and obstacles in my hodological space" (p. 328), and that some of the roads and paths lead either to viewpoints from which I see other people's space or else carry me directly into their space, where I meet immediate conflict. Fell comments: "We noted that 'hodological space', a term derived from the Greek (odos: way, path), refers to [Kurt] Lewin's theory that the physical and social environment (or 'field') is perceived as a set of attracting or repelling 'vectors' directed toward or away from various objects. In itself, this is a relatively trivial notion, merely conceptualising the obvious fact that we evaluate objects and events, and try to organize them, in terms of our purposes. Given certain goals, various objects, events, people in my perceptual field will be evaluated as useful, obstructing or neutral in relation to these goals.

"Such hodological space is a Gestalt, a unified form, a perceptual whole. Sartre, equating it with Lewin's field of 'reality', appears to have reasoned thus: if emotion consists of going-out-of-the-field of reality, and if this field of reality is the hodological field which consists of paths to be used instrumentally and of obstructions which must be surmounted, then the emotional 'space' must be the Lewinian plane of unreality—a magical space in which my goals are attainable *without* mediation: without the necessity of instrumental action, without the necessity of surmounting difficult obstacles" (*Emotion in the Thought of Sartre*, pp. 122–23).

another group. In a world of too few conveniences and happy coincidences, the Jew emerges in the bourgeois consciousness as a deserving scapegoat; not only has he accumulated a visible burden of social offenses, he has also responded to the Jewish god's angry voice by crucifying his Christian son.

In his *Réflexions sur la question juive* (1946–47) Sartre, showing a fine moral ardor in his desire to fight the virulence anti-Semitism introduces into society, further develops his notion, sketched in "L'Enfance d'un chef," that the Jew represents the Other who has been fixed and immobilized by fearful individuals. He begins with a dilemma: the contradiction between a world committed to democratic values and the simultaneous existence in that world of anti-Semitism. Democratic societies, believing in the equality of all men and their social brotherhood, should not be able to tolerate such formalized hatred. Yet, within them, men of good will, who spend their time in humane pursuits designed to improve the lot of the whole race, can also be anti-Semites. Since the other attitudes of these men—their hatred of disease, plagues, and social evils—are justified, it is possible that their anti-Semitism is justified, too. They have, after all, shown discernment in their other undertakings.

But if one admits that there is a basis to their hatred of Jews, then one has to admit that democracy is founded on a contradiction. Though its advocates presuppose the equality of all men, they also assert that there is, within the class, men, a subclass, Jew, which is not entitled to equal treatment. They thus deny their initial presupposition that there is a class, men, since they have subsequently decided either in thought or by their action that within that class there are nonmen. Since this is an unreasonable position which threatens the fundamental claims of democracy, an explanation must be sought elsewhere.

Anti-Semitism exists because the men who believe in it have the same passionate and irrational needs of their forebears who vilified God or Satan or fateful forces for whatever wasn't going well. Anti-Semitism, then, is nothing more than a structured mode of the Other, created in order to justify man's determination to consider the Other as inalienably hostile to his goals and thus deserving of his animosity. It is a passionate persuasion by which the massed super-Ego of a class or a society creates a super-Other around whose existence it organizes an essential part of its own enterprise. The super-Other, once he has been identified, serves a variety of useful purposes, but the single most important one is probably the fact that even as he reminds men of the Other, he remains the Other who can always be defeated.[17] He embodies a double deception: the first is men's creation of

17. In *BN* Sartre, though alluding to a different situation, had already summed up one of the lengthiest arguments of *Réflexions*: "The bourgeois denies that there are classes: he attributes the existence of a proletariat to the action of agitators, to awk-

him; the second is the personal profit men derive once they have created him. He makes it possible for them to tell themselves that they have faced up to the issue of the Other and met it bravely and triumphantly.

What the anti-Semite is in effect doing is demonstrating his continued fascination with being-in-itself. He wishes to surround himself with elements suggestive of permanence or unchangeability; he wishes to possess an armory of unchanging beliefs and principles which will assure him he is properly equipped against all threats from chance or from others. Against that double threat, which is always embodied in the Other, he creates an Other who, by the nature of what he is cannot gain entry to the armory and thus cannot benefit from its weaponry. The Jew exists to serve this purpose, for the Jew, no matter how long he has lived in a country, will not be allowed to claim that country as his home, will not be allowed to claim its language as his own, will not be allowed to claim its past as his past. In the eyes of the anti-Semite, the Jew exists in order *not* to accede to the goods of the country and the class; the Jew exists precisely to be denied such access as a right legitimately his.

The results of this are various. Objectively, anti-Semitism represents a commitment to that mediocrity which results from the fear of change; subjectively, the mediocrity is disguised to appear as the wisdom of the elite which conserves what it possesses, not in order to oppose progress, but to have progress at the pace it chooses; the elite is not fighting the future so much as it is preserving the rich visible traditions inherited from the past. Subjectively, anti-Semitism provides the governing class with a rallying point which it uses in order to mystify the lower classes. Though they may not be allowed access to education and to the full enjoyment of the society's riches, they can be associated with the elite by identifying with its anti-Semitism. The governing class creates a beast in order to be able to point out, when necessary, a common danger which threatens *all* the nation's citizens.

The Jew is transformed into the source of Evil in the world. It is, to be sure, extremely useful to know where Evil dwells; it is also reassuring to know that, having located the source of Evil, one is on the side of the faithful angels. But if, for the reasons and rewards indicated, men spend their lives fighting Evil, they assume a function which spares them the necessity of deciding what Good is, where it might be found, and how it might be multiplied. They equate the fight against Evil with the fight for Good. The outcome of such nonsense, Sartre insists, is that the pursuit of the Good is lost in the fight against Evil. The refusal to seek the Good is a deliberate

---

ward incidents, to injustices which can be repaired by particular measures; he affirms the existence of a solidarity of interests between capital and labor; he offers instead of class solidarity a larger solidarity, a natural solidarity, in which the worker and the employer are integrated in a *Mitsein* which suppresses the conflict" (p. 429).

policy of those who organize the crusade against Evil. The crusade suggests that their forces are organized to fight only for benevolent causes; but it also serves as a pretty cover on the ugly Evil crusaders effect in the world: they are selfish and, as a result, indifferent to the good of others.

The Jew has historically paid the cost of the crusaders' self-indulgence and self-delusion. He has been condemned to be the eternal Other; he has also been condemned to a passive role which cannot be precisely defined because the events for which he may be held responsible have not yet come to pass. In this sense, the Jew is the creation of others. He begins his extra-familial life with the realization that he is a fully defined object for a large part of humanity which, having recognized him as a Jew, practically forces him to model himself on their idea of the Jew. His initial freedom of choice is thereby significantly reduced.

We would be rash if we tried to brush away the truth Sartre reveals here, for American society is riddled with examples of the way in which the Jew is not allowed to develop freely. We do not think of driving the agnostic back to the Protestantism of his youth; yet we never really let the person whose origins are Jewish but whose agnosticism is total forget those origins, however little they may have to do with what essentially he is. The apostate Jew is trying to hide his birthmark; the apostate Protestant is exercising his birthright. Having created the Jew as a lesser being, we use any evidence that he is trying to escape from opprobrium as further proof of his race's defects.

The Jew is exemplary of being-for-Others (*l'être-pour-autrui*); he is made to exist for certain others so that they can avoid the condition in which they have placed him. He is superdetermined; he is what the formative influences of a hostile society have made him. His individuality is always darkened by the cloud of that superdetermination and his expressiveness blocked by its obstacles. As a result, he is the incarnation on this earth of the problem of authenticity. His situation is impossible because he must choose between an authentic and an inauthentic way of life in conditions which do not exist for the majority of society. He must make his choice in a situation which neither he nor his ancestors have created, but which nonetheless defines his initial space in the world.[18]

Though he remains free, the field of his freedom has narrower boundaries than the fields available to other members of society. His greatest natural inclination will be to deny their right to impose such limitations and such

18. Curiously enough, Lucien undergoes a somewhat similar experience in his relations with God, whom Lucien does not like because God knows too much about him, because God sees all he does, and because, according to the myth of his class, God will one day judge him on God's standards. It is not farfetched to suggest that, in categorizing the Jew, Lucien is seeking to model himself on God, but to pass judgment and mete out punishment here and now rather than on some future day of doom.

an unmerited burden on him. He will be tempted, because of the intolerable situation in which he is born, to insist on his right to live like others. According to Sartre, such a desire, if it is indulged, plunges the Jew into an inauthentic existence; it leads him to deny or set aside a situation which, though awful, is genuinely his. It also seems to validate the portrait which the anti-Semite has of him. Authentic existence for the Jew is to accept the situation into which he is born in order, by living it out, to show how wrong it is. In a way, though the odds he must face are enormously greater than those confronting other men and though his situation represents an objective condemnation of those who have placed him in it, the Jew is exemplary of social man. Thus, in addition to being the victim of one of society's plagues, the Jew tells us, if we would listen, who we are.

He is exemplary of social man because his torment comes to him from society; he not only experiences the kind of alienation we saw in Roquentin, he also experiences the alienation of the victim from the victimizer. He is the Other in his most radical manifestation: the Other who has been created, not as a result of intersubjective encounters, but as a result of social situations and the fear they engender in all men. He is twice the victim: originally because of the open-ended contingency he shares with all men; subsequently as the victim selected by those other men as part of their effort to forget or soften the blow of their own condition. He is exemplary of social man because he also embodies the problem of all the have-nots of society. He has been condemned to make his choices in the midst of a false situation imposed on him by others whose own situation, as a result, is equally false; theirs, however, is more comfortable and, in the pleasure derived from the comfort, its falsity is readily enough overlooked.

The Jew—and by extension all the condemned of the earth who are used by the ruling class to justify its activities—embodies in his condition the gravest problem of social reality: its historical refusal or inability to find a way of living honestly with its proclamation of a class, man, whose members all share the same basic capacities and dignity. Such proclamations are a shabby varnish trying to hide an ugly lived reality and it is the ugly reality—inauthentic because it denies in its everyday experience what it celebrates in its cherished ideological system—which is our situation. To live authentically, a society must do what Sartre encourages the Jew to do: recognize the full reality of how it lives. For the non-Jew this involves a discovery worse than any the Jew will make, since what the non-Jew will discover is that he lives in a situation which he has created against his own more accurate discoveries. No one has forced him to live as he does; he has chosen freely to live a contradiction. Like Lucien Fleurier, he has had other experiences in which he has learned more brutal truths. That they were frightening in no way justifies the later pretense that they were not true.

RELATED THEMES AND WORKS

Sartre's basic and longest discussion of the question of the Other is in *BN*, part three, "Being-for-Others." The concept and the problem it refers to is so central to his thought, however, that it appears almost everywhere in. his work. As we shall see, his treatment shifts from a presentation which suggests that confrontation with the Other can only produce conflict to a concern with showing how the confrontation with the Other must take place if there is not to be conflict. In what can be called a midpoint essay, "Venise de ma fenêtre" (*Sit. IV*, pp. 444–59), Sartre begins moving in this direction. He uses the physical situation of Venice—the city constructed from the blending of and cooperation between sky and water, liquid and solid, still-ness and motion—as a kind of metaphor for the constructs which could result if men cooperated. The essay is never quite so obvious, but the point of its indirection is surely the one I have just made.

In a brief memorial essay on the late Kurt Goldstein (*La Quinzaine litté-raire*, 15–31 October 1966), Yvon Belaval alluded to the influence Goldstein had on Sartre and Merleau-Ponty, especially because of Goldstein's insis-tence that a dualistic approach to the subject-object relationship could pro-duce no useful result and certainly not truth. While this pattern of influence is clear and unquestionable—because subject and object are intermingled in Sartre's theory of alterity to a point where no individual can be under-stood or understand himself unless he realizes he is both subject and object—Sartre differs from Goldstein on other essentials. One of the most important can be seen in the unilateral evaluation given to Lucien's forma-tion. While Lucien may be despicable or at least disagreeable, there is no doubt that his formation provided him with one immense advantage: the ability to cope with his environment and to resist shocks to his psychic stability. To decry this ability in such a way as to suggest that it is in itself evil is to misapprehend the very great importance, indeed the absolute need of some stable formation if men are to live as Sartre would have them live. I shall return to this question in later chapters, particularly in my discussion of love and in my concluding chapter.

Sartre has been vehemently criticized by many commentators, both Jew and Gentile, for presenting what they consider a caricature of the Jew in which the Jew loses all chance of individuality in order to become a total creation of his persecutors. A good summary of these criticisms is presented by Joseph Sungolowsky in his "Criticism of *Anti-Semite and Jew*" (*YFS*, 30 [1963] 68–72). Sartre clearly had no intention of caricaturing the Jew, but here as elsewhere his ardor pushes him into making a category which he then implicitly applies to all Jews, leaving inadequate space for individual differences. (He does list a series of categories, in *Réflexions*, but they remain categories despite the variety they seek to indicate.)

The solution he outlines at the end of the essay is one which has not been well served by time. There he proposed a classless society as the only kind of structure which would do away with the roots from which anti-Semitism nourishes itself. If a classless society is a synonym for Utopia, his suggestion may have some value; but there is little point in making estimates of values which have small chance of coming to pass. The solution is one of those sad proposals which, coming after a lucid and admirable analysis, shows how infrequently we can really come up with plausible remedies for our worst ills; it also shows that it is visionary to expect that human nature will change in its fundamental needs once socialism triumphs. Anti-Semitism, like so many other prejudices, answers psychological needs—and Sartre is vividly aware of this—which are not necessarily the product of social privation. There is further discussion of Jewishness and its impact on a single individual in the introduction Sartre wrote to Andre Gorz's *Le Traître* ("Des Rats et des hommes," *Sit. IV*, pp. 38–81).

A poll taken on anti-Semitism in France (for the magazine *Adam*, November-December 1966) showed that many of the situations cited by Sartre had not changed. Of "several thousand" polled, 10 percent thought there were too many Jews in France; one in five felt Jews were less French than their fellow countrymen; 50 per cent would object to having a Jew as President of the Republic; some thought the Jews had been responsible for the death of Joan of Arc.

The "affair of the gunboats" in December, 1969—when five such vessels were released under initially clandestine circumstances to Israeli agents— once again brought some of these convictions to the surface and raised, for right-wing Frenchmen, the question of the divided allegiance of French Jews. Extreme commentators reverted to the old argument, cited by Sartre in his essay, that Jews really cannot be as loyal to France as "true" Frenchmen.

Readers may be interested in consulting the following: Levy and Tillard's *La Grande Rafle du Vel' d'Hiver* (Paris, 1967) which deals with the background situation Sartre was most familiar with when writing his essay; Norman Cohn's *Warrant for Genocide, the Myth of the Jewish World Conspiracy* (London, 1967), and George Friedmann's *The End of the Jewish People?* (New York, 1967; Paris, 1965) which raises, from a different point of view, many of the issues Sartre considers.

Jean-François Steiner's *Treblinka* (Paris, 1966), the fictionalized history of the camp used by the Nazis for the extermination of Jews from Warsaw's ghetto is prefaced by Simone de Beauvoir. In her startling introduction, Mme de Beauvoir, in addition to some muddled use of terminology from the *CRD*, accuses the Jews of having been their own exterminators and sees the dealings of the *Judenrat* with the Nazis as part of a transhistorical phenomenon in which eminent persons *because of their class* cooperate with their oppressors. Readers who hope for the maintenance of consistency, if not justice, may wish to compare this analysis of a tyrannically oppressed people to Mme de Beauvoir's explanations of why, during the German occupation of France, she signed a paper certifying she was neither Jewish nor of Jewish background: "It was repugnant to sign, but no one refused to do it; for most of my colleagues, and for me, too, there was no means of doing otherwise" (*FA*, p. 478).

5 Towards Freedom

The inevitability of conflict as an underlying fact of human existence is oné of the main currents in Sartre's work. After the publication of *La Nausée* he told an interviewer that he planned "to take Roquentin away from his wholly personal life at Bouville and plunge him into the all-embracing world of modern political and social reality created by the Munich crisis" (cited in Thody, p. 40). Roquentin was no longer to be allowed the narcissistic luxury of writing a book designed to make men ashamed of their existence; he was to be plunged more deeply into existence, there to discover that no book could keep him out of the stream of events. This, as we have already seen, is not simply because salvation through books is not possible; more centrally, it is because salvation through schemes worked out by others is not possible either.[1] His book could not save Roquentin because it was a dishonest answer to an honest appraisal of the situation; social reality cannot automatically save him either, since he would surely encounter social reality with his habitual predispositions. Any such encounter would produce a further conflict because Roquentin is a fundamentally disturbed rebel whenever an exterior reality menaces what he believes is his personal integrity.

Sartre's second novel, *Les Chemins de la liberté*, presents a panoramic portrayal of the world as a battleground where individuals fight against the demands of social reality. It is a place where conflicts multiply precisely because of the hostilities which develop between man and man, between man and society, and among nations.[2] The book is not a study of how freedom makes its way in the world by steadily clearing and following one path; rather the novel depicts the several ways in which free men become aware of their freedom and the various methods they choose for living with their discovery. The book is divided into four parts. In the first volume, *L'Age de raison* (1945), Sartre presents us with a random gathering of individuals who do not comprise a true group. They are monads who knock up against each other from time to time because they are acquaintances, friends, or

1. This clearly raises a problem, one which becomes more and more difficult for Sartre since, in seeking a means by which the proletariat can become an effective and victorious force, he must urge the workers to accept the discipline and therefore the schemes worked out by the Communist party; their agreement to do so will naturally be a free one, but once they have agreed they must obey. We shall see in the discussion of *Le Diable et le Bon Dieu* how Sartre attempts to establish a formula which will justify such obedience.

2. The novel was originally entitled *Lucifer* and was supposed to be divided into two parts, "La Révolte" and "Le Serment." Revolt appears to indicate the discovery of a problem; the pledge proposes the way of solving the problem. As we shall see, the evolution of the novel does not readily allow for such a solution, though that solution will play a major role in the argument of the *Critique de la raison dialectique*.

lovers; but they live essentially apart, even when they encounter others. The single fact that brings them to our attention is their involvement in Mathieu Delarue's problem: his mistress is pregnant and he needs both an abortionist and money for the operation. Those he meets are for the most part people who live in situations whose consequences they have never examined thoroughly; they are living, therefore, in indifferent inauthenticity.

The second volume, *Le Sursis* (1945), traces out what happens when such people discover that their indifference can no longer exist hermetically. They find themselves menaced by a broader situation which comes from outside the carefully if unconsciously drawn circles of their lives and threatens to penetrate those circles. Change, which they have not willed and against which they apparently can do nothing, hovers over them like a dangerous bird whose flight gives no indication of his ultimate intentions. At the end of the book, the bird flies away; though they are out of danger for the moment, they have learned that there is danger. Thus the threat of change, even though it has gone away, has altered their lives. They cannot any longer pretend not to know what that threat has taught them: there are external powers which will treat them as a collective adversary no matter how forcefully, as individuals, they have resisted participating in the endangered collectivity.

The third volume, *La Mort dans l'âme* (1949), plunges these individuals into a situation from which they cannot escape; the bird has returned and his intentions are now only too clear. They can try to cope with the consequences of the war; they cannot pretend that their lives are what they were or that the care and management of their egos have provided them with any adequate fortress. The enemy has invaded their country and their lives. He intends to deal with them as his opponents; he has classified them. In one way or another, with cowardice or courage, they must face up to the fundamental changes which have intervened in their lives and deprived them of their erstwhile security. At the end of the book, with the defeat of France, their condition is clear: they are surrounded by a situation which goes beyond their own and determines it to a point where they feel impotent. Having always thought that they could care for their personal interests despite the claims of the external world, having persistently avoided political and social action, they find themselves obliged to think of the necessity of either acting or reacting, of the inevitability of encounters between them and the others who have now taken over their country and their lives. The irony in this is that they discover the need to act at a time when their freedom to act is severely tailored, when the possibilities of provoking change are limited, and when their hope has been absorbed by the force of hostile circumstances. The ego's insurance policy has been cancelled; with the termination of the ego's rights death enters the soul which nourished those rights.

The fourth volume, *La Dernière Chance*, exists only in fragmentary form.[3] It deals with projects which are organized in an effort to wrest hope back from the hostile circumstances. The situation Sartre describes is one in which the vacuum seems total since he is dealing with a concentration camp where men are not only no longer free to move about as they wish but where they are also liable to a kind of despair about the usefulness of freedom. All the old excuses now seem to be justified. Watched over by guards and surrounded by barbed wire, an individual can reasonably believe that he is no longer free. His action in fighting the enemy has been futile since the enemy, the Other, has vanquished and imprisoned him.

For Sartre this is a "perfect moment" quite different from those organized by Anny in *La Nausée*. This is the "perfect moment" brought about by the Other whose intention is to reduce his opponents to inaction. Like all perfect moments, it is not without risks. For those who have been blocked and incarcerated still remain free and can, even within the limitations of a prisoner of war camp, act freely. With their liberty hedged on all sides, some of these men become even more aware of what that presently restricted freedom means. They can look back to the conditions which have brought them to a point where freedom seems to mock itself; they can also look ahead to the establishment of conditions which will allow liberty to flourish; for the time being, they must seek to exercise what freedom is left to them. Typically, Sartre offers no hardy rhetoric, no brave songs, no enthusiastic slogans, not even a dreary dirge. The world of Nathan Hale and Patrick Henry—the world of resounding phrases—is not this world. To give one's life for one's country implies that the country is worth such a sacrifice; to choose between liberty or death is nonsense, since one is free, if only to make pretty phrases, until one is dead.

This is the essential revelation of the book: the inevitability of freedom. For good or ill, freedom is man's constant companion, not because he has chosen it, but because he can choose nothing else. Condemned to be free, man may very well wonder what he has done to merit such a condemnation; whatever answer he turns up will result only from a free-thinking process about freely defined choices. If Sartre, in *Les Chemins de la liberté*, brings us to the threshold of this discovery, he does not do so with the intention of showing us a stately mansion on the other side of that doorway. Indeed, as the reader looks through the doorway, he may very well decide that the noble façade of the word "freedom" hides a seamy tenement in desperate need of repair, if not replacement.

3. The fourth volume would have directly continued the narrative movement of volume three. A fragment, "Drole d'amitié," was published in *TM* (5:49, 5:50, 1959).

If freedom is considered as the gift of perpetual decision-making and the curse of never escaping from that task, it is not surprising that Mathieu, the protagonist of the novel, should define existence as the obligation "to drink himself without being thirsty" (*AR*, p. 54). Nor is it surprising that he imbibes from that beaker without asking himself too many leading questions. He is fundamentally a drifter, a Roquentin without an independent income—he must work for the salary he gets as a teacher. He has a social philosophy, but, like his ancestors throughout history, no plan for social action. He wants to be separated from his class; he appreciates the importance of changing social conditions; he believes in the need to be involved in action which will produce reform. He does nothing either to realize his visions or install his beliefs.

He is the center of the novel not simply because it is principally concerned with him but also because his kind must be the principal concern of any commentator who wishes to provoke change in the world; and, to the extent that he resembles Sartre, he is the center because his experience is the author's. He is, by default, *l'homme moyen sensuel*; though in his purer moments that is not what he would like to be, it is, in effect, what he is. Through him we meet the other characters in the book and, through them and their relations to Mathieu, we have a presentation in fiction of many of the situations discussed in *Being and Nothingness*. We encounter in Mathieu, as he deals with others, the troubled question of human freedom and the many conflicts created by the possession of that freedom.

Though *L'Age de raison* centers about Mathieu's effort to find money for the abortion, Sartre's main concern is not with forming a moral judgment on abortion. Abortion is an indifferent act; what is not indifferent are the motives behind the act, for they have to do with individual intentions. It is evident that this abortion, as an intention of Mathieu's consciousness, is a project which reveals the abject condition of that consciousness. The abortion is a sign; behind that sign is the significant act which produces the sign. This relationship between an intention and a revealing motivation behind the intention is, of course, meant to be prototypical of a broader situation. What I mean by this is that Sartre wishes to indicate that the great collectivities—classes and nations—act in the same way on a broader scale. One man's desire to abort is a small reflection of a whole society's desire to oppress. From this point of view, Mathieu's intention to rid his mistress, Marcelle, of their child is not radically different from Chamberlain's and Daladier's desire to rid themselves of a problem by turning Czechoslovakia over to Hitler. The individual intention, like the national intention, is a project whereby the individual seeks to protect himself from the consequences of his own acts.

Mathieu's weakness, like France's and England's, is that he seeks by all means to remain free. But his attempt is dependent on a nonsensical procedure: the liberty he seeks is one that will protect him from the results of all his other free acts whenever those acts lead him towards a road he doesn't want to take. In order to avoid that road, or another like it, he would have to avoid all acts. In trying to keep away from all roads which may have unsuspected potholes, he finds himself in the rut hollowed out by his caution and fear. Hoping to be free, he is a good deal more immobilized than he suspects. He is as much hemmed in by his desire to be free as he would be by what he might consider a more restrictive situation. We see this in several of his activities.

He carries on his relationship with Marcelle clandestinely, coming to see her late at night, like a thief. He accepts these conditions out of sexual need. But he is growing tired of the affair (and has another outlet in view); Marcelle is also growing impatient with it—it promises her so little. When he is with her he feels remorse over his growing indifference, but the remorse, rather than being an expression of generous pity, is more a manifestation of his increasing sense of entrapment. Because she does not have his freedom of movement and because she satisfies his sexual needs, Mathieu senses that Marcelle exercises a kind of superiority over him—the superiority, perhaps, of all victims upon whom the master depends for his pleasure. Her superiority gives her some rights. As a result, he looks upon her as someone who is more than his sexual partner. She is also his lucidity, his witness, and his judge. She reveals him to himself during his intimate conversations with her; in so doing, she is the witness of the fact that his life is happening and, in a variation on that verb, passing by. Because these two functions allow her to make comments on what he does and to suggest a meaning for his actions, she is potentially his judge.

These three functions are put into high relief once she becomes pregnant, for the imminence of new life represents a claim on his freedom and is a call to the exercise of a decency he cannot easily refuse. He is protected by an agreement that has always existed between them; but the agreement, which he can rightfully invoke, does not spare him a feeling of humiliation nor does it keep him from thinking that Marcelle hates him. Even though he considers her the judge, she considers him the master, for she must accept his decision. And he must live with the hatred his decision may set loose in her. What he is experiencing is shame; the Other who is Marcelle looks at him and determines that he must, in this situation, act one way or another.[4] The particular way he may choose does not, as she

4. See above, p. 89, where other reactions to shame are discussed. Sartre has placed major emphasis on the look as the action or the gesture which awakens the individual looked-at to the feeling of shame. See *BN*, pp. 252–302.

looks at him, matter. What does matter is that he must make an unavoidable decision whose necessity comes to him from the Other.

His reaction, while it may appear bizarre, is not without its own compensating logic. He feels a need to be away from her, in a café, where the looks of the passersby will console him against the look he has received from her. Because those others, the people who stroll by the cafe, or sit with their drinks in front of them, look at him neutrally, he can interpret that neutrality in his favor and tell himself that they know they are looking at a free man. For them he is not the man who, minutes before, was enclosed in a room, surrounded by the threat of an inevitable responsibility; he is instead the man who can sit in a café whenever he chooses. He is using others, about whom he knows nothing—certainly not their thoughts about him—to reassure himself against the claim a particular Other, Marcelle (who does know something about him), may seek to stake. He is in a paradoxical situation, but since paradox most often has to do with the tougher aspects of truth, his paradox is the essence of his dilemma: he needs the Other in order to exist, yet, when existence becomes difficult, he needs the Other in order to deny the Other. In his case, the Other does indeed tell him who he is; whenever that revelation is disagreeable or does not conform with his present desires he seeks still another. The Other who attracts him more than Marcelle, and certainly more than anonymous spectators, is Ivich, a young student whose primary attraction is her youth. What he wants her to tell him, I gather, is that time, though it is passing, is not depriving him of the chance to pluck younger rosebuds.

Youth clearly has charms to blind the most perceptive eyes; since there is little evidence to make us believe that Mathieu's perceptive equipment is in very good condition, there is little reason to be surprised about his infatuation with Ivich. But he could not make a worse choice. If he expects to receive something from Ivich, he ought first to be sure that she has something to offer and, as the giver of gifts, represents something. She represents nothing. Not only is she horrified by the Other and the act by which he would demonstrate control over her, she is also immobilized by the sheer fact of existence. Any act, any initiative, any situation which demands a response terrifies her. When she finally allows herself to be seduced by someone other than Mathieu, she does so in a fit of bad temper, seeking vengeance on her family, on her unhappiness, on her lack of decisiveness. She feels that she is surrounded by a world whose major purpose is to soil her, and thus she thinks back to another world, the Russia from which her parents have fled, as being a better space; she knows nothing directly about it. Her closest human relationship is with her brother and is clearly a manifestation of her desire to keep time and things at a standstill.[5]

5. In a later work, *Les Séquestrés d'Altona*, Sartre portrays another brother-sister relationship which picks up in a much more elemental and vivid form some of the

She lives, throughout the first volume of the novel, with the sure and sick conviction that she has failed an examination. The impression she creates in the reader is one of passionate passivity, the kind of passivity which demands an endless amount of mental activity in order to be maintained. Her greatest fear—she expresses it several times in the book; it is a recurrent dread in Sartre's literary works—is of being touched. The human hand reaching out towards her would be the transformation of the Other's look into a gesture of possession. Unlike Mathieu, she does not seek to protect a nearby space in which she can act freely; she seeks rather to extirpate herself from any situation in which another's freedom might force her to exercise her own consciously. Her only strategy is to be, if not a mighty fortress, surely a distant one.

Mathieu appreciates the distance even though he does not understand the strategy behind it. He thinks it keeps her "safe from attack, with her frail waist and her hard beautiful breasts; she seemed to be painted and varnished like a Tahitian woman in a Gauguin canvas—unusable" (*AR*, p. 59). The implication is this: if she cannot be used neither can she be abused. She has escaped from consequences as he has not, and so she represents an ideal attained and an insurance obtained to protect her from assault. She exists only for herself, in solitude, and because of that he senses that he does not exist for her. The curious result of this series of discoveries is that Mathieu falls in love with her, consciously aware that what he calls love is a project freely formed on the basis of a desire he does not choose to impede. Each of them is playing a complicated game whose goal is to stop all games which demand any kind of participation that might compromise personal aims.[6]

Ivich's distance is nothing other than her sense of alienation, an alienation produced more by her realization that the world has only too clearly been formed to include her than from the idea that there is no place for her in the world. Since the world has kept space reserved for her, this means that the world has unstated claims on her; it means, too, that she exists for the world or, more exactly, for the Other. This is what she finds intolerable because, though the space is there, it is the terrain on which the Other may refuse her as she wants to refuse him. Because she is obligated to live with the ill-defined and not easily predictable ways of others, she recognizes

concerns which tie Ivich to Boris. In the play, the use of family relationships as a protection against others is much more noticeable, as is the revolt against the incest taboo and its explicit design of forcing individuals to relate to others who do not come from the same family or tribe.

6. Their relationship is a very good example of what happens when two different hodological spaces are brought together. Mathieu, anxious to annex her space to his, can only do so by making her agree to be usable by him; he thus automatically runs up against her resistance and finds that the strongest point in that resistance is precisely her refusal to be used as a tool for anyone else. Their relationship is also a good example of the kind of love-project Sartre discusses in *BN*. See below, p. 249.

the Other only in order to refuse to be with him. In other words, before experiencing empirically the possibility which she envisages—the refusal of her by the Other—she operates on the basis of its foreseeable certainty. She has decided initially that she hates being dependent on others, and her response to that hatred brings her to a situation Sartre described in *Being and Nothingness*: "I escape the Other by leaving him with my alienated Me in his hands. But as I choose myself as a tearing away from the Other, I assume and recognize as mine this alienated Me. My wrenching away from the Other—that is, my Self—is by its essential structure an assumption as *mine* of this Me which the Other refuses; we can even say that it is *only that*" (p. 285). In brief, what Ivich is seeking is to refuse the Other before the Other can refuse her; the anguish produced as she waits for the result of her exam—where she is inescapably in the hands of the Other—only confirms her judgment.

If Mathieu thinks of her as being beyond attack, that is because, in a muddled way, her impregnability makes him impotent. He experiences the same uselessness that he has assigned to her; but where he had considered it some sort of accomplishment in her case—because he desired her *as unusable*—he does not want to think of it as a value he should accept in his own life. Being beyond use may be a desirable personal quality when it is freely assumed and when it incarnates what one seeks; it is frustrating when it impedes one from having the sort of use one would like to have. By leaving Mathieu with her alienated Me, Ivich is putting him in the position of being an object, an object which has become a thing because it has been refused; he exists for her, as does almost everything, as that which she rejects. This puts him into a tense situation; he does not want to exist as the refused Other, yet he admires the distance created by the process of refusal. Mathieu could find a relatively easy way out of his dilemma if he chose, in turn, to refuse Ivich and therefore to turn her into an object by denying her any right to influence or reify him.

He cannot do this precisely because he desires the quality of her "studied" alienation and also because he needs her assent before he can reject Marcelle definitively. What he wants is well-nigh impossible: "I want to assimilate the Other as the Other-looking-at-me, and this project of assimilation includes an augmented recognition of my being-looked-at. In short, in order to maintain before me the other's freedom which is looking at me, I identify myself totally with my being-looked-at. And since my being-as-object is the only possible relation between me and the Other, it is this being-as-object which alone can serve me as an instrument to effect my assimilation of the *other freedom*" (*BN*, p. 365).

On Mathieu's terms alone, his project is as impossible as his desire is real, for, desiring in Ivich that which cannot be got at, that which cannot be used, he wants to make use of it. To the extent that he met with success, he would possess a quality which had been seriously diminished if not destroyed by his success. If Ivich were to become his, she would no longer be elusive: possession would entail the destruction of the quality sought. Ivich, the free subject, would at the moment of possession become the submissive object. The fundamental problem we see in their relationship is the fundamental problem we have met in all of Sartre's characters: they are free subjects in their own eyes but objects in the eyes of others. Their freedom as subjects leads them to want to possess the object-Other in order to satisfy the needs of their own subjectivity. Necessarily they meet either opposition or a fulfilment of their project which destroys the goal of the project. If Mathieu is drawn to Ivich because of her apparent and total freedom—total because it rejects him—he will not, in possessing her, possess what he thought to possess since in giving herself to him she will be that much less free; in other words, she will no longer be the quality he sought.

What has been lacking to all the Sartrean characters we have encountered so far, with the irrelevant exception of Eve and Pierre, is the possibility of reciprocity, of a joint participation in the pursuit of a common goal which they could attain as free subjects. Common action, which would produce joint satisfaction and allow for cooperation in action and reciprocity in pleasure, haunts these people but finds only incoherent expression. Mathieu vaguely senses the need for some third force to serve as the mediator between him and Ivich. He seeks both to win Ivich's admiration and palliate his own unattractiveness by introducing her to beautiful things; she rebuffs him, telling him "I find it horrible that someone should try to create a duty between me and the things I like" (*AR*, pp. 86–7). She thereby echoes and develops Anny's dislike of people who claimed to share her thoughts. Joint action obviously creates the duty of going through with the whole process of acts which will bring the joint action to fruition; with Ivich's refusal to accept that duty, all roads seem blocked.

As a result, Mathieu, with wavering degrees of full consciousness, must seek detours. In moments of anger and frustration, he assumes a superior attitude towards Ivich and her brother Boris: they are only kids, afraid of death, afraid of the future, afraid of the changes which will age them; he, an adult, should not be wasting his time with them. But what the mind tells the frustrated body is not enough to dampen the unsatisfied desires which give birth to frustrations. At a later moment in the book, he tells himself that he would be willing to accept a tense, unpredictable, probably unhappy relationship with her in order to be generous in love; the generosity would, of course, redound upon him. In the end, any chance of a relationship is clearly impossible because he realizes that his generosity—or any sense of gain in an affair with Ivich—would depend on her. Whether he likes it or not—and he does not, since he breaks with her—she would call the plays by refusing to play the game. She does not love him. The "good" he seeks does not exist.

Consciousness, Sartre has always insisted, is a hollow to be filled endlessly. It is not a punctured container so much as it is one which expands throughout life; the job of filling it continues as long as the heart beats. The trouble with Mathieu and Ivich is that their consciousnesses have been filled indiscriminately and thus are full of contradictions from which they cannot escape because they have never thought out the meaning of the contradictions. Infected with the contradictions and the acts they produce, they are forced to live in solitude and even to consider solitude the sole efficacious way of life. Only by living for themselves can they protect themselves. Mathieu's desire for Ivich is in a way a desire to protect *his* impregnability against hers; to the extent that she seeks to classify him he must possess her and thus invalidate her classification; impotence is a possible if not immediately satisfying strategy. What they cannot see together is the possibility of a common project—dare one call it love?—which would serve them both. Each of them is really terrified of breaking out of his solitude in the company of another because he cannot foretell whether that act will produce a breakthrough or a breakdown.

Uncertainty is the central cause of frustration for these two. The solitude of the Other is a mirror offering a sharp reflection of one's own solitude. The mirror of the eye, as we saw with Estelle, is no better and possibly is worse since it imparts no information at all from the Other. Locked in their subjectivity, they refuse, like Estelle, to learn anything from a mirror unless it confirms their own idea of their existence. This incapacity to see, and the fear that, in common pursuits, a part of oneself will be lost, is the central flaw of Sartrean man. It dooms him to live with his fears and apprehensions; it dooms him to ignorance. To the extent that it becomes a habit, it forces him back into himself even though he may have seen a way out. The task of showing that there is a way out and that it is the only way is one of the most difficult Sartre has to accomplish.

In one of the most puzzling episodes of *L'Age de raison*—the scene in which Ivich stabs her hand and is then imitated by Mathieu (pp. 205–211)—we see what persistence in defending solitude does for the maintenance of ignorance and frustration. Ivich's gesture is a declaration of separation rather than independence; she wants to shock even more profoundly the already shocked couple sitting next to her. They represent a decency she has no part of and presumably wants none of. But the gesture is also an assertion of herself to herself and not only to them: *her* hand is wounded, *her* blood flows, *her* act produces these confirmations of *her* identity. Reacting to her gesture—and instinctively feeling uneasy with the couple's appraisal, which heavily underscores the fact that Ivich is setting herself off as "different"—Mathieu reproaches her and immediately urges that she have her hand bandaged. The coolness with which she counters his protestations infuriates him and, after suggesting that her action is only a self-indulgent game, he imitates it, despite the fact that Ivich had earlier told him how much she detested having people emulate her. Mathieu's fury quickly disappears, and he feels he has done more than comment on Ivich's original gesture. He, too, has stood up to others; he, too, has braved public opinion. For the rest of the evening he and Ivich are a couple. They laugh openly and with something not far from joy; they have, though only briefly, their most honest conversation. The shared act has for the moment brought them away from thinking about themselves and seems to have promised something better: the possibility that this moment, which "glitters like a little diamond," might go on forever. It does not, precisely because each returns to his solitude.

Only much later in Sartre's work does the significance of this episode become clear. In the transformation of Mathieu's gesture from one of mockery to one of solidarity, there is an indication that he has stumbled onto the benefit of imitation. There is an indication, too, of why Ivich earlier had expressed her detestation of those who imitated her. Imitation produces a strand of solidarity; once he has imitated her, Mathieu feels that he is one with her—her act becomes his. As Ivich had stabbed herself in order to assert herself before the neighboring and disapproving couple, so Mathieu stabs himself in order to assert himself before Ivich. Their act could become exemplary if only they could see, or, more precisely, if only they could communicate.[7]

Instinctively, Mathieu can experience such revelations and the good feelings they engender. Rationally, he can do little with them, not because he is incapable of thought, but because he does not wish to reflect; reflection produces perspectives whose prodding information cannot be ignored. We see this in his relations with Brunet, a friend from his youth who is an active organizer for the Communist party. Brunet represents for Mathieu the outcome of thought: it leads to decisions, and decisions involve you in a way of life from which there is only dishonest escape. It is easier for Mathieu, and it corresponds better with his desires, to live in another world where

---

7. Sartre discusses his ideas on imitation on pp. 352–63 of "Les Communistes et la paix" (*Sit. VI*). It is pertinent to note that the situation of the workers is graver than that of Ivich and Mathieu in the sense that their needs are dire and immediate; the necessity of working long hours in order to attain minimum subsistence, the wretched conditions of slum life, the lack of time do not allow the worker to sit in cafés and indulge in futile though significant gestures. Still, the worker's choice of imitation, in its manifestation of a desire to escape the solitary nature of his condition, is very much the option that Mathieu is electing by his gesture. He hopes, through imitation, to use a sign in order to convey an important message: he and Ivich are one in their protest against being one's. The worker's situation, in the long run, has a better chance of success since syndical organization can provide the structures which will allow him to agitate for improvement. No such structures exist for Ivich and Mathieu.

lies are possible, where change can be effected if one learns to resign oneself
to uneasy compromises. This other world has the kind of fluidity Mathieu
needs, possibly because it allows for excuses, but probably because it represents an immersion in a way of living which silences most questions. In
this other world, you never need ask yourself what you are.

Brunet, by contrast, is someone. He, too, is a manifestation of the Other,
but he is the Other who, once having been Mathieu's friend, is so no longer;
his friends are the other militants of the Communist party who share his
projects, who work with him and with whom he works. In political action
he has found a steady manifestation of a way of cooperation Mathieu had
grasped only incoherently in the stabbing incident. Because of these qualities in his existence, Brunet is a catalyst to a reflective thought-process
within Mathieu.

Before he meets him, Mathieu thinks back to his childhood, to the goal
he had set for himself, a goal not in any way different from that of the young
Sartre: salvation. That was the bet he had made with the world and in the
name of which he had read and thought and practiced his profession. But
against the pattern of acts implied by the bet, he can offer no pattern of
lived action. He has become a minor functionary, with good tendencies,
but with no acts to his credit. In Brunet's presence he is stripped of his
defenses and exposed to fundamental questions about what he has done
with his life; what is more agonizing, he feels that he is being questioned
about the relationship between what he is and the overall flow of life. Pablo,
the child of Gomez—a man who is fighting for the Republican cause in
Spain—looks at Mathieu and even in that infant's gaze Mathieu detects
the Other who is questioning him not only about his existence but also about
the single immediate project he has: to obtain money for the abortion. His
existence at the moment he encounters these others, who in his eyes have
a substance and a weight he does not possess, is that of the individual who
spends his time staving off existence. Guiltily he tells himself that he is not
planning a dark act: "I'm not going to kill anyone. I am going to prevent
an infant from being born" (*AR*, p. 49). It is obvious that he is also keeping
his own consciousness from being born into responsibility.

Like Ivich, Brunet and his milieu also refuse Mathieu; but the terms
of their refusal are quite different from hers. They turn him back on himself,
not out of opposition to him, but because he will not make the decision
which would give him a full claim on their cooperation in the realization
of a common project. In replying angrily to Sarah's (she is Gomez's wife)
plea that he not abort the child, Mathieu suggests that he is doing nothing
worse than those who allow children to be born; no one can predict what
a child's life will be like. But he is not being honest, for what he really wants
to do is prevent the birth of another consciousness. There are already too
many of them in the world, and, in Sarah's living room, all of them, from

the young Pablo to the seasoned Brunet, seem to disapprove of him. The desire to abort, like the act by which at the age of sixteen he had smashed an antique vase, is part of the desire to destroy what he cannot either dominate or possess. The destruction of the vase was an act of vengeance on the world of things; the abortion will be an act of revenge on the others, especially on those others who look upon him and his intention with disapproval.[8]

He does not tell himself this openly, of course. He looks upon the abortion as a good act. Yet, despite such encouraging arguments, he cannot keep his mind from touching on other possibilities, the most disempowering of which is that he has been engaged in such acts all along, acts which have led him nowhere. He tries to assure himself that these have been preventive acts designed to keep him available for one important act. Brunet will not indulge such arguments and bluntly tells Mathieu that he chooses these abstract justifications in order to certify his abstention from meaningful and responsible involvement. Against such abstention—and abstention, as we have seen, is only another way of acting—Brunet urges him to accept his freedom. Mathieu can find no real answer to this except to protest that such a decision serves no purpose. Again, he is lying to himself because he knows that he has indeed decided to accept his freedom; he has done nothing but that. Still, the only freedom he wants to acknowledge is that favored by the child who claims accidents and the unkind maneuvers of higher forces to explain acts for which he does not want to accept the blame. In Mathieu's fascination with the youth of Boris and Ivich, as well as in his characterization of the adult world as heavy and formless, we see the irony of the title of this first volume: having long before reached the age of reason and the negotiations with knowledge it makes possible, Mathieu is fighting againt what he is.[9]

In his efforts he has had some apparent success; yet he has made no real gains. With Marcelle he has faced the Other who is inferior to him, because she has less power than he; despite the pity he may feel for her, he can leave her or insist that she not have the child. Because of his greater freedom of movement, he makes Marcelle dependent on him; yet she has her small dose of potential revenge in the scorn she heaps upon him merely by looking accusingly at him. Though he can triumph over the Other who

8. Cf. *BN*: ". . . the recognition that it is impossible to *possess* an object involves for the for-itself a violent urge to *destroy* it. To destroy is to reabsorb into myself. . . . Destruction realizes appropriation perhaps more keenly than creation does" (p. 593).

9. Simone de Beauvoir writes: "Sartre could not resign himself to moving into the 'age of reason', into the 'age of man'" (*FA*, p. 218). "He had an absolute confidence about his future; but the future wasn't always enough to brighten up the present. Sartre had brought such ardor to being young that at the moment when youth was taking leave of him he had need of some strong consoling joys" (p. 219).

is Marcelle, he still experiences the primary reaction of every discovery of the Other: shame. Their love affair has not dismissed that possibility. With Ivich he is dealing with the distant Other, an Other who is not unlike the mysterious far-off princesses of the troubadours and with whom he seeks a relationship which, initially, is not much different from the *amour lointain* of the Provencal poets. Yet his ultimate project, like the ultimate project of the *trovères*, is to reduce distances and intensify fondness by bringing the distant Other under control—which amounts to the same thing as making her inferior. Intimate love may be better than love from afar; it is not the same thing.

Even as he seeks to bring Ivich under control, Mathieu, as we have seen, is not quite sure what life will be like under the new circumstances. What he discovers at the end of *L'Age de raison* is not what life with Ivich would be like; rather he comes to understand what their relationship has been and, like Swann in Proust's novel, realizes that he has spent his time pursuing a girl who was not what he thought and who could not be what he hoped. With Brunet, he has been offered a way out—the way of emulation whereby he would join with others in pursuit of a common goal. He does not accept this for the reasons I have pointed out: the absence of persuasive arguments in favor of one way of action as opposed to another.[10] He does not accept Brunet's way because in so doing he would also be accepting a judgment on the way he has lived his life up to now. Whatever decisive action he has been holding himself in readiness for cannot be the commitment proposed by Brunet since Brunet does not place any value on Mathieu's formative years. As far as Brunet is concerned, they have prepared him only to cherish nothing, since their intention had been to abstract him from everything except his own petty concerns. Brunet is the Other who tells Mathieu too much about himself for Mathieu to want to listen. The tunes that Brunet plays have too much cacophany and not enough melody. Mathieu wants something sweeter—a music of absence to celebrate what Mathieu has not done.

Ironically, Mathieu, who does not wish to emulate, is emulated; Mathieu, who does not wish to accede to an age of reason he already possesses, becomes an ideal for Ivich's brother Boris, who looks upon him as a remark-

---

10. Simone de Beauvoir writes: "Sartre had not found a means of incarnating the sympathy which attracted him to the proletariat; his was the weakest of positions" (*FA*, p. 121). "More than once during those years [the early 1930s], Sartre was faintly tempted to join the C[ommunist] P[arty]. His ideas, his projects, his temperament were stumbling blocks; but though his taste for independence was as strong as mine, he possessed a fuller sense of his responsibilities. . . . we concluded—our conclusions were always tentative—that if one belonged to the proletariat, one would have to be a Communist; but that struggle, while it concerned us, was still not really ours; all that could be demanded of us was that we always be on the proletariat's side. We had to pursue our own undertakings which were not in harmony with membership in the party" (p. 140).

able example of how one should live as an adult. For Boris, Mathieu incarnates a kind of mastery of freedom which is altogether admirable and therefore to be imitated. Mathieu thinks and does whatever he wants; he has no sense of responsibility towards anyone save himself; Mathieu is open-minded because he constantly interrogates and reexamines everyone and everything; Mathieu, in the current expression, is cool. Despite Mathieu's apparent lucidity, there is an opaque side to him which puzzles Boris. This puzzlement has to do with the place ethical judgment would have in Mathieu's world or, in other words, with the limits of coolness. Incoherently, Boris is aware of a potential flaw in Mathieu's attitude: it is no more than an approach; it does not allow for predictions about how to act in particular situations; it is not a code of conduct. What Boris tries to determine through a needless theft—he proposes to steal a semi-valuable book—is what Mathieu's attitude to such a meaningless free act would be. (Since it is intended to provoke a response, the act is not as gratuitous as Boris pretends.) It is futile because Boris never learns what Mathieu's judgment is. Mathieu, in desperation over his efforts to find money for the abortion, is too close to accepting theft as a solution. In the end, he does indeed steal the money he needs from Boris's aging and neurotic mistress, Lola, and, through a complicated chain of reactions, creates a situation in which Lola believes Boris has stolen the money.[11]

In all these encounters and relationships, Mathieu's apprehension of the Other remains on a very primitive level!—the level of *Being and Nothingness*. Here I must once again stress that the philosophical work, rather than

11. Boris initially proposes that he, Boris, try to borrow the money from Lola; Mathieu refuses the offer, but Boris persists and tells Lola a concocted story which she adamantly rejects without speculating too much on why he might really want the money. She then asks Mathieu if he is aware that Boris is looking for a loan; Mathieu twice denies all knowledge of the situation. Lola concludes that it is some kind of test that Boris is putting her to; she still refuses to give him the money. The next morning Boris confuses the aftereffects of drugs on Lola with her death and comes in panic to Mathieu, informing him of her decease and asking that Mathieu go to her hotel room to recover a packet of Boris' letters to her. Mathieu takes the letters; he is also tempted to take the money which he finds in the same trunk, but hesitates, concluding, as he leaves Lola's room, that he is a weakling. Disturbed by this indication of his lack of courage, he goes back to steal the money and discovers that it is too late; Lola has come out of her torpor.

That evening he returns once more to the hotel, during Lola's absence, and steals the money which he then gives to Marcelle, admitting under questioning that he has stolen it. This act indicates to Marcelle how far apart they have grown and precipitates a break which Mathieu accepts with relief. Still later on the same evening, a distraught Lola arrives at Mathieu's apartment looking for Boris, claiming that she has complained to the police, and strenuously repulsing Mathieu's confession that he is the culprit; she *must* believe that Boris is guilty. Daniel finally arrives, her money in hand, which he obtained from Marcelle; he returns it to Lola and, when she has departed, informs Mathieu that he is going to marry Marcelle. Sartre's intention here is to show how rings of bad faith eddy out from patterns of slovenly intention and devalue all the acts produced by those patterns.

being a summary of Sartre's thought, is the starting point for the systematization of that thought. The situations it deals with are very much the situations dealt with in *Les Chemins de la liberté*, and its terminal point is the one Mathieu reaches: the beginning of ethical conduct. The primitive level is that on which the ego seeks to defend what it possesses and to incorporate, as a reinforcement for that possession, what is denied to it. What it possesses is very little, and that little is increasingly impoverished. Mathieu, like the "I" in *Being and Nothingness* loses all the battles; whatever remains intact after the defeats is something of no great value, a series of questions without answers, an expense of passions which produces no useful result either for him or for the Other.

Yet he does make progress in this book, much as Roquentin had made progress in *La Nausée* and as Lucien failed to make progress acceptable to Sartre in "L'Enfance d'un chef." At the end of the first volume, Mathieu must accept the fact that he has reached maturity. He recognizes that he has wrapped a protective shell around himself and then coated the shell with a gummy substance designed to repel others and to hide him further from reality. In so doing he has only accentuated the fact that he is surplus being. As he looks at the drugged, somnolent body of Boris's mistress, he understands that existence is composed from the future much as a body is put together from the void. As the body then fills space, so acts should fill his future. Up to this point he has behaved in order to protect a void: an isolated, personal space which would keep him from consequential activity and the ethical problems it would produce. At the end, he knows that ethical behavior is unavoidable, for there will be neither good nor evil unless he invents them. Action will demand a process of choice designed, not to protect, but to select. He is alone and at liberty, condemned to make decisions, sentenced to be free. Until now, in his fight against the Other, he has lived in total dependence upon the Other. The future must be used to set up another kind of relationship with the Other in which he will exist for the Other and the Other will exist for him. This clearly is not a victory since the major question has yet to be answered: is it possible to have that kind of reciprocal relationship? Still, to know what the question is represents some progress. At the end of the first volume Mathieu has at least found himself; and in so doing he has found, in Pirandello's expression, that there is no self—there is only an endless process of creation. Maturity brings lucidity, an understanding of what must be done; that lucidity, unfortunately and inevitably, is no more than a feeble light to carry into the unillumined reaches of the future.

Mathieu's progress represents a breakthrough in the sense that he escapes, none too happily, from circularity. Where Roquentin's progress led him to the desire to create a circle which would respond to the circle he rejected, and where Lucien's progress led him away from uncertain paths and back to the safe circle of his class, Mathieu learns the impertinence of circles. Before making that discovery, he has been prowling, like Milton's Satan, about the edge of the circle in which Lucien had enclosed himself; he has not joined another social circle—for there the circle of his individuality would lose its perfect shape—nor has he succumbed to the force of any other influence which would lead him into the future. Along with most of the other characters in *L'Age de raison*, he is an existent [12] who has deliberately immobilized himself in order to fight against an open world which holds no appeal for his consciousness. He and most of the others do not want either to exist in the world or to make the world exist as the result of their actions; they have placed themselves in compartments, closed the doors, and are hoping for the best. What communication they have with others comes about only when they need the Other for the maintenance of their self-defeating project. And their project is almost a nonsensical one since it aims at allowing them to have no further projects.

There are exceptions. Brunet's involvement with the Communist party is obviously an opposite kind of activity, as is that of Gomez who has gone to Spain to fight for his socialist beliefs. But their presence in the novel is for the most part shadowy; indeed, the activities of the rest of the world are shadowy. As I have said, we are here living with monads who from time to time knock up against other monads and who fight against the possibility that they are very much like the rest of the world. Though they represent feeble protests against a bourgeois world which is in its last agony, they have no program for replacing that world and run the risk of being entombed with the class they despise. They live in disillusion with a world which has not honored the promises it made to its members. An ill-defined disquiet eats away at the heart of these people because the recipes and prescriptions written out by the bourgeois cooks and doctors have neither nourished them properly nor drugged them adequately against the assaults of fact.

We see this during Mathieu's conversation with his eminently successful and eminently bourgeois brother, who enjoys playing with the evident contradictions between Mathieu's abstract liberalism and his actual activities. The conversation points up all of Mathieu's weaknesses, especially that disparity between his assertions and his actions. But the chat concludes in nonsense. His brother refuses him the money for the abortion but counters his refusal with an offer to give Mathieu the same amount if he agrees to marry Marcelle. It is nonsense not only because it fails to pay adequate attention to the poor chance of success such a marriage would have but

12. The word *existent* is Sartre's. He uses it in order to allude to and convey an active quality which is not caught by the expression *human being* with its suggestion of an already defined or ideal quality.

also because it incarnates the bourgeois attitude against which most of the characters in the book are modestly rebelling. This is that "serious attitude which involves starting from the world and attributing more reality to the world than to oneself; at the very least the serious man confers reality on himself to the degree to which he belongs to the world" (*BN*, p. 580).

Such an attitude can propose no solutions since it refuses to accept at face value the terms with which it is presented; the class which holds it prefers to cow its rebellious members once it perceives that their rebellion may contain a truth which endangers the class. This attitude is also no solution because the individual's rebellion may indicate that he has a better comprehension of what the world ought to be about: it should not have necessarily to do with protecting what is established, especially if what is established does not adequately respond to individual human needs on all levels. As Mathieu and others in the book have gone their way because no other way corresponds to what they know about themselves, so, too, the world has gone its way, refusing to obey the dictates of the bourgeois conscience. The bourgeois world presupposed a solidity and a universality which some of its members have begun to interrogate; so long as the bourgeois world can beat these members back, it can deny the pertinence of the information conveyed by their refusal. It can live enclosed, pretending that its space is the only relevant space. But it is living in a dream which will soon turn to nightmare.

The class, in its attitude towards the Other, is no more than the individual writ large; unlike the individual, it derives benefits of mass and force from its size. What it fights for in its very organization is the right to remain a we-subject (*BN*, pp. 423–30), to direct the world so that the world will respond to its needs. What it fights against is the danger of becoming an us-object (*BN*, pp. 415–23), of being used by another we-subject for the exploitation of that other's needs. We saw with Lucien how the risk of becoming an object drove him back into the massive support of his class and the privilege of becoming there part of the we-subject. We saw, too, how anti-Semitism provided a prototype of the kind of Other created by the class in order to absorb, in a safe way, the danger of the Other. What we have seen with Mathieu is the refusal of one individual to take Lucien's way out; we have seen, too, that so far his decision has produced nothing of great value. What we shall see in *Le Sursis* is the transformation of the class into an us-object by the threat of an Other it has not created and thus cannot control. It is not the Jew who menaces now; it is another anti-Semite.

As Mathieu's shell fell off under the pressure of his recognition of the inevitability of acting with conscious freedom, so the class's shell falls off with the arrival of an unpredictable Other. The fight for mastery which has occupied both individual and class, and sometimes set the individual in opposition to his class, is, with the arrival of the war, overshadowed by the discovery that the individual, the class, and the society, each of which bears the common name "French," are all now confronted with the possibility of being victims. They have all becomes Jews in the sense that they have become for the German what the Jew is for the anti-Semite.

The phenomenon of conflict which is, according to Sartre, at the basis of all encounters with the Other, now becomes, under the guise of war, the main force of *Les Chemins de la liberté*. The war is an inverted pyramid built from the stones of individual hostilities and conflicts; because it is inverted, its topheaviness threatens to destroy all the individuals who, by indulging their personal hostilities, have prepared the way for global hostility. Mathieu's sister-in-law's reaction to the war is typical of that of her class and most of its members: someone should have protected her from it. The impending war—the book covers the period of the Munich crisis—touches them all and confronts them with the information they have been trying to avoid. It reduces the possibilities of escape to a limited number: one can compromise with the Other—a process which bears the problematical name of appeasement; one can decide, like Mathieu's brother, that the Other who is the potential enemy is really not so bad; one can discover the usefulness and even the beauty of Switzerland and decide to seek refuge there, beyond the melee, enclosed once again in oneself. The paths of escape may be few; the reactions of the individual are many. What is of central importance is that the war is a provocation which cannot be ignored, even if it is the fault of someone else, even though Switzerland beckons one to its neutral haven.[13]

For Boris the war provides the way out he has been seeking from his involvement with Lola; for Ivich the war is just another cause of shame, another of those forces which come to shake her up without first asking her opinion. But it brings one advantage: it gives her an external justification for giving up the studies which hold no great interest for her anyway. For Mathieu's brother the war is an opportunity to use reason and compromise in order to stave off the war's worst threat. The Germans, he tells himself, are not irrational and intransigent individuals; terms can be

13. By contrast with *L'Age de raison*, which is presented in a fairly traditional episodic technique (though with a prose style which is peculiarly Sartre's), *Le Sursis* attempts to be quite innovative, a kind of intensification of the Dos Passos technique. Sartre has chosen a cross section of French and European society at the time of the Munich arrangement. He creates a flow of events through individual consciousnesses by jettisoning the usual paragraph divisions and frequently by making one sentence join together the thoughts or reactions of two widely separated consciousnesses. This technique is clearly of great value and import to him. In *BN* he had already suggested what the technique would seek to accomplish: "So long as the detotalized totality 'humanity' exists, it is possible for some sort of plurality of individuals to experience itself as 'Us' in relation to all or part of the rest of men, whether these men are present in 'flesh and blood' or whether they are real but absent" (p. 420).

worked out with them, concessions can be honorably made. The bourgeois club, in his judgment, need know no frontiers. For Maurice, a worker who is also a militant of the Communist party, the war provides a chance to fight against fascism abroad as a prelude to the future struggle against fascism and oppression at home. For Pierre, an Army brat returning from a visit to North Africa, the war will be the fundamental test during which he will find out whether he is the coward he fears being. More than that and worse, it will be the risked exposure to a new level of experience which may demonstrate that his swagger and his cruelty have been attitudes he has deliberately chosen to disguise that cowardice. For Mathieu, the war is the end—a kind of baptism of fire which is coming to ceremonialize his arrival at the age of reason.

For each of these people, the war has become the Other, the mysterious and unavoidable Other whose arrival is as inevitable as its intentions are unknown; it is the Other in an incarnation powerful enough to convince each individual that he is not its sole enemy but rather is part of a larger group it is attacking.[14] The war is a monstrous Other set loose to prowl about the world for so long as it chooses; it is a force which will oblige every individual to live on its terms until the moment when it goes away: ". . . the war broke out: it was there at the other end of that luminous inconsistency, written as though it were evidence on the walls of the vulnerable city. . . . It had always been there, but the people didn't know that yet" (*Sursis*, p. 21).

We see its arrival through many eyes, but recurrently through Mathieu's. The war is there, not simply as a conflict in which one fights, but more significantly as a force stronger than any idea. The war is the project which cannot be dismissed or avoided. As such it is not a projection of Mathieu's mind, as was his love for Ivich, though it *is* a projection of the fundamental hostility between him and his idea of the Other. His love for Ivich was an idea manufactured in his head; it had no external validity because what he sought from her was the chance to get hold of the Other in order to bring her under his control. The war, by contrast and also by comparison, is a real possibility and a genuine hostility introduced by the activities of an Other to whom he had never given much thought.

Faced with this new kind of possibility—that is, with a project he has not chosen but which becomes his all the same—Mathieu undergoes a major transformation. The possibility of war destroys something in him and sets him to the task of rebuilding: "Something which was attached to him only by a strand loosed itself, was compressed, and fell away behind him. It was his life. His life was dead" (*Sursis*, p. 73). His life is dead in the sense that Mathieu is aware that life is not a cluster of attitudes and tendencies

14. We have here an expression of an idea which will be brought to full term in the *CRD*: an assemblage of people, under the influence and stress of an outside force, is becoming conscious of its reality as a group with a common concern.

bound tightly together and eventually brandished as a poor weapon against the unexpected. Life is open-ended; life has to be existed. In an ironic moment he feels that the war will be a great vacation from life since life's terms will henceforth be dictated by the exigencies of the conflict. When the threat of war fades, this excuse is also denied him. He has no way out now except to live his life within whatever terms happen to circumscribe it.

The resolution of the Munich crisis represents a quite literal reprieve for many of the characters in *Le Sursis*. With the threat withdrawn, they can go back to their old ways and pretend there is no conflict to which they must pay prolonged heed. Most of the characters have learned nothing from the situation except possibly that optimism is always justified, fragility is never to be unduly feared. Mathieu's sister-in-law, Odette, can well breathe a sigh of relief; in the end someone had come along and protected her.

But the reversion to old attitudes is no more than folly reinforced. There are a few who know that. Daladier, as he leaves his plane at the Paris airport, looks into the surrounding crowd which is shouting "Vive la paix!" and says to Alexis Léger: "The asses." He knows that the war has only stepped back, like the pitcher, in order to deliver a more powerful ball; it is futile to wish long life to an already dead peace. And Mathieu knows that what the crisis really represented has neither disappeared nor withdrawn for more than a few paces. Because of what he knows, he would not even think of crying "Vive la vie!" Life needs no encouragement to go on being what it is: no thing.

I have written that Mathieu makes progress in the book. Though it is exclusively personal progress, it does bring his consciousness to a level of keener perception. He no longer lives in the protective circle designed to nurture his fear-ridden and desire-laden ego; he has discovered that both fear and desire are connecting ropes thrown from his being towards the world of others. He has accepted the full range of freedom and the possibly paradoxical discovery that by agreeing to live with freedom and its consequences he is narrowing his field of action. Freedom is involvement before it is liberation. This is what he knows at the end of *Le Sursis*. Knowing it, he utters no joyful cries; the acceptance of the inevitable provides no cause for self-congratulation. While his decision does not lead to a lightning conversion—he does not, for example, decide to join Brunet in a well-defined program of social action—it does allow for the possibility of rebirth, the acceptance of a new perspective which may lead him to ethical behavior. He leaves for the army without protest. In the train that carries him towards his duties, he reads a letter from an oldtime friend, Daniel, who had played an important role in *L'Age de raison*. Despite his wealth,

Daniel had refused to give Mathieu money for the abortion; at the end of that novel Daniel had decided to marry Marcelle—whom he had been visiting on the sly—and allow Mathieu's child to be born. Mathieu reads part way through Daniel's letter and then throws it aside.

Mathieu's gesture is significant for a number of reasons, the most important of which is his new cast of mind. The letter makes no sense to him because it attempts to do something he now knows is impossible: to fix life in a definition, to encase it as though it were an object in a museum. Daniel's ideas are ruins left over from Mathieu's ancient history, and they crumble as that history had crumbled. Earlier Mathieu might have understood what Daniel is trying to do in the letter. But his past is gone; only the future remains. What Daniel is trying to do in the letter is to deny the future. Mathieu and Daniel had met on the paths of freedom in their discussion of Marcelle at the end of *L'Age de raison*. They talked; they looked at each other; they took momentary leave of each other. With Daniel's letter they take leave of each other completely and on all levels. The conclusions each has derived from the experience of the Munich crisis are completely different. Mathieu has decided that he cannot avoid the paths of freedom; Daniel has decided to abandon them.

His decision is no swifter than Mathieu's; it has come in small degrees which, when accumulated, form the circle he has always wanted. Daniel is a more extreme manifestation of a phenomenon we have already seen in the Inès of *Huis-clos*. He is the individual who hungers after the absolute, and the absolute he seeks is what Sartre has called "the absolute indifference of identity" (*BN*, p. 174). He wants to be all of a piece with himself, to live as the manifestation of a category—his homosexuality, which for him has all the qualities of being-in-itself; in so doing, he wants to claim as particularly his an honesty which other men haven't the courage to avow. The honesty in which he wishes to drape himself will produce nothing more authentic than trompe l'oeil; but, like all trompe l'oeil, his effort has the appeal of cannily devised deception.[15] Like Inès, whose frankness in refusing to deny the impact of her lesbianism was impressive when compared to the phoniness of her surrounding company, Daniel strikes us by the rigor with which he accepts his condition. He creates the impression of a man who has faced his situation bravely in order to see it clearly; he also strikes us—and at times this is touching and wins admiration—as the man who fights, despairingly and with little chance of success, against the state into which nature has immersed him. He is devoured by homosexual desires

15. Many years later, Sartre described Flaubert's project in remarkably similar terms: "Gustave's aim—to detach himself from himself by perching himself, as a steely witness, above his own life—is that of all those who, for example, believe they have escaped from guilt by recognizing themselves as guilty" ("Flaubert: du poète à l'Artiste," *TM* 22 [1966]: 467).

and by the anguish they produce. And he is fully aware of this; he is aware, too, that his failure to dominate his instincts may be a manifestation of cowardice.

The portrait Sartre presents of Daniel elicits the reader's sympathy especially because, by comparison with Mathieu and Boris, and most particularly by comparison with Marcelle, he seems honest. He hides nothing from himself; he seems to tell himself no lies and therefore he justifies his claim that he is the only protector of reality, the Archangel who soars above others and understands what motivates their actions. His gaze, as it surveys the surrounding world and narrows in on particular situations, provides the perspective and the evaluative equipment which otherwise would be missing. He shows Mathieu up as the shit (*le salaud*) he is; he understands straightaway all of Marcelle's complex motivation (she wants a child more than she wants Mathieu—the child will depend on her as Mathieu does not; motherhood has sweet and discreet modes of revenge). Daniel's gaze and his observations, as he prowls in the homosexual haunts of Paris, or as he roams the streets of the capital abandoned by its citizens to the onrush of the invading Other, show that there is as much pretense in the world of the solid citizen as in the world of the queers. Though himself stricken, he appears to have an edge on those who, stricken with other illnesses, refuse to recognize either the existence or the cause of their malady.

He joins a distinguished French literary tradition which began with Rousseau and found verbose if not virtuous expression in Chateaubriand. He is *l'homme fatal*, the individual who bears in embryo the destiny of every individual who is separated, for one reason or another, from the surrounding collectivity. His distinction—or his point of differentiation—forces him to live apart. The collectivity does not want him; nor does he want it so long as it cannot answer his needs. He lives in solitude, aware that he has not merited the collectivity's condemnation; what has earned it for him is the fatal stigma which he brought into the world at birth. This awareness provides him with a special outlook; because of it he can see—and here he is close to Roquentin—that the others are also stricken. Still, their condition is noticeably graver than his because they lie to themselves, pretend they are in good health, and refuse to look any more closely within themselves for fear of what they may detect. In the face of their refusal, Daniel takes on the responsibility of doing what they decline to do. He will be the witness of their refusal, the examining magistrate who will pierce through their masks and reveal what is behind them—the devices employed by the young homosexuals to hide their tendencies; the maneuvers Marcelle uses to win his sympathy and justify her dissatisfaction; the bluffing behind Boris's theft.

He sums up his attitude economically and pertinently when he announces to Mathieu—who has encouraged him to accept his homosexuality—that he will accept being a pederast when Mathieu accepts being a shit. He doesn't keep the wager or at least he doesn't pay when he has lost. When he sends his letter to Mathieu he does not know of the changes which have taken place in him. That knowledge, if he possessed it, would change nothing because Daniel does not believe in change. He is beyond change, firmly ensconced in the world of magic. If the others whom he judges wear shabby, thin masks, Daniel wears one that is as subtle as it is false. He is a charlatan whose most stunning tricks are performed in the theatre of his mind. [16]

His honesty is pretense which uses artifice to produce an artefact. Instead of lying to himself, he tries to be a lie and thereby seeks to subtract himself from the dynamism, the long involvement with involvement, which is existence. Sartre will not accept this as a sensible solution. Daniel himself knows that it is not a solution, not even a response; it is only an escape. Early in the novel he had said: "I am not . . . one is never anything" (AR, p. 94). Despite this awareness, he can later write to Mathieu of the great discovery he has made and the important news he has to announce as the consequence of his discovery:

> At last I know that I am. I have transformed, for my personal
> use and your greater indignation, that idiotic and criminal expres-
> sion of your prophet: "I think therefore I am"—which has made
> me suffer so much. And I say: I am seen therefore I am. I no
> longer have to bear with the responsibility of my pasty dissolu-
> tion: I am just as I am seen by the one who sees me and makes
> me be; I turn my nocturnal and eternal head towards the night,
> I raise myself up as a challenge, I say to God: Here I am. Here
> I am as you see me, as I am. What can I do? You know me and
> I don't know myself. What else is there for me to do except put
> up with myself? And you, whose look escapes me eternally, bear
> with me. Mathieu, what joy, what torment! At last I am changed

16. In the bad faith chapter of BN (pp. 47–70), Sartre writes: "The basic concept which is thus engendered utilizes a double property of the human being, who is at once a *facticity* and a *transcendence*. . . . Bad faith seeks to affirm their identity while preserving their difference. It must affirm facticity as *being* transcendence and transcendence as *being* facticity, in such a way that the instant when a person apprehends the one, he can find himself abruptly faced with the other" (p. 56). Further light is cast on this kind of attitude, which justifies fixity by seeing it as dynamism, in remarks on Flaubert: ". . . even when he is talking of himself, Gustave remains insincere: he does away with one of the temporal dimensions and pretends that he has only a past when the future is the genuine source of his torment. From that stems the strange undertaking of restoring his real life from the point of view of a fictional other (the old man he has not yet become) and, as a result, giving his memories . . . a fictional character. Everything happens as though the young novelist could only present reality by stripping himself of reality in order to make it at least *formally imaginary*" ("Flaubert: du poète à l'Artiste," TM 22 [1966]: 426).

> into myself. I am hated; I am scorned; yet someone bears with
> me, a presence props me up to being forever. I am finite and
> infinitely guilty. But I am, Mathieu, I am. Before God and all
> men, I am. *Ecce homo* (*Sursis*, pp. 331–32).

Translated into Sartrean terms, Pontius Pilate's Latin phrase means: behold nothingness in the futile task of trying to be something in the aftermath of its abandonment by God. What Daniel seeks is an essence which will excuse him from the task of existing. He wants fixity, a place, a role, the assurance that what he is, is guaranteed by another who is out of this world and therefore out of the way. God is conveniently there to provide Daniel with the assurance he craves. God is the Other who can be manipulated, who has all the suppleness and pliability we choose to attribute to him. In avowing that he has become abject in the eyes of God and has decided to live in abjection, Daniel is nihilating the more proximate Other as a threatening being and replacing him with a more convenient *deus absconditus*.

Similarly, Daniel's apparent honesty in asserting his homosexuality is a gesture born of his fear of the Other; it is the tactic by which he seeks to escape from shame. It is more than that, too. If his avowal that he bears his homosexuality as a cripple bears his infirmity is a confession made in bad faith, whatever satisfaction the Other receives from knowing that Daniel is a homosexual—and therefore identifiable as a fixed, predictable quantity—is derived from bad faith, too, even though it may mask itself as sincerity.[17] Daniel is ashamed of his homosexuality, not because of moral scruples, but because his tastes lead him inexorably to the Other who by satisfying his needs may in return be empowered to judge him. In the earlier part of the novel he cannot accept himself because he identifies such acceptance with capitulation to the Other whom he needs. To console himself he has recourse to all kinds of ruses which condition if they do not justify his periodic lapses: he gets drunk; he refuses to give in readily to his desires and nurses them with sick indulgence; he chooses his bed companions from among the poor and the dull; he exhausts himself winning a tussle with a young hustler in order to show that he has the upper hand; in marrying Marcel he joins the company of the holy martyrs by sacrificing

---

17. In the "Patterns of Bad Faith" subsection of his chapter on that question, Sartre discusses the homosexual as an almost comic example of the man who is in bad faith (pp. 63–67) and also as one who cannot escape from a dilemma. If he refuses to admit to his homosexuality, he is denying a quality he possesses; if he admits to it as though it were a state which he must confess to sincerely, then he risks slipping into just another form of bad faith; this, then, raises the question of the good faith of the man who, invoking the value of sincerity, urges the homosexual to admit to his homosexuality. The homosexual will be reluctant to do this because he senses the risk of being reified; to the extent that this is the intention of the man who urges sincerity on the homosexual he, too, is acting in bad faith.

his heterosexual virginity. And, once he has fallen, he justifies himself by saying that he has paid dearly for his penchants.

If he confesses his homosexuality to Mathieu, that is because he feels particularly ashamed before him. But even in this effort he aims at hoisting himself far above the Other in the hierarchy of honesty in order subsequently to be able to look down on the Other. His challenge to Mathieu—I'll accept being a homosexual when you accept being a shit—is indicative of this aim. The cruelest irony is that God's gaze is not enough for him, as we learn from his eager anticipation of the Germans' arrival. Simply because he has stayed on in the capital, Daniel feels superior to those who have fled. The stout defenders of humanism, honor, and heterosexuality have taken to their heels towards provincial havens, abandoning their home city, leaving behind the monuments erected to a glory which once again is being tarnished: the taxis of the Marne have become the vehicles of exodus. Daniel, once the Archangel, now becomes the Angel of Death; he strolls through the city as though it were both his possession and the late-found symbol of his life, for he has been destroying *their* values for years, he has been the witness of their defects and defeats. He has won the right to be the welcoming committee for the other angels of death who are arriving to install evil in the city and eventually in the world. He sees himself as the Guilty One who rules over what will soon become openly the capital of guilt. Truth, of a sort, is finally going to exhibit its naked power. God has left his heaven and somewhere on his earthward journey has engaged the demiurge and has been destroyed.

> He was alone on this long avenue, the only Frenchman, the only civilian, and the whole enemy army was looking at him. He was no longer afraid: he let himself go confidently to those thousands of eyes; he thought: "Our conquerors," and he was filled with delight. He returned their look stoutly, he drank in the blond hair, the bronzed faces whose eyes were like glacial lakes, the narrow builds, the incredibly long and muscular thighs. He murmured: "They *are* good-looking!" He no longer walked the earth: they had raised him into their arms, were hugging him to their chests and flat bellies. Something was toppled in heaven: the old law. The society of judges collapsed, the sentence was erased; those frightful little soldiers in khaki, the champions of human rights and of the solid citizen, were routed. "*This* is freedom," he thought and his eyes were moist. He was the sole survivor of the disaster. The only *man* who stood before these angels of hatred and rage, these angels of death whose looks brought back his childhood. "These are the new judges," he thought; "this is the new law!" Above them, the marvels of the

> soft heaven, the innocence of the small clouds seemed derisory;
> this was the victory of scorn, of violence, of bad faith; it was
> the victory of the Earth (*Mort*, pp. 83–84).[18]

As Lucien's class runs off, Daniel—who is what Lucien might have been
if he had believed himself a homosexual—repeats Lucien's basic decision.
He has had to wait longer, of course, since the approving class he sought
was not available. Finally he has encountered it, and he greets it with tears
in his eyes.

Bolstered by these observations, Daniel feels that everything is permitted
to him. In the past, he had imposed limitations on himself, had kept evil
at a short distance; now that evil is installed as the law of the earth, he is
exalted. He no longer has to undergo the experience of being an object
in the Other's field of vision; he has become one with the Other, sharing
the same field of vision and the same orientation. There is no more guilt,
once guilt has become the way of life. Justified, invested with the authority
of the new governing force, he looks upon the young Philippe—a soldier
who has deserted his post—as his possession, not simply because he has
kept the young man from suicide, but also because his superior consciousness authorizes him to possess the youngster. Since everything is allowed
to him, and since the ambience is favorable, he is shrewd and patient about
the seduction. There is no reason to hurry, there is no need to think in
terms of privation; this is the time of prolongation, of the slow spinning
out of anticipation so that the culminating pleasure will be greater. The
world is his because he and the invaders share the knowledge that they
are a superior race. Daniel no longer needs to abstain from desire, he
no longer needs to reject his particular projects; now, for the first time in
his life, he can look to the future with pleasure. In that future he will cooperate with the forces of evil; in that future he will have a stable love affair
with Philippe. Once again he is lying to himself and once again he knows
it.

> [*Finie la Terreur!*] He sat on the bed and began to undress:
> "This will be a serious affair," he decided. He was sleepy, he
> was calm; he got up to get his things, he noticed that he was
> calm, he thought: "It's funny that I'm not troubled." Just at that
> moment there was something behind his back, he turned, saw
> no one and the anguish broke him in two. "Again! Once again!"
> Everything was beginning over again, he knew everything, he
> could foresee everything, he could tick off minute by minute

18. Of Genet, Sartre writes: "I can testify that during the occupation he had no particular liking for the Germans. No doubt he admired, on principle, Nazi malevolence.
But then what? They were victors, the triumphant Evil was likely to become institu-
tional; it would be a new order, a new Good. And this order, like the other, would
condemn theft and common-law crime" (*SG*, p. 170).

the years of unhappiness which were going to follow, the long, long commonplace years, full of ennui and without hope and then the filthy and sorrowful end: it was all there. He looked at the shut door, he was puffing, he thought: "This time, it will kill me," and in his mouth there was the bitter taste of future sufferings (*Mort*, p. 146).

Whatever terror is over is over only for the time of a few thoughts. Immediately it comes back, probably because once terror stops there is a good chance that slavery may be beginning. If terror is both reaction to an intolerable situation and the necessity of doing something in order to change that situation, terror can lead to two possibilities. It can inspire carefully tailored programs designed to produce needed and desired changes; once the changes have been effected, there is no longer need for terrorist methods. Or it can lead to the acceptance of dishonest situations— for example, Daniel's desire for immobility—where, precisely because it cannot work, it cannot be abandoned. In such cases, its devotees becomes its eventual victims. The deepest source of Daniel's terror has nothing to do specifically with the Germans or even with his homosexuality; it has to do with the difficulty, the impossibility of becoming what he wants to be.

Though collaboration with the Germans will clearly call for acts on his part, the idea behind that collaboration envisages the goal which has attracted him all along. He is still seeking fixity, stability, the calm unconsciousness of the things; he hopes that the victorious Other with whom he will associate will invest him with these immobile qualities. Simultaneously, he hopes to establish a permanent relationship with Philippe. But such a relationship, since it is built on desire, is potentially fragile. The man of desire is the man who needs the Other in order to have his desire satisfied. Once the desire has been satisfied the future becomes again uncertain. Nothing, neither bad faith, nor the reign of evil, nor the time of scorn can eliminate that insecurity. As Daniel moves more and more deeply into inauthenticity the dangers multiply. Despite all his efforts, despite all the cautionary tales and apparent truths he tells himself, the Other has not disappeared from any of the several levels on which life is lived. In his personal existence, Daniel risks losing Philippe to someone else, or discovering that he no longer wants Philippe, or desiring some Other he cannot have. On the plane of social reality he risks being the victor for a bitterly short time. For outside Paris, outside France, the Allies are grouping to fight the Other with whom Daniel has associated himself. The terror is not over; it has been pushed deeper down inside him; it has been removed to an island on the other side of the Channel. When it returns to deal with him as an Other, Daniel, according to Sartre's plan for his unfinished novel, will find only one solution: suicide.

Suicide, rather than being a solution, is a dissolution (see below, pp. 160–62). In Daniel's case it is also a comment on how little progress he has made since, in the first volume of the novel, he had already contemplated suicide, and, when his courage failed, the smaller-scaled destruction of castration. It has all been futile: the suicide comes at the end of a ruined life; the castration, contemplated earlier, would have been senseless, since it would only have removed equipment and not the mental fantasies that set the equipment in motion. Daniel is a coward, by which Sartre means that he is the man of ruinous compromises who, in *L'Age de raison*, admitted that he was killing himself in little ways in order to avoid decisive action: his drinking, his contemplated murder of his cats, all the minor restraints on his conduct were metaphorical actions for the final action which comes years later when there are no other ways available. But, even while they are metaphors for suicide, they are also examples of decisions constantly made, projects repeatedly undertaken to avoid the major project: an authentic life. That project, as we have seen, has been replaced by a hopeless one: the desire to annihilate the Other. There is something of willed schizophrenia in this since, in his fight against the Other, Daniel is objectively two people: the man who acts in order not to act, the man who thinks that the possibility of not acting is realizable. Yet, as the above quotation shows, he knows both are false—and that knowledge "breaks him in two."

By contrast, Mathieu, who had experienced the same schizophrenic desires, has taken an altogether different path. At the end of *Le Sursis*, and especially at the moment when he crumples Daniel's letter, he is passing through a crisis of consciousness. He has been forced to accept his maturity, but he has accepted it as a recognition of all the difficulties which are posed by a life freely lived. His life is not made, it has not been organized on the basis of unshakable principles or even a steady orientation. Everything remains to be done, everything will always remain to be done. In terms of the enterprise which he nourished in *L'Age de raison*, this realization is a defeat, the replacement of the idea of freedom he wanted to have—a state in which he would protect himself from all the bother and the encumbrances others would try to impose on him—by the idea of freedom as a very febrile, undetermined, open-ended condition. I have already said that the major catalyst for Mathieu is the war; what I should also note is the extent to which the war serves as a parallel force to freedom. The war, too, is indeterminate, uncertain, unpredictable; the war will keep creating challenges to which one must respond in one way or another. And the way in which individuals meet their challenges will necessarily affect their fundamental attitudes.

Since Daniel saw French society as a hostile force which condemned him, he could easily invoke, as further support for his choice, a nonfact: the universal homosexuality of the Germans. He could look upon the war and the Occupation as an epiphany: the installation in his midst of the evil with which he would live and in which he could operate. Mathieu did not have the same kind of total hostility to his environment. While it is true that he is alienated from bourgeois ideas, his way of life—even of mental life—has been bourgeois: there was always tomorrow. Precisely because he was the abstainer, the man of abstract thought Brunet had accused him of being, his egotism was no different from that of his class, and his desire to protect it was only a slightly distorted reflection of the class's desire. He loved justice but didn't get involved in areas where it was under assault; he never voted; he had thought of enlisting in the Spanish Republican cause, but had done nothing; he supports the aspirations of the working class but leaves the task of abetting those aspirations to others. The war changes this by cutting down his range of choice; he must go, he must participate, he must apply his abstractions to real situations. At the moment when the range of his free movement is most severely reduced, he has his fullest experience of freedom.

As the final rout approaches, he seems to have nothing but free choices. The principal one is this: how should he organize the last moment of his resistance? He and his fellow soldiers know instinctively that resistance will be futile; they will be overwhelmed simply because they belong to a defeated and abandoned army. But beyond inevitability is the question of the *value* of carrying on a fight which will end in defeat. For Mathieu the question is even more complicated. When we pick up the strands of his life in *La Mort dans l'âme* he is not yet fighting. Others are continuing the struggle in the north and are being beaten back; that they should prolong the prelude to sure defeat seems, on the face of the evidence, silly. But Mathieu does not feel that he is authorized to have any opinion about the value of their action. Though they are all members of the same army, they are not all in the same situation; the ties of solidarity among them have been destroyed. They still fight; he is immobilized. Even in war, his situation is a résumé of his life: the struggle is for others to carry on. No one has asked his opinion; no one has ever asked his opinion. His immobility is only momentary, however, since the enemy is drawing near and some sort of encounter is bound to take place. While no *one* may have asked his opinion,

> *Everything* asks for our opinion. *Everything.* A great question
> encircles us: what a farce. We are asked the question as though
> we were still men. But we're not. We're not. We're not. What
> a farce: that shadow of a question asked by a shadow of a war
> of men who are men in appearance only (*Mort*, p. 51).

Still, the war, however shadowy and insubstantial, is approaching, a moment will come presently when he will have to make a decision about his reaction and the nature of his participation. The great temptation is to let go—and he has a lifelong habit of letting go—with the sure knowledge that letting go or fighting back will not in any way change the outcome of onrushing events. He and the other soldiers have no sense of patriotism left. Why should they when their officers have abandoned them? They have no sense of being tragic; the situation is too banal for lofty thoughts or great emotions. They have no sense of participating in history; masses play no role in history. They are no more than supporting footnotes to the great text of the world which tells them and us: there is no order over which you have any real or lasting control.

Mathieu's mind at this point is a confusion of vision and blindness. He seems to think that he is the only one preoccupied with the idea of futility; the reactions of his fellow soldiers are only instinctive responses to an enemy. They want to fight the Germans because the Germans are the enemy and one fights one's enemies. What he learns is that the motives behind their desire to fight run much deeper and therefore much closer to his. What they are fighting on a large, almost impersonal scale is the battle that, as individuals, they have fought all their lives: they are struggling against their feeling of shame before the Other who is this enemy, the Other who is going to defeat them and imprison them. While they do not have a philosophical view of their situation, they are conscious of themselves; their final struggle will not be a banal fight for a country which, having cheated them and then abandoned them, does not merit their blood. If they offer final resistance, they will do so in the name of their individual freedom. In so doing they will discover that every man is not necessarily or eternally a hostile force before whom one must know shame. Since they are all plunged into shame, and since they all breathe in the odor of scandal which will come to encircle them and enclose them in a situation not of their own choosing, they can make a common cause of their shame. They learn—and, most especially, Mathieu learns—that even in the midst of desperation, fear, and uncertainty their liberty provides a bond between them because it makes it possible for them to act or react in concert.[19]

Mathieu's accession to this knowledge is not quite so instinctive, for he is obsessed with the overriding absurdity he detects in the situation; he feels isolated from these others who want to fight. He goes through a moment when he feels that he is radically the Other because he is reluctant

19. Colette Audry provides a helpful comment on this situation: "They have just undergone the shame of defeat. They recognize vaguely that they are responsible for it even though they have been *subjected* to it in spite of themselves. In order to free themselves from it, they take flight from an imposed shame, they affirm their scorn of themselves, they *choose* to be ignoble. They are proclaiming their freedom of being" (*Connaissance de Sartre*, p. 74).

to share their situation, not of Frenchmen on the point of defeat, but of human beings. Realizing this, Mathieu undergoes a slow transformation. Despite his disgust with the beverage the soldiers offer him, he drinks it in order to associate himself with them. Earlier he had looked upon existence as the necessity of having "to drink himself without being thirsty"; now he looks upon it as an act performed, in the midst of disgust, in order to be united with the others who are performing the same act. From this point on, in the midst of precipitous actions, he is living as a free man.

The shell of his old defences falls. The ego goes first; it had only served to make him more thoroughly the victim of others who did not respect its goals. His earlier idea of liberty as the maintenance of constancy and a certain level of pleasure disappears. There are no solid states, there is only movement whose arc is generally traced across unpleasant experiences. He learns of the need for acts rather than gestures: ". . . gestures, those little destructions . . . where do they get you? I took them for freedom" (*Mort,* p. 137). Even as he pronounces this judgment on his former way of life, he thinks of the imitative gesture he had made in stabbing himself; that gesture, as we have seen, was futile because it had no orientation towards the future. His progress is not easy because each time a thought comes to confirm the idea of freedom he is elaborating, another comes to stress once again the futility of being free generally, and, under the present circumstances, even specifically. Though there may be no neutrality in decisions made, there is a process of neutralization in decision-making.

A small item, a portent of great forces, tips the balance. Mathieu learns that one of his fellow soldiers is Jewish. For this soldier a German victory will mean more than defeat; it may mean annihilation. The issue is greater than who wins or loses: the issue is what motivates the victor. For Mathieu, Germany is beyond being inspired by territorial acquisitiveness. It is inspired by its desire to impose a way of life which has its roots in evil and which stretches up and out in order to spread the shadow of universal death. Once Mathieu begins to act, the scales tip decisively on the side of committing his freedom in a particular direction. He has seen Germany's intention as that of plunging the world in mourning; as he looks down on the corpse of the enemy soldier he has killed, he thinks:

> "He felt it [the bullet] go through him, Jesus Christ he did! He understood. That guy understood." *His* dead man, *his* work, the trace of *his* passage on the earth. The desire to kill still others came to him: it was diverting and easy; he wanted to plunge Germany into mourning (*Mort,* p. 190).

The conditions of this epiphany are frightening; for, in order to discover himself and approve of what he is doing, Mathieu has first to kill the Other who has come to kill him. From the point of view of finding some tolerable way in which to live with a single other, or with many others, nothing seems to have been gained. There is always still another who is the enemy. Mathieu acts only because that Other is there, dispensing fear and producing fear's reaction: conflict. But that is only a partial view of the situation. The terror produced by the possibility (or necessity) of living-for-others has been diluted by several newly apprehended factors: Mathieu is fighting with *other* men against this particular Other; he is fighting in the name of certain principles; the awareness of a death in life, which seeks to produce the same immobility as real death, has forced him to accept his freedom. Such knowledge is a sparse, joyless possession; but it is something, and what it is is better than what has been.

> He was firing on man, on Virtue, on the World: *Freedom is Terror*; the fire was burning in the town hall, was burning in his head: the bullets whistled, free as the air, the world will blow up and me with it, he fired, he looked at his watch: fourteen minutes thirty seconds; he had nothing else to ask for except a half-minute delay, just the time to fire on the handsome officer, on all the Beauty of the Earth, on the street, on the flowers, on the gardens, on everything he had loved. Beauty took an obscene dip and Mathieu fired again. He fired: he was pure, he was all-powerful, he was free (*Mort*, p. 197).

The equation, freedom is terror, comments, of course, on Daniel's earlier assertion that the terror was over. It comments in two ways since Daniel's project to end his freedom was a project enunciated in order to end the terror; but it also indicated that, since freedom is inevitable, the possibility of terror remains no matter what arms or masks one puts on. The terror comes from the *fact* of freedom, from the obligation of having to create oneself through one's acts, and from the necessity of living with the consequences of those acts. Terror comes from the individual's solitude in the midst of other men—a solitude which horrifies him but which also pushes him to the deeper horror which is his discovery of the Other. Terror forces him to decide what he must do with that Other who wants something from him. There are times when he will learn how to cooperate with the Other; there are times when that cooperation will produce another moment of terror—when the damned of the earth, in order to escape from their condemnation, must turn against the forces of oppression and use their methods in order to fight against them. Terror engenders terror. A question—and Sartre will be a long time answering it—remains. Is there no end to it?

Daniel had thought to see something pure in his choice; Mathieu has found that there is no purity which does not attach itself necessarily to bad faith. Acts muddy you because they are no more clearly delimited, no more purposeful than the actor. By a companion process the actor cannot hope for tidiness when he is inescapably involved in untidy situations; there is an unending reciprocity between individual and situation which obscures quite as much as it illumines. Because of this there is an equally lasting temptation to abandon the situation in order not to be compromised by it, or to blame the situation for the compromise, or to exploit a fresh situation in order to escape from another whose staleness has become claustrophobic. Thus Schneider, whom we meet in the final, incomplete volume, has left the Communist party because of the Russo-German pact. Thus Boris plans to fly off to England to join the Free French Forces and, in the process, break off with the mistress he has been trying to abandon throughout the novel. Thus Gomez (who has been faithful to his principles if not to his wife), exiled in New York and depressed because of the defeat of the Republican cause in Spain, is tempted to smugness because the French, who had not helped that cause, have now fallen under the heel of Fascism; he also decides that his career as a painter is over—it cannot continue once he has fired on men.

What all of this shows is that man's situation, as I have already stressed, does not liberate him, it merely provides him with the context in which he must act freely. Each one of these people is still free, despite the personal dilemmas which eat away at their sense of perspective, despite the depression that comes with defeat. In an even narrower context—the context in which the book ends—the French prisoners in the German camp remain free. There, surrounded by barbed wire, freedom may very well seem to have come to an end. The Other has triumphed, the future is undetermined and undeterminable; the prisoners have won the right to consider themselves immobilized and extracted from all possibility of action.

The prison camp is no more than an intense example of a more general situation. For most men, if they emerge from Plato's cave into the light, walk almost straightaway into some other prison—that of the ego, the family, the class—which they either accept freely or suffer to be imposed upon them. Brunet responds to the prison's challenge with the sense of discipline and purpose he has learned in the Communist party; he begins to organize and proselytize, not because he thinks that his activities will change much now, but because he is thinking ahead to the future. He has few illusions and a cautious dream. Sartre has no illusions, and whatever dream may have semed to pass into reality with Mathieu's triumph over himself in *La Mort dans l'âme* is quickly shattered with the return of quotidian human relations.

War may unite the citizens of one country in joint action which seeks to respond to a particular threat. But war, as the colossal manifestation of basic hostility between men, and as a form of violence which men choose as an inst ument of policy, does nothing to eliminate the forces which cause it. War solves nothing; and the example of joint action it offers manifests no beauty. That action still involves the presence of a hostile Other; whatever unity war brings to disparate groups within a nation comes only from a temporary dislocation of the Other. Men who have been uncooperative and hostile may, under the presence of an external threat, put aside the hostility; it comes back again once the common external menace has disappeared or, in the context of the prison camp, triumphs. The broad implications are clear: if war brings out the best in men—their courage, their willingness to defend an ideal, their generosity in laying down their lives for a cause—it brings out those qualities at a time when the worst in life is triumphing. It also brings confusion to those who in peacetime were trying to work towards general human betterment. The French Communists cannot avoid a feeling that Russia has betrayed them by signing a pact with the Nazis; power struggles among those who are the leaders of reform are not unknown. Commitment, even to a recognized ideal, does not eliminate fundamental problems because commitment does not dispel either confusion or complexity.

War suggests that Anny's perfect moments could indeed be brought about and useful lessons derived from them. Sartre risked suggesting that war could be the exemplar whose ravages and ruins could be brandished over the heads of a testy humanity as a reminder of where its testiness and petty hostilities would bring it. But in war, as in peace, there is no absolute purity either in motives or in action. Fidelity to high motives may bring an individual like Schneider inner peace and a sense of consistency in his beliefs. But since this fidelity has driven him to resign from the Communist party in protest over the Russo-German pact, it has driven him out of history. He no longer has any agency through which to help change the world, and that world, despite his dissent from one method and his hope for a better, keeps changing under the influence of those who have not entertained his scruples. Loyalty to higher or more promising causes may also involve disloyalty to particular emotions and situations; it thus undermines the very base of its own structure. This is the dilemma Brunet faces. Party discipline, which he respects even to the point of ceding his command position to a higher party functionary who arrives in the camp after the organization has been set up, requires that he condemn Schneider because Schneider believes that his freedom to criticize supersedes his obligation to be loyal. Yet Schneider's position entails greater fidelity to the cause of the workers than does the position of the Russian Communist party.

Brunet's dilemma is Sartre's; it is one which finds its most complex expression in the *Critique de la raison dialectique* where, after the disillusion of discovering concentration camps in Russia, of watching the crushing of the Hungarian Revolution, of being perplexed by Khrushchev's condemnation of Stalin, Sartre seeks to give a coherent, purposeful statement of the individual's conflict with the social forces which try to save him. In "Drôle d'amitié" he attempts a much more limited response by suggesting that a friendship which goes beyond blind defence of dogmatic positions, which is nourished with reciprocal respect, can make fruitful collaboration possible. The last and unwritten volume of *Les Chemins de la liberté* was to show how a group of individuals, of different shades of belief and commitment, could cooperate in meeting a common menace.

In *La Force des choses*, Simone de Beauvoir summarizes what the last volume would have been about (pp. 213–14). Brunet makes a second escape attempt and is successful (in "Drôle d'amitié" he had made a joint attempt with Schneider in which Schneider was killed and he was recaptured); he returns to Paris and is shocked to find that the party has once again done a somersault after Russia joined the Allies; his concern over the individual's freedom within the discipline of the party grows. By contrast, Mathieu, called back to Paris by Daniel to become editor of a collaborationist newspaper, refuses the post; instead he goes underground and, in collective, disciplined involvement, finds a useful employment for his freedom; he also finds a durable love with his brother's wife, Odette; finally, he dies, after courageously resisting torture and thereby showing, in Mme de Beauvoir's words, "not that he was heroic by nature, but that he has made himself a hero." Daniel's lover, Philippe, joins the Resistance in order to prove that he is not a coward but also as an act of revenge on Daniel; he is killed and his death leads Daniel to commit suicide by setting a bomb at a meeting of important German authorities. Boris is parachuted into France to become part of the maquis. Mme de Beauvoir notes: "With almost everyone dead, no one remained to raise the questions posed by the postwar period."

That is the most succinct explanation of why the novel remains unfinished. It was not completed because history had gone its own way and had seemingly undone, even before they had had a chance to be applied, whatever solutions the final volume might have outlined. You answer one riddle and find, like Oedipus, that your reward is the slow, steady acquisition of further disempowering knowledge. You construct a paradigm of how men should behave and find, like Sartre, that once the war is over, the old hostilities are back, the former hierarchy of privileges and privations is reimposed. Individuals concern themselves once more with imagining vain things, and the nations prepare yet again to wage furious annihilating war together. It is not only Lucien who moves in circles. The world, too, seems to move in circles and returns always to where it started: conflict.

RELATED THEMES AND WORKS

The note to chapter 1 provides bibliographical information on Sartre's most significant essays and interviews on the subject of language. More specific comments on the novel as a form can be found in *Litt.* and in his introduction to Nathalie Sarraute's *Portrait d'un Inconnu* (*Sit. IV*, pp. 9–16). As the Chapsal interview (*Les Ecrivains en personne*) indicates, his attitude towards the new novel has changed; later interviews confirm this. Opposition to Surrealism has also been a constant in his thought, beginning with a long note to *Litt.* ("Situation de l'écrivain en 1947," n. 6, pp. 317–26) where in effect he accused the Surrealists of a determined inconsistency which is not far distant from bad faith. This estimate received a curious variation in "Orphée Noir" (*Sit. III*, pp. 229–86), his introduction to an anthology of African verse, where he finds that the Negro poets of Africa have brought a genuine and valuable surrealist vision to poetry. Michel Beaujour presents a dissenting appraisal of these views in his "Sartre and Surrealism" (*YFS* 30 [1963]: 86–95).

Readers interested in establishing parallels between Sartre's personal experience and the incidents and characters of *Les Chemins de la liberté* are referred to Mme de Beauvoir's memoirs, especially to *FA*. For further variations, readers may wish to read her *L'Invitée*, whose inspiration is partially drawn from the same experiences which furnished the raw material of *Les Chemins*. In that novel, Mme de Beauvoir is primarily concerned with the problem of the Other which, at the end of her book, remains very much a problem since the solution found by the female protagonist is murder. One of the chief characters in *Les Chemins* is inspired, not by Sartre's personal experience but by his mental experience; the character of Philippe seems to be clearly modeled on Baudelaire and thus is an interesting example of one of the possible processes by which Sartre goes about establishing perspectives on certain historical personages who interest him. The general lines of the characterization are very much derived from the details of Baudelaire's life; however, the portrait is on the whole more sympathetic than the portrait of the poet traced by Sartre in his *Baudelaire*. There is also an interesting adjustment to be seen in the redemption Sartre planned for Philippe in the final, uncompleted volume.

Readers will find valuable comments on Sartre's experience of the Occupation and his immediate postwar hopes in the first four essays printed in *Sit. III*: "La République du silence" (pp. 11–14), "Paris sous l'occupation" (pp. 15–42), "Qu'est-ce qu'un collaborateur?" (pp. 43–61), "La Fin de la guerre" (pp. 63–71).

Terror is a concept that recurs in Sartre's writing. In his earlier work it is said to be inspired by Jean Paulhan's discussion of literary terror in his *Les Fleurs de Tarbes* (Paris, 1941). Readers might with some justice believe that Sartre has done a rather major job of emending Paulhan's use of the concept, since Paulhan is primarily concerned—if I read correctly his mandarin style—with terror exercised by critics who, refusing to read carefully and insisting on novelty rather than meaning, impose a burden on writers that they do not deserve; the burden is that of having irresponsible critics. Sartre allows some room for this interpretation in *Litt.*, but in *Les Chemins*, as in his later writings, the concept seems to be derived from the Marxist (and Hegelian) notion of terror as the acceptance of the burden of seeking change through violence because there is no other way available.

In more recent years Sartre seems to have become concerned with his too casual invocation of violence as the only solution to social problems; this orientation has been visible since, roughly, 1965, in the pages of *TM* where it is now admitted that "pure" programs may not be capable of achievement and that against purity one is sometimes obliged to choose what is politically feasible. This seems to be *TM*'s politic way of handling the very hot potato of China. Mao's intransigence and the Red Guard's roving revolution should have had much appeal to the staff of *TM* and certainly could be justified by much that has appeared in that journal and in Sartre's theoretical writings. But neither Mao nor the Red Guard seems to hold much promise for the global revolutionary movement, and one senses that *TM* is a little embarrassed at the risks China has been taking in the name of ideological firmness—risks that may erase many gains made by China since 1949. I shall discuss the issue of terror in later chapters when writing about works where the concept is even more present than in *Les Chemins*.

Sartre tried diligently to convince me

that every life had a term properly its own,

that it is no more absurd to die at nineteen than at eighty-four;

I didn't believe him.

— Simone de Beauvoir

6 *Waiting for Death*

War may be the abrasive which rubs away the various outer coatings of life in order to reveal deeper realities and to produce a sharper sense of what existence should be about; war may also create modes of cooperation which usually do not exist in peacetime. If these are the profits of war, they do not compensate for its principal deficit: the possibility of imminent death. Warfare in the twentieth century is impartial to an unparalleled degree in this respect; whatever guidelines politicians may draw up and whatever elastic norms theologians may recommend, modern warfare allows for the survival of the innocent only until such time as they get in the way of massive retaliation, slow escalation, or other forms of generalized savagery. War today threatens more than the professional soldier; indeed one of its crueller ironies is that it may endanger the professional on the front lines less than those who live in cities. The little reality which T. S. Eliot claimed human beings can stand is too determinedly present in wartime; the end is always immediately possible. It is not surprising then that, when the war is over, the old ways come back; despite their defects, they seem, by comparison with war, good ways. War does not lead to a deeper view of the realities of conflict in life and therefore to better social awareness; it is simply an interruption. The paths of freedom, discovered in battle, may lead, once the war is over, straight back to where the warriors started.

Nations, Giraudoux wrote in *La Guerre de Troie n'aura pas lieu*, die like men, as a result of imperceptible impolitenesses. But both men and nations refuse to accept the fact of their death with any enthusiasm. That refusal, better than anything else, may explain the origin of bad manners among men and among nations. I have already touched briefly in a preceding chapter on the fixation with death that began to appear in French literature once skepticism about a life after death set in. That uncertainty produces disturbing consequences, for if there is no life after death, then death seems to become the central and awful fact of human existence.

Death, even more than man's discovery of his freedom to shape his life according to his desires, becomes the major guiding force of every life; but since the principle is so unsettling by its very nature, it is also life's greatest absurdity. We live in order to die, and the world is indeed Sir Thomas Browne's hospital in which everyone is sick with mortality. If death is the central fact of life, and if there is nothing beyond death, fundamental questions about how life should be lived crop up. It is not simply a question of determining *how* one should live; it is more disturbingly a question of deciding *why* one individual should make any effort to reduce the amount of pleasure he can obtain during his days on this planet. Death is the situation beyond which there is no other; as such it can become the situation whose shadow qualifies, if it does not darken, the whole of life. It also becomes one of the most influential elements in ethical thinking and choice.

To live in order one day to live no more, to exist a life knowing that one day that life can no longer be existed, is objectively absurd. Subjectively, it is a cause of potentially permanent anguish which can produce a quantity of different individual reactions. But since a man's life is all that he possesses which is really himself, its loss is the loss of whatever weight he has pulled and whatever space he has occupied in the world. As a result, one of the simplest and most brutal observations he can make is that he does not want to lose one moment of pleasure during his life in order to serve some principle which is going to subjugate him to others or expose him to pain. Such a response is, perhaps, simpleminded. It is also instinctive. A more complex reaction would lead men to consider the relationship between life and death, between that which allows for experience and that which puts an end to all experience. And the most common reaction is that life is perhaps a bit too busy, time a bit too short, for overindulgence in meditations about its most ordinary fact.

For a number of existentialists, the fact of death, however commonplace, is one of the main obstacles men must clear before they can live freely; if that fact reinforces the notion that existence is absurd, it may infect all other actions. Men have not chosen to be free, but since they are free, they might just as well benefit from that freedom; yet no matter what they do, the use of that freedom will not forestall death. Life begins in absurdity— man is born free without having been allowed a choice as to whether he wished to be born at all. Life ends absurdly—man knows only that he must die and possesses none of the details of his end. Death may be man's deliverance from the freedom which has haunted his days, but until the moment when those days come to an end he must live with his unasked-for freedom.

The great value of Christianity, and of some forms of paganism, was to provide sense for a life which otherwise would have had no fixed ideal. Believing Christians did not have to speculate about the value of life since life was given to them as so much clay from which they were to mold an object whose value would win them a final reward: either salvation and—if the object made was of first-rate quality—a high place in heaven; or damnation and—if the object was especially bad—a chilly spot on hell's lowest lake. The world's injustice, and the misery and cruelty it produced for the world's masses, was neither foolish nor unintelligible; it provided the gantlet the faithful had to run in order to win the prizes which a just and merciful God would hand out on the dreadful day of judgment when even the saints would need consolation against his mighty ire. What otherwise would have been insufferable in life was made tolerable because God would eventually adjust the books. There was an admirable emotional and psychological economy in such divine cost-accounting which no subsequent philosophy or ideology has been able to equal for assurance and certitude in face of ontological perplexity. The Christian prisoners in "Drôle d'amitié," gathered together by the Catholic chaplain, meet in order to meditate together on the meaning of their present predicament in relation to the overall sense of life. The task to which the priest urges them is one of profitable resignation which will earn them more credits for salvation.

Brunet is infuriated by this. He can offer no equally attractive sense for life. Against the priest's encouragement to his faithful to seek an inner peace which will hopefully toughen their moral skin to meet all of adversity's assaults, Brunet can only offer a program of disciplined joint action which *may* provoke favorable changes in the lives of some of his followers; others will surely die either in the fight for terrestrial progress or before that progress is achieved. Brunet's anger with the priest and his followers is also Brunet's anguish that he, living with no belief in God, has no equally efficient myth to offer. He must work in a world stripped of myths where accomplishment is very uncertain and where the assorted horrors are all the more unbearable because no date can be fixed for their end. He must ask men to work together, to suffer indignity and adversity in common, without being able to offer them any but the vaguest promises.

He thus faces the basic problem of all ethical programs which, confronted with the meanness of man, must aim—and in the absence of any metaphysical support—at establishing patterns of behavior that will transmute meanness into munificence. It is hard to convince individual mortal men to work together if their cooperation is going to reduce the amount of pleasure or serenity they can find in life. The inevitable reality of death, rather than encouraging or even necessitating joint action, may do just the opposite by encouraging men to work only for their own egos and the satisfaction of their own desires.

There seems to be no reason to work with or for others when those others can do nothing for the individual at the moment of his death. Since he dies alone, he might just as well live alone. Since the Other can do nothing helpful for him at the moment of his death—tears do more for the living than they do for the dying, and somewhere in the mind of the living there is probably speculation about what they will derive, through inheritance, from the dying—there is no commanding reason why he should do anything for the Other while he is still vigorous. If one man hurts another by profiting personally at the latter's expense, his act is cause neither for regret nor sorrow; it is the outcome of a struggle which might have had the opposite result. The consequence of such an attitude is that obsession with death can prevent men from working in the interests of any agency wider than the self. A fair amount of nineteenth-century French literature was concerned with precisely this situation and, with great frequency, exalted every effort which armed the ego against incursions from the surrounding society.

Baudelaire, who, despite his agnosticism, was infected more than he knew by Christian mythology, might try to avoid the deeper aspects of the question by writing, in "La Mort des pauvres,"

> C'est la mort qui console, hélas! et qui fait vivre;
> C'est le but de la vie, et c'est le seul espoir . . . .

He could do so only because he believed, as he showed in "Le Voyage," that death was a consciously experienced state and not the full end to a life. At the conclusion of "Le Voyage" he could await death with anticipation, for he hoped to find something novel in it; the search for new escapes from old and recurrent ennuis had been his lifelong quest.

Later French writers have not been able to profit from either involuntary or unexamined beliefs where death is concerned; with them death becomes more and more a central preoccupation of life. Death is, as Baudelaire said, the end of life, a terminal point and possibly a goal, but it is an absurd end since beyond it there is no longer consciousness; at the edge, there may be purpose. The ancients had the same preoccupation, but they, too, had their mythologies which, if they did not promise individual immortality— the end of *Oedipus at Colonus* is probably exceptional—at least described a universe operating with purpose and order in the interests of a known ethical system. They had their rebels, too, for if Aeschylus and Sophocles were able to suggest that man could learn to join in the greater harmonies, Euripides invariably returned to raising questions about *whose* harmonies they were and whether, at the end of the catastrophe, they could offer melodies to soothe any breast; the interventions of the gods at the end of some of his plays suggest that the machine from which the gods come to reimpose order was made in the factory of human despair.[1]

Professor F. J. Hoffmann's book, *The Mortal No: Death and the Modern Imagination* (Princeton, 1964), has shown the degree to which concern with death is a major preoccupation of the literature of our times. A pre-

---

1. It is not, as a result, surprising that the two Sartre plays derived from classical sources, *Les Mouches* and *Les Troyennes*, should be based on Euripidean texts; *Les Mouches* is the less directly derivative of the two. Whatever there is of the deus ex machina in *Les Mouches* is present primarily for farcical, though not necessarily comic, purpose. In *Les Troyennes*, where the gods are presented as colossal and colossally dangerous forces, there is no deus ex machina other than fate, or proliferating error, or the frightening example of human avarice which, not content to seek its own wretched goals, ties its ambitious star to a god who, in turn, has tied his star to shrewdness and chicanery in his dealings with the other gods. Ultimately, what is of interest in the Sartrean derivatives is the heavy evidence demonstrating that Sartre's spirit is Euripidean: skeptical, complaining, ironic, not yet plunged into despair but close to it, fundamentally convinced that no extra-human force exists.

occupation with mortality is at the center of all of André Malraux's work; and that preoccupation has a direct relevance to this study because of the influence Malraux, both as a man of action and a writer, had on Sartre's imagination. Both in his novels and in his esthetic works, Malraux has been haunted by death as the end to a struggle which can be either purposeful or purposeless. If an individual life has been adorned with purpose, the individual's death initiates a process whereby a steady, feeble light is cast across the otherwise drab reaches of time. The possibility of contributing one's life to the intensification of that illuminative process ought to encourage men to live so that their acts will help reduce the shadows and eliminate the darkness. Death may silence voices; it does not obliterate the handsome objects men leave behind them and which museums exhibit and libraries enshrine.[2]

Efforts like Malraux's, which seek to reassure men and to reduce their anguish when confronted with death, are all efforts to respond in some way to the truth suggested in Heidegger's observation that our life among others is our life towards death (*Dasein ist Sein zum Tod*). Since death afflicts us all, we should not attempt to disguise the inevitable, but should live together as beings who seek to justify our deaths by the quality of our lives or, as with many of Malraux's characters, justify our life by the dignity of our death. According to Heidegger, concern with death should help form the collectivity rather than divide it into self-protecting egos.

This pleasant idea (which soured totally when it was used to defend Nazism as an adventure into a higher form of courage) can serve to encourage the young to live full and active lives—until they meet their first paralyzing disappointment. The young, before that first frustration, accept all encouragement with enthusiasm because, like the child in the early part of Baudelaire's "Le Voyage," they have the impression that the world presents an inexhaustible panorama of experiences and thus a rich source of continuous refreshment. There will always be new places to go, other things to do. But they risk learning the same lesson that the narrator of Baudelaire's poem learned: everything is everywhere more or less the same, life is always overshadowed with ennui and disappointment, death will at last come as a consolation against accumulated deceptions. There are ways of rebounding from the early paralyses; in the end, however, the damage is too great and besides there is nowhere else to go.

2. The idea is not new with Malraux, though his repeated insistence on it is perhaps novel. Baudelaire had put forward the same idea with the greater economy of fine poetry. In "Les Phares," after having given one-verse summaries of several painters, he writes in conclusion about the works they have left behind them:

> Car c'est vraiment, Seigneur, le meilleur témoignage
> Que nous puissions donner de notre dignité
> Que cet ardent sanglot qui roule d'âge en âge
> Et vient mourir au bord de votre éternité!

We shall see presently how Sartre responds to Heidegger's analysis of death and shall examine Sartre's own position on the importance the living give to death and to the dead. We shall, however, be able to appreciate better the broader context in which Sartre looks at the issue if we consider the various reactions Simone de Beauvoir has experienced when confronted with death.

Mme de Beauvoir's steady and usually self-conscious gaze at death has been accompanied by various and shifting reactions from her, none of which can be said to show that she fears no resultant evil. At the end of the *Mémoires d'une jeune fille rangée*, she traces out, in what are perhaps the most moving pages of her needlessly long and often fatiguing autobiography, the romance and early death of her friend, Zaza. For Mme de Beauvoir personally, that death represented a deliverance from the norms of her class, which had deprived Zaza of the love she might otherwise have known. From that experience and all that she saw in it of the repressions and inadequacies of her class, Simone de Beauvoir worked out the terms of her encounter with life: "It was my mission to attend to the multiple splendor of life; I was going to write in order to pluck life away from time and from nothingness" (*FA*, pp. 18–19). As a young woman she set out to explore the world with the kind of organization and deadly seriousness usually associated with military campaigns waged by ambitious young field-grade officers. There is a kind of gray determination both in the way she proposes and disposes of her mission, but her point of departure is very much Baudelaire's—she will conquer.

Yet the idea of death as the inevitable end of her explorations keeps coming back. At first it is a simple observation; in recent years, and despite Mme de Beauvoir's sturdy periodic denials, it has become an obsession. Death has brushed her closely on several occasions: an unexpected illness whose effects are described both in *La Force de l'âge* and in *L'Invitée* (Mme de Beauvoir is not one to hesitate about going over the same minute territory many times with a finicky attention to every lugubrious detail); a bicycle accident which might have killed her; more recently, an automobile accident while driving from Italy to Paris. Since she emerged from each of these experiences intact, her basic or residual optimism was reinforced. She could write: "The idea of dying did not seem at all scandalous to me, for death is never anything if not deferred—we live on reprieves" (*FA*, p. 470). The implication is that we should be grateful for the reprieves we are allowed. At the same time that she was finding such limited consolation, she was also formulating sharp and jabbing ideas on the nature of death as a state: "Death is nothing," she writes, "one never *is* dead since there is no one there to experience death" (*FA*, p. 511). One is no longer the consciousness which lived a life; one is a cadaver and a cadaver, precisely, is not a man.

The experience of war, Sartre's imprisonment—with the uncertainties it created—and the unforeseeable dangers of the Occupation invalidated some of these attitudes and reduced the effectiveness of earlier consolations. Death increasingly terrifies her and she finds that she can no longer face it with chilly rationalism: courage in the face of death strikes her as no more than wilful giddiness. Though her optimism returns, she is never again fully with the stoics. She recognizes that it is the living's obsession with death which is atrocious and writes of "this book [as] my supreme recourse against death" (*FA*, p. 618); her earlier declaration that death is nothing is now more horrible than reassuring. She seeks another path to cheerfulness: "We must accept dying when there is no other means of saving life; death is not always an absurd solitary accident: it creates living ties with others . . . it has a sense and justifies itself." The conclusion is astonishing, perhaps only because what comes before it doesn't really make much sense, but also because nothing in her earlier experiences legitimates a phrase as mysterious as her claim that death justifies itself. She had long been troubled in her search for such justification and had hoped that Paul Nizan, a longtime if misunderstood friend of hers and Sartre's, might bring back some sort of reassurance from the Soviet Union, where intimate, socially purposeful ties with others supposedly existed before death. "He had often wondered whether socialist faith helped to conjure away [death]. He hoped so and had questioned the young socialists at length about it: they had all replied that, in the face of death, camaraderie and solidarity were of no help and that they were afraid of it. . . . It was a blow for him to discover that [in Russia] each man died alone and fully aware" (*FA*, p. 213).[3]

Death then offers no justification, and Mme de Beauvoir, having had her moment with bravado, returns to meditating on the frightful aloneness one must experience at death's arrival. She tells us that the idea of dying becomes more and more unbearable as age sets in. At a certain moment—a moment which lasts no longer than the time needed to convey it to the reader—she writes that she would like to die with the man she loves, but she immediately recognizes that that would change nothing. They would not become either Paolo and Francesca or Romeo and Juliet. If anything, they would be Wagner's Tristan and Isolde, singing difficult tunes as they stared into the approaching nothingness. The horror of such meditations

3. In his essay on Nizan, Sartre writes apropos of the same subject: ". . . the revolution would deliver men from the fear of living; it did not remove the fear of dying. He had questioned the best of them [the Russian revolutionists]: they had all answered that they thought about death and that their zeal for the common tasks did not save them from this hidden personal disaster" (*Sit. IV*, p. 180). Nizan was expelled from the Communist party because of his opposition to the Russo-German pact. It is possible that, in this sense and perhaps in others, he is the model for the character of Schneider in "Drôle d'amitié."

is that after death "there is no place [in the world] for those who no longer have any space. It is complete separation, complete betrayal . . . one day I shall be that absent individual" (*FA*, p. 620).

At the end of *La Force de l'âge* she seems to share the hope of the Stranger in Saint-John Perse's poems: there are still many places to see, things to do, conversations to be had, causes to be supported, witness to be given through her books. In the subsequent volume, *La Force des choses*,—which remains, for the present, the last and the longest—we are given exhaustive descriptions of what she saw and did. The title is not untouched with sadness, for where in the second volume it was the force of life which seemed dominant, in the third it is the primacy of things. The impression one has is that things govern in this world because they last, or do not suffer, or do not see; Simone de Beauvoir is only a traveler in their midst, a trainee at a permanent installation she must one day leave. There is something mournful in the book which goes beyond its tedious length; it is the impression that she is writing, like Lord Byron in the last cantos of *Don Juan*, to keep from crying and that, unlike Byron, she has driven all laughter away as obscene. Only the diligent and arduous task of telling where ardor leads remains.

Writing may have been undertaken as a way of plucking life from time and nothingness; life, as the days pass and the imagery of night grows dominant, is fully determined to get away from time and back into nothingness; writing is the slowing metronome marking vitality's decline. At the end of *La Force des choses*, all bravado is gone and with it rather a lot of common sense. After a long description of her relationship with Sartre, she can no longer restrain herself: the world and its adventures have not been enough; death is always there; it has taken possession of her face and she can no longer bear to look in a mirror. Something—age—is victimizing her without her having assented to being a victim. The last sentences catch the disarray of her deceived spirit and express the cry she cannot restrain:

> At best, if I am read, the reader will think: my, she did see a lot of things! But the unique ensemble, *my* experience, with its order and its chance—the Peking Opera, the arena of Huelva, the *candomblé* of Bahia, the El-Oued dunes, Wabansia Avenue, dawn in Provence, Tiryns, Castro speaking to five hundred thousand Cubans, a sulphurous sky above a sea of clouds, the purple holly, the white nights in Leningrad, the bells of the Liberation, an orange moon above Piraeus, a red sun rising over the desert, Torcello, Rome, everything about which I have spoken and other things about which I've said nothing—nowhere will any of that be resurrected. If it had at least enriched the earth; if it had produced—what? a hill? a missile? But no. Nothing

shall have taken place. I see the hedge of hazel trees rustled by
the wind and remember the promises with which I made my
heart pant when I contemplated the gold mine at my feet—a
whole life to live. The promises have been kept. Still, turning
an unbelieving look towards that credulous adolescent, I measure
with stupor to what degree I was cheated (p. 686).

I have taken this long detour into Simone de Beauvoir's thought because
it catches the "tone" of much existentialist discussion of mortality; it also
gives us a detailed and at times moving image of the situation of some
modern intellectuals whose preoccupation with other issues, like social
reform, does not spare them anguish about the fact that no amount of
involvement over the space of a lifetime can involve others in their death.
At one point Mme de Beauvoir expresses her hope that she will die before
Sartre; she does not pursue her wish in any detail since that way lies the
whole unresolved question of the Other. For even if one succeeds, as she
and Sartre so clearly have done, in overcoming the instinctive hostility they
claim every man has towards his fellow men, that hostility, in the guise
of eternal absence which might be mistaken for abandonment, returns.
Having been with the Other we have loved throughout life, we are left
with nothing, at the moment of his death, except a diminishing reservoir
of memories. I have also presented this résumé of Mme de Beauvoir's attitudes as a prelude to the presentation of her companion's ideas; these are
radically different, possibly because he is a more rigorous thinker than she,
probably because he has enormously more optimism and joie de vivre, certainly because of his conviction that obsession with death is likely to have
a major influence on the way men live together.

Sartre writes about death with something of the cool remoteness of Lucretius, and, under the calm disciplined surface, there is something of the
same bleak passion which inspired the Latin poet. Sartre has no theory
of a world full of atoms where the dead, if not raised, are at least reab-
sorbed; nor has he any far-off gods who serve as models of how humans
should conduct themselves. All he has is a packet of observations and arguments which he hopes will provide the reader with a stunning appreciation
of the value of life and which will encourage men to live it to the fullest
by recognizing that death is a happening with which men have little or
nothing to do. In the sense that death comes to us, uninvited and unwanted,
it is a terminal situation, an unyielding wall to which we are forced. Though
that wall is always before us we cannot know, even when we think we are
in a clearly delimited situation, with the death sentence pronounced and
the time of execution set, whether the execution will surely take place on
schedule.

That is the situation of Pablo Ibbieta, the narrator of Sartre's short story,

"Le Mur" (1939). The hour and conditions of his death are as sure as anything can be in this world; he has been arrested by the Franco forces and
condemned to death by a firing squad the next morning. In the intervening
hours he takes leave of everything. His illusions and aspirations now strike
him as foolish, not only because they have not been realized, but also because
they depended on a kind of enthusiasm which is not too far removed from
a belief in eternity. He draws no reassurance from the idea of humanity
or from the presence of those nearby; they cannot do anything for him
except reflect his own nervousness in theirs. He takes leave of his past which
no longer has any meaning because there is no longer any future in which
that meaning could be used or further evolved. He has only one hope—a
hope that will be shared by some of the characters in *Morts sans sépulture*—he would like to die with dignity.

That hope is frustrated by the rebelliousness of his body, which sweats
despite the efforts of his will and the chilliness of the night; it is also frustrated by the presence of a Belgian doctor who apparently is making a study
of how condemned men react physically during the last hours of life. Ibbieta
is clearly close to that unyielding wall with only two remaining tasks: the
first is to die without being seduced into any bargain which might result
from his revelation of where his companion in arms is hiding; the other
is to meet the actual moment of execution honorably—though whatever
honor surrounds his demise will be known to him alone and then only for
the brief moments of consciousness which remain after the bullets have
struck.

He decides to play a final trick and tells his jailers that his companion,
Ramon Gris, is hiding in the gravediggers' hut of a nearby cemetery. This
is a pure invention on his part, but by force of other circumstances, it turns
out to be true. His death is postponed; Gris is arrested and will presumably
be executed shortly. The wall has withdrawn from Ibbieta who now must
go on living though he has stripped himself of all motivation for life. In
looking back upon his former motives, before his reprieve, he had found
them hollow and irrelevant to a world of mortal men.

Sartre's intention is transparent; he wants to show, for thoroughly non-
theological reasons, the accuracy of the Bible's warning that man knows
neither the place nor the hour of his death. While accepting the accuracy
of the description, Sartre rejects its advice that men should therefore be
prepared for death at every moment. Since neither place nor hour is certainly known, such preparation serves no purpose except, as in Ibbieta's
case, to produce disillusion with life and the energy men need to live it
out. Though there is some justification for Ibbieta's attitude, it cannot help
him once he is reprieved. Had such attitudes existed throughout his life,
his freedom and his capacity to act would have been seriously affected.
Neither by the way they live, nor by the mood in which they prepare to

die, can men determine the mode of their death; death is something they go through, something they endure.

It is thus the nonhuman phenomenon par excellence precisely because, unless he commits suicide, man does not choose it. Sartre, to be sure, is aware of the many modern attempts which have been undertaken, notably by Malraux and Heidegger, to define death as a kind of tonic chord which comes to justify the melody of life. If that final chord is especially resounding, they imply, then deeper harmonies and lovelier melodies will be heard and appreciated. Such explanations, Sartre insists, represent no more than an attempt to redeem death by idealizing it; that sort of undertaking has to do with poetry and not with philosophy. Since such efforts try to present death as the phenomenon which gives sense to life, they make death life's great project; it is the event which men should interiorize early on in order to make it a lifetime goal and value. A life so committed prepares a man to die in dignity rather than in despair. He knows as he leaves this planet that he has been a conscientious instrumentalist in its search for ultimate harmonies.[4]

Sartre considers this view to be nonsense which is only periodically redeemed when a Vigny can make a fine poem of it. The principal characteristic of death is that it resolves nothing. Men consent no more to dying than to being born; life, therefore, is bounded by two events which have nothing to do with human freedom. Living for death, he insists, is a senseless project. A man can plot out all the actions by which he will die nobly and then be unexpectedly carried off by plague. His anticipations have been a waste of time, much as Ibbieta's meditations have become a waste of time once he must go on living. The way in which men die does not necessarily make any comment on the way in which they have lived. Thus Heidegger's insistence on the unique quality of *my* death makes no real sense and derives no authority from Heidegger's companion assertion that this uniqueness exists because no one can die for me.

Though Sartre agrees to the truth of this assertion, he immediately begins to show that it is a trivial statement. While no one can die for me, no one can love for me either, or think for me, or eat for me. But someone can do all

4. While Claude Lévi-Strauss has not given expression to any thoughts about death which can be said to fall into the existentialist camp, he insists in the opening chapter of his *Le Cru et le cuit* that music, because it is at once a creation, an ordering of melody to a specific end, and a stimulus which evokes a physical response from the listener, is an excellent paradigm of a basic, perhaps *the* basic mode of human thought. Since thought operates in such a way, Lévi-Strauss insists that man, in order to understand his experience, must in a certain way let himself go to the spontaneous development of that experience within him. A society preoccupied with death, or which has placed death rituals firmly within its structures, is a society which would demand an understanding response from its individual members, not simply in order to have their allegiance, but also in order to have their support as members contributing to the maintenance of a very complex and symphonic social system.

of these in my place. If I die another can love my wife; and another can die in my place, as the characters of *Morts sans sépulture* must do, in order to protect me. Any effort made to convince me that my death is my chance to present others with a good example, or to leave a noble legacy to humanity, must take into consideration two things. First, another human being can do exactly the same thing. Second, I will not be here to appreciate others' reactions to my final performance.[5]

Men can expect death as they can expect the arrival of any calamity. But they would be fools to spend their lives waiting for death. One waits for a train and one waits for a friend with whom one has an appointment because one has the certitude that train and friend will arrive. One can also expect that a disaster may befall friend or train and that that disaster will render the period of waiting useless. But those are exceptional circumstances; for the most part we are behaving rationally when we wait for a scheduled train and a friend with whom an appointment has been made.

By contrast, when we are planning a trip which will take place several months hence, or awaiting the return of a friend next year, we do not stop all activities; we expect that the trains will be running for our trip (or that the inevitable strikes will last only a day or so), and that the friend will return at the date foreseen. This, Sartre says, is what man's attitude towards his death should be. But, as we have seen in Ibbieta's case, even when the date of death is set and immediate, we are not, because of that, removed from the world of action. Even as we wait for the train, something else may happen to which we should respond. Even while we, or the characters in *Le Sursis*, are preparing unenthusiastically for the arrival of war, an international conference is going on; when it succeeds, we are plunged for a time back into a "normal" life.

To wait for death, even in such circumstances as we find in *Morts sans sépulture* (1946), is ill-chosen behavior. Chance and hazard remain the rulers of this world; the unforeseen, one of its surest forces. Action is no more likeable for being uncertain, but it is no more avoidable either. Even at the moment when I have assumed the disposition I favor in preparing myself for death, situations can be developing elsewhere which will oblige me to further action. This is the idea at the heart of *Morts sans sépulture*. The members of the Resistance who are imprisoned in the school attic are certain that death is near. They are also certain that their meeting with it will be grim because, before it comes, they will be tortured. Rather than being able to prepare themselves for noble deaths, they must live with the

5. Sartre had worked with this idea in *Huis-clos*, where the three characters are witnesses to their complete disappearance from the earth. Not only has their consciousness disappeared as a force in the world, but their influence is gradually and totally lost as those they had known forget about them. By the end of the play, they realize that they have left *nothing* behind except vacant space in which others can operate—for themselves and against them.

possibility that all dignity will be wrested from them if they succumb to the torture. They have one assurance. Though physical weakness may force them to cry out or collapse and thus suggest a debility which will make their torturers feel superior, it will not force them to reveal the whereabouts of their companion, Jean, because they do not know where he is. The immediate future may bring shame and produce pain; it cannot force them to reveal what they do not know and thereby betray other members of the Resistance. The memory of their immediate past is more unsettling because they live haunted by the futility of the act which has brought about their arrest. That act produced the death of other Frenchmen and, since its ultimate purpose was frustrated, it produced nothing else. The last planned act of their lives represents no achievement: their last hours may only multiply their shame.

Chance complicates their existence even further and intensifies the risk of augmented shame with the return of Jean, who has been arrested for a banal reason and brought to the attic. His captors do not know his true identity. Everything is now changed. His comrades can no longer wait passively for death since Jean's presence means that they will have to act; they are living rather than dying because, under the pressure of torture, they will have to resist further and refuse to reveal what they now know. That "little bit of posthumous life" which one of their members had spoken of (p. 201), has become a dangerous even though small patch of time which they must cross under excruciating circumstances. Having thought they were dead, they find—and this is surely the sense of the title—that there is no death, no release from action, until one is buried. Before Jean's return, their remaining hours seemed determined; with Jean's arrest, that determinant, and the relative peace it brought, are gone. Another determinant has come, forcing them to act even unto the moment of death.

Morts sans sépulture is a play which deals with two forms of waiting. One is the expectation by the prisoners of a force which is going to determine their destiny; the other is the expectation of what Sartre would call themselves. What he means by the latter has to do with the nature of men's reaction to circumstances and the quality of the project which will be produced by that reaction. Even with death sure and proximate, men are not at rest; there are unanticipated forces which may still arrive. Men remain free, free to choose their reaction to determining or, more accurately, conditioning directional forces; these forces are always there. Here Sartre is reverting to an idea which he has often expressed: freedom is a kind of slavery because it is a condition from which one never escapes. Death writes the finish to this enslavement as birth wrote its beginning. In between is the period of servitude wherein acts will determine the nature, the quality, and the value of each human life. By the nature proper to them, neither death nor birth can provide life with a sense, though they may provide it with apparent determinants which can be invoked as excuses. Whatever sense an individual life has is provided by man, the pure subjectivity who lives it out. All that death provides is the end to the pattern of acts which have, on the basis of a variety of inspirations and intentions, given definition to that life.

Suicide might seem a mode of death which at least places the individual in a position of mastery. If life is absurd and, contrary to the bland assurances of cheerful clergymen, not worth living even when one has learned to think positively, then suicide can appear as the act which best comments on the absurdity. It would have the beauty, so long dreamt of by the Marquis de Sade, of insulting an all-powerful Nature by robbing her of her claims, by acting before she can. Sartre does not agree. The very act of suicide, he says, is senseless, given that its sense depends not on the act itself but on the commentary the act seeks to make. If an individual survives a suicide attempt, he can then live with the consequences of his commentary and decide that it was the wrong one or that he was too cowardly to make a truly efficacious commentary by living purposefully. If he succeeds in killing himself, he won't be around to make any evaluations whatsoever. Suicide only succeeds in plunging a man into an absurdity he cannot enjoy and which has no consequences for him since he is no longer there to know what they are. It will have no consequences for nature either since nature is unconscious and cannot be made aware, even by violence, of any messages left behind for her attention. The nature which provoked men to self-violence was only an idea in their minds; once the mind is gone, the idea is gone too.[6]

Attempts at suicide which we have encountered so far in Sartre's work have for the most part been gestures—Roquentin stabbing his hand, Mathieu and Ivich repeating that gesture though with bloodier results, Philippe thinking of throwing himself into the Seine, Daniel making elaborate unfulfilled plans to castrate himself. As gestures they indicate that the actors have been only too aware of the finality of suicide: they wanted what amounts to a propitiatory gesture but they also exercised enough control to avoid turning gestures into sacrifices. In the cases of successful suicide, the consistency of Sartre's observations only appears to be compromised. Daniel's suicide would have been the despairing gesture of a man who, having reached the end of one line, did not have the energy to look for another; it would have been more an expression of fatigue than a commentary on deeper issues.

Sorbier's suicide in *Morts sans sépulture*, however, goes beyond both gestures and fatigue, though it does not escape the influence of fear. It is

---

6. Of Genet, Sartre writes: "To kill himself: never! It would horrify him to slip out of the world and leave it just as full. But if he could drag *everything* along in his gradual disappearance suicide would tempt him" (*SG*, p. 375).

an act designed to produce consequences. By killing himself he eliminates the possibility of revealing Jean's whereabouts and thus protects the cause to which he has dedicated himself. His act comes as no surprise since he has been haunted by the fear of buckling under torture. So long as he was ignorant he could bear that possibility, though he had admitted on his return from his first session with the collaborationists: "They asked me where Jean was, and if I had known I would have told them . . ." (p. 209). He adds, shortly afterwards, when he knows that Jean is in the attic: "It's unjust that a single minute is enough to rot a whole life" (p. 210). His suicide is the act he chooses in order to avoid betraying another; conceivably, it is an act which he hopes will cast some retroactive dignity on the rest of his acts.[7]

This raises the question of the objective value of his suicide. Sartre would probably insist that it was a free choice of the easier way; Sorbier could have resisted torture and thereby achieved sturdier and fuller dignity by denying his torturers any dominion over him. In resisting to the end, he would also have stayed alive to enjoy the improbable but possible situation in which he might have been freed. Though his suicide is not exempt from the general evaluation made of suicide in *Being and Nothingness*, it does take place under those extraordinary circumstances which Sartre described in *Qu'est-ce que la littérature?*: "We could not find it natural to be men when our best friends, if they were caught, could choose only between abjection and heroism, i.e., between the two extremes of the human condition beyond which there was nothing. Cowards and traitors, they were below the rest of men; heroes, they were above them" (pp. 249–50).

The value of Sorbier's suicide as an intentional act effected in the interests of someone else is further enhanced by the growingly unsettled situation of the collaborationists. The terror they administer is worse physically than the terror they expect; for, as the play unfolds, the Liberation is near, and they do not expect to be tortured by the Allies. The radio's reports of Axis resistance only underscore the Allies' advance. The torturers are having their last brutal moments, and though they derive satisfaction from believing that those they torture are cowardly or suicide-prone, at least one of them realizes that in others' memories the members of the Resistance, no matter what kind of reactive behavior they were reduced to, will be the victors.

What Sartre opposes in suicide which takes place under less extreme conditions and with less clearly generous motivation—for Sorbier does after all die with the hope that others may live—is that it is ultimately a refusal of existence, a desire to incorporate oneself into being-in-itself; if it brings no other results, death does accomplish that. As such it becomes

7. Suicide as a device, a way out of an insoluble situation, occurs later in Sartre's work in *Les Séquestrés d'Altona*, which I discuss in chapter 10.

part of the range of gestures employed to put an end to consciousness and responsibility; it joins the other similarly pointless gestures we have seen: the desire to slip into the viscous, to be dominated by others who can then be blamed for what one has made of oneself. Since the measure of man's humanity is the degree to which he decides to live as a free being in a world of other free beings—that is, in the world of being-for-others—suicide is a refusal of his humanity, for in it he accepts death as the goal of his freedom. What he should do is recognize that death is the end of his freedom and, in that sense, is his enemy because it is the force which will make of him what, if he is honest, he has refused to make of himself: a being-in-itself.

Once dead, the individual depends on the memory of the Other. As a result, the dead are potentially victims since whatever remains of their existence can be manipulated by the Other for a number of reasons, the worst of which would be the Other's triumph. The Other can say what he wishes about the dead; no voice will come from the grave to say otherwise. Those who have been celebrities in life can expect to maintain some kind of particularity in death because of the works or the deeds they have left behind. But those who have been part of the earth's humble masses will in memory remain only part of a remembered mass: one of those who died of famine, who was slain in a massacre, or who stormed the Bastille. Even those who are famous and keep some kind of particularity after death are subject to the caprices of the future. If they were writers, they will be subjected to the needs of Ph.D. candidates who will have the task of saying something new about them; or, if they have been Baudelaire or Flaubert, they will be subjected to Jean-Paul Sartre who has his truth to tell about them. To expend one's life trying to prepare oneself for immortality, inspired perhaps by the hope contained in Mallarmé's phrase—*Tel qu'en Lui-même enfin l'éternité le change*—is to waste time, for the future treats the dead as it chooses and on the basis of reasons which may be capricious or imperious. Since such an effort is absurd, it would be equally absurd to pass one's life trying to contribute consciously to a process over which one will exercise no control.[8]

One concern with the dead who have preceded us on this globe and then into the nothingness of the grave is not absurd at all, however. The dead have prepared the world in which we live. The dead have formed our

---

8. Later, in the concluding chapter of his book on Genet, Sartre will stress that, with proper comprehension and a commitment to intelligent and justified investigation of a man's work, we can derive much profit from his experience despite its intention and even despite what may have been wrong in what the intention aimed at achieving. In the case of Genet, Sartre stresses the immediate value Genet has for a contemporary audience: he shows the present, as it is manifested in the bourgeoisie, how the future will look at it. In this sense, Genet has already put the present in the past, has already made an in-itself of it. I discuss this further in chapter 11.

parents and shaped the institutions which form us; they have also tried
to influence the thought which inspires both parents and institutions. At
the moment when we surge forth as consciousnesses in this society we must
take some sort of position with regard to those who are dead and towards
what they have left behind; we can accept them, as Lucien did, or we can
insult them, as Roquentin did in the Bouville museum. But one way or
another, we must decide upon their role in our lives and, in so doing, make
our contribution to their fate. We can make use of them as we wish; but
whatever the use we ultimately decide upon, we reveal our intention not
only towards them but also towards life.

Like Parson Weems, we can glorify Washington out of reality in the
hope of making virtue more commonplace than it usually is; or, like Edward
Albee, in *Who's Afraid of Virginia Woolf?*, we can make inferences about
Washington's barren marriage in order to make statements that are none
too clear but which apparently have to do with tarnishing overly bright
reputations. Washington's uses, to be sure, are limited when compared
to God's. The deity has been more often invoked to justify human evil than
to explain divine good. But whether one is Washington or God, and whether
one's will is interpreted by Parson Weems, Edward Albee, or casuistic
churchmen, the situation is the same: the dead and absent are the prey of
the living.

By a reverse process, the living can choose to pretend that they are the
prey of the dead, either because this is really although limitedly so, or because it provides an excuse for otherwise reprehensible conduct. We shall
see variations on this situation in *Les Mouches* and *Les Séquestrés d'Altona*,
where the influences are momentarily inescapable and where the arguments
for accepting and rejecting them are at loggerheads. In *La Putain respectueuse* (1946)—quite far and away the worst thing Sartre has written and
perhaps one of the silliest plays produced in this century by a serious
artist—the situation is straightforward; it is clearly a question of letting
the dead govern the living.

There are three types of dead in *La Putain respectueuse*. The first type
is the most obvious: those who have breathed their last and been interred
but who, despite their departure from this world, have become fireside
deities whose force is not unlike that of the Eumenides. Then there are
the living dead, the white inhabitants of the American South who justify
their actions in the name of a tradition they have inherited from the past
and which they must protect because the tradition is long and, more significantly, because without it they would have no claim to the seedy aristocratic heritage they confuse with dignity. They do not seek to make anything out of themselves; they seek, and in the vaguest of fashions, to slip
into a tradition which can provide them with nothing more honorable than
an explanation for resounding bad faith. This is the bad faith they express

in actions they do not wish to accept as their own, but which they are compelled to perform out of personal need or in order to maintain the tradition. In a way, they are examples of that captive thought Sartre had written of in *L'Imaginaire* which "is constrained to realize all its own intentions" (p. 97). We have an example of bad faith, rooted in need, in Fred's explanation that ". . . with the Devil you can only do evil. [My cousin] put his hand up your skirts, he shot a dirty nigger, so what? Those are only gestures you do without thinking; they don't count" (p. 289). His other brand of bad faith is manifest in the speech he makes to Lizzie, the whore of the title, when she threatens to shoot him: "My father is a senator and I'll be a senator after him: I am his last male heir and the last of my name. We made this country and its history is ours. There were Clarkes in Alaska, in the Philippines, and in New Mexico. Would you dare shoot at all of America?" (p. 315).[9]

Lizzie, unfortunately, is not persuaded by the deliverance she might bring to the world were she to rid it of this last male heir and the rest of the tribe he might engender; she is more persuaded by the argument of tradition, even though that tradition has allotted her the narrowest of berths and a single function to perform in it. She assents to Fred's description of her state: "A slut like you *couldn't* shoot a man like me. Who are you? What do you do in the world? Did you even know who your grandfather was? *I* have the right to live; there are a lot of things that need doing: there are people waiting for me" (p. 315). By her assent, she agrees to turn the world over to them, to their traditions, to their obsessions, to their needs—one of which she will satisfy on Tuesdays, Thursdays, and weekends when Fred will come to do the black act with her and bring her to orgasm. Everything, as Fred says at the end, "is back in place."

This includes the Negroes, who represent the third kind of dead in the play. They are dead because, though they can make the same claim to freedom as other men, they, like the Jews, are other men's victims. As such they are necessary to the maintenance of a system which needs enemies it can control; as such, they feel guilty. The Negro and the prostitute are the forces of evil in the world. Though the whites shoot the Negro and screw the prostitute, the Negro and the prostitute take the burden and share the blame.[10] Sartre does not excuse the Negro; his admission that he

9. Cf. *SG*: "Evil is a projection . . . it is both the basis and aim of all projective activity. . . . the evildoer . . . is a man whose situation makes it possible for him to present to us in broad daylight and in objective form the obscure temptation of our freedom. If you want to know a decent man, look for the vices he hates most in others. You will have the lines of force of his fears and terrors, you will breathe the odor that befouls his beauteous soul" (p. 29). Sartre's specific reference in this passage is to white men who lynch Negroes.

10. Cf. *SG*: "For peacetime society has, in its wisdom, created what might be called professional evildoers. These evil men are as necessary to good men as whores are

cannot shoot the white man is an unnecessary capitulation. He could very well shoot him; since he is being pursued by white men with lynching in their eyes, his fate would be no worse. His refusal, like Lizzie's, is free; with it he recognizes the right of the dead to rule in his life as much as they rule in the lives of the "aristocrats" who pursue him.

Thus the dead, and the living who allow themselves to be ruled by the dead, still exercise a role which is a genuine force in the world of the living, of the here and now, of tasks endlessly to be done. Since the dead cannot manage their destiny—what has been made of them—it is clear that all responsibility falls on the living.[11] The dead not only tell no tales, they justify no excuses either. The dead may, when living, have acted with the hope of determining the future by telling their children that the Negro was a threat and the prostitute a useful way of coping with evil sexual needs. The living can continue to believe in such injunctions; the decision remains theirs exclusively. The dead, since they leave formative influences behind them, have a kind of transcendence, but that transcendence depends on the transcendence of the living, who can just as readily decide that the dead were wrong as that their counsels must be slavishly followed.

All the characters in *La Putain* have embraced a form of inauthenticity precisely because they refuse to resist the influence of forces inherited from the past. In allowing themselves to be governed by the dead they, too, are dead—dead to their possibilities, to the mindful formation of their future, to the widest apprehension of their conscious comprehension of the world. They are also fools: there is no death this side of the grave and the pretense of being dead or being governed by the dead is a declaration of servitude freely and knowledgeably made. Death in both its manifestations—as that which controls me from the past and that which will dominate me in the end—remains a great temptation to make excuses. As we shall see in the next chapter, it is only one such temptation and thus is only one of the obstacles on the road to conscious exercise of freedom.

---

to decent women. They are fixation abscesses. For a single sadist there is any number of appeased, clarified, relaxed consciousnesses. They are therefore very carefully recruited. They must be bad by birth and without hope of change. That is why one chooses men with whom the decent members of the community have no reciprocal relations: so that these bad people cannot take it into their heads to pay us back in kind and start thinking of us what we think of them" (p. 30).

11. The notion of destiny—of people and more explicitly a group or class *being destined*—is one that Sartre attacked very early in his career because of its limiting and claustrophobic consequences for others. In his essay on Mauriac he writes of destiny as that "which envelops and goes beyond a character, which represents, at the heart of nature, and the very vile psychological work of M. Mauriac, the power of the supernatural" (*Sit. I*, p. 40). In the essay on Dos Passos he saw the idea of destiny as the product of a capitalist society, but also as an idea which, because it only applied to the managing class, necessarily robbed the other members of the society of the chance to have a destiny properly theirs (*Sit. I*, p. 19).

RELATED THEMES AND WORKS

Sartre's discussion of death is found in *BN*, pp. 531–53; the preceding sections of that chapter, "Being and Doing: Freedom," should also be consulted in order to have the proper context for his discussion of death; of especial importance are the pages on "My Past" (p. 496–504). His determinedly objective and analytic exposé of what is involved in suicide should probably be considered as no more than that, by which I mean that Sartre does not intend to pass judgment on or even to investigate causes; his later writings, especially his appeal for the need to "understand" in the *CRD*, indicate that in talking about suicide as an act he does not mean to evaluate the conditions which have provoked an individual to self-destruction. Certainly, anyone who has been exposed to suicides or near-suicide, is most forcefully struck by the extent to which the potential suicide is incapable of thinking in terms of any other solution. There are, however, disturbing incidents in Mme de Beauvoir's memoirs which indicate that, at least when they were young, she and Sartre had little patience with, because they had less understanding of, the emotionally distraught, particularly those who were contemplating self-destruction.

Mme de Beauvoir's ruminations and lucubrations on death spot her memoirs a good bit more heavily than my discussion of the subject indicates. Her *Tous les hommes sont mortels* (1946) deals, again at great length, with the same subject and seems to suffer from what the late Yvor Winters called the intentional fallacy. The point of her novel is that immortality gets wearisome; the point is made. Whether it is well made depends on the individual reader's willingness to expend his patience improvidently. More recently, in a tell-it-all account of her mother's death, *Une Mort très douce* (1964), Mme de Beauvoir returns to the subject. Her basic outlook has not changed, though she seems puzzled at being moved so deeply by another's death and at discovering latent residues of affection she had thought exhausted. In that sense, *Une Mort très douce* is a kind of liberation for her; in the past, the death of others had sent her into immediate speculation about her own.

Francis Jeanson, who unfortunately has turned from critical analysis to hagiography in discussions of either Mme de Beauvoir or Sartre, deals at length with the concluding paragraph of *FC* in his reverential and cloying *Simone de Beauvoir ou l'entreprise de vivre* (Paris, 1966). His argument is ingenious, tedious, ultimately not persuasive, because it depends on a line of spurious reasoning which amounts to saying that Mme de Beauvoir did not say what she meant or mean what she said, and that, in any case, readers' reactions to her dismay resulted from their giving a "literary" reading to her text. Since books take rather a lot of time to produce and since authors see them more than once before they are published, it seems rather unfair, and perhaps even a little bit in bad faith, to blame the reader for evaluating a text in the emotional context in which it is offered.

Morts sans sépulture and *La Putain respectueuse* were originally presented on the same bill, thus creating an interesting juxtaposition of the almost sublime and the unquestionably ridiculous. *Morts* has not fared as well as the shorter play and has never been given a Parisian revival, though an amateur group in Neuilly-sur-Seine did present it in 1967. Two of Sartre's essays, "La République du silence" (*Sit. III*, pp. 11–14) and "Qu'est-ce qu'un collaborateur?" (*Sit. III*, pp. 43–61), provide helpful background comment on the play, especially in their discussion of the mentality of collaborationists and the experience of living in an occupied country where death is always proximate.

    La Putain respectueuse—which was originally (and is even presently) more discreetly entitled *La P . . . respectueuse*—has had a comparatively more successful history. It has been turned into a film, more closely related to American gangster thrillers of the 1930s than to a document of social protest. Yet social protest, in addition to a certain amount of comedy, was what Sartre was after. In the year of its presentation, 1946, he told a UNESCO audience that he considered the Negro problem a worse social evil than any forced population removals the Russians had conducted after the war. Sartre apparently has not taken the play too seriously as an artefact since he was willing to tamper with it for a production in the USSR where Lizzie, at the end, came to her existentialist senses. The play has generally been accorded a better reception in France than it has in this book.

Pertinent writings about Heidegger's attitudes towards Nazism, along with a brief commentary, will be found in *The Worlds of Existentialism* (ed. Maurice Friedman [New York, 1964], pp. 525–33). A broader study of the German philosopher's political concerns has been done by Jean-Michel Palmier, a young French disciple of Herbert Marcuse, in *Ecrits politiques de Martin Heidegger* (Paris, 1968).

7 The Goods of This World

The argument I have been conducting in this study represents an effort to follow the development of Sartre's thought as it is expressed in his philosophical and literary works. I have been trying to isolate those moments— for there are several and, with different emphases, they recur—when an individual becomes aware of his existence as both gift and curse and reacts with corresponding ambiguity or confusion. What we have been seeing is that the sense of being cursed is stronger than the sense of being endowed. The growth of that awareness has seemed to produce only fleeting moments of pleasure which serve as a prelude to ensuing unhappiness. A reader might well wonder whether the constant reversion to such saddening results is worth the effort of following Sartre's thought, which seems relentlessly to retreat to the edge of despair. There is no doubt that Sartre believes that the search for a modus vivendi is worth the light expended; there is also no doubt that up to this point no steady light has been found. Each new source of current has been quickly exhausted, and it will not be until the *Critique de la raison dialectique* that some more reliable supply of energy will be located. At this point we are still living with damaged and despairing individuals, with long and apparently futile struggles against overwhelming odds. We have seen several types of men: those who give up before they get started; those who start and then give up; those whose commitment and patience are not enough to assure them of victory.

Roquentin took his leave of the viscous on a note of optimism audible to him alone; Mathieu took leave of his past on the promise of better future attitudes. Each revealed a kind of truth to the reader; the one that authentic moments of understanding were inevitable; the other that freedom was the only possible mode of experience and that, despite its curses, it merited being lived. Still, each took his leave before having shown *how* one lives either authentically or freely. A not unmeaningful silence falls over them when the time for continuous action approaches. By contrast with them, the greater number of characters we have encountered in Sartre's work have been defeated either because the project they had selected for their lives was unrealizable on its own terms (Hilbert, Eve and Pierre); or because the victory they thought they had won was fictitious (Lucien, Daniel, and the three characters in *Huis-clos*); or, finally, because they were convinced that liberty was a luxury available only to others (Lizzie and the Negro in *La Putain respectueuse*, the inauthentic Jew in *Réflexions sur la question juive*).

We have also heard the justification offered by the defeated or overwhelmed in explanation of their conduct and their failures: the massivenesses (*massivités* is the word Sartre uses) of a world which allows them no privileged or protected place; the threat incarnated by the Other against which one must fight if one does not wish to be engulfed in the Other's designs; the mysterious forces which hedge life with uncertainty, among which are chance and the lag between the individual's wants and the world's possibilities. *Morts sans sépulture* provided a vivid and almost ruthlessly cruel example of this, for at the end of that moving play the maquisards' efforts to find a justification for continuing to live were rendered pointless by their murder. They had argued with themselves and with others in order to convince themselves that, despite the violence they had done and the violence which had been done to them, they could rightfully look forward to the future with modestly circumscribed hopes. Expecting to live, but knowing fully the difficulties they would encounter, they were sadistically killed on orders of one of the collaborationists. Whatever difference can be seen between their courage and his abjection offers no consolation to them.

Implicit in Sartre's unyielding exposure of what seems a stacked deck, is his optimism. It may well seem, on the basis of the evidence presented so far, unjustifiable to speak of him as being optimistic. Yet what he continues to look for is some way of finding the force and justification to deny the arguments of this mass of negative evidence, to show that the apparent solutions accepted by certain individuals are no longtime solutions at all. The data accumulated so far, even as it places the evidence in a sorry light, also suggests that since life is nothing but a long agony, and human experience no more than a game carried on in the most savage jungle, the only way to survive is to become one of the strong. Rather than pretend to be nobly inspired men who seek the greatest good for the greatest number, human beings would do better to reap the profits of bad faith even at the cost of appearing disagreeable and detestable. Their personal qualities matter little if they can win for themselves the only meaningful prizes: more time and a tolerable life. Sartre's goal, which invites men to risk either their lives or their happiness in the pursuit of causes that promise them nothing better than what they already possess, is not designed to appeal to such individuals.

Since those who possess what they consider to be happiness are not readily going to yield any part of that happiness, and since those who are miserable are so because of the happy, Sartre's work seems to bring us unavoidably back to the same observation: the human enterprise, as he envisages it, cannot be brought into reality. As a result, Sartre's descriptions are not divorced from a kind of Sade-like rigor; they keep bringing us back to the futility of man. Sartre risks appearing as Nietzsche with a new but not especially promising message: there will be no more Nietzsches. He risks, too, resembling Roquentin in his lesser moments: he is the individual who has a special and therefore superior wisdom; having discovered the uselessness of any struggle, he has settled for being the chronicler of all the defeats. Historical situations, individual motivations, and social conditions may change; behind each change, there is the same permanent message—man remains the same.

Everywhere in Sartre's work we have searched for or hoped for a solution; everywhere the uncovered evidence has shown us how scant is the basis for any hope. The promised land which he espied in that early essay on Husserl—and it was indeed a promised land, for Sartre was inviting his readers to join him in a journey towards human betterment—seems further off than ever. Putting oneself in the midst of men is an act which seems only to reinforce pessimism. The paths of freedom, not necessarily glorious, have so far led through disillusion to the grave.

There are reasons for this which are more serious than a Parisian newspaper's appealing explanation that Sartre is just a nasty man. Changes in his personal life and in the political situation in France after the war were partially reflected, as I have suggested, in his decision not to finish *Les Chemins de la liberté*. In that novel Sartre had sought to implement his idea of "situation" by projecting individuals against the background of a world they could no longer bracket in ways designed to protect their egos. His hope had not only been to show the inadequacies of the characters in his first fictional works by setting them off against the example of men committed to action by the unavoidable sweep of events, but also to show that productive and generous modes of action were possible.[1] In his earlier books, his imagination had been dominated by ideas of hostility. The crisis and shock of the war justified an attempt to show that dangers which were a peril for the individual became, when they were expressed in war, dangers for everyone. As a result, the war had lessons to teach individuals, lessons which had to do with both the reality and the value of the collectivity. But the paradox of war is that it creates enthusiasm for what, in peaceful cir-

1. Not only is there a clear sense of mission behind this undertaking, there is also a wide awareness of how easily, and in the name of apparently honorable reservations, people who believe themselves to be of good will can refuse to get involved. Both Sartre and Simone de Beauvoir had lived through such a period in their own experience. About it Mme de Beauvoir writes: "On a great number of points I was— and Sartre, too, though perhaps to a lesser degree—deplorably abstract. I recognized the reality of social classes, but reacting to my father's ideologies, I used to protest whenever anyone spoke to me about the French, the Germans, or the Jews; only individual people existed. I was right in refusing to accept essentialism. I already knew the kinds of abuses that stemmed from notions like the Slavic soul; the Jewish character, the primitive mentality, the eternal feminine. But the universalism to which I was rallying carried me far away from reality. What I still did not possess was the idea of 'situation' which is the only way of getting at a concrete definition of human ensembles while avoiding the risk of subjugating them to a timeless, fatal force. But, once I had moved away from the context of the class struggle, there was no one to supply me with [the notion of situation]" (*FA*, p. 172).

cumstances, would be rejected; it reduces the dimensions of the other dangers which frighten us: my neighbor, for example, is less my enemy than the troops who are billeted in my home town.

It is those other dangers, which have recovered their original importance, that I am looking at now. One of them is death, which separates man from the collectivity and makes him question the value of any self-sacrificing commitment to that collectivity. In peacetime, he dies alone, far from any battlefield and its bloody promise of glory; in peacetime, he dies for no reason, certainly not *pour la patrie* since his demise represents no contribution except perhaps that of a space abandoned for the nation's burgeoning population. In peacetime, the collectivity may appear to do nothing for the individual save to remind him day after day that the Other is not only massively there, the Other will also survive him, comment on him, pigeonhole him, and bury him in a grave which will be his only until such time as the space is needed for others.

On this side of death, there are other obstacles which hinder the creation of a meaningful collectivity or which prevent the individual from offering his full cooperation to existing collectivities. The projected final volume of *Les Chemins de la liberté* would have offered a model of how such cooperation could be effected; it would also have attempted to show that through cooperation the individual would come to a fuller and more honest understanding of himself. What happened in the aftermath of the war was that the collectivity created by it fell apart, especially in France where members of the Resistance returned to their older and internally divisive allegiances. What had allowed for meaningful collective action during the Occupation was the existence of an external, that is, a non-French threat. When death at the hands of the Other, who has clearly declared himself the enemy, is a daily possibility, local violences may be set aside. Once that menace has withdrawn, the danger is no longer there; death at the hand of the declared enemy, like Camus's plague, has withdrawn. It may, like the plague, come back; but for the moment the threat is no longer imminent and what is not imminent is usually not thought to be important. With the war over, the collectivity formed by the Resistance no longer had a common enemy or a common threat. Individuals or infragroups moved back into their old shells; the enemy was no longer the German, the enemy was the neighbor, the fellow citizen who impeded, either by his beliefs or his actions, the progress of groups or movements to whose goals he did not ascribe.

The country then returned to a situation where the threat of death no longer had a significance for the collectivity; the implication which an individual could draw from this was that if his death had no meaning for the collectivity, then his life had little or none either. In such circumstances, a man is on his own to earn whatever he can of the goods of this world.

He is thrown back on the fact of his individual existence and private needs. With the return of national peace, the old problem comes back: the solitary man who has the slightest feeling of revolt senses at the same time that he is hardly an individual because he has no collective importance. He is a meeting place of needs and frustrations, of free purpose and limited means, of being and nothingness; no single cause or act or event explains, and thus solaces, the tensions that are at the saddened heart of his being. He has fallen back into the multiple problems raised by his *facticity*.

His basic problem is this: despite his potentiality for a life of free and perhaps freewheeling decisions, and despite the assertion that the value of his life can only be judged when he is dead and all his actions are completed, the fundamental *fact* remains that he *is* something. He is Jean, who owes his life in the newly peaceful world to the silence and death of his fellow warriors; or he is Gustave Flaubert, the son of Achille-Cléophas Flaubert, the distinguished physician who belongs to a certain class, who has certain beliefs and guiding principles, and who also has ideas of what his son should be. Once consciousness arises, or is thrown back on itself, it finds that it is surrounded by a certain number of "givens" which condition, if they do not determine, its reactions. It finds, too, if it comes to wakefulness in a bourgeois world, that it is invited to immerse itself in those givens; if it is born into the lower classes, it finds that it may have no choice save to resign itself to the dominance of whatever givens have been imposed from some higher and unattainable rung in the hierarchical ladder.

Thus man comes to awareness as a free agent who discovers the simultaneity of his freedom and the ontological conditioning of that freedom. External circumstances limit his freedom; his situation places him to a greater or lesser degree in servitude. With the discovery of these limiting conditions, he has an inkling that they cut against the grain of his freedom even as his freedom represents a threat to the stability of those conditions. He realizes, if he is Lucien, that his freedom is contingent upon the tolerance of his class. He realizes, if he is Mathieu, that one can live without or beyond the tolerance of the governing class. In rarer cases, he understands that the class's existence, if it is not exclusively dependent upon his tolerance, nevertheless is made possible only by the assent of all the members of the class. If his existence makes no sense on its own terms because it contains no inherent rhyme or reason, it makes only practical sense on the supplied terms of the surrounding milieu, since assent to the supplied terms implies dissent from the fullest expression of one's own freedom. The individual discovers that he "is an insoluble contradiction" (*Sit. I*, p. 154).

He can agree to take daily life as he finds it, to restrain (or perhaps confirm) his ego by accepting a place in the surrounding society and by giving himself over to the efficient fulfillment of his role. Or he can choose to live only for himself, inspired by hedonism or, on a higher level, a desire to perform feats no one else has performed or could have performed. By so doing he will make himself into what Sartre, in *Les Mots*, calls the most irreplaceable of beings. The individual can react uneasily to the first possibility for a number of reasons. In working cooperatively with the society, he discovers a series of what Marx called fetishes: idols of the tribe which he is invited to worship on a continuous basis and whose worship involves such restraint as produces a partial loss of the self. He becomes alienated. Or he discovers, in a highly technological society, what increasing numbers of college students believe they are discovering: he is to be the man of function, highly trained to perform efficiently in a society of complex and not easily appreciated roles. He is summoned to be a cog in a wheel so large that its overall operations cannot be seen or even understood; when he refuses the summons in an organized way, he is subpoenaed to explain why he should not be punished.

If he chooses the other option—of living only for the fullest expression of his own being—he runs other risks. In the egotistic pursuit of his own goals, he may become a menace to others—a menace not only to the oppressed, but also to those who have ample power to fight against him. In moments when his pursuit produces stress and frustration, he may fall back on the assurance provided by loyalty to the class or the assumption of a role. In more vulnerable moments, when he is aware that his capacities are not adequate to achieving his task, he may join with others in order to continue the pursuit of his program. In this instance, of course, he risks replacing one kind of limiting structure with another—a consequence Sartre discusses lengthily in the *Critique de la raison dialectique*.

The human contradiction seems unresolved, not only because of this apparent either/or choice, but also because of man's both/and nature. Man is free *and* fixed; individual human existence, if it is able to wander where it will, nonetheless has a home ground; Sartre calls it the being-in-itself of being-for-itself. Gustave is Achille-Cléophas's son, with all that that implies; he cannot *not* be Achille-Cléophas's son without raising embarrassing questions about the fidelity of his mother. And even in that case, he becomes someone else's son. But Gustave can choose not to be what Achille-Cléophas wants of his son and in that sense he will cease to be Achille-Cléophas's idea of Achille-Cléophas's son. As a free creature, man has a sense of being unrestricted, of having a capacity to transcend his initial situation and its possible limitations; yet as a being bound to be free he has the sense of immediate restriction. Freedom is not simply the power to create and deal with a situation; it is also situated, conditioned, and possibly contaminated by external circumstances. The significant question then becomes that of discovering to what extent the surrounding circumstances of one's freedom (its *facts*) influence one's behavior. Attached to this is the more worrisome fact that one cannot *not* be free to cope with and possibly control such surrounding circumstances.

Connected with this observation about the initial conditions of freedom is a very old and honorable idea of Western civilization: the worth of the individual. To say that every man is unique is to give him pleasant encouragement to believe that he is indeed an individual; but it also suggests that those individual differences which distinguish him from other men must be preserved if he is to maintain his individuality. If he is too quickly or too totally absorbed into class or group, he will no longer be himself. We encourage the individual to believe in his own worth; in so doing we may be accentuating his hostility to the Other and to his milieu. Yet simultaneously, part of his individuality is supposed to be infected with a desire to serve the greater good: he is to achieve his individual worth by losing some part of his individuality.

This is paradoxical, and the paradox is complicated each time we try to take an overall view of man or to enunciate a philosophy of man. Most philosophies, since they are inspired more by instinct than by empiricism, have sought to establish systems which accentuate what is common to men rather than the differences noticeable among them. Sartre's ultimate goal is the same, for he wishes to replace those particular points of view, which are the cause of division and hostility among men, with an idea of the collectivity which will underscore the need for men to recognize the indispensable necessity of that collectivity. The war did not succeed in doing that in any durable way, and the problem Sartre now confronts is that of imposing his point of view on a universe peopled by too many individuals too immersed in their own carefully nurtured hopes to pay much attention to his. The difficulty can be summarized in a fairly banal way: a man might expectably answer Sartre's invitation by replying, "What you want me to do is to accept your point of view and give up mine. Why should I? All hothouses work on the same principle." What they grow is another matter.

Part of the answer lies in the contradiction I have alluded to above. In escaping, in the name of personal freedom, from the restrictions of one's initial milieu one may be escaping only in order to create a more personally advantageous model of those conditions. As Hannah Arendt has pointed out, totalitarians can pass from the far Left to the far Right, from Communism to Catholicism, without ceasing to be totalitarians; the Waffen SS as well as the Harvard SDS can disrupt universities in the name of urgent, immediate, and apocalyptic reform. The assertion of one's individualism, as we shall see in the case of Hugo in *Les Mains sales*, may be made in the name of a fine goal: liberation from an oppressive class. But the result, in the end, may be similar oppression of or by others. If one is not successful in effecting the passage, as Hugo is not, one can claim that the oppressive factors were too strong and too determining.

What Sartre must now seek to do is effect a threefold strategy. Retaining faithfully the notion of unavoidable freedom, he must first show that freedom is never exercised outside a situation which conditions it and which it conditions; then, he must isolate areas where the conditioning is by its nature evil because it is interlocked with the oppression of a particular group; finally, he must indicate another kind of condition in which men would yield some part of their individuality in the name of a greater exercise of freedom for everyone—the reward will be a clearer conscience for all. Free and restricted, when not oppressed, man must find a way of creating a situation in which self-imposed restriction will be the small price paid for the disappearance of oppression.

Several elements of this notion of facticity are present in the intriguing essay which Sartre wrote in 1957 about the relationship between Tintoretto and Venice ("Le Séquestré de Venise," *Sit. IV*, pp. 291–346).

The study is concerned with Tintoretto's career, with the role his sometime mentor Titian played in his ambitions and in the possibilities open to him, with the refusal of the city to accord Tintoretto the sort of welcome he sought, and with his efforts to impose himself on the city. Finally, the essay turns to the question of the broader implications of the relationship between painter and city-state. What interests Sartre principally is the pattern of disquietude and misunderstanding he finds in the relationship. Tintoretto begins his career with a general goal he has imbibed from the city; he wishes, through his painting, to give pleasure to his fellow Venetians. The idea of pleasing the public in no way repels him; he does not seek to be a rebel and thus seems to have secured the basic qualifications for winning favor. He is not, however, without ambition. He wants fame, glory, and honor; he is also willing to work in order to obtain them. The place of honor is, unfortunately, already occupied by Titian who seems in no hurry to die and relinquish his eminent position. Titian's obstinate longevity is only one of the obstacles Tintoretto meets.

The city itself is resistant. Despite her bourgeois interests, she is a city of generally conservative aristocrats. Though she derives her wealth from commerce and must constantly seek new markets and outlets, she wants to preserve her old ways. As a young man, Tintoretto succeeds in pleasing the city as an apprentice in Titian's workshop. He is acting as the wise, docile child by associating himself with a painter whose reputation has been assured by most of the crowned heads of Europe. But Tintoretto does not stay in Titian's atelier, and there is some evidence that he was dismissed because the older painter saw in him a threat to his privileges. Despite the rupture with Titian, Tintoretto continues to please the city with his first works. He even manages to win that rarest of favors: Aretino's compliments. But slowly the attitude of the city changes as she discovers what she considers a "vulgar" side to Tintoretto's ambition; the docile child has too much of it and will resort to any maneuver in order to impose himself on the public. When a certain brotherhood chooses not to buy his paintings, he offers them as a gift, knowing full well that the group cannot refuse donations. Any ruse is valid in his effort to keep himself in the limelight, and his desire to woo and win the city is so great that he will not accept commissions which come from elsewhere. He lives in order to please Venice, and Venice more and more seems to want no part of him.

The city, having formed him and having refused to accept his offers and his work, is rejecting her own creature; she thereby robs him of the chance of reaching the goal she has instilled in him. Her refusal is based on an insight which may be no more than a vague appreciation that something in the painter's work undermines the city's conservative vision of herself. Similarly, his artistic vision imprints his work with elements which confirm the city's disquiet. City and painter see dimly in each other traces of a dissolution which neither is willing to avow.

According to Sartre each has established an impossible goal, because each has sought to stave off the changes produced by the indispensable and ever-present dynamism of life. Tintoretto's vision of the city contradicts the city's idea of herself, for Venice is seeking to preserve an idea of her structure that is mocked by her commercial involvements. Though she wishes to remain an aristocratic center, she is in fact becoming bourgeois; commerce holds an increasingly important place, producing new facts and forces the aristocrats preferred not to see. Since those forces find expression in Tintoretto's works, the city has either to close her eyes to what she sees or to deny her approbation to the painter. Consciously or not, he expresses on canvas the forces of that future against which the aristocrats are fighting a holding action. What he sees is the growing importance of a new type of endeavor and an almost Calvinist emphasis on work and productivity.

The disparity cut deep precisely because the aristocrats saw in Tintoretto's work the disquiet they were trying to ignore in their lives: their class was being driven to extinction as the dominant force in the life of the city. Tintoretto's paintings thus became the symbol of their liquidation, for what he expressed on canvas was the passage of traditional art and the arrival of new, violent, and tempestuous forms. Common to both painter and the city was a reaction to a thoroughly novel situation which, beginning in the sixteenth century, was to become the great new force of the modern consciousness and the cause of its anguish. The traditional absolutes, and the stability they provided, were passing away with the aristocracy. An old order was falling, and whatever new order was forming had not yet provided enough information, did not yet have a clear enough shape, to allow spectators to know what it would be. Against the unknown, the Venetians preferred to hold on to what they already possessed. Tintoretto, seeing more deeply and perhaps more innocently, was less aware of the imminence of loss even though he was one of its agents.

The disparity between the painter and his native city had to do with more than social change, however; it had also to do with a change that would strip away order and replace it with a force which, when compared to the order, could only be identified as chaos. As Tintoretto had accepted the role of giving pleasure to the public and as he had gone in pursuit of the means which would allow him to fulfil that role, so the city had accepted the role of preserving the values she had received. City and painter thus resemble each other in their efforts to strike impossible bargains. Each has lived dynamically—the city pursuing her commercial interests, the artist realizing his artistic vision; but each has tried to deny the ultimate consequences of that dynamism—the city by thinking she can possess two contradictory worlds at once, the painter by seeking favor through paintings bound to disturb his public beyond any possibility of pleasure.

As far as Sartre is concerned, Venice was more culpable than Tintoretto since she had not only her own inklings of the disturbing future which she was preparing for herself, she also had a verification of her foresight in the painter's work. But Tintoretto himself was not altogether innocent since, despite his fidelity to his insights, and his awareness that he was painting in a world where God no longer justified the painter's vocation, he was seeking from the city the assurance he could no longer obtain from an absent God. The city fell back on God, or more exactly on the idea of pattern and purpose she derived from belief in God, in order to reassure herself. Tintoretto, knowing that no God could justify him, fell back on the city and sought her assurance against his own disquietude. For the city to have given him what he sought, the city would have had to admit the appropriateness of his request and thereby, in reassuring him, admit that there was no God, no sure base to assure her of her own justification.

In this essay, Sartre is stressing that in a world without sure ideological or theological moorings, men cannot assert their freedom and simultaneously lean on inherited beliefs. Both Venice and Tintoretto sought to assure themselves of a mandate which validated and justified their particular enterprises. But, in those enterprises, each showed, the one by her dedication to the pursuit of new markets, the other by his fidelity to his inspiration, the basic contradiction of every effort to establish a stable base for unstable and mobile existence. In the end each canceled the other out and was left defeated, with its original disquietude magnified.

Painter and city have each had an idea of what they are and a project for what they want to be. The disparity in each case is the disparity between the two poles of the self-description; what one is and what one wishes to be does not make sufficient allowance for what one may become. The Cartesian formula, "I think therefore I am," does not necessarily yield a third clause to define more precisely the range of the second. On the contrary, the formula places thinking man at the edge of unexplored terrains which he must traverse as best he can and with whatever honesty or dishonesty he finds useful. The Cartesian assertion, whatever its goal, is forward-moving and not recuperative; we know that that was Descartes' intention since he wished to break with the categories and claustrophobic systems of the scholastic philosophers. What I am tells me very little about what I may be; the fact that I am does, however, allow me to employ whatever tools or weapons I can lay my hands on in order to help me negotiate my way through the slopes, crags, and plains of the future. By contrast Montaigne's implied question, "What am I?" allows for almost nothing except tomes of essays. The search for a less voluminous answer to Montaigne's upsetting question is the central preoccupation of *Kean* (1954).

Theater concerned with theater, plays within plays, the use of illusion to comment on illusion, essays about the reality of the actor's stage-actions—these matters are no novelty in our literary tradition and may even be one of its staler staples. From *Hamlet*, through Diderot's meditations in the *Paradoxe sur le comédien*, to the majority of Pirandello's plays such issues have been the stuff of theater; concern with a kind of schizophrenia, incarnated in the actor, which catches the division between reality and the imagination has allowed those who are stimulated by such questions to worry them more than perhaps any actor has.

Sartre's curiosity about the nature of theater predates his first plays. In an early book, he had alluded to the role of emotions in the theater and observed that ". . . the actor mimics joy and sadness, but he *is neither* joyful *nor* sad because this kind of behavior is addressed to a fictitious universe. He mimics behavior but he is not behaving" (*Emotions*, p. 72). In somewhat the same vein of reservation about the reality of the theater, he had written a conversation between Roquentin and Anny in *La Nausée* in which he suggests that the theater was a means whereby Anny, an actress, achieved some of her "perfect moments." But she had rejected them for a number of reasons: one was that they were perfect moments created for others; another was her increasing temptation to laugh aloud while she was acting; and a third was her realization that "the essential for all of us was that black hole in front of us and at the end of which there were people we didn't see; they were the ones, of course, to whom we were presenting perfect moments" (p. 191).

His own experience in writing plays and his study of Jean Genet may very well have changed or developed these notions, for *Kean* shows that while the actor may be mimicking behavior on the stage he may also be establishing an otherwise unavailable perspective on behavior. The play shows, too, that perfect moments, organized in the theater for the benefit of the spectators, may not be very different from perfect moments organized in daily life for the deception of the Other or, in more precise terms, for the deception of a Roquentin. It shows, finally—and here the influence of Genet is clear—that the theater has uses not only as a commentary on life or as a perspective on human conduct, but also as a force shaping life. If theater symbolizes life, the old question of a division between reality and the imagination, between spectator and stage, is irrelevant, especially if one can show that in life, as in the theater—but with less honesty—one is always playing roles.[2]

The Alexandre Dumas play upon which *Kean* is based has really nothing to do with such issues. It is concerned with inserting a bare minimum of social protest into a wobbly romantic framework which has to do with the unhappy disorder produced by genius. In that sense, it is a hack repeat of a tired and possibly false concern with the man of genius as one who, possessed by some vague daimon, risks embarrassing others and threatening his own stability. In the end love comes to impose a promise of order; the hierarchical organization of society, having been gently assailed, presumably remains unchanged. Sartre surely must have considered this an example of bad faith—Dumas is playing with explosive issues which he drops as soon as a match is brought too close. Sartre must also have been much attracted by the temptation to play with the Dumas play in order to show how much Dumas had played with reality; for play—that is, the conscious assumption of roles—is essentially what *Kean* is about. As Sartre plays with Dumas, so his characters play with and against each other; by playing or pretending, each is seeking either to confront or avoid reality. And Sartre is suggesting that reality will express itself most exactly in the interplay between the efforts to avoid it and the efforts to confront it.

The play's point of departure is the conflict between a world which follows its ways happily and an individual who is allowed to entertain that world and even to associate with it, if he remembers to keep his place. As he acts on the stage, so he must act in upper-class society. He is the gentle victim who need never feel his victimization so long as he accepts it; but he is also the man who has used his talent to win a place for himself and

---

2. Sartre later looks at the broad issue involved here from two other angles of vision. In *SG* he discusses the use of imagined gestures as the basis for real actions; he writes: "*In reality*, Genet steals because he's a thief; *in the imaginary*, he steals in order to become a thief. Consequently, he derealizes himself entirely, he rivets his attention on a fictive interpretation of his behavior, he becomes an actor" (p. 350). In the *CRD* he discusses a somewhat more conscious process—what is involved when an actor, like Jean-Louis Barrault, interprets Hamlet—and writes: "It cannot be denied that the undertaking of the imaginary prince expresses in a certain devious and refracted way his real undertaking, nor can it be denied that the way in which he believes himself to be Hamlet is his fashion of knowing himself to be an actor" (p. 38). ". . . the truth of the imaginary praxis is in the real praxis and the former, to the extent that it acknowledges itself as imaginary, contains an implicit return reference to the latter as though to its interpretation" (p. 39).

who thereby has discovered that the free use of skill is not enough to carry him beyond all obstacles. He has discovered that ". . . if freedom is defined as the escape from the given, from fact, then there is a *fact* of escape from fact. This is the facticity of freedom" (*BN*, p. 485). He has escaped from poverty into glory of a limited kind, limited because he has also learned that if it is true that "we can be nothing without playing at being" (*BN*, p. 83), it is also true that the games we play are hedged by rules. Having experienced his freedom, Kean wants to change the rules because the rules, since they exclude him at what he considers an arbitrary point, place unjustifiable limits on his freedom and thus on his sense of existence.[3]

Kean is a play concerned with the limits placed not only on social ambition and the exercise of freedom, but also on all the other possibilities which tempt man and eventually restrict him. It deals with lies—lies that hurt and lies that help; with function—when does an actor cease being an actor and an ambassador an ambassador? with the refusal to play roles and with the kind of role-playing which is a refusal of life. In dealing with limits, it deals with puzzles and thus profits from being concerned on the surface with the conflict between the actor's role as a professional pretender and his existence as an unacceptable pretender to the rights of a class whose tolerance of one kind of pretense does not imply tolerance of other kinds.

The play works because the problem is very much that of the Kean who is created sympathetically in the play; but it works, too, because Kean's problem is presented as a metaphor for the problem of all men who run into obstacles and limits which make them recognize that, all the world being a stage, some men are inevitably invited to play parts not necessarily of their own choosing. This is a truth Sartre will never get around to denying outright; here he simply wants to air it and make it visible to others as a poetic insight which differs from a philosophic one by protesting against this truth instead of explaining it. In the *Critique de la raison dialectique,* Sartre will return to this insight again, not to deny it, but to redefine and redistribute the roles and to encourage the endless analysis and, where necessary, the rewriting, of the script. The verbal and ideological plays around these issues go on throughout the play and add as much to

3. In *SG*, discussing a somewhat similar situation in which Genet seeks through gestures to establish his reality and position, Sartre writes: "Mircea Eliade tells us that in archaic and traditional ontology 'reality is acquired exclusively by *repetition* or *participation*; whatever does not have an exemplary model is "devoid of sense," that is, lacks reality. . . . the man of traditional culture recognizes himself as being real only insofar as he ceases to be himself . . . and is content with *imitating* and *repeating* the gesture of another. In other words, he recognizes himself as being real, that is, as "truly himself" only insofar as he ceases precisely to be so' " (pp. 328–29). (The quote is from Eliade's *Myth of the Eternal Return*.) That Sartre should quote Eliade does not mean that Sartre subscribes to Eliade's general theories. The historian of religion and the scribe of religion's demise do, however, agree that the fundamental anguish of modern man is due in significant part to the loss of religion and with it the sense of a specific and available sense or meaning in life.

the fun as to the profundity. *Kean* is the work of Sartre in a jovial mood, the fun-loving Sartre Mme de Beauvoir alludes to in those unintentionally mournful portraits she draws in her memoirs; yet, for all its wit and good spirits, the play is about essentially serious issues.

At the very beginning of the play, Eléna, the ambassador's wife whom Kean is attempting to seduce, asks whether there is *a Kean*, by which she means: which of the characters he interprets gives the best indication of the real Kean? And by which she also means: how much of the real Kean dwells in the several Keans who most tempt her? She pursues the issue later with the Prince of Wales when, in response to the Prince's statement that Kean is an illusion of a man whom women pursue, she asks (p. 29):

> *Eléna*: An illusion? Does that mean that he isn't a man?
> *The Prince*: Why no, madam. He's an actor.
> *Eléna*: Well, then, what's an actor?
> *The Prince*: A mirage.

She then asks if princes are not also mirages, but her question is deflected by a flirtatious remark from the Prince and the almost immediate arrival of Kean. The basic terms of the "problem" have been supplied along with implications: if an actor is someone who acts, and if what he acts out produces mirages, then what is there in the nature of his action that differentiates it from those actions which apparently are not mirages—the actions, for example, by which a man indicates that he is a prince? The further implication, of course, is that all actions may be no more than mirages, man-made to be sure, but manufactured nonetheless to be deliberate, enticing, and enviable deceptions.

The Prince can readily define what another man is and can shrewdly deflect leading questions whose answers might define the Prince himself. Kean, unfortunately, does not possess the same facility. He can supply glib comments; what he cannot do is believe them, because he lives as an individual who has *made* his function and, unlike the Prince, not as one who received it at birth. Because his function is not hereditary, it lacks the respect accorded to those which are part of a birthright. While the source of his resentment is clear, his methods of explaining or dealing with the source are not. By attributing the difference in roles to accidents of birth, he seeks an external explanation which his valet-manager, Salomon, will not accept: men are men and not overgrown children. At other moments Kean seems to be trying to convince himself that he likes his role. Addressing invisible flowers—they are not visible because Kean hasn't enough money to buy them—he says: "I like ruling over mirages, and I like you all the more because you do not exist" (p. 45).

But because the others who limit him do exist, they are not mirages; he then tries to establish a special relation between them and him: "Do you think they *pay* me to perform? I am their priest: each evening I celebrate mass and each week I receive their offerings" (p. 52). He is the celebrant at the mysteries other men need. That observation, which might make him feel superior, is compromised by his belief that those other men, for whom he creates indispensable illusions, have created him in order to serve that function: "They take a child and change him into a trompe l'oeil. . . . I am a fake prince, a fake minister, a fake general. . . . Can't you see that what I want is to have my own weight count in this world?" (pp. 64–65). The only place where his true weight seems to make itself felt is on the beds of other men's wives. There are limits even to that role since his desire to seduce an ambassador's wife creates political difficulties and leads the Prince of Wales to order him to desist. But there is another and sadder limit which he does not discover until later. With whom are the women he seduces having intercourse: with Kean? or Hamlet? or Romeo? or Othello?

In an alcoholic moment, when wine produces truth in its almost impenetrable complexity, he announces: "I am playing at being what I am" (p. 75), a phrase which, if turned about to read "I am what I play at being" would help to explicate the fundamental and paradoxical truth. Fundamental, because acting is an act which represents something; paradoxical, because, despite his protests, what Kean is actually seeking is being—a fixed identity and not the stock of characters over which his ego wanders evening after evening, like Hansel and Gretel in the forest, looking for nourishment. He wants a function that is less fluid and more precise than the one he has, a function which will define him as a being possessed of the same rights and privileges as the other beings with whom he associates. He subsequently catches all the contradictions of his project when he says:

> One doesn't act [the word throughout is *jouer*] in order to earn his living. You act in order to lie and to lie to yourself, in order to be what you can't be and because you're fed up with what you are. You act in order not to know yourself and because you know yourself too well. You play a hero because you're a coward and a saint because you're a sinner; you play a murderer because you're dying of envy to kill your neighbor. . . . You act because you would go mad if you didn't. You act. And do I really know when I'm acting? (p. 81).[4]

This is a fine portrait of Sartrean man, for whom each action has a purpose and a motive that is speedily undone or which immediately produces further frustration once the action is completed. It is precisely what Kean does

4. Cf. *SG*: "Genet's world resembles that of the chronic paranoic: while playing his own role, he helps Stilitano [a criminal Genet desires] play his, he tries to find for him situations and types of behavior which enable him to *appear*" (p. 317).

not want to be, since what really tempts him is the desire to possess the kind of fixed being he thinks identifies the members of the upper classes.

When he returns briefly to the milieu of knockabout actors from which he comes, he senses that he has returned home, gone back to what he is. What he is really experiencing is the importance he has for them, an importance he attributes to the fact that they look upon him as a man; still that feeling cannot be isolated from the impact his success has had on them. He meets them as their superior, a better, because a more renowned, actor. And he is unsettled when Anna, the wealthy young woman who is pursuing him, follows him into this world. She is an intruder both because she comes wearing a mask, offering him yet another role to play, and because she is identified in his eyes with that other which spurns him. Still, drawing assurance from the milieu in which he is superior, he contemplates avidly an encounter with the nobleman who, in turn, is pursuing Anna. "I can pummel him! I can really pummel a nobleman. That's been my dream" (p. 108). It remains a dream because the nobleman refuses to admit that an actor can engage in such diversions with a peer of the realm. Kean is immobilized by this assertion; and though he knows he can still pummel the nobleman if he so chooses, he retreats towards rhetorical victory, telling the nobleman: "You are free to withdraw" (p. 112). It is a fine gesture of noblesse oblige; a sourer interpreter would assert that it is the nobleman who has been convenienced and not Kean who has obliged.

Kean cannot escape theatrical gestures because what is deliberately done in the theater is also deliberately done in daily life, though with less art and weaker consciousness than in the theater and generally in the absence of influential critics. Ambassadors play at being ambassadors, princes at being princes. Ambassadors' wives play offstage at being Desdemona with the man who, onstage, has interpreted Othello; their hope is that, in the two-way shift, the Moor become ordinary man will forget the play's ending while supplying most of its thrills. Businessmen's daughters decide that they want to be actresses and, more incredibly yet, actors' wives. Everyone hides his motives and creates those of others. A clear dividing line, not between the stage and the spectator, but between reality and imagination *everywhere*, exists perhaps only in the theater.[5]

At the climax of the play, Kean, who is acting in a play within the play—the scene is Drury Lane where he is interpreting *Othello*—reaches across the footlights of the Shakespeare play in order to challenge the spectators who are, of course, other actors in Sartre's play. Here Sartre is trying to isolate two levels of utterance. The first is the utterance of the Shake-

5. Cf. *SG*: ". . . when action is repressed by the world, it is internalized and de-realized, it is play-acting; reduced to impotence, the agent becomes an actor. Such is precisely the case of Genet: his idle will never moves into the realm of the imaginary; he becomes an actor despite himself and his rejection of the world is only a gesture" (p. 345).

spearean play, which is a symbol because what Kean-Othello is experiencing provides information about what Kean-Kean feels. The other level is that of the connections which exist between the play, *Othello*, and what is happening in its audience, where Eléna, talking loudly to the Prince of Wales, is trying to arouse Kean's jealousy.

What is happening on the stage has the reality of an artwork which is concerned with jealousy and, in Sartrean terms, with what happens when individuals like the Moor retreat into their emotions. What is happening in Eléna's loge in the audience has to do with playacting in real life, with the use of real but dishonestly motivated actions to provoke genuine emotional responses. What is happening between the stage and the loge, once Kean stops playing Othello in order to play Kean, is real: this is genuine fury and, as he moves from playing Kean into playing Othello and from playing Othello into playing Kean, this may be the authentic Kean. And the fury of the genuine Kean produces results: the play on the stage stops, as does the playacting on Eléna's part.[6] Kean, claiming that he is king in his theater, tells the Prince of Wales that the play will not go on unless the Prince keeps quiet. The public, goaded by the nobleman Kean had hoped to pummel, turns away from the actor, making him realize that he is alone in his fury. He discovers that his audience's love for him is not as boundless as he had supposed.

Summing up the situation he says: "*Voici l'homme.* Look at him. Aren't you going to applaud? *((Hisses.)* Still, it is funny: you like only what's false" (p. 166). The *Voici l'homme* repeats Daniel's *Ecce homo*, but it offers an entirely different kind of man since Kean at this point is refusing roles whereas Daniel was accepting one. What Kean has seen is that the role is a straitjacket: on the stage you must recite the lines of the play; in society you must recite the lines expected by others. Once you refuse to say those lines, you will be hissed because, by wanting to speak independently, you become a threat. He goes on to tell them that Kean died at an early age and is met with laughter. But when he tells them "You're the ones who took a child in order to make a monster of him" (p. 166), there is "frightened silence in the audience." That accusation could be a tidy summary

---

6. Jeanson comments: "What Sartre is condemning, through the magic of the play, is the 'magic' attitude of the man who has taken on a certain faith, who has allowed himself to be possessed by a role or by a mission, and who allows himself to be endlessly dizzied and blinded in order to be able *to take seriously* characters who are dressed in similar garb. Though it is a theater concerned with freedom, the Sartrean theater is at one and the same time concerned with *bad faith*. For bad faith is not an evil which overcomes us by accident; it is the original situation of every consciousness because that consciousness is free" (*Sartre par lui-même*, pp. 114–15). There is good reason to claim that while the profit Kean draws from his rage does not cancel out Sartre's theory of the emotions, it does suggest an adjustment in it. In this play, Sartre seems to be indicating that there are emotional moments when the sheer expense of energy produces an encounter with real situations and motivations; under other circumstances the encounter might never come about.

of the theme of Sartre's study of Jean Genet, and the silence and fright
of the stage audience are clearly meant to suggest that Kean has touched
at a deep truth which, when discovered, throws into question the kind of
formation society gives to the young and the sort of reaction it expects from
them.[7] At the end of his tirade, Kean does not quite know what he has accomplished, but he does know what he has discovered: "I don't really exist,
I've only been a pretense" (p. 166).

One of the reasons why he doesn't exist is that he does not want to and
has sought not to. His anguish over who he is has at least kept him existing,
because the question of who he is has been a recurrent one. What he and
the others discover in the last act is that, for the most part, none of them
has wanted to exist. Eléna, her husband, and the Prince of Wales have
roles rather than functions, and they have been happy to play them; Kean's
desire to enjoy a freedom like theirs has in effect been a desire for just
another role. In crucial moments, the others break out of their roles: Eléna
under Kean's prodding, for he has had too much of making plays with her
when he thought he was making plays at her; the ambassador when he
thinks his wife has been unfaithful—dignity disintegrates under the rage
of the potential cuckold. In the last act, Eléna misquotes the Prince of
Wales's earlier comment about Kean when she says that "an actor is a reflection [as in a mirror]" (p. 192); what the Prince had earlier said was
that the actor is a mirage. The slip is no accident, however, for the Prince's
definition needs Eléna's astute gloss: actors reflect real characters, as plays
reflect real situations. They do so in order that, by playing, they can present spectators with images of the amount of play that goes on in all life.

There are some who will not see, and the Prince of Wales is one of them.
He alone at the end of the play has learned nothing; what especially he
has not learned is that, despite the social distance he keeps between himself
and Kean, he can desire only the women Kean has desired. In order to keep
the Prince happy and blind at the end of the play, Kean and Anna must
lie to him by insisting that Kean still loves Eléna, who has rebuffed him.[8]

7. The same idea is presented in *SG*: "Once upon a time, in Bohemia, there was a
flourishing industry which seems to have fallen off. One would take children, slit
their lips, compress their skulls and keep them in a box all day and night to prevent
them from growing. As a result of this and similar treatment, the children were
turned into amusing monsters who brought in handsome profits. A more subtle
process was used in the making of Genet, but the result is the same: they took a child
and made a monster of him for reasons of social utility. If we want to find the real
culprits in this affair, let us turn to the decent folk and ask them by what strange
cruelty they made of a child their scapegoat" (p. 23). Later, in his introduction to
André Gorz's *Le Traître* (*Sit. IV*, pp. 54–55), Sartre takes up this idea again and
speaks of the effort made by all societies, primitive and sophisticated, to form children who will defend already established values. If the child accepts the value, he
finds an identity; in the bargain, he is too often degraded.

8. Cf. *SG*: "Genet can say: 'I am Stilitano' as Emily Bronte's hero said: 'I am Heath-
cliff'. He is Stilitano, as much as is Stilitano himself, since the one seeks to appropriate

Though she lies at the end, and forces Kean to support her lies, Anna, throughout the play, has been the only major character who has shown a sound understanding of what reality is. She has seen Kean's limitations in the theater—under the influence of alcohol he tends to slip from one role into another—and her keen observations there, as elsewhere, indicate that in purusing him she knows what she is after. She also knows what she is offering: a chance to play a human role with someone who will respect him because she loves him. There is more to her than her wit and more to what she offers than the conventions demanded by the theater. For Anna represents a new kind of character in Sartre's work and, especially, a new kind of woman: the woman who is open-eyed and steady before the general confusions of life and the particular confusions in the man she loves. As a result, she represents a kind of feminine force which heralds a significant development in Sartre's theory of love. In *Being and Nothingness*, he had drawn a rather dismal portrait of love as a choice between sadistic and masochistic maneuvers (see below, pp. 251ff.). Here love is both the way out of old confusions and stubborn lies and the beginning of a more honest future.

Kean's claim that the formation he received as a child had made a monster of him might have the power to silence an audience and bring its fears to the surface; it is not yet an excuse acceptable to Sartre. That Kean can formulate such a statement, that he can break out of the boundaries society has set for him, that he can decide to marry Anna—these are facts which compromise the accuracy or the irremediability of the basic fact. The monster can cease being a monster. Any claim of facticity—his assertion that he has been *made* by those other influences—must also recognize the facticity of being-for-itself: it can effect change or offer resistance. Man does not come into the world with the choice of being; he comes into the world free. That freedom is the condition he can never renounce. We can no more choose not to be free than we could have chosen not to exist.

This is the situation which confronts Hoederer and Hugo in *Les Mains sales*, a play which predates *Kean* by seven years. Hoederer, a Communist chieftain in disfavor with the more dogmatic members in his party, never questions whether the human condition—relentless freedom—is pleasant; he lives with it. Hugo, the young bourgeois who has joined the Communist party, does practically nothing else. He does not want to *live* free; he wants to *be* free only in that moment or in those moments when the exercise of freedom will give him what he wants—an absolute. Hugo's trouble is that he does not exactly know that he wants absolute direction; indeed he does not often seem to know what he wants. He would like to profit from certain

by amorous practices the ideal hero whom the other is attempting to copy in his bearing. They exchange gestures" (p. 325).

specific acts in order to attain a state wherein further action would not be necessary. His choice of the Communist party has less to do with a desire to help the party achieve its program than with a need to get away from a background which, having hampered him, still haunts him. His enlistment is thus based on a contradiction. Revulsion with his past and the moral claustrophobia it has produced leads him to join the party. This would be laudable conduct were he not seeking from the party another but more comfortable form of claustrophobia; for what he seeks from the party is a program of action which certifies his condemnation of his past and thus justifies his rupture with his family. The very structure of the play indicates the form of facticity which fascinates Hugo: it is the past as the inescapable burden, but also as the bunker of accomplished fact to which one falls back. If he hates the past, he is also fascinated with its fixity, its perfection, its apparent clarity.

The play unfolds in time present. Hugo is in Olga's room, having been released from prison where he has been serving time for the murder of Hoederer. Olga, a party functionary, must determine whether he is reliable enough to be reintegrated into the party. The play is thus spent in a review of what happened when Hugo, who had become Hoederer's secretary in order to murder him, succeeded in that aim. What were his intentions then, and what is his attitude now, when the party which caused Hoederer's death has turned to praising him? Because of that metamorphosis, which relates crucially to the nature of his act, Hugo is once more gazing into the past. In the flashback which reproduces his relations with Hoederer we find the second level of the past. For as Hugo, in dealing with possibilities which open before him on his release from prison, thinks back to his past with Hoederer, so the Hugo who had become Hoederer's secretary was continually thinking back to his past with his family. The play, as a result, has to do with a whole life and not simply with the single incident around which the initial action revolves.

No one of Hugo's projects—and, in a way, he has only one—looks to the future. They are all designed as a response to a past in which he had known the classical experience of the Sartrean protagonist: the sentiment of being surplus being, of having been shaped by others, of wanting to reshape himself in such a way as to lose the traces of that other formation, of hoping to escape from hazard by enclosing himself in some impenetrable shell. His intention in joining the Communist party was to associate himself with the workers in their fight for justice, but he also hoped to escape from those who oppressed the workers and to have that escape consecrated by the workers; in that way his past would be condemned by those whose approval he needs. Though he breaks all ties with his family, he retains a silk bathrobe and, what is more important, photographs which assure him, when such assurance is needed, that his past did take place and under pampered conditions.[9] He begins to work with and for those suffering others; but he is not at ease in his new situation because the workers are profoundly suspicious of him—he has joined the party voluntarily and not because he had no other choice; the militants will not allow him to undertake a daring act which, in proving his valor, might conceivably, at least in his eyes, make him superior to them.[10] Instead he is given a newspaper post where, rather than performing his own acts, he chronicles the acts of others. Finally, he convinces the directors of the party to let him become Hoederer's secretary and carry out the mission of killing Hoederer before he can make an unsavory deal with reactionary forces in the country.

Up to this point, Hugo has not accomplished very much. The act he is going to perform is ultimately one of obedience. He does not know the reasons for Hoederer's policies; the only reasons he possesses are those he has received from the branch of the party with which he is associated. He unquestioningly assumes that those are right reasons. What happens when he meets Hoederer is that he encounters free man; the result is one Sartre had described in *Being and Nothingness*: ". . . the appearance among the objects of *my* universe of an element of disintegration in that universe is what I mean by the appearance of man in my universe. . . . suddenly an object has appeared which has stolen the world from me" (*BN*, p. 255). The result is disarray. From the disarray comes a dilemma: Hugo either carries out his mission and thereby shows himself to be an obedient inferior, or he lives in the independence which Hoederer incarnates and to which Hoederer invites him. He thus would acknowledge Hoederer as the Other but with a significant difference, for Hoederer is the Other who recognizes the anguish which the discovery of the Other produces within man.

Hoederer is also a man who has abandoned everything; there are no childhood photos in his valise, no silk bathrobes in his closet. He does not drag his past behind him as the cocoon into which he can retreat when the present becomes difficult. And, to make him especially annoying to Hugo, he has great compassion for those men who hold onto the traces and evidence of their past. Hoederer is a man who lives fully conscious of the range of freedom; as such, he is the only completely authentic

9. Cf. *BN*: "The for-itself discovers itself as engaged in being, hemmed in by being, threatened by being; it discovers the state of things which surrounds it as the cause for a reaction of defence or attack. But it can make this discovery only because it freely posits the end in relation to which the state of things is threatening or favorable" (pp. 487–88).

10. These are Hugo's *motives* and about motives Sartre has written: "I can have motives: a feeling of pity or charity for certain classes of the oppressed, a feeling of shame at being on the 'good side of the barricade', as Gide says, or again an inferiority complex, a desire to shock my relatives, etc.," (*BN*, p. 447). Sartre makes this comment in the context of a discussion of the fact that motives do not necessarily become causes, that is, they do not lead to appropriate action.

character in the play. Because of his honesty, he is both an ideal and an obstacle for Hugo. He is an obstacle because he can exercise the same kind of influence on Hugo as Hugo's father had. He is an ideal because he represents the individual who, while independent of others, still works in the interest of those others. He is what Hugo would like to be and at the same time what Hugo can never be, for Hugo could never live with such unstructured freedom.

The relations between the two men are modeled on the relations which existed between Hugo and his family, though Hoederer is not aware of the resemblance. Such things do not concern him; they concern Hugo entirely too much. There is a moment when Hugo thinks he has found a solution: he can work with Hoederer because he recognizes that, even though Hoederer is superior, his superiority is cut with compassion as a bitter wine is cut with perfumed water. He can also work with him, and this is perhaps the stronger motive, because he is convinced that Hoederer is stronger than the members of his wing of the party. By associating himself with Hoederer, he will be drawing closer to the powers who really rule in the world.

As I have said, Hugo does not wish to act in order to act again; he seeks a single act which will fix his nature for the rest of his life. At a critical moment, when he decides to model his life on Hoederer's, his act becomes an acceptance of dependence. It is an honest act since he has always needed to be subordinate, if only to have something to protest against. It is a beneficial act since he will still be working for a good cause. And it will be a wise act since Hoederer respects him. In Hoederer, Hugo finds the father he has been looking for: a father who is tolerant, kind, and apparently unpaternal. The respect Hoederer shows for him keeps him from feeling that he is the child he always was with his family and that he still is with his wife, Jessica, a spoiled, sensual woman who takes neither him nor his talk seriously. They are quite consciously playmates in a stop-and-go game which they undertake everytime reality comes too close; Jessica wins most of the time. For Olga and the other militants of the intransigent branch of the party, Hugo is an inferior. They don't take him too seriously either; they are skeptical of his endurance and uncertain about his ability to carry out the mission he has been assigned. It was not a lack of perception which led them to baptize him Raskolnikoff—the man of theory who is so little acquainted with action as to be overly familiar with self-pity.

Since Hoederer respects him, Hugo is tempted to respect Hoederer; the temptation, of course, goes beyond his sentiments for Hoederer and touches on Hugo's freedom. Respect for Hoederer further dampens his already soggy resolve to kill him, and pushes Hugo to a point where shooting Hoederer will have to be an act totally his rather than obedience to orders issued by others. Ironically, the Hoederer he respects has little to do with the real Hoederer. What Hugo seeks in him is a fixed quantity, a massive resolve, the same kind of solidity and set function he detects in a coffee urn. He does not see Hoederer as a free man who faces situations as best he can, manipulating and maneuvering in order to win the best advantage, concerned less with ultimate success than with the solid try.[11] Hugo cannot see this because the last thing in the world he wants is an open situation.

The situation which Hoederer is trying to exploit is an example of this, for Hoederer knows that only through compromise can he keep the future open for Communist operations. The other political forces in Ilyria are not yet clay he can work; they are forces he must work with in the hope that his greater skill will one day reduce them to malleable clay or useless dust. This shocks Hugo's sense of purity; he had wanted cleanliness and not compromises, clean hands and not the grime that Hoederer plunges into because there is no other way ahead except through the grime. But shock only produces immobility; in a situation where he could easily kill Hoederer, he is paralyzed by Hoederer's confidence that impurity is the garb necessity has chosen as the staple of its wardrobe.

Hugo's obsession with purity is at the base of all his difficulties and uncertainties. He tells himself that his concern has to do with the pursuit of justice and the improvement of human conditions; but Hoederer reminds him that that kind of purity does not seek to change the world so much as to blow it to smithereens. And that, imprecisely but surely, is what Hugo wants to do. The world remains the place where he must live in company with the Other who makes him ashamed. And Hugo is haunted by the dream of another better world where he would exist in the kind of moral comfort that would make him, if not the king de jure, at least the boss de facto.

When Olga asks him *why* he finally did kill Hoederer, Hugo pretends that he has no answer and describes his act as though it had been committed either by a hypnotic or a robot: "An act happens too fast. It gets away from you brusquely, and you don't know whether it's because you wanted to do it or because you couldn't control it. The fact is that I shot him" (p. 33). Yet, to the spectator, the motives of Hugo's act are transparent. In discovering Hoederer caressing Jessica, he had the impression of being played, not so much for the cuckold, as for the fool; Hoederer's kindness was only a cover for his scorn and sexual desires. Once more reduced to the position of an inferior—father has been asserting his superiority again—he reacts as an infant: all of Hoederer's ideas are false and dangerous because Hoederer's real attitude towards him is not what it should have been. At the moment when he shoots Hoederer, Hugo hates

11. Cf. *BN*: ". . . our freedom . . . constitutes the limits which it will subsequently encounter" (p. 482). ". . . success is not important to freedom. . . . the choice . . . supposes a commencement of realization in order that the choice may be distinguished from the dream and the wish . . ." (p. 483).

him as the sulky child hates the parent who has just reprimanded him. He falls back on the act, defined by others, that he had originally volunteered to perform. But when he shoots Hoederer, he is acting dishonestly since his intention is not to kill a rebellious party chieftain, but rather the Other who scorns him from a position of authority and paternalism.

The question with which the play begins is whether Hugo is still of some use to the party. It is a question which poses a paradox rather than a dilemma because Hugo has made one small step forward. He recognizes Hoederer's value as a free man. Hoederer remains the authoritative figure in his life. But Hugo's fascination with immobility also lingers on. He wants now to become the guardian of Hoederer's image even if that role demands that he sacrifice himself. While he does not want to change the nature of his act—if he has any idea of what its nature was and is—neither does he want to recognize its genuine nature, that is, that his act had nothing to do with the real value of Hoederer or even with his real danger; it had to do with Hugo's own unresolved problems.

To be of use to the party and to have the party believe that he still can serve, he would have to accept the lived idea of Hoederer—the man of action—and not the immobilized idea of Hoederer that he cherishes most fully—Hoederer as the man who, by living in freedom, had escaped from the Other. In the final moment of the play, Hugo is still pursuing purity in some form even if that form has to be created in his imagination; he is pursuing it because, once he finds it and fixes it, his life will be justified. He tells Olga that he has always wanted to hang a crime about his neck but that once he had done so he felt nothing. In prison he had only to wait—to wait for his colleagues, the others, to deliver him. The murder he committed has now become his destiny—something external, something whose weight he doesn't feel, but whose impact and consequences are going to govern his life. Without realizing the truth of what he is saying, he confesses: "I haven't changed; and I still talk as much" (p. 246).

He hasn't changed, and he talks too much in order not to change; yet the talk is all bluff and bluster because it has nothing to do with external events but only with internal desires. Hugo doesn't want to change; Hugo doesn't want to feel the weight of his existence; he wants instead to isolate outside forces which govern him and explain him. For this reason he refuses the terms of reintegration into the party, for he would have to start afresh—"completely stripped, without encumbrance" (p. 255). That means he would have to give up all the explanatory and ultimately blameable forces upon which he has always relied. He would no longer be Raskolnikof but Balzac's Rastignac, who had taken on the vast challenge of Paris in order to meet it on its terms, or Stendhal's Julien Sorel who, in the end and in prison, had at last seen clearly and had decided he wanted no part of the world available to him. Hugo wants no part of such visions, nor does he want to accept the amnesia that would blot out his past. Where he wants a destiny, reintegration offers him only an uncertain future purchased at the price of denying that his murder had any significance.[12]

That especially is what he cannot accept, for his act has to have a meaning. Yet he cannot himself determine that meaning and has therefore been counting on the party to supply it. But now that the party has changed its opinion of Hoederer's policies, it cannot provide the meaning. Hugo is thrown into the uncertainty which comes with knowing that he performed a political act for egotistical reasons. In a very brief space of time, he goes through extraordinary mental gymnastics. In the end he decides that, in order to save Hoederer's reality, he must refuse to be reintegrated into the party. Before his own death—for he is to be shot by party members—Hugo must create an ideal which will justify his refusal to go on working with the party—he will die in order to defend the reality incarnated in Hoederer.[13] That reality exists only in Hugo's imagination; it has nothing to do with Hoederer. And so he goes to his death in the same frame of mind which has governed his life, lying to himself, trying to find external justifications for his internal confusions. The Other triumphs over him as surely in death as in life. The Other, who had set up Hoederer's murder, kills Hugo because he refuses to adjust, because he abjures living free. Hoederer, the Other seen as an ideal—and, in Hugo's mind, the Other who demands Hugo's death—would have approved the party's gesture and so, from the grave, Hoederer does not approve of his first martyr; the cult Hugo has tried to create dies with him. It had never existed elsewhere than in his imagination.

Against all the evidence, he has persisted in believing in the value of purity and tried to make Hoederer part of it. Yet the only purity revealed by Hoederer was his steady understanding of the exigencies of freedom and situations. Those demands kept Hoederer from any possible involve-

12. Of Genet Sartre writes: "He hopes for Saintliness, he wants to acquire it. What is it that he wants? To be. To be a saint, to be an evildoer, it doesn't matter: to be his being" (*SG*, p. 239). This is the destiny he seeks. In the Genet book Sartre offers an economical definition of destiny when he describes it as "the reverse of freedom" (p. 93).

13. Sartre views similar efforts on Genet's part as attempts to create the terms of a kind of mystical potlatch, a process of exchange which will assure him of possessing the greatest merit. He writes: "The reasons for the sacrifice are inverted: if one renounces the goods of this world, it is no longer because they are false goods; rather one offers them to God because they are true goods. The lord who has been touched by grace sells his beautiful palace. But not because he has contempt for the beauty of its architecture. He will use the money from the sale to build an even more beautiful church" (*SG*, p. 223). Hugo is willing to sell his past in order to buy a more beautiful future. Like the lord who exchanges his palace for a church, temporal comfort for eternal security, he wants an appreciative audience for his gesture as well as the future the gesture is supposed to guarantee; and, like the lord, he wants his gesture to be expressed in something as solid as a structure—a hard, unalterable, translucent act. Sartre's original title for *Les Mains sales* was *Les Biens de ce monde*.

ment with the kind of purity Hugo is seeking. Confronted with the world's flux and the chameleon character of political maneuvers, Hugo pulls back; in the end he tries to place Hoederer in a pantheon Hoederer would be astonished to inhabit. There is a pitiful beauty in Hugo's final gesture and in his determined attempt to preserve Hoederer as the ideal he has sought throughout his existence. Yet the gesture's small beauty is swamped by its vast futility, since the ideal betrays Hoederer thoroughly. Hoederer's life was nothing if it was not a long demonstration of the impossibility of living for any ideal which sought to install itself as purity incarnate and immutable on this earth. The earth, Hoederer saw, was the field of man's liberty; as the earth turns, so must man, but with less regularity and probably with no serenity. Recognizing this, Hoederer also recognized that all individual engagement in the world's affairs dirties hands and muddies intentions. Hugo's last gesture changes nothing of that. He lets himself be killed in order not to risk being dirtied by further actions and other people. Yet his life has been nothing if not a long involvement with others in which his hands were dirtied anyway.

RELATED THEMES AND WORKS

The concept of facticity is discussed in *BN*, pp. 79–84 ("The Facticity of the For-Itself") and pp. 481–553 ("Freedom and Facticity: The Situation"). It is one of the central Sartrean concepts which develops throughout the works subsequent to *BN* and which is eventually closely linked to the concept of the practico-inert (see my discussion below, p. 295n.). The practico-inert, which later, perhaps a bit casually, I label as the bog, is a situation which one can exploit either by escaping from it or else by asserting that, imprisoned in the bog either because of what others have done or because the situation has become something other than what was originally intended, one has no other choice but to remain there. "[To live in a world haunted by my fellow man] means also that in the midst of this world *already* provided with meaning, I meet with a meaning which is *mine* and which I have not given to myself, which I discover that I 'possess already'" (*BN*, pp. 509–10). In the *CRD*, Sartre will give much greater weight to the importance of this "meaning already possessed"; he will also stress that individuals who have been reified have not *become* things but have fallen into a situation where they treat themselves as though they were matter or are so treated by other men.

Sartre originally intended to write a full-length study of Tintoretto. In an essay in *L'Arc* ("Saint-Georges et le dragon," 30 [1966], pp. 35–50) he comments on two segments of the London National Gallery canvas in an effort to show how, in one of his paintings, Tintoretto depicted the conflicts Sartre discusses in "Le Séquestré de Venise."

A radically different interpretation of *Kean* will be found in Robert J. Nelson's *The Play within a Play* ("Sartre: The Play as Lie," pp. 100–114), New Haven, 1958.

In addition to the earlier title already mentioned—*Les Biens de ce monde*—*Les Mains sales* was at one time called *Crime Passionel*. To add to the possible confusion, Sartre's scenario, *L'Engrenage* (1948), was originally entitled *Les Mains sales*. Sartre explains in a prefatory note to the scenario that there is no relationship between the two works. To a limited extent—involving mainly plot details—that is quite true; in a wider sense, the two works share many common interests, since *L'Engrenage* pits a Hoederer-type figure against another who has much sharper definition and clearer commitment than Hugo and who also elicits more sympathy in his insistence on the need for pure intentions and precise motivations. His concern, while it is indeed linked with the effort not to soil himself needlessly, is also with the infected carry-over that personal soiling brings to the issue being defended. The ironies are sharper and the ambiguities more shadowy in the scenario than in the play. Though never turned into a film, *L'Engrenage* was produced on the stage in Paris in early 1969. Simone de Beauvoir treats a somewhat similar theme in her only play, *Les Bouches inutiles*, where she shows the problems in moral decision-making which are brought about when a town, fighting for its freedom as for an ideal, chooses momentarily to engage in a quiet unideal policy by denying food to those who cannot join actively in the defense of the besieged city.

Les Mains sales is an interesting example of a work which got away from its author both because, on its own terms, it manages to raise more and broader issues than he had intended and because it had significances for others which Sartre had apparently not meant to put into it. Since its conflict took place within the Communist party, the play was not cheered by party members; because it showed such conflicts, anti-Communists welcomed it into their camp without giving much attention to the meaning of the conflict. Sartre's own remarks about the play indicate, not so much radical oscillations of his opinions, as the density of the play; he has spoken of it as a study of ends and means presented as objectively as his skills permitted. He has also suggested that it was written to present a model to other confused young Hugos in the hope that, warned, they would not waver and then wither as Hugo does. Simone de Beauvoir (*FC*, pp. 166–68) views it as the presentation of the confrontation which takes place between praxis (Hoederer) and morality (Hugo), morality here meaning an unwilling but unshakeable conviction that there must be firm standards even in shifting situations. There was a successful production of the play in Paris in 1963 with François Perrier playing the role of Hugo.

8 *Living Free*—I

If we look upon the slogan of the French Revolution—*Liberté, Egalité, Fraternité*—as an equation rather than as a proclamation of three simultaneous possibilities, we begin to perceive the difficulty Sartre has been trying to deal with. If, in order to assure equality, men must link their liberty to a sense of fraternity, the inferential consequence is this: fraternity demands some sacrifice and that sacrifice reduces an individual's quantity of liberty. If men do not make that sacrifice, fraternity becomes impossible. Once there is no fraternity, there is no real equality either. Individual men may be free; their collective existence cannot be free if it is not fraternal. Though slogans may allude to truths, they stumble constantly against facts and lose their appeal when they are measured against real situations. The faded revolutionary legends on the façades of French public buildings indicate more than indifferent maintenance.

The difficulties inherently contained in the French slogan are those we encounter in Sartre's works. So far we have seen only a handful of people living with an open consciousness of being free; very little in the way of equality has resulted from that consciousness since it has only rarely been accompanied by any desire to create a fraternal society. The defect has not been the consequence of any scarcity of free men. Lucien, the three characters in *Huis-clos*, Brunet, Schneider, and Hoederer have all been aware of their freedom and have known how to use it. Yet, with the exception of Schneider and Hoederer, no character in Sartre's work has been living both freely and authentically, by which I mean that all the others have chosen to ignore crucial discoveries they have made; they have preferred to live in bad faith, to choose what they want, to make their lives constant battles. Some of those who have not exercised their freedom have resorted to excuse-making; since they have been ballasted with influences which, for a number of reasons, they either have not dumped or else could not dump without losing an already precarious balance, they have been victims.

Even in those cases where men have sought to exercise an informed freedom and have had a clear desire to use that freedom in order to create a fraternal society, the results have not been happy. Schneider, and eventually Brunet, felt that the restrictive influences of the Communist party were so strong as to make freedom at least momentarily irrelevant: they are boxed in by a party discipline which, however justified, replaces rather than replenishes freedom. The party does this, Brunet presupposes, in the name of greater future freedom; Schneider, disillusioned by the Russo-German pact, no longer considers such presuppositions reliable.

Hoederer, who possessed the toughest and least romantic idea of free-dom, was obliged to maneuver against his party colleagues; finally he was felled by an assassin who could not explain his motivation, either to himself or to others. One cannot say that such dismal outcomes are the inevitable product of Sartre's point of view. Man's dedicated inhumanity to his fellow man had established a bulging dossier long before Sartre turned his atten-tion to human freedom—so much so that Karl Popper's claim that human history is the chronicle of savagery shocks only those who have the ability to overlook the facts Popper presents. Humanity pegs its history on the wars it has fought; men do not talk about what happened before the peace or after the peace; instead they organize their sense of chronology around their periods of brutality and, in times of peace, wait expectantly, if ruefully, for the next holocaust. Sartre's defeats are not what he sought. Certainly they are not what he expected; he had had better hopes from which naiveté was not altogether absent. But he has been discovering that the dossier of human cruelty is not simply a record of disasters, it is also a description which depicts, on a universal scale, the more limited interpersonal hostility he had portrayed in *Being and Nothingness.*

Behind that work was a hope that a new ethical climate could be created once men had seen the dismal realities and dreary prospects born of their fear of freedom. What the fictional works have shown is that men prefer to continue supplying further data for future forlorn philosophical works to reading the chronicle of their failures and learning something from it. Sartre, as a result, is living with the failure of *Being and Nothingness* to supply an adequate program; for, while it may appear promising to en-courage men to live freely, what happens when they do choose freedom may turn out to be not at all promising. Men are a good deal more condi-tioned by external circumstances than that massive work was willing to concede; where those circumstances exert vast influence, individual declara-tions of freedom may change nothing at all and conceivably may produce more harm than good. There is a certain unreal purity and intellectual rigor in Sartre's early insistence than man is free under all circumstances to select his response to those circumstances; the sad fact is that any one of the responses available may inevitably produce a worse situation, not because the individual wants to worsen the situation but because he cannot foresee all the consequences of the response he carefully chooses. The world of action is vaster than the paltry attempts of any one man to influence it; it is composed of mysterious interactions upon whose elements historians, even hundreds of years after the fact, cannot agree. Yet there is no doubt that acts and the interactions they produce are the result of men living together and responding to surrounding conditions.

This is no paradox; it is a problem, and *Being and Nothingness* has not solved it. In an unintended way it may have contributed further to it since,

if you encourage man to declare himself to be free and to live authentically
with his discoveries, you may very well be inviting him either to destroy
already functioning collectivities or to believe that there is an unbridgeable
chasm between him and the collectivity in which he lives. It would be silly
to join the chorus of critics who accused Sartre, in the aftermath of World
War II, of disillusioning a generation of young people and driving them
to despair. That certainly was not his intention. It is nonetheless a fact that
Sartre's postwar works have been a steady, brave, and sometimes wilful
effort to fight against despair from amidst circumstances which seem to
allow for no other reaction.

The plays which I am going to discuss in this and in the following two
chapters trace out this development in Sartre's thought. In each there is
no question of man's ability to act freely. There is, however, serious question
about the methods free men use when they encounter and surmount various
obstacles to their liberty. Though these obstacles may cause individuals
to stumble, those individuals fully realize that they have stumbled; they
fight against falling. They are not men who are seeking originally to place
the blame elsewhere or to find an excuse for their weak behavior; rather
they are men who have elected freedom only to find that, if such an election
represents something, that something is as poor as it is troublesome. What
they discover are the conflicts which develop between men who have an
equal interest in being free but whose means for attaining that freedom
are more than different: the means chosen depend on the exclusion of all
other means and sometimes, on the exclusion of all other men. They discover that one man's good may be another man's evil, with the result that
good and evil become labels with less and less meaning. They discover,
finally, that the exercise of freedom brings a few rewards; too often, those
rewards are less agreeable than Lulu's shrewd and cheerful adjustments,
Lucien's capitulation, or Pierre's madness. Free men can become unjust
men; they can also become slaves and while, from the bonds of slavery,
they can continue to react freely, slavery is not what they sought.

If *Les Mouches* (1944) traces out the process whereby one individual
exuberantly embraces his freedom and its implications, *Le Diable et le
Bon Dieu* (1951) shows that exaltation is short-lived, that freedom cannot
be personal *and* efficacious (the individual must live in terms of the collectivity); and *Les Séquestrés d'Altona* (1960) suggests that had the young
hero of *Les Mouches* known all that awaited him, he might have decided
to return to Corinth and leave the city of Argos either to solve its own
problems or to go on pretending that they were not real problems. Such
a decision is unacceptable to Sartre; but the contrary decision produces
a situation which, with its continuous discord, seems no better. The citizens
of Argos, since they had come to terms with their existence, knew a form
of tranquillity; the Gerlach family in *Les Séquestrés d'Altona* has come

to terms with nothing and lives in a house shadowed with madness, defeat, and death; no maneuver has worked as planned though every available one has been tried. Free man, having negotiated all the obstacles as best he can, falls across the accumulated horror of his own maneuvers and comes to believe that it would have been better if he had never set forth at all. While his defeat elicits Sartre's sympathy and forces him to temper some of his early rigor with understanding, it cannot win his approval. If this is where freedom leads—and Sartre's persistent honesty will make no contrary and deceitful claims—then reform must take place on a scale more vast than any he had foreseen in his earlier works.

Relentlessly, in those first works, he set about to show that freedom is inescapable; the implication in such determination was that the conscious use of freedom promised more than did enslavement to the various subterfuges I have discussed in earlier chapters. The argument Roquentin and others developed against freedom did not derive its terms, or even its evidence, from what would happen if one lived freely; rather it drew its force from various degrees of envy for other nonhuman states: the solidity of matter, the indifference of the universe, the easiness of letting go in order to imitate the presumed serenity of all fixed quantities. Relentlessly in those works, Sartre seemed to be discovering that freedom, because it plunged man into authentic living, made man better. Mathieu at the end of *Les Chemins de la liberté* was considerably more tolerable and valuable than he had been at the beginning of the novel.

If Pascal rejoiced in his conviction that rational man was potentially noble man, Sartre seemed to rejoice no less in his belief that free man was better than man enslaved. Once man accepted his freedom he could begin to manage the world and determine the conditions of his existence. Indeed, those conditions would reflect his desire only to the degree that he resolutely worked for their establishment; and the degree to which he worked to bring about those conditions would, conversely, serve to measure the extent to which he was accepting his most specifically human endowment. The joy derived from this discovery seemed to be validated, not by Sartre's works alone, but also by the outcome of the war. The line of demarcation between good and evil during the Resistance had been clear; the victory of the Allies had verified the belief that good did win in the end if free men risked all in order to safeguard their liberty.

Such assurances did not last long into the postwar period and with their death came disillusion; the temptation to model one's life on the search for absolutes or on the imitation of fixed quantities produced less distressing individuals than did the open exercise of freedom. The result was that exhortations designed to lead men to an acceptance of their freedom were exhortations which encouraged the creation of unpredictable situations and worse dangers. A Pierre locked in his room, awaiting the next appearance of his hallucinatory visitors, was certainly harmless when compared to two great political forces confronting each other with arsenals of annihilating weapons which they were willing to rattle and presumably use in the defense of what each identified as "freedom." The grave problem is not what happens when man refuses to be free; the grave problem is what happens when he chooses both to be free and to fight to the death for his idea of freedom.

The shifting emphasis in Sartre's work reflects a deeper understanding of the world's major influential forces. The insistence on *individual* attitudes and patterns of behavior which had underpinned *Being and Nothingness*, and which had been the ethical stuff of the early creative works, was justified; it was perhaps even necessary. It was also very partial with the consequent risk that the fragment might be mistaken for the whole or, in a wider sense, that the Resistance might be considered the unquestionably finest of human moments. Sartre also had reason to believe that his wisdom would have powerful sway in the world since, immediately after the Liberation, he found himself a celebrity. Since few intellectuals, especially those who have been professors and felt the pinch of relative poverty in both fame and fortune, can resist celebrity, there is no particular point in taking Sartre to task for what he himself quickly discovered: one can talk to packed halls, journey about the world, be discussed and demeaned in the popular press, be interviewed by as many reporters as a fairly full day can accommodate, and still not manage to become the world's savior. In fact, the world's adulation may be no more than the best strategy it has devised for not being one whit influenced. Sartre was aware of this; Simone de Beauvoir tells us that he knew he risked becoming the intellectual who was listened to avidly precisely because no one believed what he was saying. He risked becoming the latest diversion of those who like to hear discussions of moral questions because, as Elaine May once said, they are so much more interesting than real questions.

There were other disenchantments behind Sartre's shift in emphasis. Those who together had said no to the Germans during the Occupation could not, once the Germans had been defeated, find any way of saying yes to one another; the Fourth Republic was shortly to become a dismal continuation of the Third, and the Communist party, quickly expelled from the government, quite as quickly went back to saying no to everything the party had not devised. Individuals who had cooperated during the Resistance and who had jointly looked forward to the initiation of major reforms after the war could not, even though they were all on the Left, agree on ideology or strategy.

Increasingly they spent their time scrapping with each other—a hallowed and forlorn French tradition which Sartre has followed more in the observance than the breach. His polemics with Camus, Martinet, the Communist party, and eventually with Merleau-Ponty are, to the Anglo-Saxon mind, no more than further sorry examples of the Latin hunger for dogmas and absolutes. On a personal level, however, they were an indication of how difficult it is, even for men whose hopes are ultimately the same, to cooperate in programs designed to realize those aspirations. Above these fratricidal disputes—and the temper of their language fully justifies such a description—was the conflict between the Communist and non-Communist worlds which Sartre considered a scandal, apparently because he expected greater politeness and patience in international relations than he himself manifested in interpersonal associations.

What Sartre's subsequent work begins to show slowly and with increasing emphasis is his realization that all these opposing forces are acting out of a commitment to their idea of freedom or to their program for the redemption of man. The basis for commitment to one or another of the opposing groups became almost arithmetical: the man who hoped for change should put himself on the side which promised the most to the greatest number of the suffering. That group, in Sartre's mind, was the Communist party, not necessarily as it existed in France, but as it existed on the international level. Since the promise, and the international organization which bore it, were inevitably connected with the Soviet Union, Sartre's choice was bound to become periodically uneasy. The burden of unpleasant and sometimes murderous facts that Stalinist Russia could neither hide nor explain wounded the purity of purpose that world Communism was supposed to be pursuing. The purity of motive which inspired Hoederer and sustained him in moments when impure political maneuvering seemed the only way to proceed was the kind of purity which, in the Communist bloc, would have put him in a slave-labor camp or, in a broader context, would have put a nation in the isolated position of Yugoslavia.[1] Too often, those who sought the dictatorship of the proletariat seemed to have become accustomed to dictating to the proletariat.

Because of these circumstances, Sartre was obliged to reconsider his fundamental categories. With the dispersion of the common front of the Resistance, Sartre began to appreciate the importance of the political structures he had disdained before the war because he believed them irrelevant to his abstract solutions. Somewhat later, in the early 1950s, he began to

---

1. The case of Yugoslavia early became a matter of interest to Sartre. In an introduction to Louis Dalmas' *Le Communisme yougoslave depuis la rupture avec Moscou* (Paris, 1950), he presented a deft and impassioned defence of Tito's decision to break with the Politburo and go his separate Marxist way. That essay ("Faux Savants ou faux lièvres," *Sit. VI*, pp. 23–68) is of capital importance in showing Sartre's earliest hesitations about the kind of monolithic system pursued in Stalinist Russia and imposed on Communist allies and in indicating the direction in which Sartre was moving: towards a recognition of the indispensable need for some sort of friendly critical voice within the general movement of world Communism. The essay thus contains in embryo many of the concepts which will be systematically developed in the *CRD*.

recognize the possibly dominant role of economic realities and the impossibility of effecting fundamental social change within a framework of arrested economic growth. (It is not certain that he has ever learned to place adequate emphasis on the role of power in the lives of men, nations, and blocs or that he fully understands international economics.)

Though Sartre's approach has changed in a major way, his earlier observations, rather than being nullified, are projected instead against a broader background. Freedom still resides in individuals; but the most important tension is no longer that between accepting freedom and hiding from it, though that dilemma still persists in the lives of individuals; the most consequential tension is that which springs up when men have radically different notions of what they are pursuing when they speak and, worse, when they act in the name of freedom. *Les Mouches*, *Le Diable et le Bon Dieu*, and *Les Séquestrés d'Altona*, considered as three different examinations of what it means to be free, show that the problems which one meets on the highways of freedom are not so much the fault of the driver's motives as of his vehicle's capacities and the road's condition.

While the war was a shock severe enough to jolt all individuals in some way and to inspire certain among them to degrees of commitment they had not earlier thought themselves capable of, it was not without its own problems. As an event, it helped to bring a socially divided nation to a sense of being a threatened collectivity and produced the kind of response which found its bravest expression in the Resistance.[2] Still the Resistance, as much as the war, raised questions of disturbing importance, not the least of which was that of justifying activities which were bound to bring reprisals on other Frenchmen who, if not altogether innocent, were not directly involved in the sabotage which led to the reprisals. *Les Mouches* is less concerned with this question than it is with two other issues: first, the question of whether one should become involved at all in what might justifiably be considered the troubles of others (the others here being the politicians and generals who bore the brunt of responsibility for France's defeat); second, the accuracy of the Vichy government's claim that the French defeat stemmed from a trinity of causes which had sapped France's strength—the

2. The Communists in *Les Chemins de la liberté* are not hoodwinked by this argument and insist that, rather than fighting for France, they are fighting against Fascism because, if it is not defeated, their program for universal reform will be that much more delayed. Still, in *Réflexions sur la question juive*, Sartre had argued that anti-Semitism was used by the governing class as an instrument of national unity; implicit in his discussion was the suggestion that the instrument produced effective results. Similar inferences can be seen in his other essays with the result that a reader feels that, while Sartre would prefer that nations not be unified in this way—that is, unified through their opposition to something—he recognizes the fact that at times they are.

rejection of traditional values, the secularization of the state, and the mis-
treatment of the army.

The propaganda of the Vichy government stressed that the Occupation
was no more than the punishment sent by God to the eldest daughter of
his church to remind her that she had wandered too far astray and thus
had lost sight of where her duty lay. The Vichy government also argued
that a punished France would be a purified France; she would thereby
be prepared to join with Germany in a grand alliance against her oldest
enemy, England. The coalition which gathered in Vichy was not there to
take the waters but to bathe France in her guilt, reduce her to shame in
the hope that the present would be eradicated and the past recovered.
Those misguided and misinformed men—misguided because they hoped
for a return of their privileges, misinformed because they did not read
accurately the all too clear indications of German intention—could not
countenance the existence of organized resistance; the worst threat they
posed, however, was that their recriminations and their readiness to identify
the sources of blame might persuade other Frenchmen that resourceful
cooperation with the victor was more prudent than determined resistance.

Sartre's purpose in *Les Mouches* was clearly polemical since, in elucidating contemporary situations through the terms of an ancient myth, he was
seeking to show the futility and the shame of Vichy's acceptance of defeat.
Beyond that, he was seeking to show that the fact of the Occupation demanded a personal response from each individual; he was thereby urging
each individual to a particular kind of response. The play is humanistic
in the sense that it is on the side of the free man who refuses to yield to
apparently overwhelming forces; it is revolutionary in the sense that it aims,
in that process, at overturning a whole humanist tradition. It strikes me
that this, rather than the desire to camouflage the play from the German
censor—who must have been colossally stupid if not just illiterate in French
when he approved it for production—explains why Sartre chose the history
of the house of Atreus for his basic material. In that material he had a well-
known myth which had been elaborated by noble writers whose works
had traditionally been counted among the high moments of Western
civilization.

Sartre could have presented his ideas without using the classical story,
but it is evident that he wanted the Orestes legend precisely because it
had long served as a vehicle for expressing a fundamental human situation;
more crucially, he wanted it because he disagreed with its earlier resolu-
tions. If Aeschylus and Sophocles addressed themselves to the right
questions, they came up with the wrong answers. In their rigorous analyses
they traced out a portrait of man plunged into a world where he was
pursued and harassed by the dilemmas which haunt every man who has
elected to respond to his environment by acting upon it. Orestes, as they

portray him, is a fine prototype of Sartrean man to the degree that he has the sense of having been needlessly set loose in the world, there to be burdened with problems he did not create. This is where the classical writers and Sartre diverge. Aeschylus, Sophocles, and Euripides simply could not conceive of a human intelligence placed so far above human life as to have the leisure to muddle over whether or not it would plunge into the fray. For them, Orestes has no choice about what he must do. If he wishes to remain Orestes, a person endowed with a function that must be exercised in a particular place, he must recognize that both place and function have been usurped by his father's murderer. He must also, if he wishes to maintain his honor—and honor is not very different from virility, from being *someone*, in the Greek outlook—he must also respect the grisly observance of blood feuds. Than shedding blood there is only one worse deed: the refusal to shed it.

These presuppositions are not Sartre's; the preoccupation with justice and with the difficulty of establishing it is his, however, as is the realization that the search for a justice based in freedom inevitably knocks up against the resistance of established systems. Here again he and the classical writers diverge, for he cannot accept their solution of the conflict between the individual and the system since that solution depends on the intervention of Apollo and Athena. In invoking the god, the Greek writers cheat. At the moment of most intense conflict, when Orestes has done everything expected of him, the hostility between him and the system is total. He can do nothing to curb or control the forces he has opposed; he cannot by himself create circumstances which will carry his civilization beyond the customs of the vendetta with its endless bloodletting. Up to that point of greatest hostility, the Greek writers are honest in their presentation of his and any similar individual's anguish. There are few nobler or more accurate portraits of human freedom pushed to extremes than Orestes at Apollo's temple or Oedipus in the Sacred Grove; but, according to Sartre, this cannot be—as the Greek writers insist—the end of human action and the beginning of divine intervention.

To bow before the will of the gods, or to hope for an answer from them, is to engage in thinking as futile as it is wishful. The gods, since they do not exist, have neither will nor answer. Just as it is inconceivable to hope that Athena will really install the reign of justice on earth by striking a bargain with the Furies or that Zeus will take suffering man, if not home to some happier haven, at least *away* from a troublesome world, so is it inconceivable to hope that the Germans will one day give France back her freedom if only France purges herself of her defects and sins. There are no sure or even magical processes for Orestes or France. On the porch of Apollo's temple, as under the German occupation, there is only one choice left for man: to clear his way by renewed action.

Though they unquestionably cheat, Aeschylus and Sophocles do so in the interest of high purposes. The gods intervene in the end, possibly because the playwrights believed in them, more probably because they were a device necessary to the task of encouraging men to believe that, against a hostile nature, and in a world of aggressive men, it was better to believe in justice than to revert to savagery. The existence of the gods was less important than what the gods represented—an effort to give a sacred quality to important ideas which should be respected *as though* they were divine, which should be recognized as the finest concepts discovered by man in his search for purpose and in his flight from despair.

Aeschylus and Sophocles were aware that the older order, which had been efficient only in sustaining violence, was one that might at any moment return. They were aware, too, that because of this the new economy was fragile; it needed to be defended and praised with whatever means they could find. Their solution may seem to involve them in nonsense, but in a world where justice has so few chances it, too, can be considered nonsense, and the use of the gods, or poetry, or lengthy philosophical argument is no more than an example of one kind of sublime nonsense needing another, possibly less sublime, in order to survive. It remains to be seen whether Sartre's approach has any greater validity; if you throw man, unsupported by anything except himself, back on his humanity, you may discover that you have thrown him back to reliance on savagery.

Sartre's purpose is evident; it is also bold. He wishes to condemn all systems which mystify man with promises that, in the end or before long, can only have sinister consequences for him. The worst of these consequences is that the man who has allowed himself to be guided by faith in supernatural forces or by fear of overwhelming external powers will forget his true nature and live a disempowering contradiction. In occupied France, he will become passive and justify his passivity either by saying that he has merited his suffering or that he can do nothing about it—the enemy is too strong. He can go even further in sophisticated self-justification and claim that, if he is well-behaved and doesn't cause too much trouble, his freedom will be given back to him as a reward for his docility. There are several things which Sartre finds reprehensible in this attitude. One is the idea that liberty can be given. This, he claims is impossible; since liberty and man are indistinguishable, man must seize his freedom in order to exist.[3] Another is the danger that, once man has assumed the habit of passivity, he will never again choose to live freely, fearing that some other force will

3. Discussing the independence celebration in the former Belgian Congo, Sartre writes: "The Congolese who participated in the ceremony, no matter what their party affiliation was, wanted no part of a gift: freedom cannot be given, it can only be taken. If we turn those phrases around we perceive that independence which is granted is no more than another kind of servitude" ("La Pensée politique de Patrice Lumumba," *Sit. V*, p. 227).

come along to punish him. A third is the tendency of divinized justice to lodge in the capricious will of cruel gods who are no more than projections of the arbitrary will of powerful and capricious men.

Sartre's method is shrewd but dangerous. By insisting that justice is the affair of all men and cannot come to pass on this earth unless it emanates from free men, he is seeking to show that it can have no basis external to man. The saga of Orestes must thus undergo a fundamental change, not because its basic data are inaccurate, but because any solution must be based on man's realization that justice comes about through him alone and not through any supernatural intermediary. This may be a sad truth, precisely because human means for installing justice seem inadequate; it is a brighter truth, however, than belief in God. To a very significant extent, *Les Mouches* is Sartre's most vehement attack on any form of deism; the strength and at times the vulgarity of the attack are a direct result of his disgust with the uses Vichy found for God. Whatever honor those uses offered to God did not keep them from dehumanizing and deceiving men by encouraging them to accept defeat and servitude.

I have already discussed Sartre's atheism (see above, pp. 13ff.) and the vital role it plays in his philosophy, since the absence of God is the absence of steady guarantees and the indication of the total job that men must perform quite on their own. If elsewhere Sartre has expressed regret over the nonexistence of God, in this play he takes an almost joyful view of the freedom which results once man has put aside all thought about God. He portrays Jupiter as a cynical, somewhat urbane man who possesses a single skill and is obsessed with a single truth. He can claim a limited repertory of tricks; he cannot forget that, having created man free, he has potentially put himself out of business. As a result, he is obliged to use his small bag of cheap devices to implement a tactical policy designed to prevent men from discovering what he knows about them: they can get along without him. He is not a benevolent being whose providence supplies the world with a gracious plan, but a conniver who seeks to block men and who intervenes in their affairs only when he can multiply their misery and increase their dependence on him. So long as he can do this, Jupiter has a place in the world. But once a man has discovered that he is free, there is no longer any place for God:

> When freedom has exploded just once in a man's soul, the Gods can do nothing more against that man. Everything's up to him, then; and other men—acting on their own—will have to decide to let him go or to strangle him (p. 86).

God in this play is seen as the kind of folly men cannot afford, simply because, like Zola's Nana, he will ultimately bring most of them to ruin and leave them there to fend as best they can without either help or sympathy from him. God is an idea which has lost its original attraction because powerful men have interpreted his will as being strangely and contradictorily in accord with their private needs; they have even fought particularly grotesque wars to decide his affairs for him. God is also an idea which, so long as it is maintained, clogs the intellectual processes.

As an idea which identifies a being who possibly exists, God must either be with men or against them. If he is with them, then he is like them and shares all their qualities. That means that he *exists*, with a consciousness which is present to the universe and obliged to respond to it with projects and intentions; his future is as uncertain as men's and thus is no sturdy pole to which they should be fettered or around which they should dance. If he *is*, that is if he is a fixed quantity like matter or like Lucretius's god, then he has not even the use Lucretius found for him since, in imitating him, men would be denying their inescapable dynamism. God, as being-in-itself, is outside the range of meaningful human concerns because he is outside the range of human anguish. He provides no example and less wisdom because, whatever intelligence he might have to offer, is established, as is all wisdom, through men.[4]

As an idea created by men, God represents two quite different things. On the one hand, the idea helps us to know something about men: that they have a hunger for reassurance which is expressed in their desire to be seen by some third force which is above both them and the others who, so much like them, are yet so frighteningly different. They create God out of a sense of their own insufficiency or, more likely, out of a needless kind of humility which stems from a suspicion that, as individuals, they have no universal significance. Men recognize their particularity; they do not spontaneously discover any direction for that particularity and thus they enlist themselves in the activity of believing in God in order to believe that their particularity serves some higher cause. While men's reasons for doing this may be understandable, they are not good reasons since they create a structure for life which turns out to be a self-imposed straitjacket.[5]

4. Cf. *BN*: ". . . it is the For-itself which establishes this coexistence [of things in the world] by making itself co-present to all. But in the case of the presence of the For-itself to being-in-itself, there cannot be a third term. No witness—not even God—could establish that presence; even the For-itself can know it only if the presence already is" (p. 122).

5. This is one of the most durable of Sartre's concerns and is an essential note in his description of contemporary man who, deprived of God, is not as easily deprived of a desire to have the benefits provided by God. In an early essay on Francis Ponge's *L'Homme et les choses* (*Sit. I*, pp. 245–93), he wrote: "This effort to see oneself through the eyes of a foreign species, to find rest from the sad task of being a subject is one we have already met a hundred times in different forms—in the works of Bataille, Blanchot, and the surrealists. It is no less than the meaning of the modern fantastic, as well as of Ponge's materialism" (pp. 288–89). He continues in a note: "It represents one of the consequences of the death of God. As long as God was alive, man was tranquil; he knew he was looked at. Today, when he alone is God

On the other hand, once he has been created, God serves the nefarious purposes I have already alluded to and which are detailed in *Les Mouches*. As incarnated in Jupiter, God is the loftiest and therefore the worst expression of sustained bad faith. He exists and exerts influence only for such time as he serves some men's purposes; there are secondary consequences of his presence, however, and they touch other men. For all that he is the creation of *some* men, God, once existing, can influence and even condition all human attitudes. Egisthe may know of God's limitations; he nevertheless allows himself to be dominated by the idea of a supernatural overseer and, as much as the other citizens of Argos, who do not necessarily have his perspicuity, he becomes the victim of his own creation. The title of the play catches this divinely infernal circle since it alludes to Zeus' role as the lord of the flies, a lord who was invoked to drive the pests away, but who, as his bill for this minor service, demanded that his faithful live paralyzed with guilt. He replaces the natural nuisance of flies with the eminently more profitable psychological plague of remorse. In order to keep operating, he needs the collusion of men, which means, more often than not, that he needs their crimes. And criminal men need him in order to survive the aftermath of their crimes. Since the natural movement of events generally threatens the criminal with punishment for his crimes, the invocation of God becomes the only means of escaping from that threat.

Thus Egisthe has imposed on the Argives a belief that they share his guilt because they did nothing to stop him from murdering Agamemnon; in so doing he has imposed the reign of Jupiter on himself as well as on the citizens. He must keep Jupiter alive in order himself to remain alive; it is significant that, during the time of the play, he finds he has had too much of such moral acrobatics and looks forward to dying. He has no escape other than death, for if he were to deny Jupiter, the citizens might take things in their own hands; even if he does not deny Jupiter, Jupiter will continue to have psychological reality after his death. Because Egisthe is no longer a danger to his designs, it becomes essential for Jupiter to win over Oreste, the new ruler, either by cajolery or threats; since he is Egisthe's enemy, Oreste is also Jupiter's.

The Jupiter of *Les Mouches* is a bad device by which Sartre is trying to achieve an understandable end. That end aims at showing men the reprehensible and inhuman uses which have been made of God. The device is bad because it is handled maladroitly. By putting Jupiter on the stage, Sartre gives him a real weight which, even though it is only meant to be

and when his look pierces everything, he breaks his neck in the effort to see himself." He picks up the same theme, years later, in *SG*: "[Consciousness] thinks that this abstract and eternal universality transcends it and that this universality is God. It therefore attempts, since it is ashamed of its singularity, to destroy the particular in itself in order to raise itself to him" (p. 204).

the personification of a human construct, achieves a density which, no matter how pedestrian it is, is more substantially and potentially durable than any Sartre allows God. Sartre also endows him with a capacity to do tricks; while those tricks may be more flashy than helpful, the fact that Jupiter can perform them might reasonably persuade some men that it is better to be with the magician than against him, since there is no way of knowing what further mysterious capacities he possesses. The tricks (the play could do without them and not be deprived of its basic line of argument) compromise Sartre's insistence that God is no more than a human projection and muddies his intention of showing the basic contradictions manifest in all belief in God.

A God involved in history, first of all, would have to keep acting in order to keep his role as stage manager of the universe. The inconveniences of such behavior on his part have been the source of anguished and sometimes twisted thinking on the part of more than one theologian; strange formulas have been devised in order to show that while God in theory can choose to intervene at any time in history, in fact he doesn't. God, it most often turns out, is as prudent as the theologians need to make him. If he doesn't intervene, then men cannot count on him to do anything in time, and eternity—whatever the rewards it offers to the dead—does nothing to help the living through the next crisis. When God intervenes, as Jupiter does in this play, he quickly learns what all stage managers already know: there are some actors who simply won't cooperate, despite threats and curses. A god who tries to manage directly the affairs of men is a god who becomes just another man and, in the Sartrean view, a very shabby one at that.

Shabby because his basic philosophy must of necessity be the opposite of Sartre's. At the point when Oreste refuses to cooperate, Jupiter thunders forth with the noble poetry of the God of Job—a poetry which loses its nobility in this play because Sartre, by indicating that Jupiter's tirade should be pronounced melodramatically over loudspeakers, is using the arguments for laughs. Jupiter accuses Oreste of being an intruder in the universe; that precisely and irreversibly is what man is in Sartrean terms since he makes human reality by assuming a position vis-à-vis the universe. Jupiter exhorts Oreste to return to nature, only to be told that while he may be the king of the universe he is not the ruler of men; men and nature have never been on good terms, and there is no conceivable purpose to be served by men's enslaving themselves either to nature or to her defender, God. If God made men free, and if he is omniscient, he should have been well forewarned about what to expect. Since he did not foresee what would happen—and Jupiter admits to Egisthe that he made a mistake in creating men *free*— God is not omniscient and there is not much point in subjugating oneself to a bumbling Creator. There is, after all, no way of telling what other mistakes he might make.

If Sartre's stage devices are maladroit, his intellectural arguments are only slightly less so, primarily because his dismissal of God is based on argumentation which derives from Sartrean categories alone. Saying that God is either a being-in-himself, and therefore irrelevant to human affairs, or that he is a being-for-himself, and therefore no God, may take care of God in terms of *Being and Nothingness;* it does not provide the kind of sophisticated discussion that the idea and even the ideal of God demand; and it presupposes, without adequate argumentation or justification, that if there is some other category of being to which God might belong that category has no present meaning since men do not know what it is. Sartre has latterly responded to this muddle by not talking about it at all or by creating his own replacement for God: history. One myth may merit or even need another; a critic wonders whether in isolating history as the dominant force in the lives of men Sartre has really got very far from what other men, over the centuries, have been trying to identify when they talk about God.

A spectator at the play might very well decide—all the while agreeing that Vichy's uses of God were indeed reprehensible—that Sartre's denunciation of God and his encouragement of men to take the affairs of the world in their own hands offer neither consolation nor inspiration and therefore are of no interest. What is of interest, primarily, is the spectator's tranquillity; any explanation, whether it be myth or not, which allows him to live in relative peace would be better than the message of *Les Mouches.* He might also decide that Sartre wanted no more than to make himself God—he had, in *Being and Nothingness*, said that this was the passion of every man and a useless one at that—and that he, the spectator, preferred the traditional God who did not make so much noise and did not announce such sad news. Sartre seems to have been aware of the eventuality of such a reaction; he has therefore organized his play in such a way as to place Oreste in the most favorable light. At the same time, Sartre traces out other positions. There are three attitudes towards human freedom expressed in the play: that of those who try to curtail the freedom of others in order to act in their own interests; that of those who seek for awhile to recoup their freedom only to withdraw in horror from it once it is in their grasp; and that of Oreste, who accepts freedom, possibly for impure reasons, and certainly without fully knowing that it may turn out to be another curse disguised in the flattering rhetoric of further blessings to come.

Oreste is a hero delineated on a grand scale; he evokes the ardor and scintillating language of Corneille's young enthusiasts. Heroism, however, is a soft currency in the Sartrean world because its use is designed to create immediate benefits only for the individual; its exchange value is low. In this sense Oreste is the last of the Sartrean protagonists who falls within the terms of *Being and Nothingness*; his problems are traced out against the background of a collectivity which is an obstacle to his acceptance of authentic living. Once he has fought his battle, he is indeed free, but neither he nor the collectivity can be said to be anywhere. Intellectual and social debris has been moved about and redistributed; what happens as a result of the new arrangement is not precisely indicated though the implication is clear: if the debris has not been reduced or destroyed, that is because the lesson of the play, clearly taught, has been badly learned.

Oreste is one with Roquentin and Mathieu in that he makes progress—and of a remarkable kind—in the play. He comes visiting in Argos with foggy intentions which emanate from foggy ideas. He is suffering through what the present younger generation likes to call an identity crisis; he is confused because his mental categories are confused. More simply, it may be that all categories lead to confusion by suggesting an order in life which life does not respect. He comes to the city believing that there are two kinds of men. Some have no choice in selecting their way through life; they have been set on a certain path which they must follow until such time as they encounter an act which is clearly labeled as theirs. Others are those upon whom a troubled burden weighs because some event enacted in their child-hood—the murder of a father, for example—has radically changed their lives and thus deflected them from the path they might otherwise have followed. The act which should have been theirs has been confided to another, or the function they should have inherited has been usurped.

Initially, Oreste does not believe that the second category, to which he belongs, is necessarily the category reserved for superior men. Those who belong to that category have been deprived of certitude; they live exiled and alienated on the earth, deprived of all the baggage which would indicate that they possess something. No act awaits them; all that awaits them is the knowledge that one day they will have to choose to act. Since he sees no sign in Argos that the city either belongs to him or wants any part of him, Oreste is tempted to withdraw; there is nothing for him to do in a city which has reserved no specific act for him. What Sartre is saying, of course, is that while Oreste's distinction between two types of men is accurate as far as it goes, his evaluation of the two breeds is wrong or, better, his implied preference for the first category is wrong since that category is the haven of men who, like Hugo, seek a conditioned freedom. What Oreste discovers is that his preference boomerangs; once he thinks he has found *his* act, he discovers that that act has placed him irrevocably in the second category.

He is an example of the persistent schizophrenia Sartrean man suffers from. He wants to feel his identity, and he seeks to have it validated by external means; yet his search for a link of solidarity either with the city as a whole or with its individual members irresistibly shows him that the price of solidarity is one he does not choose to pay. He would then have to cease being in revolt, which means in effect that he would have to live on terms dictated by others. Those terms cannot assure him that his act of acceptance is the act he had described nostalgically. When he finds what seems to be solidarity with his sister, he discovers that she no longer wants to define her identity on his terms. Identity, when it depends on the Other, offers a yield the suppliant cannot accept.

The temptation to be one with the city remains strong since, if he achieves it, he will have a mandate. But an apparently insurmountable obstacle remains; by working on the principle that "a king should have the same memories as his subjects" (p. 29), he is setting an impossible goal. There is, to be sure, more whimsy than wisdom in the principle since it establishes a rule of behavior which asks no questions about the nature and purpose of the people's memories and gives initially inadequate weight to the variety of reactions shared memories can produce. At this point, Oreste's project is not essentially different from Hugo's: he wants to be validated, confirmed by an external force, not in the interests of that force, but in his own. He is a good deal more inspired by egotism than by generosity. His position is replete with the ironies we have seen in other Sartrean characters. By seeking to be confirmed by others, he will alienate those others; but the reason he alienates them is that he does not seek to dominate them. Having initially sought an act which would provide him with his identity, he performs a series of acts which saddle him with the knowledge that he is free; that is a quite different answer from the one he was seeking.

Though he is confused, he is not cruel. The hatred which devours his sister is not his, nor is her apparent belief in determinism. When she tells him that crime and misfortune run in her brother's blood, Oreste (who has not yet revealed his name) immediately begins to talk about Corinth, whose citizens have less contaminated blood; he suggests that Electre flee there with him. While that seems to be a more than reasonable proposal, and while it answers his pedagogue's objection that life in Argos would demand voluntary acceptance of abject remorse, the proposal has little attraction when measured against the other factors which are washing through Oreste's mind and flooding his emotions. To the degree that he offers Corinth as a solution, he ceases to conform to the idea of her brother that Electre has cherished; he thus moves further away from his expressed goal of *being* Oreste in order to be someone. Since Electre can confirm his being by recognizing him as her brother, he experiences shame and some fear when he realizes that she is rejecting him because his history, his background, and his possibilities are not hers. Haunted as he is by the idea "that no one is expecting me, I go from city to city, a foreigner to others and to myself" (p. 67), he cannot easily reject the temptation Electre offers. "I want my memories, my part of the earth, my place. . . . I want to be a man of a particular place, a man among men" (p. 68). This is a vital need for him, so vital that he turns his eyes immediately and supplicatingly to heaven and asks Jupiter to map out his route for him.

Electre, strong in her independence, mocks his falling back on the gods in search of wisdom and, in the same condescending tone, urges him to go back to Corinth. This is no solution since Electre, the Other with whom he wishes to identify in order to be identified, is counseling him to do what still others want him to do. He balks. If he leaves Argos and returns to Corinth, he will be living on terms dictated by others without finding the specific personal gravity he is seeking; he will exchange a hodological space on which he has some claims for another which is not his at all. He immediately decides to stay and seek another way, which is none other than the elaboration of a project which will be personally his. That project implies a thorough separation from the others, from all the others, even from Electre. She now strikes him, not so much as one who can help him achieve his identity, but as just another among the many who are separated from him and from the project he is in the process of formulating. His project still lacks sharp definition; he wants to steal the remorse of the city, not in order to expiate the city's guilt, but in order to possess it as something personally his. Yet, even as he desires to possess it, he does not know what he will do with it once it belongs to him.[6]

What is significant is his recognition that possession will bring the duties of ownership and management; that is what Electre does not want to recognize. As a result the solidarity of joint action they have both dreamed of is short-lived. Their common project does not survive the murder of Egisthe for, while Oreste discovers through that act that justice is the affair of men, Electre discovers only the horror of having to live with what they have done. Oreste must kill Clytemnestre alone, and in the aftermath try to convince a wavering Electre that their actions have set them free. But his exaltation, his knowledge that he has found both himself and his place— and it is important to note his awareness that both self and place are wide open and unfixed—is not Electre's; she wants no part of joint ongoing projects whose road signs are not clear and whose destination is unknown. She is haunted by her belief that they cannot in the future undo the murders they have committed. Faced with her refusal, Oreste experiences neither his original shame nor any sympathy, for he is now at the point where the Other, rather than provoking fear, stimulates pride. He tells Jupiter: "I love her more than myself. But her sufferings come from herself; she alone can rid herself of them; she's free" (p. 65).

6. Cf. *BN*: ". . . what freedom posits by the simple upsurge of its being is the fact that *it is as having to do with something other than itself*. To do is precisely to change what has no need of something other than itself in order to exist; it is to act on that which on principle is indifferent to the action, that which can pursue its existence or its becoming without the action" (pp. 506–7).

Electre is a creature whose apprehension of reality has been shaped only to enhance her romantic ideas of herself. Her vivid description of her parents' dirty underwear reveals more than close examination of the world's less consequential items; it shows how she selects objects in order to support her position. In an era before *True Confessions*, soap operas, and maudlin popular songs conveyed with all the unexpected urgency of sonic booms, she has been thrown back on her imagination only to come up with the same kind of acuity one finds in those other media. She is not living in the world but in her imagination, where she writes a scenario which might be called *The Tribulations of Agamemnon's Daughter*. That scenario is expressed in technicolor, melodrama, and stereophonic sound; it is scattered with episodes designed to excite and stimulate pity for her. It is the creation of a young girl who wants to play at being a moral virgin and not at being Electre. She is threatened and, in her imagination, she has an answer to all the threats. But when reality comes too close and when she is touched by the action of which she has dreamed, she withdraws and blames Oreste for her violation. She is very much like the woman Sartre discusses in *Being and Nothingness* who allows herself to be caressed all the while pretending that she is not cooperating; the Other is performing all the action and her body is an object quite detached from the more educated wishes of her consciousness.[7]

What Electre seeks is not complete freedom, but just enough freedom to allow her to feel very sorry for herself and very angry with those who have debased her. So long as she can perform little acts of independence, whose purpose is to remind her that she is being ill-treated, she can view them as the first cobblestones for the path to complete freedom that she is laying out. Fundamentally this is because her project has at best a questionable basis and no future: ". . . the shrewd person can hope for nothing on this earth except to deal out one day the evil that has been done to him" (p. 63). When that day comes and when the reciprocal evil has been meted out, what she has imagined becomes real; that was never her intention. What is done can no longer be dreamed about or, more appropriately, the

7. Cf. *BN*: "But then suppose he takes her hand. This act of her companion risks changing the situation by calling for an immediate decision. To leave the hand there is to consent in herself to flirt, to engage herself. To withdraw it is to break the troubled and unstable harmony which gives the hour its charm. The aim is to postpone the moment of decision as long as possible. We know what happens next; the young woman leaves her hand there, but she *does not notice* that she is leaving it. She does not notice because it happens by chance that she is at this moment all intellect. She draws her companion up to the most lofty regions of sentimental speculations . . . during this time the divorce of the body from the soul is accomplished; the hand rests inert between the warm hands of her companion—neither consenting nor resisting—a thing" (pp. 55–56). A fuller discussion of the caress as a reciprocal gesture, involving the motivations of two people, is conducted on pp. 379–90 in the chapter on "Concrete Relations with Others." I shall have some remarks to make about those pages in the next chapter.

dream, accomplished, becomes a nightmare for two reasons. As a dream it could be adjusted as her emotions dictated; as a nightmare it robs her of the fun and some of the consolation of the dream.[8]

She rejects Oreste at the end because Oreste is reality and reality is precisely what she does not want. She does not want it because, as we have seen, it is bedrock and not the malleable clay of dreams; but she also does not want it because she envisions it as something Oreste is trying to impose on her. Oreste in her dreams was someone whose actions she controlled; Oreste in reality is the Other who is trying to make her belong to him without offering any clearly defined reward for the sacrifice. In her dreams she had complete, though imaginary, control of her situation. In the aftermath of the murders, she can only choose between modes of domination. Nothing in her experience has prepared her for what Oreste offers since, never having thought the murders would really take place, she had never felt compelled to consider what would happen after them.

The experience of a city living fairly comfortably with guilt and the limited, self-consoling litanies of Clytemnestre—"no one has the right to judge my remorse" (p. 39)—have subconsciously prepared her for the way she finally accepts. That her final choice is thoroughly dishonest is clearly indicated by her late declaration that Jupiter can provide her with no hope. Still, faced with uncertainty, she is willing to barter hope for a role; she will live, as Clytemnestre had several times forewarned her, with remorse for her irreparable crime. At the end she decides that she can live better with her enemies than with her supposed friends and cries out to the Furies: "Defend me against the flies, against my brother, against myself" (p. 116). The period of romance is over, the period of remorse begins. One pervasive element has not changed, however—Electre is still trying to live in an imaginary world.[9]

By insuring the dominance of that faculty she has to some extent preserved her identity. She will go on operating with the same means if not in the same framework. Oreste, at the end of the play, has found no equally stable principle. Having asserted that he is free, he has begun to discover

8. Cf. *L'Imaginaire*: ". . . reality is always accompanied by the collapse of the imaginary" (p. 281).

9. Doubrovsky comments: "Freedom must move away from the proudly isolated Ego of Oreste in *Les Mouches* and of Hugo in *Les Mains sales* to that relationship of pure reciprocity and of total integration where each is an Alter Ego for the Other. Examples are found in moments of fervor and revolutionary action. The misfortune is that the Apocalypse—and Sartre refers directly to the Malraux of *L'Espoir*—like all moments in which man bypasses his normal condition, comes in a flash. The difficulty, though it has been mitigated by an ingenious deployment of theory, reappears in all its force. Sartre will meet the same dead end, in his effort to move from the revolutionary instant into a revolutionary order, that Corneille met in his effort to move up from the heroic instant to the heroic order" (*Corneille, ou la dialectique du héros*, p. 508).

the questions raised by freedom; initially, he answers those questions with heady enthusiasm and little precision. He rejects the throne which Jupiter offers him—and which he has won. With airy insolence, he replies to Jupiter's threatening observation with a demeaningly casual question (p. 106):

> *Jupiter*: If you dare to think that you're free, then you have to vaunt the freedom of the prisoner in chains at the bottom of a dungeon and of the crucified slave.
> *Oreste*: Why not?

Oreste thinks he has been through the worst, and the better, if not the best, is yet to come. He is sure that life can now begin because he has passed to the other side of despair; what he does not know or even consider is that some of the despair may have rubbed off on him as he passed through it. He takes his leave of the city confidently:

> I want to be a king without a kingdom and without subjects. Farewell, my friends, try to live: everything is fresh here, everything has a new beginning. For me, too, life is beginning. A strange life. Let me just tell you this: one summer Skyros was infested with rats. It was a terrible plague which ate away at everything; the inhabitants of the city thought they would die. But one day a flute player came along. He stood up in the middle of the city—like this. (*He stands up.*) He began to play his flute and all the rats gathered quickly around him. Then he began to walk away in great strides like this (*he steps down from the pedestal*), crying out to the people of Skyros: "Out of the way!" (*The crowd steps aside.*) And all the rats raised their heads hesitatingly—the way the flies are doing. Look at them! Look at the flies! Then suddenly they rushed after him. And the flute player disappeared forever, taking the rats with him. Like this (p. 120–21).[10]

In the sense that he guarantees nothing to Argos except a clean start— and it is not all that clean because Jupiter has vowed to go on fighting and has already won one victory with Electre's capitulation—Oreste achieves very little. He has not guaranteed that the city will be any better equipped

10. The language is very much like that used by Sartre in a play, *Bariona*, which he wrote for Christmas festivities while he was a prisoner of war. At the end of the play, Bariona says: "I am free, I hold my destiny in my hands. I march against the soldiers of Herod, and God marches at my side. I am buoyant, Sarah, buoyant—if only you knew how buoyant I am. Ah joy, joy! Tears of joy! (Quoted by Burnier, *Les Existentialistes et la politique*, p. 20). The play has been reproduced (1964) in multigraphed form for distribution to Sartre's friends. It also appears in Contat's and Rybalka's *Les Ecrits de Sartre*, pp. 565–633.

than Electre to live without its remorse or some equally blameworthy attitude. He has found *his* identity and, in his initial exaltation, may very well have the wrong hopes and impossible desires; but the identity he has found, though it is floating rather than fixed, openminded rather than contained, is the right one. He is free, which means that he is and will remain nothing. It may be poor wisdom, but in the works of Sartre there can be no other unless one starts with this. And even then nothing more promising is assured.

That wisdom is much more important than anything that may happen in Argos as the result of Oreste's action. Since the play is a metaphor, the last speech is intended, not for the Argives, but for the audience which has been slowly seizing the sense of the metaphor. It is not Oreste who speaks at the end so much as it is the playwright who turns directly to the audience in order to issue a challenge and who, in passing, informs them of what his role will be.[11] The spectators have seen what their choice is and, on leaving the theatre to find themselves once more in occupied Paris, could not have avoided realizing, if only for the moment before the old blinders were back in place, the immediacy of that choice.[12] The playwright has also discovered what his function is: to draw the parallels, to mediate between the public and its experience, to live a strange and possibly isolated life. And to the extent that the playwright is indeed the piper he will be back, looking for other rats and playing whatever tunes may be required by new situations.

RELATED THEMES AND WORKS

Marc Beigbeder (*L'Homme Sartre,* p. 15) says that the stark, sunbaked, primitive setting of *Les Mouches* had been inspired by Sartre's visit to a deserted Greek village during his travels in the 1930s. Beigbeder speculates

11. Champigny comments: "A reconciliation between Orestes and the Argives would have defeated Sartre's moral purpose. The only *deus ex machina* is the spectator, the 'Other'. It is in the mind of the spectator, if possible in his life as a social being, that the third part of the trilogy stands a chance, a small one to be sure, of being more than a theatrical gesture. The spectator has to decide between the moral systems which have been presented, between the search for freedom and the search for psychological comfort, between violence and abstention, between Orestes and the Argives" (*Stages on Sartre's Way*, Bloomington, Ind., 1959, p. 99). Jeanson (*Sartre par lui-même*, pp. 150–51) speculates that Oreste's departure was principally indicative of Sartre's belief "that the Resistance [was] the personal adventure of each of its members; to this test of freedom, he did not yet envisage any other response than a sort of heroism of consciousness."

12. Andre Gorz comments: "The moral attitude implicit in Sartre's philosophy at that time was a purely individual ethic of authentification ('a writer's morality', as he later put it). It showed that freedom was at the source of all conduct and the permanent possibility that freedom comes to terms with itself, renounces the project of being, elects itself as the highest end by a commitment to action" ("De la Conscience à la praxis," *Livres de France,* 1 [1966]: 5).

that the village was probably not deserted but rather was enjoying its siesta. Simone de Beauvoir (*FA*, p. 521) says that much of the general background of the play was derived from Etruscan funeral ceremonies about which she had read in a book which she then passed on to Sartre. Charles Dullin's 1943 production was, in Thody's words (p. 77), "a primitive production . . . a mixture . . . of Surrealist exhibition and a display of African dances." In 1951, a revival was put on in Paris, using a text which Sartre had abridged and apparently changed in other ways. This text has not been published and I am not familiar with it. The most recent production by *La Compagnie Jean Deschamps* used a very bare set and made no attempt similar to Dullin's to create a background designed to place the play in a special focus.

The play strikes me as suffering from a basic weakness which Dullin's treatment sought to overcome. Though it is set in a city where primitive beliefs and practices are strong, and where ceremonial life holds a central position, its language, on all levels, is Latin Quarter Paris, circa 1943. Dullin's production tried to overcome this difficulty by presenting the play as an imaginative construct; in so doing it attempted to overcome the dangers of literalism which would have exposed the play's contradictory esthetic techniques. I have never seen a production of the play which was convincing. This is partially because the language remains a problem, but it is also because the argument is too often expressed through sermons, or debating speeches, which make it very obviously *une pièce à thèse*. It is also because some of it—especially the physical movements and speeches of the Furies—comes dangerously close to being silly. My hesitations are not those of French drama critics, who consider it one of Sartre's best plays.

In the preface to *Les Troyennes* (1965), his adaptation of Euripides' play, Sartre discusses the question of the language and metaphors which should be used in presenting ancient plays to modern audiences. His general argument insists on the need to find a modern idiom because reliance on the original idiom would create an unbridgeable gap between the modern audience and the meaning of the play. I find this an extremely dubious argument which is canceled out by the fact that Sartre was inspired to do his adaptation by Euripides' original text. The presupposition that others cannot be equally moved unless they are given a treated text is gratuitous. Sartre's adaptation is in a colorless prose, arranged to look like verse but possessing no kinship to poetic utterance. One result is that directors and actors naturally tend to interpret it as though it were poetry; what emerges is ludicrous, as the version broadcast by the French Radio in the spring of 1967—with a fine cast—showed. One of the more amusing ironies of that broadcast was an introductory explanation by a French professor who, in trying to prepare the listening audience for what he considered Sartre's "harsh and crude" language, was in effect undoing the theory and practice Sartre had outlined in his introduction to the printed text.

The friends of God have until recently been no friends of Sartre. A vitriolic example of the ininimity can be found in Robert Troisfontaines' *Le Choix de J.-P. Sartre* (Paris, 1945). An equally intemperate attack can be found in English in Kurt Reinhardt's *The Existentialist Revolt* (1960). Gabriel Marcel, whose existentialism is of a brand acceptable to Troisfontaines and Reinhardt, has been a faithful member of their company. Wilfrid Desan briefly discusses Sartre's concept of God in *The Tragic Finale* (Cambridge, 1954; Harper Torchbooks, 1960); his treatment is concerned only with the philosophical aspects of Sartre's thinking. Regis Jolivet, a Catholic churchman, has written a sympathetic study in his *Sartre ou la Théologie de l'absurde* (Paris, 1965). Francis Jeanson's *Sartre* (1966), in the *Ecrivains devant Dieu* series, contains a bibliography of works which discuss this aspect of Sartre's thought. Jeanson's book is on the whole a disappointment. He seems uncomfortable with his topic, despite his early disclaimers; he does not provide a really good summary of Sartre's thinking but seeks instead to do some imaginative theorizing. Some of the theorizing, notably his discussion of the role of Christ in Christian theology, is not at all uninteresting. Sartre himself has recently been less vehement in his discussion of God than he was in either *BN*, *Les Mouches*, or *Le Diable*. At a 1966 talk during a UNESCO conference on Kierkegaard, he presented a sympathetic and temperate analysis of the meaning of God for the Danish philosopher. (Excerpts were published in *La Quinzaine littéraire*, 15 June 1966). The next chapter of this book goes into some further details of the idea of God as it is presented in *Le Diable*.

Sartre's position on human freedom is the aspect of his philosophy which has perhaps been most severely attacked by other philosophers and psychiatrists because, highly abstract in nature, it corresponds to lived reality only as theory corresponds to fact. Sartre, as we have already seen and as we shall see further, is not unaware of this and in the *CRD* and the work-in-progress on Flaubert puts the fundamental theory pretty much to rest as he concentrates on the discussion of the enormous difficulty most men encounter in trying to exercise a faculty which is early impeded by their encounter with the world. His most recent statements are not, as a result, much different from the position of Stuart Hampshire. Readers can profit from reading Professor Hampshire's brief but dense *Freedom in the Individual* (New York, 1965) both because it is an excellent discussion and because it presents a more moderate position than Sartre's original position.

Today's men are born criminals,

and I must claim my share of their crime if I want

to have my share of their love and their virtue.

— Le Diable et le Bon Dieu

9 *Living Free*—II

If Oreste's pledge to live his freedom completely and constantly has earned him admission to some sort of pantheon, and if Oreste is Sartre, both he and Sartre are bound to discover that pantheons are not places of repose for the living; they are colonnaded passages through which one moves only to find, at the other end, the components of earlier situations rearranged to suggest a novelty which turns out to be superficial. Freedom is not a state of mind; it is an orientation, an intention to behave in a certain way; once embraced, it produces the momentary pleasure that comes with any decision. The ensuing movement promises change and progress; what it does not straightaway indicate is that one may have begun moving towards the dark places of further conflict. The trouble does not necessarily stem from the new situations; the trouble comes from other individuals who may also have won the right to pass into and through the same pantheon. They, too, have decided to live with their freedom. While their decision and Oreste's have to do with the same thing, the implementation of their decisions may take a quite different form. They are not people who, like the Argives or Electre, have renounced freedom for a more promising slavery; they are men who, like Goetz, the protagonist of *Le Diable et le Bon Dieu* (1951), know what human freedom means; they do not delude themselves. What they discover—or what they are going to discover with increasing frequency in Sartre's works—is that the exercise of freedom, in noble as well as ignoble causes, creates new problems, further dangerous situations none of which could have been foreseen either in its true nature or its full consequences. Freedom exercised with discrimination may extricate an individual from the bog of egotism only to plunge him into the maelstrom of a world in conflict.

Up to this point—with the exception of his portraits of Oreste and Hoederer—Sartre has been concerned with those obstacles which, because of their bulk and the fact that their existence predated his discovery of them, encouraged the individual to renounce freedom before taking any risks with it. In the cases of Roquentin, Mathieu, and Oreste, Sartre drew the portraits of men who had eventually realized that, however forceful and alien the obstacles might appear, *every* reaction to them was an exercise of freedom; one gave into them or one fought against them or one forgot about them *freely*. In each of these works his concern was with the equation: man=freedom. His concern was also with the attempt to show that authentic living depended on the acceptance of that equation. He has not yet turned his attention to the barriers which appear after the ceremonies of purification. Only with Gomez, and in the fragment which brings *Les*

Chemins de la liberté to a close, have we seen some of the troubled situations that come after those rites.

The direction in which the militant of freedom moves has been indicated, but little has been said about the nature of his new life. The result of this kind of partial survey has been that the decision to live free has seemed to be a great victory over a range of temptations and, because of that, adequate and even valuable in itself. But, in a world of need, where masses of men have neither enough food, enough clothing, or decent habitation such a victory risks being a scandal before it can ever become a triumph. It is a scandal because the victor's success depends on a luxury of movement and a richness of choice which is not at the disposal of large numbers of men. Sartre has had the time and the leisure to worry about the question; he has also had an education which has made him articulate enough to be able to argue with himself or with others about such issues. The encouragement Sartre has been dispensing liberally to all men—the encouragement to exist their freedom—might, however, appear to have little relevance to the man who, living on the scarce side of affluence, has to spend so much of his time and energy trying to survive that he has no leisure left to worry about either the great or small questions of life. One of the peasants in *Le Diable et le Bon Dieu* gives a terse summary of this situation when, in the act of buying an indulgence from Tetzel, he says that the man who labors sixteen hours a day hasn't the time to worry about his salvation.

As there are men whose condition does not allow them to think about whether they are living authentically or not, so there are individuals who having made the decision to live honestly find themselves beset with unexpected troubles. What they discover are the horrors which are enacted not only in the name of freedom but also as a result of the open use of freedom. These are horrors so great that the same honest men may very well ask themselves if they wouldn't be purer and the world a little less contaminated if they had chosen Pierre's or Lulu's solutions; in the long run Pierre and Lulu did little harm to anyone except themselves; and, as we shall see, had they chosen another more authentic way, they might have done considerably more damage both to themselves and others. The easy answer to this—that so many small absences eventually amount to an enormous presence of passivity and indifference which clears the way for greater threats and more pervasive evils—contains an implication which is not demonstrably true. For, if it is suggested that the individual's refusal to act freely is a contribution to some kind of evil, then it is implied that his agreement to act will make some contribution to the flourishing of good in the world. Too often the individual finds that this is not true. His lonely protest avails him nothing; in too many cases it increases the weight of evil.

His well-intentioned act does this because the world is not a multiplicity of individuals who, if they act individually in answer to noble inspiration, will automatically make this planet a pleasant place to be. The world is a collection of collectivities whose existence preceded and conditions the life of every individual. At best, each of these collectivities has its own ideals which it embraces with fervor and defends at the price of the life and liberty of the individuals who belong to it. At worst, in the defence of its ideals, it may resort to either manifest or hidden terror on the grounds that freedom or national autonomy or economic independence are goods precious enough to require a bloodbath from time to time. Manifest terror is open violence: the slaying of prisoners of war because it is inconvenient and perhaps even impossible to do anything else; the establishment, in the name of the greater good of all concerned, of slave-labor camps or of collective farms whose operations seem to have more to do with savagery than with progress. Socially productive terror loses its value because of the possibility that a man like Stalin may be less interested in the good of the workers than in his own apotheosis.

Hidden terror is usually manifested in economic practices: the policies of French entrepreneurs which depended, according to Sartre, on keeping the French worker firmly ensconced in his misery;[1] the pressures exerted by the United States to deprive countries of food or democracy when one or another of the deprivations appears to serve the needs of American planners. Whatever the nature of the program which makes use of terror, two things are clear. First, the terror is directly involved with the pursuit of an ideal which, superficially, can be made to seem good: America wants only peace and freedom in the world; Russia wants only to release the workers of the world from their economic slavery. Secondly, whoever cooperates with either agency in the name of the ideal being pursued is necessarily a part of the terror. By his free act of cooperation with his government, an individual is involved in the maintenance of Batista in Cuba or the suppression of the revolution in Hungary.[2]

The old framework of Sartre's thought does not so much crack as find itself forced to expand beyond its capacity in order to take account of the larger body of information he acquired during the 1950s. The Sartrean

1. Sartre discussed this issue in a series of articles published in *TM* between 1952 and 1954 and gathered together as "Les Communistes et la paix" in *Sit. VI*, pp. 80–384. Sartre later avowed that the article's insistence on the Malthusianism of French employers and industrialists referred to an economic policy which was just then beginning to change.

2. In *Les Séquestrés d'Altona* Sartre will deal with this issue in its widest possible ramifications for an individual. For the moment, one moving phrase from that play is appropriate to this discussion: "There are two ways of destroying a people: you can condemn them as a group or you can force them to denounce the leaders they have given themselves. The second is the worse" (p. 43).

individual still must go on negotiating with himself and with his temptations
and weaknesses; but the negotiations are carried on within the larger framework of the community and world in which he lives. It is not that the
individual is irrelevant in a world of superpowers; rather the world of superpowers—whether they be parents or nations—achieves a relevance which
Sartre had not before given it. He had partially depicted it in *Le Sursis*
as a kind of evil which came from elsewhere; and there, as well as in *La
Mort dans l'âme*, the need for reciprocal terror was understandable: good
and evil faced each across the Rhine, and there was no trouble in discerning
which was the side of light, which of darkness. In the aftermath of the war,
Sartre learned the impotence of formulas. That lesson stirred his realization
that neither workers nor "right" ideas were going to triumph simply because
they existed in large numbers and were "right." He saw himself as a man
who had always lived in relative comfort and therefore as a man who had
raised fundamental questions about the meaning of existence without ever
having experienced fundamental difficulties in possessing its means. A full
belly, a steady income, and long academic holidays allowed his body to
stay healthy while his mind contemplated what possibly were horrors for
others; but there was a significantly different portrait evoked by the metaphysical statement that man is nothing and that evoked by the more
mundane observation that most men are always underfed. Hungry man
may not care about whether and what he is; he cares very much about
whether and what he is going to eat at his next meal.

This realization led Sartre to conclude that the ideas he had formulated
in his philosophy and experimented with in his literature were irrelevant
to the immediate situation of the great majority of men. Given their misery,
there was something indecent and quite possibly wrong in telling them
that their misery and hunger and poverty were states to which they had
freely assented and thus states from which they could escape by a similarly
free act of the will. Whatever truths or accurate descriptions were contained
in *Being and Nothingness* could only be appreciated by those who had the
funds to buy it, the leisure to read it, and the moral force to do something
in answer to its charges. Any worker who might stumble across it could
justifiably consider it little more than another clause in the big lie which
tyrannically conditioned his existence. Man, or men, did not strike such
a worker as useless passions at all, since some men had put *his* labor to *their*
very profitable personal uses. Sartre, in brief, realized that he had had no
genuine communication with the have-nots of the world and jotted down
this note: "Speak to the person who can't be convinced (the Hindu who
is dying of hunger): otherwise all communication is compromised. This
has certainly been the meaning of my development and of my contradiction" (quoted by Beauvoir, *FC*, p. 262).

The contradiction to which he alludes was an upsetting discovery for a man who had sought to establish a universally applicable definition of man. Sartre's intellectual background and his economic condition had exposed him to a mode of freedom which not only had set him apart from the majority of men but which had also conditioned his experience to the point where his individualism had become something of immense value to him. Mme de Beauvoir tells us that he set such a high price on this freedom that he would have had to oppose anyone who tried to deprive him of it. In another working note, Sartre amplifies what he means: "The contradiction was not [only] in [my] ideas. It was in my being. For the freedom *I* was, implied the freedom of all. And all were not free. I could not, without snapping apart, put myself under the discipline of all. And yet I could not be free alone" (*FC*, p. 262).

I mention these notes, not simply because they show a broadening of Sartre's outlook, but also because they provide an essential background for the mood in which he wrote *Le Diable et le Bon Dieu* and his subsequent works. Though the claim may at first seem exaggerated, this play is profoundly autobiographical. In it Sartre is looking for himself; he is also trying to find out where to go beyond *Being and Nothingness* and the ultimately ineffectual involvement in social programs he had experienced after the war; finally, he is trying to find some sort of resolution for the contradiction between his refusal to let himself be directed by all and his concurrent need of others, a contradiction which was made all the more bitter by his hope of resolving it in terms of a freedom which could serve a public function without ceasing to be coincident with his individual aspirations.

That contradiction, and the fundamental issue it rests upon, can be seen at the end of *Les Mouches*, for, if Oreste has found his way and has some confidence about its value, the fact remains that the merit of that way depends in some part on a comparison between his victory and Electre's capitulation; it involves, too, the fact that he has left the Argives behind to look after themselves. The implication is that he has done a good thing for them by assuming the remorse and guilt which so narrowly circumscribed their existence. In so doing he may, in fact, have deprived them of a psychological bolster which, if it did nothing else, furnished security and a limited number of rewards; he may also have won his victory by leaving them with nothing except an unpredictable and undesired future. Two issues are placed in relief by the resulting situation. How can the Argives, who have been habituated to a particular mode of existence, govern themselves in a meaningful way once Oreste has taken away both their sense of existence and, by his murders, the forces of government? What is Oreste's value when he leaves the town just as its real, its authentic, problems begin? *Being and Nothingness* provided evident answers to these questions. Oreste has brought the Argives the authentic existence their freely accepted remorse tried to hold at bay; he has thus created the situation wherein they can establish a government of their own making rather than accept the one imposed by the combined self-serving of Egisthe and Jupiter.

Sartre's introduction to Roger Stéphane's *Portrait de l'aventurier* (*Sit. VI*, p. 7–22) indicates the changes that took place in his thinking as the result of issues which haunted him in the years immediately preceding the composition of *Le Diable et le Bon Dieu*. His concern in his introduction to *Portrait de l'aventurier* is with the clear distinction between the adventurer—a man like Oreste whose commitment is to the formation of *his* personality through a program which *may* serve the needs of others—and the militant, the man who, like the worker enrolled in the Communist party, must hitch his hopes to a program outlined and directed by others before he can expect to possess any personal dignity. The Argives were unaware of such a choice, since Oreste offered them no clear program of militancy; his eye was on further undefined adventures. In the absence of a program, the Argives are neither fully liberated nor properly directed. Oreste, the adventurer, has left them to their own inadequate devices which means, in effect, that he has left them in abjection. There they will derive solace from their belief in the gods. Heaven, then, provides them with both meaning and excuse. The Argives can go on sinning and repenting; indeed the repentance will continue to ease the momentary stress of the sins. Though Oreste has cleared the terrain of their existence of all the old debris, the regrading of that terrain depends on them. In 1943 Oreste's gesture seemed to be all that was needed; by 1951 it appeared to be futile. Sartre grew to appreciate that abject men may have been so affected by abjection as to be incapable of formulating any program. Oreste's departure is an unthinking abandonment of a situation Oreste has created; it thereby raises the fundamental question of Oreste's social worth. Sartre's new purpose, which reflects the contradiction already mentioned, is to justify the adventurer while recognizing that nothing he undertakes is motivated by the same need or stamped with the same value as the militant's enterprise. He has come a long way from *La Nausée*.

The militant inspires more confidence because his membership in the Communist party is the result of otherwise inescapable necessity. He is not like Hugo who, in order to be a successful member of the party, would have had to renounce all concern with the preservation of his ego. The militant does not have an ego; that is Sartre's way of saying that his class has not provided him with the kinds of inestimable treasure Hugo had inherited from the bourgeoisie. What Hugo, or even Sartre, tries to preserve is something the worker is not conscious of until he has become a member of the party—something which loosely and dangerously might be called human dignity. The militant cannot have the kind of assurance about individual worth that the child of comfort has because the militant, as a worker, has lived too intimately with two threats: first, another can as easily be found to do his work if he rebels; second, because of circumstances beyond his ken or control, there may be no job at all. In an incoherent fashion, the abused worker is aware of being interchangeable; the Other consequently does not represent quite the same problem to him as he represents to Lucien. The worker by his condition forms a unity with all the others who may be let go when he is let go; he is also one with those who in times of economic depression may find no work at all. Hazard rules his life, not as the possibility of catastrophe, but as its probability.

Unlike the bourgeois child, he has no reason to believe that there is something irreplaceable about him, nor does any element in his situation encourage him to believe that he is unique. It is precisely because he is not unique that he has trouble finding work. Yet, though he does not share the comfort of the moneyed classes, he does not necessarily share their radical solitude either; once he has become a member of the Communist party he certainly does not share their *kind* of solitude since his accession to a sense of his possibilities, which is a comparable development to the bourgeois' recognition of his ego (that is, of special interests to be preserved), is made in the company of others. The young Communist becomes aware of his personal interests as interests he *must* share with others if he is ever to satisfy them.

While he may not solve all the problems that crop up in encounters with the Other, the Communist solves many of those problems by discovering the Other as the individual with whom he must cooperate and who must cooperate with him. In contrast to the bourgeois, who lives imbued with the ideal of preserving his individuality against the collectivity, the Communist endows himself with the need to act collectively in order to become a human being. The bourgeois seeks to have his singularity ratified by the woman he marries—the woman Lucien envisaged waiting somewhere in the wings for him to beckon her to make her appearance on the stage of his life. The young worker who enters the Communist party has no ego before he begins to love; he discovers himself and his possibilities in the gift of himself which he makes to others and which the others make to him.

We have seen at several points the contradictions Sartre finds in the attitude of the young bourgeois: seeking to preserve his ego or his interests, he must constantly act; he cannot be sure of himself without being confirmed by another in some way, and yet each collusion with the Other risks becoming a collision. The bourgeois, cherishing his ego, detests his solitude; still the only way he can be sure of preserving his individuality is to live alone and that, as we saw with Roquentin, is not what he really wants to do. "Through action one becomes other, one pulls violently away from oneself, one changes oneself in changing the world" (p. 12). This is a truth most Sartrean protagonists do not wish to admit; when, like Lulu, they admit it through their actions, they make a determined effort to deny it in their thoughts.

This is because their project is intimately connected with self-interest. That self-interest does not have a public dimension except in those instances where, if their self-image is to survive, they must manipulate that part of the world which threatens them. This was the case with two of the characters in *Huis-clos* who denied the public consequences of their evil because their projects never turned out as they had hoped. The militant cannot initially have such concerns, nor make such razor-thin distinctions, if only because he has so little to protect; instead he has fundamental claims to assert about the basic physical conditions of life. In joining the party, he begins to be human; more importantly, he is sustained and created anew by the party's project which, incorporating his, also carries it beyond its initial humble goals. He thus comes to serve a greater interest than might have been expected; in serving that interest he receives certain rewards. He has the sense of having enlisted in a cause whose success will work to his profit and also to that of those who come after him.

His life is not only a struggle against the haunting fact of death—though finally, like every man, he dies alone and possibly in anguish—his life is also a struggle for the amelioration of conditions which will still obtain after his death. He is not concerned with achieving personal glory because his immediate needs are too bitterly mixed with reality to allow for fantasy. He has nothing to lose by fraternal cooperation with others; possibly he has everything to gain. The bourgeois youth has everything to lose in such cooperative projects; glory remains his ideal because, glorious, he will become the ideal of his fellow bourgeois, the embodiment of what glory means. Glory ratifies the bourgeois notion of individual dignity since the glorious man exists as an ideal for everyone. The bourgeois does not work for the good of the overall collectivity; were he to do that, he might have to give up some part of what he treasures in himself. He works in order to win the collectivity's respect.

Sartre is here touching on an idea which he treats more expansively in *Saint Genet.* It is summarized in his assertion that the saint exists because of the criminal, since the criminal creates the standards by which we judge the saint. The ramifications of such an idea are clear. What they imply is that traditional ideas of excellence mean no more than this: the man who triumphs over others by whatever means, is better than those others. But in order for him to be better there have to be those others than whom he is better; and in order to know what "better" means, and if what it means is worth anything, it is necessary to see who the others are and to analyze the process by which a single individual has become their superior.

Roquentin's sense of superiority stemmed from a conviction that he had a wisdom about the others which they could have had but which they consciously chose not to possess. Lucien's apprehension of dangers had led him to accept identification with his class and thus to trim down any dreams of the glory he might earn by triumphing, after the fashion of the young Rimbaud, over his class; his consolation was the sensation of glory he experienced in becoming a junior entrepreneur and in undertaking his crusade against Jews. We are seeing Sartre's work as a brief against a class which allows little possibility for valuable individual excellence; threatened, the leaders of the class must enlist the solid support of all of its members in order to maintain their economic and "moral" superiority. In this sense the leaders are the managers of uneasy contradictions. The ideal they present to their recruits is not an ideal which can be pursued within the class; if it were, the leaders would be threatened both from within and without. To insure their special status and protect themselves from the consequences of the contradictions, the leaders must conjure up other menaces which threaten all the members of the society they govern: the Jews, the Germans, the workers, and especially the Communist party, which is looked upon as evil incarnate, not only because it is materialistic but also because, as some clergymen never cease saying, it is "atheistic materialism." (There is, of course, a divine materialism, expressed in lavish churches and episcopal palaces, which is quite acceptable.) The fundamental distinction between the bourgeois youth and the young worker comes down to this: if the worker receives his purpose from the party, he also receives a program to which that purpose can be applied; if the bourgeois youth receives his ideal from his class, he finds that the class's program—its self-preservation—immediately calls for a tailored approach to the pursuit of that ideal.

In writing of *Les Mots* and of the "Merleau-Ponty" essay, I showed the effect that this contradiction had on Sartre. His education and family background had imbued him with a sense of optimism, a desire for renown, and a realization that there was something false about the whole arrangement: the bourgeois chiefs would not only call in their promissory notes if the young man strayed too far beyond tolerable bounds, they would also demand exorbitant and unannounced interest rates. Though Sartre can and does issue declarations of hatred against his class, he cannot shake off completely the formation he received, which means that he cannot effectively deny that the bourgeois emphasis on the possibility of individual excellence goes beyond being the myth of a class in order to express a fundamental truth about human drives and capacities. The irony which allows him his revenge is that the class does not want to live with the implications of its own emphasis; its younger members either capitulate to its demands or become, as Sartre has become, adventurers.[3]

3. Writing about Paul Nizan, Sartre describes the consequences of such a decision: "What a strange kind of life: at first alienated, then stolen, then hidden and saved

This option plunges the bourgeois youth into a very ambiguous ethical situation. If one member becomes better than the other members of the class, and if those other members remain comfortable, one has done no real harm to anyone. A company vice-presidency is a more than adequate consolation prize; and, in the constant jockeying of today's corporate board rooms, Monday's vice-president can live with the hope of Tuesday's shake-up and, the award, on Wednesday, of a slippery slot at the top. But if, inspired by the class's expressed ideal, one decides to live it, one may find that it cannot be lived in the class because neither presidencies nor vice-presidencies adequately express the ideal, especially in a world where there are so many others who can aspire neither to presidencies nor to ideals. The adventurer, compelled to action by something learned within his class, may have no choice except to turn against his class.

If revolt appears to be a solution, it is only a partial one, not because the struggle against the bourgeoisie may be wrong, but because the motives one brings to the struggle may be tinged with insincerity. The adventurer may become a parasite on the militants simply because, like Hugo and, of course, like Sartre, he *chooses* to embrace their cause; he also chooses the methods, means, and moment of his identification with that cause. If he gets tired or finds other interests, he can always withdraw. One can imitate Lucien's (and Rimbaud's) example in one's forties as readily as in one's twenties. This, in Sartre's opinion as in that of others, is precisely what André Malraux has done. The reference to Malraux is not made out of malice; his influence on Sartre's generation was enormous precisely because he, along with Lawrence of Arabia, seemed to provide an alternative to Lucien's choice. Malraux, fighting successively if not successfully on several of the world's battlefronts and, between engagements, writing books that were eloquent descriptions of those battlefronts, was a herald. But time not only produced change in the location of his battlefronts, it also supplied glosses to his more ringing statements with the result that, if in *La Condition humaine* he spoke of creating a world whose factories could testify to human dignity as the medieval cathedrals had done, in his later utterances he showed that such dreams stemmed from obsessions produced by a bourgeois formation. No worker would have disturbed his sleep with such entertainments. Malraux's preoccupation with death, for example, is a bourgeois obsession which the worker does not share since, already possessed of so little in life, he has only that little to lose when he dies. Poverty does not offer romance to those for whom it is an inescapable fact.

---

right up to the moment of death because it was a life which said no. But it is also an exemplary life because it was a scandal, as is every life that has ever been made and as are the lives being manufactured for young people today; but it was a scandal which knew itself for such and which was made known as such to the public" (*Sit. IV*, p. 187).

The problem, for the adventurer who wishes to look directly and unflinch-
ingly at his situation, is this: though he may find a way to express his ideal
by associating himself with the workers' cause, he cannot really become
part of that cause. He always remains the Other for those in whose cause
he enlists, simply because he shares their concerns *voluntarily*; his goal
is not theirs. What he seeks has a circular pattern. His may be a better
because a more inclusive circle than the erratic orb finally traced by Lucien;
still it is a sketched line which brings him back to his original ideal by ful-
filling that ideal in his life. Having been educated to believe in his individual dignity, he expends his life in order to prove that he does indeed have
that dignity. The worker cannot have such concerns since any line he sought
to draw would only enclose him more tightly in his misery and that precisely
is where he does not wish to be. The worker's project is forward moving
and, in a carefully restricted sense of the adjective, visionary; it aims at
breaking out of the real or willed circle. It provides the essential force for
the adventurer; yet, once the worker's goal is achieved, there will be no
place left either for the adventurer or his project.

This, Sartre says, is right and good; it should also be inevitable because
the militant's cause is just. But it is nevertheless the cause of some melancholy reflections since it implies two things: first, the adventurer will
be doomed to solitude because of his essential isolation from the experience
of the worker; second, the disappearance of the adventurer from a future
world where social justice will finally be installed suggests that that world
will then be a sterile place. Everything in Sartre's previous psychological
analyses testifies to the impossibility of such sterility; in those works he
had presented conflict as something which arises with the individual's initial
discovery of the world; it is predictable that once the worker is adequately
fed and tolerably comfortable he will stumble into the same antinomies
encountered by man in *Being and Nothingness*. At this point in his career
Sartre seems not to want to probe too deeply into that possibility. There
is something depressing and conceivably self-defeating about urging
reform programs which will pluck the worker from economic misery in
order to plunge him into psychological misery. Yet, having always insisted
that man never is but is always trying to be, Sartre cannot really anticipate
that there will one day be a world in which this very fundamental and vexa-
tious situation—and it will remain fundamental as long as man is mortal—
will be done away with by social reform. Such a bland world, with its evoca-
tions of the *Brave New World*, so disturbs Sartre that he knows almost
instinctively what his role would be: Mr. Savage, the adventurer, the tireless
voice which utters the latest refusal to go along with any system that derives
part of its force from the sacrifice of his individuality.

Curiously but understandably, Sartre concludes his introduction to
Portrait de l'aventurier by saying that he does not want to see the adven-

turer's heritage obliterated by the triumph of the militants. The statement is curious because Sartre has recognized that the adventurer's project results from social evil and that the adventurer is thus the by-product of evil: what he is depends on what others are not. Sartre is fighting here to assert his own individuality against what might appear a puzzling general position: he urges the workers to accept the Communist party's discipline even though he himself refuses to accept it. Part of Sartre's refusal may indeed stem from the fact that no necessity forces him into the party. A far larger part of it stems from the fact that he could not submit to such discipline and remain Jean-Paul Sartre. That in turn suggests something which, on his own terms, would be an ugly truth: against the anonymity of being another worker in the cause, he prefers the celebrity of being the independent critic. He writes:

> Adventurer or militant—I don't believe in this dilemma. I know too well that an act has two faces: the negativity which comes from the adventurer and the achievement which results from discipline. What we must do is reestablish negativity, disquietude, and self-criticism within discipline. We will never win unless we draw all the consequences from this vicious circle: man remains to be made and it is only man who can make him (p. 22).

In saying that he does not believe in the dilemma he is actually saying that he does not want to believe in it. What he wants to believe is that the radical dichotomy between militant and adventurer which he has just traced out can in some way be reduced. A harsh critic might suggest that there is no such problem since the dichotomy is not a real one but a Sartrean one. A Sartrean problem, however, is a real problem for Sartre, and while its statement in the introduction to *Portrait de l'aventurier* sometimes brushes on nonsense it never altogether abandons sense. Sartre has always had a tendency to depict complex situations in sweeping general lines and then to presuppose that every detail repeats the overall pattern; every worker is without ego and potentially ready to fight the good cause; furthermore, every worker is endowed by history with the right to do so; every bourgeois is lonely, confused, and seriously or slightly schizophrenic. In any strict analysis, this approach is ill-informed and suffers from its own ardor; in a polemical sense, it isolates an undeniable truth: some men are free to refuse to live in the situation where they find themselves; others are not. The freedom to get out, to say no *and still survive*, creates an essential distinction between categories of men; unfortunately what it does not create is the fixed and eternal distinction Sartre insists upon.

The worker whose situation is improved to the point where he no longer lives hedged by misery may quickly cease to have any interest in the world's remaining poor; the bourgeois may enlist his energies in the service of causes which are so essential to his structure of belief that no force other than illness or death can dissuade him from his support of those causes. There are measurable differences between the first Henry Ford and Walter Reuther, between Lawrence of Arabia and John F. Kennedy. While the concepts of the militant and the adventurer provide useful categories for describing kinds of activities, they become less useful when applied to particular individuals since, in the latter occurrence, they fail to take account of sometimes crucial details. Surely it is easier to deal with a world divided into camps and a humanity broken down into categorical groups; it is not, unfortunately, very prudent, if only because such a technique presents a false and unsophisticated portrait. It also risks becoming a caricature of the reality it is trying to portray.

This, as we shall see more completely in the last chapter, is persistently the greatest weakness in Sartre's outlook. As a good product of the French educational system, he sees the world in schemas. Because he is infected by Manicheism, those schemas are concerned with locating the disposition of the forces of good and evil; because he is French, he is not spared that Gallic arrogance which presupposes that Gaul is the macrocosm of which the rest of the world is the microcosm. What results too often is a wild West adventure. The forces of good, though sparse and weak, fight against organized evil; surprisingly, they triumph. They triumph because they should; and if, in reality, they don't win, then they must win dialectical arguments. Though they are not now winning in France, they can be assured that, because they are good and their oppressors evil, victory must one day be theirs.

If they have no other visible resource, Sartre's militants are mighty with rectitude; by contrast, the adventurers are new soldiers who, not wanting to be the hoplites of their class, seek to become the heroes either of that class or of the militants. Because they are morally androgynous, they have an indeterminate relation to the good-evil dichotomy. The stubborn part of Sartre's mind is uncomfortable with them—as it is with workers who, no longer living in misery, opt for bourgeois values and possessions. The speculative part of his mind is tempted by the seduction the adventurers offer; precisely because they confuse the old distinctions, the morally androgynous help prepare the way for a new moment. Even when they do not perform such a major function in the service of novel distributions of social and moral forces, they raise the questions and express the doubts which keep already existing categories from becoming rigid.

Sartre has been willing to run the risk of appearing morally androgynous because he wishes to avoid the greater risk of sterile orthodoxy. His refusal to join the Communist party or to be controlled by it was an implicit recognition that the French party in crucial moments of decision-making or self-evaluation preferred orthodoxy—with its dogmatic statements and periodic rashes of interdictions and excommunications—to experimentation, rectitude to reality. Steadfastly playing its purely negative role in the Chamber of Deputies, the party assumed that it was acting in the name of the highest morality, which wished plagues on every house that did not enshrine Marx.[4] In the bargain, it condemned the worker to a stagnation which was no less fetid for being morally or ideologically inspired.

In the same bargain, it instilled uneasiness in men like Sartre. There was never much chance that the bourgeoisie would believe Sartre was working in its behalf; there were constant accusations from the Communist chiefs that he was doing nothing else. Thus, from the realities of the French political scene and his oscillations between its various poles, Sartre attempts the difficult task of meditating on his situation in universal terms. The child of the bourgeoisie has exiled himself from its beliefs and practices only to learn that as a convinced Marxist he has been interdicted by the local branch of that church. The two houses in which we might have lived are no longer hospitable to him. Knowing which is the home of evil and which the home of good, which he rejects and which he accepts, he still finds himself living in the hinterland; he is the prophet without honor and also the prophet who is skeptical about visionaries and prophets and solitaries. He wonders how the prophet gets invited into the house of the lord when his prophecies suggest that the lord's policies need to be changed and when the lord, well aware of the interloper's proposed reforms, is determined to maintain his policies unchanged.

Sartre firmly believed that the house of the Marxist lord was, despite its signs of shabbiness, a sturdier structure than the crumbling bourgeois mansion. There should have been no reason to criticize his desire to shore up that sturdier structure before going to live in it—no reason, unless one was already living within the structure and therefore was unable to see how certain stresses were splitting seams. Men like Merleau-Ponty grew to believe that the only place to be was in the hinterland; they believed

4. This raises a thorny issue because Sartre, while condemning the French Communist party for its useless intransigence and for its dogmatic condemnations of those who, if not its friends, are certainly not its enemies, has tended to act in the same categorical way towards those who do not fall with the confines of his orthodoxy. Though he was a passionate supporter of Algerian independence, he was an equally passionate opponent of De Gaulle and argued vehemently in a series of articles that no possible good could come from the General (*Sit. V*, pp. 89–166). Yet, even as he argued, De Gaulle was setting up a strategy which made it possible for Sartre's wish to be realized. There are, of course, many other things which separated Sartre from De Gaulle, but his opposition in this particular instance is an indication of something I will discuss later: his inflexibility, his refusal of compromise, and, most tellingly, his failure to note and accept what appear to be the most promising processes for producing change in this world. One of his and Simone de Beauvoir's young friends once said to them: "What's tiresome about you . . . is that others must have your opinions *at the same moment as you*" (*FA*, p. 37). In the spring of 1969, Sartre headed a committee which urged voters to abstain from voting in the referendum which led to De Gaulle's retirement.

this, not because it was an "honorable" position to take, but because it was an honest one. That attitude implied the legitimacy of a third position and attributed a value to it. Sartre is uneasy with this because he is bothered by certain questions: who confers the value or, in terms more precisely his, who mandates the third position which is neither intermediary between the existing poles nor visibly committed to another? His fear seems to be that the mandate comes from nothing more honorable than human cowardice; and cowardice achieves no great distinction by being related to a desire for purity. When it is no more than the absence of the courage needed to walk boldly into the Communist structure, the Communists may be right in saying that those who are not with them are against them; the hesitant are no more than another breed of adventurers who stray in and out of social reality unwilling to commit themselves, unable to effect meaningful change because of their reluctance to accept discipline and the programs of action discipline makes possible.

If you are Sartre and have polarized the world into good and evil—only to discover, because you are honest, that those poles are slippery to a degree that excludes stability—and if you have several times expressed your conviction that there is a universally applicable truth, your presence on the plains of indecision can superficially be ascribed to a fear of encumbering commitment; for indecision in a polarized struggle where everything is at stake, has no ascribable value whatsoever. While there is legitimate reason to question, as Merleau-Ponty did, the validity of believing in the necessity or even the reality of that polarization, we must recognize that it was the only reality for Sartre; it therefore allowed him no other choice. He knew to which pole he was attracted. His observations told him that the pole he preferred was off-center; his admirable hope of real and profitable improvement of the workers' cause warned him that, if he allowed himself to be tied to that pole, he would certify its dislocation and possibly impede the proletariat's progress. What he henceforth had to do was show that his presence away from the pole was maintained in the greater interests of the pole; what he had also to do was find some way of making those who were already clustered around the pole see that he was indeed working for them and not for himself. His refusal to join the party was a strategy plotted out in order to guarantee that the workers' membership would be more meaningful.

From 1951 on Sartre allows no question of where he stands; if he is not in the Communist house, he is firmly encamped on the surrounding terrain from which he hurls scathing condemnations at the bourgeoisie. Politically, he becomes concerned with the nature and possibilities of social man. His literature will no longer be exclusively concerned with why men live apart, in fear, making use of each other for personal rather than communal purposes. Rather it will be dedicated to presenting situations in which advance-

ment becomes possible only through cooperation. Philosophically, he will
be concerned with extending the basic structures of *Being and Nothingness*
in order to show that being-for-others, despite the fears it creates in individual man, is the only way man can accede to the fullness of his potentiality
for creating, along with others, a genuinely human world. Personally, he
will be concerned with demonstrating, through the combination of these
activities, that the place for Oreste is on a promontory overlooking Argos.
From that vantage point, he can give generous encouragement to the
Argives, inform them of what is happening in Corinth, and warn them about
all forays organized by the happy city against the emerging new and *right*
order.

Le Diable et le Bon Dieu is the first step in this new direction, the implementation of the speculations expressed in the introduction to *Portrait de
l'aventurier*. By its very title, the play alludes to the question of polarization;
in its presentation it demonstrates, not that polarization is a reality to be
discarded, but that it represents an inevitable distribution of the world's
active forces. The devil and God, as symbols of a particular theory of good
and evil, may not be the exact symbols of the true opposition and therefore
may have to be redefined. Once the redefinition and redistribution have
taken place, human reality still remains wedded to conflict. Each of the
two armies in the conflict gathers around one of the forces; each produces
surprises. For it may turn out that, in the process of rearrangement, the
forces of good are not the forces of God, which implicitly means that the
forces of the Devil are not necessarily engaged on the side of evil.

The particular backdrop against which the process evolves is the Peasants' Revolt; the more general background, as a result, has to do with the
nature of revolution, the forces that produce it and the reasons why it comes
about. The play therefore has to do with the kinds of redistribution and
change which are implicit in all revolutions, whether they be in sixteenth-
century Germany or twentieth-century Europe. The meaning of revolution
here implies both an overturning of a present order and the installation
of a new order; more significantly, it means that, once the reversal has taken
place, a process of purification has also come about. The terms on which
the old order sought to effect its destiny and maintain its sway have not
disappeared; they have been assigned to new forces and other individuals
who presumably will act more honestly in seeking to bring about what
those terms promise. In other words, good and evil do not disappear as
meaningful terms once the revolution is under way. Quite the contrary,
they emerge as even more powerful and meaningful terms because they
label spades as spades rather than attempting the more difficult task of
calling suffering serenity.

The center of the play is Goetz, who cannot be called its chief protagonist
because he is as much passive as active. To be a man of decisive action

had been his chief hope; yet, as the play unfolds, he learns that individual action, no matter how resolutely it is sustained and no matter how susceptible it is to change, is not strong enough to eliminate the influence of other forces. Goetz, since he is a bastard, exists naturally as the foe of legitimacy—something which he can never possess. This allows him one of two reactions: he can compromise with his instinct and accept the uncertain role, with all its unpredictable consequences, that falls to him because of his bastardy; or he can undermine legitimacy's claims by refusing to accept their validity. The latter is what he opts for and, as a result, he becomes the perfect image of free Sartrean man. He does not accept the situation into which he is born because that situation imposes stern limitations; it categorizes him in the terms of others and, in the process, tells him that he has no terms properly his own. His refusal to accept those terms passes gradually into open opposition to them, an opposition which is expressed in his decision to live in full personal freedom; he will do only what he chooses to do, change his programs to suit his caprices, meet situations according to present will or whim.

This leads him, in the first critical moment of the play, to abandon the evil to which he has committed himself in order to fight for the generally accepted notion of good; he will stop ravaging the earth in order to redeem it. In making his decision he pretends to accept the authority of chance: the dice will decide.[5] The dice, however, do not decide because Goetz cheats. His decision to work in the name of good results from fraud on his part and not from the lay of the cubes. At this point in the play, the cheating is meant to do no more than underscore the fact that his choice is a free one; it also emphasizes the perennial Sartrean conviction that even the acceptance of honestly read dice would be a voluntary decision on a man's part to pretend that chance has some defensible claim to his attention. Later in the drama, cheating will play a more crucial function when it becomes a method of response, a way of saying no to existing authorities and institutions in order to say yes to the human beings who are oppressed by those authorities and institutions.[6]

Goetz sets about to install the reign of good on the earth; he establishes the City of the Sun whose citizens are encouraged to love one another and

5. The image of the dice is derived from Mallarmé's hermetic *Un Coup de dés jamais n'abolira le hasard.*

6. Cf. *BN*: "These conversions which have not been studied by philosophers, have often inspired novelists. One may recall the *instant* at which Gide's Philoctetes casts off his hatred, his fundamental project, his reason for being, and his being. One may recall the *instant* when Raskolnikoff decides to give himself up. These extraordinary and marvelous instants when the prior project collapses into the past in the light of a new project which rises on its ruins and on what as yet exists only in outline, in which humiliation, anguish, joy, hope are delicately blended, in which we let go in order to grasp and grasp in order to let go—these have often appeared to furnish the clearest and most moving image of our freedom" (pp. 475–76).

to join with Goetz in proving that goodness can find a home on the earth. The trouble is that it finds no more than a spot. The Peasants' Revolt still rages in surrounding territories; the force of those other ruling authorities is undiminished; those who had once been associated with Goetz in his enterprises, as well as the woman he is tempted to love, will have little or nothing to do with his City of the Sun since they see it as an expression of the kind of neutrality which serves the cause of legitimacy. The bastard may well have made some statement about good by founding his City of the Sun. An accurate translation of that statement into the language of reality would read: good serves evil when it refuses to enter into combat with it. That is what Goetz has refused to do. He will not join with the peasants in their cause because the cause is doomed; he will not join with the barons either. His double refusal serves the interests of the latter even as it works against the interests of the former.[7]

His project, though it is unquestionably successful on a local scale—the city works, its citizens are happy—is irrelevant to the country's bigger and more genuine conflict. He has abstracted himself from the world and risks being abstracted from his own city until he cheats once again, simulates a miracle, and thereby maintains a dishonestly won influence over an irrelevant corner of the earth. He has lost his wager about producing good in the world because his brand of good has nothing to do with the world. At worst, like Andorra, his city is a curiosity; at best, like Switzerland, it is a convenience. In either case, its existence means that he has retired to the sidelines where he benefits from the world's need of curiosities and conveniences, not from its respect for virtue.

This leads him to conclude, self-pityingly, that good cannot exist in the world; it also inspires him to withdraw into a hermit's hut from which he can condemn all and sundry for impeding the realization of his project. Since he cannot live apart from men without condemning them, he is in effect precluding the possibility of cooperating in any project which will make him a man among men. A major change in Sartrean emphases takes place here with the indication that radical Otherness is inhuman if only because, by separating one man from other men and for whatever highly motivated reasons, it eliminates him from the human race. With the failure of the City of the Sun, Goetz is nowhere; he is neither with the peasants nor with the barons. He is thus nothing but a complaining voice, with an

7. In "Les Communistes et la paix" (*Sit. VI*, p. 238 n.), Sartre dismisses the example of the Scandinavian countries and the United States; he sees them as nations where socialism has no real expression because they depend for their relatively good standards on the misery of others. He raises the hesitations mentioned above as questions. He then goes on to criticize trade unions in the United States because they have not put any brakes on American imperialism. As is frequently the case, Sartre is looking at the side which supplies the best footnote, at George Meany rather than at Walter Reuther.

audience of one—Hilda, the woman who loves him—whom he tries hard to dissuade from her fidelity. He seems to understand that if he wishes to be alone he can be with no one and therefore must deny an essential part of what it is to be a man—to know love, for example. Yet the renunciation of solitude means the acceptance of a particularly delineated force within the overall conflict. He can hope to live alone or he can hope to live with some men; he cannot live with all men.

If the project of living with some men does not promise everything, the project of living alone promises nothing, especially once he discovers that all qualitative behavior in this world demands the sanction of other men— other sanctions, such as the divine, having lost their meaning. Once he realizes this, Goetz can no longer be self-justifying. He cannot invoke a non-existent god to validate his decision; he must have the approbation of some men. In brief, he needs the Other and his participation with the Other in a common project in order to have a mandate.[8] The Other, though he may in many circumstances be the enemy, is essential to man's achieving a sense of function in the world. In the end, Goetz agrees to *serve* the peasants as their ruthless leader because ruthlessness and leadership must go hand in hand if leadership is to perform any meaningful role in winning victory for the peasants' cause. In agreeing to be ruled by the peasants who are the militants, Goetz, the adventurer, is reconciled with them.

At an earlier moment in Sartre's thinking bastardy had seemed a most appropriate state since, by knocking aside all the usual bolstering props, it made man aware of his true situation. Every major Sartrean character who has come to grips honestly with himself has passed through a crisis in which he recognized the purely conventional authority of legitimacy. What Goetz recognizes is that illegitimacy, while it may be a better starting place, is no more qualitative a resting place than legitimacy, primarily because resting places have nothing to do with inevitable human dynamism. He also recognizes that illegitimacy only describes a point of departure; it says nothing about how one gets elsewhere or, on another tack, if it tells man more powerfully than legitimacy that he is free, illegitimacy does not tell man what he is free *for*. Other Sartrean characters have learned what they could be for by accepting the claims and the compromises of legitimacy; Goetz is the first Sartrean character who learns from the Other what he is free *for*, rather than what he must be free *against*. In that puzzling French euphemism for bastardy, he is *un enfant naturel*. What he learns, before his reconciliation with the militants, is that neither natural nor

8. In *SG* Sartre writes: "We are reminded of the strange perplexity of Kafka: 'I am mandated', he said, 'but by *no one*'" (p. 116). Simone de Beauvoir discusses this question of mandate at several points in her memoirs. Early in their career the sense of mandate was so strong that there was no question of wondering from where it came. "Sartre lived to write; he had a mandate to be a witness of all things and to account for them under the light of necessity . . ." (*FA*, p. 18).

unnatural children find their justification in nature; they find it in their relationship to the Other.

Until now, the Other in Sartre's work has been perceived as a cause of fear and thus did not achieve much definition as a person; prior to this play we have seen the Other as a menace and have not had a detailed presentation of what he is, both as an individual (who, we must presuppose, also fears the Other) and as a participant in social reality. In *Le Diable et le Bon Dieu,* the Other, as the source of fear, is still present; the justification of the fear is gravely questioned, however, by the presentation of a multitude of Others. These Others, as they rub up against each other, learn who, from among the category Other, share their fears and who create them. Though the world remains the locus of radically polarized conflict, what this play shows is that at either extreme of the conflict men are cooperating with each other in opposing the organized force of the Other who is the enemy. This play then, while remaining faithful to Sartre's principal ideas about the Other, represents a diversification of the idea and thus begins to suggest a valuable function for Otherness. In effecting the diversification, Sartre has been admirably shrewd, not in the sense that he has indulged in chicanery, but in the sense that each of the principal characters in the play begins with a basic personal certainty which he wishes to maintain against his apprehension of the Other; each character who survives into the moment of cooperation has to yield some part of his original notion. This does not apply to the peasants, however, because they are still militants and thus have only begun to accede to the human; they have not yet encountered the problem of the Other in its bourgeois formulations. The Other who is their enemy—that is, the grouped barons—has openly declared his enmity.

Nasty, the peasants' ringleader, begins with two certainties; the first is that anyone who is not clearly with the peasants must be completely opposed by the peasants; the second is that his strong commitment to the peasant cause is clear proof that his inspiration comes to him from God. The commitment thus justifies his wholesale condemnation of his opponents. He incarnates a new category in the Sartrean system, a kind of harmonization of the subject-object conflict. He is an object in that he accepts his condition fully and allows it to determine the mode of his behavior, that is, he does not flee either from his position or his place. He is an oppressed peasant (an object) who affirms his condition and thus acts as a subject by asserting that his condition must be changed and with it that of his fellow peasants.

Buoyed by this conviction, and the divine sanction he believes it has received, he initially knows none of Goetz's disquietude or of Goetz's determined resolve to preserve his individualism. Believing, as he does, that nothing is forbidden when one is fighting in the name of humanity, Nasty has inexhaustible energy to bring to the fight for his cause; he is the perfect militant in his devotion to the cause, as he is the perfect man of action in his dexterity and suppleness in effecting programs. He does not flinch from brutality; he knows that proclamations produce rhetoric rather than results. The process of involvement eventually compromises his militant status, however, since the very nature of his commitment involves him in decision-making and choice. He comes to believe that the God who mandated him does not exist; but the support of the peasants has also convinced him that he has a better mandate—theirs. He learns, too, that the rectitude of his cause in no way assures that it can be achieved by pure means; he must lie and manipulate, compromise and hedge, make promises he is not sure he can keep but which he knows will never be kept if they are not made now. He is the chief militant who must dupe the other militants in order to supply them with the energy they need to fight for their own interests. The dupery, of course, has to do with a time-lag rather than with wicked deception; he cannot honestly tell them when they will win or that they will win at all; realistically he must let them believe victory is near in order that one day victory may come. He is Hoederer at any early stage.

At the end of the play he knows—and significantly it is Goetz who points it out—that he is alone because of his role as a man involved with decisions. But his solitude is diluted, as is Goetz's, with the knowledge that it exists because of his commitment to man's struggle against the forces which would annihilate him. What remains as the essential difference between him and Goetz is that his militancy is the result of his social status; he becomes a chief because the peasants provide him with his mandate. Goetz, who has never been a peasant, does not receive the mandate he has sought from the people; he receives it from Nasty. He thus will never know the kind of direct confirmation of his function that Nasty knows. The peasants will always be suspicious of one who does not come from their class precisely becaue—and here we return to the observations found in Sartre's introduction to *Portrait de l'aventurier*—he will always be free to abandon their cause.

Immediately adjacent to Nasty and slightly below him in what is clearly intended to be seen as a naturally emerging hierarchy is Karl. He is another militant who has moved, on the strength of his commitment, from a condition of servitude to a position of leadership. He shares all of Nasty's commitment to the peasants' cause; what he does not share is Nasty's mysticism and his desire to remain pure in the pursuit of his ideal. Karl is all pragmatism; if men must be duped in order to fight in their own interests, he has no hesitation about duping them. The ideal is in no way affected since, were they not duped, there would no longer be an ideal. He is, because of his hard-headedness, as essential to Nasty as Nasty is to Goetz.[9]

Heinrich, the priest who originally shares Nasty's concern with the peasants, is essential to no one because he must try to believe that everyone is subservient to his personal needs. He is the adventurer who wanders among the poor and needy hoping they will tell him who he is. Yet when the cause of the poor does not elicit his superiors' approval or Goetz's interest—in other words when he cannot, by identifying with the poor, become the ideal of the powerful—he is ready to abandon that cause. He needs to be validated by the Other without becoming involved too directly with the Other. What Heinrich basically hopes for is that the Other will have the courage of Heinrich's convictions. When once the Other materializes and shows the makings of courage, Heinrich becomes afraid and seeks to deny the Other either by forgetting about him as he forgets the poor or by dominating him as he seeks, late in the play, to dominate Goetz. His major purpose is to protect himself even as he persists in his search for a new Other who will validate him. In the end his only safe reliance is on God because God, being remote, poses no threat; more significantly, once Heinrich convinces himself that he will spend eternity in hell, God as the Other poses no threat at all. Finally, God, as the judge, validates the impossibility of Heinrich's goal.[10] In hell, Heinrich will be able to live complacently with the notion that success was impossible; and total failure, if it offers no other reward, does provide a sense of purity maintained against all assaults.

Heinrich is the perfect moral schizophrenic, the self-created contradiction brought about by the impossible desire to want to live at both poles at once, with good and evil, with God and the devil, with action and inaction, with loyalty and treason. His schizophrenia is not the result of an incapacity to make decisions, but of the consequence of a passion for making impos-

9. Speaking of militants who move into leadership positions, Sartre writes: "That does not of course mean that the militant does not move out of the masses; but, if he moves out, he achieves a point of distinction. But only in this: mass man is weighted down by his particular interests from which he must be plucked away; the organism of the relationship must reflect a pure act; if it bears the slightest germ of division, if it preserves any passivity whatsoever within him—heaviness, interests, divergent opinion—who then will unify the unifying apparatus? The ideal would be to have it follow the same kind of pure relationship which is visible whenever two workers are together" ("Les Communistes et la paix," *Sit. VI*, p. 249).

10. In a somewhat analogous vein, Sartre writes of Flaubert: "The Artist as God's witness—even when he only speaks about the devil—that, without doubt, is the most secret and yet the profoundest of Flaubert's ideas. And, of course, there is no need for the witness to believe: quite the contrary, since the image is nothing but a decoy he must ruin himself in despair and unbelief. The only demand made by the Creator is that the Artist give his witness of the unreal through an *imaginary creation*" ("Flaubert: du poète à l'Artiste," *TM* 22 [1966]: 628).

sible decisions, the most extraordinary of which is his creation, near the
end of the play, of a companion devil who, being a product of his imagination and thus readily serving all its needs, answers the most critical of
Heinrich's questions. The devil shows that human existence is impossible
for the individual who doesn't want to be touched by it or who hopes to
live apart from it and who, at the same time, seeks humanity's approbation.[11]

Unlike the madman's, Heinrich's schizophrenia is deliberately embraced
and carefully nurtured in order to allow for the most essential need of his
mind: he must always find someone else to blame. He would like to love
the poor and might succeed in doing so if only they would take the first
step and love him. He would like to act, if only he did not have to live with
the consequences of his actions. Eventually, the perfection of his schizophrenia is unable to protect him because it is brought into question by
Goetz's final development. If Goetz, by embracing a new program of action
thereby denies that exterior forces run the world, then Heinrich has no
external validation. His devil remains his own creation unless he can subject
Goetz to that devil, and, in so doing, finally achieve what he has always
been seeking: the confirmation of what he is by the Other who, having
given that confirmation, immediately joins him in living out their common,
externally mandated being.

Goetz refuses this kind of mutuality, and Heinrich, when he sees his
personal devil failing to function effectively in the resultant void, falls apart.
Once again the Other has failed him; henceforth the Other must bear all
the blame. The Other becomes the real devil, the force which will never
mandate him because what he seeks from a mandate is the right to deny
that Other as part of a permanent process whereby the Other is always
the agent who expiates Heinrich's sins.[12] At the very end he has no choice
except to fall back on God, offering his belief in the divinity both against
Goetz's atheism and as a reparation for his own theological infidelities. That
does not work either. Men stand before him. They have voices; they could
tell him what he needs to hear. God is invisible and silent, and when Goetz
tells him that God's silence means there is only the voice of man, Heinrich
grows desperate: "Goetz, men have called us traitors and bastards; they've
condemned us. If God doesn't exist, then there's no way to escape from
men. O God, this man has blasphemed; I believe in you, I believe. Our

11. Of a contemporary French writer, Marcel Jouhandeau, Sartre writes: "Jouhandeau . . . wants to play the dangerous game of betraying God out of love. It
is because of his faults that he brings contempt upon himself and he is the first to
recognize that he deserves the slurs which are cast upon him. He thereby knows true
humility" (*SG*, p. 221).

12. Cf. *BN*: ". . . as soon as we posit ourselves as a certain being, by a legitimate
judgment, based on inner experience, or correctly deduced from a priori or empirical
premises, then by that very positing we surpass this being—and that not toward
another being but toward emptiness, toward *nothing*" (p. 62).

Father who art in heaven, I prefer to be judged by an infinite being than by my equals" (p. 268).

In the face of Goetz's insistence, Heinrich tries to kill him but instead is killed by Goetz. It is clearly an act of self-defense and its meaning is equally clear, for what Heinrich has tried to do is to stifle the truest voice of man. And if man is to survive, he has no choice save to defend himself against those who try to kill him. In a more particular sense, what Goetz kills is his alter ego, the other possibility he might have become. Like him, Heinrich has been an adventurer; but Heinrich has been the adventurer who could never do what Goetz ends up doing: accepting an extreme which enlists him in the service of other men. If Heinrich sought to kill Goetz because of the message Goetz was transmitting—"there are only men" (p. 268)—Goetz kills Heinrich in order to silence the voice which conveys a temptation he has known more than once: the desire to set himself above men and to make use of them for his own causes.

What saves Goetz is neither the hazard of chance nor the wisdom produced by skepticism about God's existence; what saves him is Hilda. Hilda is thus a necessary device in the play since, without her, chance would indeed seem to be the only differentiating principle between Goetz and Heinrich. But she is more than a *principium ex machina*, since her mere presence in the structure of the play would not automatically require that Goetz change. What produces his change and explains Heinrich's intransigence is a different deployment of the same basic energy. Faced with the presence of the Other, Heinrich remains faithful to his fears; Goetz learns to love.

Hilda is an immensely appealing figure both because she represents a high level of human existence and because, if she ever heard of Polyanna, she quickly decided she wanted no part of her cloying sweetness. Hilda seems to be a combination of Simone Weil, whose deep involvement with Christianity apparently in no way affected Sartre's great admiration for her, and Simone de Beauvoir, whose faithful companionship over some forty years has clearly effected an amplification of the idea of love Sartre presented in *Being and Nothingness*. In the play, Hilda represents the only way by which the bourgeois—she is the daughter of a well-to-do baker— escapes from solitude. She gives herself completely to others, not out of generosity, but out of selfishness. She explains quite simply that she needs them. Her need, however, is quite different from that of women in Sartre's previous works, though conceivably it represents a sophisticated version of Marcelle's need of Daniel and Eve's patience with Pierre. Unlike Anny, Estelle, Inès, Ivich, Electre, and Jessica, Hilda possesses a self-assurance and knowledge which have prevented her from asserting her egotism as a defense against others. Instead she asserts it with them, in their midst, and in function of their needs which join with hers in order to oppose forces rather than individuals. In working for the peasants, she openly seeks fulfillment; but that fulfillment would be marred if her service did not help them to a better existence. Patience and fidelity—qualities which exist only when one joins with the Other—are her signal virtues; and she holds steadfastly onto them despite various provocations of Goetz and the general bleakness of their common situation.

The tone of Sartre's subsequent presentation of women suggests a growing conviction that such female patience and fortitude are the steadiest bases on which the race can rely. Woman, though she recognizes the danger of some Others, is instinctively committed to protecting her own. This sense of possession, and the protective instinct it produces, fundamentally though very quietly alters the Sartrean theory of the Other as the radical opponent; it suggests that a major group in the race does not have that experience of continually renewed hostility. This is not because woman is weak but because she is wise and, when circumstances require, wily. Hilda's eyes are as wide-open as any other's in the play; they flutter less frequently than Goetz's. Atheism for her is not a cause so much as it is an observation which conveys a judgment: if God exists, then he should be asking men's pardon. Those she loves are not guilty, they are the victims of injustice. Patience wins more battles than polemics. Her fidelity will bring Goetz to a realization of their love faster than either flight or threats; the reign of folly necessitates greater fortitude. The struggle may not be won, but it certainly will not be lost because of worthless, unproductive maneuvers.

Sartre's presentation of love in *Being and Nothingness* (pp. 364–412) was cast in a quite different and more dismal mode, primarily because his discussion fell within the general terms of being-for-others as a repugnant experience. Love was treated there principally as a hope which produced a number of strategies organized to neutralize the threat represented by the Other. Since he placed the phenomenon of love within the context of his observation that "conflict is the original meaning of being-for-others" (p. 364), because the Other "founds my being" (and I resent this), it was inevitable that Sartre should conclude that love is the source of a series of gestures whereby an individual seeks to recover his subjectivity by capturing the Other in some way.

Complicating this choice of a point of departure were two other influences on Sartre's thinking: one was the attitude towards human sexuality which he inherited from his class and which produced within him a belief in certain categories, such as the obscene, which have no fundamental empirical justification, and a general orientation towards the physiological aspects of sexuality which is not easily distinguishable from puritanism.[13] The other influence was an allegiance to abstraction which accorded a more significant role to ratiocination than to either biology or psychology. In this sense, Sartre's original discussion of love produces a Sartrean construct which, while it is not entirely devoid of empirical credibility, is a singularly partial and inadequate survey of the phenomenon. Its greatest single defect—greatest because it ignores an important source of the human being's sense of his experience—is to look upon love exclusively as a strategy developed by ratiocinating (and conniving) adults and to overlook the fact that the experience of love, initially known in childhood, is a legacy before it becomes a tactic. As a consequence of this, his discussion of love pays only the scantest attention—an admission that sexuality begins with birth—to the almost undeniable fact that adult attitudes towards love are, more frequently than not, the product of childhood experiences. Love, as it is described in *Being and Nothingness*, is an experience between adults who unhappily believe that they confront each other as equals and who share similar apprehensions of hostility and danger. It is an intellectual argument conducted by extracting from lived experience only those fragments which support the movement of the argument.

The argument is also deliberately and therefore curiously fragmentary since Sartre, after having related love to fundamental human conflict, immediately distinguishes between two kinds of love. The first, which he alludes to but does not discuss, is a kind of pragmatic agreement, "an enterprise; that is, an organic ensemble of projects toward my own possibilities" (p. 366). He elects instead to discuss what he calls ideal love, by which he does not necessarily mean the best kind of love but love as a project designed to realize man's ideal of incorporating the Other and the Other's disturbing look. Since that look seems to identify me as an object and thus to destroy my subjectivity, I wish to neutralize the person who looks at me and to divert his gaze. This project creates difficulties. If it is to be successful, it must incorporate the Other as a free agent freely consenting to be incorporated; in other words, it does not seek to destroy the Other.

---

13. Jeanson, without identifying the source, quotes Sartre: "When one makes love, one finds nothing to reproach in it. Yet everything changes if the act is seen by a third person. In making the reader that third person, one has the very best chance of making him feel—where the flesh is concerned—the horror of contingency, all the more so because in the greatest number of cases he will recognize his own adolescent reactions where the sexual act is concerned" (*Sartre par lui-même*, p. 124 n.). What such a statement means, of course, has little to do with objective experience on any independent scale; it has a great deal to do with the experience of the individual who makes such observations, casting them into a vocabulary which implies (or presumes) objective analysis. Nothing in it supports either the contention that a third person reacts to the sight of others engaged in sexual activities in a particular way or to the other contention that adolescents have a universally similar reaction to sexuality which allows the word *adolescent* to be used as a qualifying and normative adjective.

Destruction would only do away with a hostile look; it would not do away with the fact of my being-for-others. What the lover seeks is to have the beloved work freely with him in protecting his subjectivity, the subjectivity which was threatened when she looked at him and suggested, by her look, that he was an object for her.

On the most fundamental level, this attempt to capture a consciousness is impossible since, as we have seen, the unendingly dynamic nature of consciousness means that it cannot ever be frozen or controlled by another simply because it cannot control or freeze its own dynamism. Pragmatically, the endeavor is absurd since a captured consciousness would have to take on the semblance of an automaton and in that mode of existence would not satisfy the lover's ambition: he seeks to possess a consciousness, not a robot. Though Sartre is not too precise on this point, what apparently drives man to seek this kind of love, rather than the pragmatic love which expresses itself in a joint enterprise organized in order to achieve common goals, is passion. Passion seems to be the essential and confusing part of this operation since Sartre writes: " . . . the lover cannot be satisfied with that superior freedom which is a free and voluntary engagement. Who would be content with a love given as pure loyalty to a sworn oath?" (p. 367).[14]

This is a very curious element in the theory; it is surrounded by an even more curious pair of value terms. What he is saying is that men renounce a superior freedom and, by their discontent with oaths, deny the terms of their most common institution: marriage. The high rate of divorce in many countries may lend some validity to the general assertion contained in the statement. What seriously compromises it is the fact that Sartre's question can be readily answered with other facts. Many people can be content with a love sustained by an oath of loyalty. He and Simone de Beauvoir began with just such an oath which they renewed for a number of years until they decided that it had become a needless ceremony. Goetz and Hilda finally arrive at the same sort of agreement; and it is justifiable to believe that Johanna's loyalty to and expectations from her husband in *Les Séquestrés d'Altona* are not unrelated to the obligations which come with a pledge.

My guess is that the passion which impels men to this mode of love—which refuses higher freedom and protracted loyalty—is the passion to be God. Two factors condition my guess. One is the fact that people learn to love in Sartre's work only after they have come to the conscious realization that there is no God and have learned to live with that fact. The other is based on the subsequent terms of the discussion of this form of love in *Being and Nothingness*. There we are told that what the lover seeks is to

14. In the *CRD* such an oath serves, if not as the cornerstone, certainly as the indispensable buttress to all meaningful human social or collective activity.

have the beloved voluntarily curtail her freedom in order to serve him, to become a fixed quantity for him, and to avoid resembling a robot by constantly remembering her consent to fulfill this function. In those renewals her essential freedom will still be visible. The chief motivation behind the lover's purpose is his desire to be known as a value in himself; with the beloved's assent, he becomes that value by becoming the source of her system of values. She confirms his value by living on his terms.

The lover's chief motivation stems, of course, from his first experience with the beloved before she consented to live with him as the center of existence. In that earlier moment she had fixed her gaze on him and made him feel he was an object. In wanting to become a value, he wants to escape from that moment, prove that he is not an object, and thereby resume his subjectivity. If he must be an object, then the best kind of object to be is that upon which the world depends. No matter how much success the initial motivation achieves, it is doomed to subsequent unhappiness for a number of reasons. The first threat it encounters is two-pronged: the fact that an Other agrees to validate him does not mean that the other threatening Others have therefore been neutralized; the fact that he has fallen in love with Annie and that Annie has agreed to be loved is the result of chance alone and not a verification of some planned order in the universe. He might have met Mary instead of Annie, and Annie might have met Paul instead of him. Or, like Anny in *La Nausée*, she may come back to tell him that their "love," on which he has been counting, no longer exists. Love proves nothing; neither does it reduce the power of contingency in the world.

In the presence of another development these discoveries are of minor importance. The greater development is the lover's realization that, if the beloved's consent to his love validates him and justifies his existence—he is because he is loved—then it is the beloved's consent which establishes his essence. He is still dependent on the Other, and this outcome is precisely the opposite of what he sought. Added to this unhappy fact is the possibility that the beloved—who, despite her consent, remains free—may at any time pull all the props away and topple the lover's project by removing its essential justifier.[15] The awareness of this cluster of dangers is what produces love's further strategy.

The lover must seduce the beloved which means that, rather than solicit her reactive love and the validation it produces, he must make himself something she needs. He must offer himself as a fullness of being adequate to

---

15. The meeting between Anny and Roquentin near the end of *La Nausée*, which I have discussed above (pp. 48–50), is a most pertinent example of this kind of desire and of the stalemate which results when the desire exists within each of the two partners. Each wishes to exact that kind of total love Sartre speaks of, and thus both lose.

satisfy her sense of emptiness and capable of calming her fears. Through his body he must fascinate her consciousness in order to captivate it and firmly attach her body's needs to his body's capacities. This cannot work either, because of the elements which Sartre discusses in the following quotation:

> the beloved . . . will be transformed into a lover only if he projects being loved; that is, if what he wishes to overcome is not a body but the Other's subjectivity as such. In fact the only way that he could conceive to realize this appropriation is to make himself be loved. Thus it seems that to live is in essence the project of making oneself be loved. Hence this new contradiction and this new conflict: each of the lovers is entirely the captive of the Other inasmuch as each wishes to make himself loved by the Other to the exclusion of anyone else; but at the same time each one demands from the other a love which is not reducible to the "project of being-loved." What he demands in fact is that the Other without originally seeking to make himself be loved should have at once a contemplative and affective intuition of his beloved as the objective limit of his freedom, as the ineluctable and chosen foundation of his transcendence, as the totality of being and the supreme value. Love thus exacted from the other could not *ask for* anything; it is a pure engagement without reciprocity (p. 375).

There is no reciprocity because the fundamental goal of the project of "ideal" love is to do away with reciprocity, with dependence on the Other. If the project is to enjoy success, the Other must become dependent on the lover. This kind of love, instead of being an emanation from freedom, is the haven of alienated freedom. The lover's freedom is alienated at the outset from any cooperation with the beloved since it aims at denying the other's subjectivity, which always threatens to reassert the lover-as-object-looked-at rather than as the subject-to-be-capitulated-to. Potentially, and all too frequently, actually, the couple is involved in an impossible exchange: each wants from the other precisely what the other will not and cannot conceivably give: his essential freedom. "I demand that the Other love me and I do everything possible to realize my project; but if the Other loves me, she radically deceives me by her very love" (p. 376). She deceives me, I gather, because she is annulling my hope. By loving me as I love her, she is getting from me what I projected getting from her. Reciprocity is there despite the fact that reciprocity is precisely what the lover did not want; reciprocity reinforces rather than reduces the role of the Other.

The fact that love of this type is impossible in no way reduces the reality of the impulses that have made it a project. Those impulses still exist and their final hope is dashed. The reciprocity might be acceptable if the lovers could live in solitude, removed from the glance of a third person who would remind them anew of the existence of the Other. From strategies which aimed at success, the lover moves into strategies designed to cope with failure. Since the lover cannot incorporate the Other, he can embrace the shame of his failure and decide to live imprisoned as an object in the Other's subjectivity. This is masochism, but it is also bad faith, and it is the latter for the usual reason: the lover can only sustain the masochistic attitude by a series of free decisions, with each decision serving as a reminder that he is deliberately living in a false situation. By a contrary process, the lover can elect the sadistic posture and seek to make the beloved delight in being an object imprisoned in his subjectivity where she becomes the victim. This fails, too, Sartre says, each time the beloved looks at the Other and reminds him that she can terminate at will her voluntary imprisonment.

It is, of course, highly questionable that Sartre's analyses here have much validity where actual masochists and sadists are concerned since, to have value, his observations would have to be correct in presupposing that masochists and sadists deliberately play at their aberrations, or in suggesting that the masochist is worried by his masochism or that the sadist's victim at any point contemplates an end to his passive role. What Sartre provides is a compelling description of why such attitudes exist and reasonable explanations of why they are aberrations; what he cannot supply is a convincing proof that they are consciously lived as aberrations.[16] Part of the reason for this, as I have already suggested, is that he takes too short a view and makes dangerously little allowance for the conditioning influences which exist within individuals before they confront other adults in a situation likely to give rise either to sexual desire or the prolonged relationship we call, however inadequately, love.

Psychiatrists like Balint have offered more persuasive structures of argument and observation to suggest that the situation which Sartre describes as the discovery of the Other ignores, to its peril, that men discover the Other as a source of fear only because they have already experienced

16. Robert Campbell (*Jean-Paul Sartre* [Paris, 1945], pp. 276–77) quotes Ferdinand Alquié: "My sexuality is not chosen by me, and the sadist, far from choosing to be a sadist, experiences more than anyone a trouble which comes from his body or from his unconsciousness. This trouble muddies his thought, surrounds it with its illusions and, with fulfillment, ceases in so abrupt a fashion that consciousness, returned to clarity, is altogether astonished by a vision implying a crime whose effects consciousness takes note of without being also able to understand its source; it is a crime which dislocates consciousness and in which consciousness no longer recognizes itself. Can we then say, with Sartre, that the sadist has changed his project? Is it not rather clear that there is something determined in us, something of a qualified in-itself, something which comes to us from society, something of psychic unconsciousness which I do not set up but which I must take into account?"

the Other, in infancy, as the source of sustenance and comfort. In this structure, men do not fear the Other because he is the Other; they fear him
because he may refuse to provide them with the experience that they have
already known with the Other. The hidden fear that adults have when they
meet in potential love situations is not that the beloved cannot love but that
he will refuse to love. In this sense, we seek from the Other what we know
the Other is able to give; tensions arise on one or both sides because of a
lack of knowledge or the absence of adequate communication. If the adult
did not learn as a child that the Other who succored him was also comforted
by him, he may in adult relationships demand without being able to give.
If, as a child, he has had too many experiences of the Other as a hostile
force, he may enter adulthood having thoroughly forgotten his initial experience of having derived nourishment and pleasure from the Other.

Only in that case would Sartre's discussion in *Being and Nothingness*
apply, for what Sartre is talking about in those pages can have reference
only to the sick or immature which does not, of course, mean that the
majority of adults are not sick or immature. What it does mean is that at
this point Sartre's theory of the Other is so incomplete as to be wrong as
a general description of humanity. His subsequent description of indifference and hate are striking explanations of how the individual who has
grown skeptical of the Other reacts to him. And his description of hate is
a vivid presentation of what the goal of hatred is: ". . . hate is the hate
of all Others in one Other" (p. 411). Hate is the way I try to do away with
all others because—and we have seen a striking example of this in Heinrich—some others make me fearful. Or, as we have seen in the case of the
anti-Semite, hatred of a particular group absorbs all my hatred and justifies
it because of the hateful nature I attribute to that group.

In later books—the first section of the *Critique de la raison dialectique*,
in *Les Mots*, and in his work-in-progress on Flaubert—Sartre partially
repairs the defect in his theory by ascribing very great importance indeed
to the formational influences of childhood. That is an advance but, as my
discussion of *Les Mots* suggests, it is an advance effected in a curious way.
It limits itself mainly to insisting that adults can so form a child as to ruin
him; it fails to pay any attention to two other possibilities: first, that the
quality of an adult's life is not only influenced by the quality of his childhood but also by the nature or state of childhood; second, that certain
numbers of children receive the kind of formation which allows them to
encounter hostile others without falling into the error of believing that all
others are hostile.

It is not malicious to say that Sartre's general theory of human relationships is based on the presupposition that *his* experience of human relationships can rightly be the source of a universally applicable theory. The
fact that he had few friends as a child, added to the fact that a significant part

of his life as an adult has been spent breaking off relations with one-time friends or collaborators over ideological issues, makes it hardly surprising that the principal premise of his general theory predicates a greater chance for the breakup of human relationships than for their maintenance. Where other men, with different experience, might predicate a system based on the belief that men can get along together without, at crucial moments, engaging in ruinous, divisive, and even hateful polemics, Sartre must, in the *Critique de la raison dialectique*, create an intellectual structure whose purpose is to convince men that they had better get along together or else live in perpetual hostility. He answers the threat of the Other with a threat of his own. The solution of the problem, like its statement, is worked out on his terms, possibly because that is the proper way to effect a solution, but more probably because Sartre cannot think outside such terms. Dialectical thinking, as we shall see, has its advantages; it has the major disadvantage of forcing an essentially gray or compromised world to be seen in sharper hues, and in terms of fundamental oppositions. This implies that polarizations must be maintained, not because they reduce tensions in life, but because they perpetuate the essential ones.

Le Diable et le Bon Dieu gives a good example of this thinking by showing that love and cooperation in Sartre's world are strangely intertwined with hatred, as progress is interwoven with violence and terror. Though hatred of one man was described in *Being and Nothingness* as ultimately involving the hatred of all men, in *Le Diable et le Bon Dieu* and in *Saint Genet*, it is considered as a necessary impulse on the way to love. What is not yet made clear is how one will rid the world of hatred if one needs it to keep the world moving. Heinrich comments at one point: "All that hatred needs as a start towards taking over the world, little by little, is for one man to hate another" (p. 117). That is meant principally to be a comment on him and the danger he represents. It slowly releases other resonances in the mind of the spectator when he realizes that if, in this play, love is envisioned as a project towards something, the organization and acceptance of the project is a declaration against something else. When Goetz accuses Nasty of being a prophet of hate, he is told that hatred is the only path that leads to love. This emphasis is reinforced a bit later when Karl, counteracting Goetz's invocation of love, tells the peasants: "You were animals and hatred transformed you into men; if your hatred is taken away from you, you will fall back to crawling and rediscover the mute unhappiness of the beast" (p. 232).

While Sartre is no longer pursuing the implications of "ideal" love in *Le Diable et le Bon Dieu*, neither is he doubting the sources of its impetus. Those sources remain. Their goal, perhaps pursued unconsciously, turns out to be pragmatic love; and its achievement depends upon that higher freedom which leads to sworn fealty. This does not seem to mean, especially since the same basic attitudes of *Being and Nothingness* are still present, that Sartre has rejected out of hand the old theory. What it does seem to mean is that he intended his earlier discussion to show the futility of that kind of ideal; he must be concerned with pragmatic love now because it exists. The inference is that others may continue to pursue futile ideals; Sartre henceforth will be concerned with those who, discovering the futility of the ideal enterprise, settle for what can be accomplished—pragmatic love. What does not change is his conviction that pragmatic love must be discovered as something not experienced before. In that sense, his theory still does not attribute any significance to the primary love men experience in infancy.

That absence creates a certain number of awkwardnesses; a reader wonders, for example, why Sartre has had to take such a long and round-about way in order to arrive at fairly commonplace ideas. The answer is probably that Sartre, like Simone de Beauvoir, cannot understand what he has not experienced and, tends to contemn, rather than explore further, what he does not understand. The awkwardness is compounded by the fact that, having denounced a bourgeois institution like marriage, and discussed personal obsessions as though they were general problems, Sartre claims that he has come up with new solutions. What he does not explain is their novelty. The bond he has had with Simone de Beauvoir, like the bond which develops between Goetz and Hilda, may be admirable because of the sure knowledge the partners have of the limitations, dangers, and risks they face; the institution of marriage has been aiming at the same achievement for millennia, and theorists from Aristotle to Freud have looked upon friendship or marriage as being at least a partial response to the needs of man's social nature.

Sartre, if he believes at all in a positive social instinct among men, does not appear to believe that it is as strong as its opposite. The burden of his writings suggests that he believes such an instinct has to be learned, usually to the advantage of the few and the misery of the many. In this sense, he and Goetz are again one, for in *Le Diable et le Bon Dieu* Goetz must learn that only love will allow him to survive. Earlier in the play, he had shied away from love because he saw it as an expression of or response to anguish, anguish apparently being a synonym for the cry of need which confesses weakness. Goetz has also shied away from reciprocal love out of fear that in such an exchange he will lose some part of his identity; he thus rejects his mistress, Catherine, in a gesture of scorn behind which can be detected his fear that love may seize hold of him and impose unmanageable responsibilities on him. What finally brings him to an acceptance of reciprocal love is the discovery of needs only love can satisfy. These needs are not sexual so much as they are social. Set off against the risk of being with another is the worse fact of being alone; set off against the compromise demanded by cooperation is the cataclysm of exclusion. If his social conditions contribute to man's fear of love, only love, as the energy necessary for cooperation, can bring forth programs designed to change those conditions. Love supplies a crucial social matrix and allows for accomplishments which would not otherwise be attainable. The major question remains. Where does love come from? Or, in another formulation, how does an individual arrive at an understanding of the need to love?

Broadly speaking, and in those instances where higher reason has not been in operation, love is all that remains when everything else has failed. Since, after the failure of everything else, love is still possible, the implication is that love has always been there but has not been seen; this in turn implies that there are some people who have been willing to love all along. Thus, if Goetz passes through a number of stages before he sees love as a common project rather than as the subjugation of the Other to his superiority, he does so because, initially, he could not see that love was available; he could not or would not admit that, in order to love, he would have to give up some part of his ultimate desire and, through that renunciation, satisfy the greater part of his needs. Thus, too, if Hilda has always been available as the woman who is willing to love she, too, must give up some part of her idea of love—a sense that it will not involve her in the acceptance of accompanying evils or defects—if she is to establish a meaningful joint enterprise with Goetz.

She gives up much less than he, of course, because she has not had to dump as much excess ideological weight. She has not known his obsession with absolutes, his repulsion at the corruptibility of the body (which he associates with certain facets of sexuality), and his fear of too close an involvement with other men.[17] By not having experienced those obsessions, she incarnates what Sartre believes is the only fresh recent contribution to the general theory of love. This comes from Jean Genet and has to do with seeing love as a ceremony which does away with vileness by its insistence that real love must entail total love of the whole person: his weakness as well as his strength, his sickness as well as his health. Having discovered this advance in theory, Sartre writes "that one loves nothing if one does

17. Sartre writes of the young bourgeois: "In order to refuse [solitude] one must take note of it, which is a manner of making it exist in extreme form. To flee from it is to recognize it and to make it the spring of all our acts. Will he seek to escape from it through love? Such love would be that of the solitary who is running away from himself: 'To love is to flee', Malraux writes. And he is right if love is not willed for its own sake but rather as a way of getting out of oneself. And that's all that's needed to make escape impossible. . . . The advantage of the young worker who enters the party is that he has no ego before he loves; he discovers himself in the gift which he makes to the other and which the other acknowledges" ("Portrait de l'aventurier," *Sit. VI*, p. 11).

not love everything, for true love is salvation and safeguarding of all men in the person of *one* man by a human creature" (*SG*, p. 532).

A reader may reasonably wonder what is new about the discovery. Human history is so full of experiences in which mothers care for sick children and wives look tenderly after husbands suffering from appalling and objectively disgusting terminal illnesses as to make these experiences the stuff of life rather than its exceptions. Nor is there anything especially new in the latter part of the formula. Many observers have pointed out that love is always compromised when hate exists, since hate denies the very possibility love envisions. What is new and undeclared is the introduction into Sartre's theory of the special role woman plays in love. Woman, because of something in her nature, is love's special deputy and witness. What Sartre, who accords no strong function to the role of the subconscious, may be expressing unwittingly here, and in his other writings on love and the Other, is the ancient male fear that woman will not respond to man's desire and, by her refusal, may bring the race to an end. In this sense, love is not impeded by the fear that the Other is necessarily inimical; it is impeded by the fear that the Other, the woman beloved, will refuse to exercise her social function or will give it an emphasis different from that sought by the male. The fear of the Other, then, is not based on a denial of the social nature of man; it is based on the dread that some men will refuse to honor the function that flows from that nature.

The invocation of Jean Genet as an important theorist of love, coupled with the observations already made about the role attributed to hate in *Le Diable et le Bon Dieu*, appears to leave us with a puzzle. On the one hand, we are asked to accept a principle—the need to love all men through one man—enunciated by a man who has much hated in his life; we are further told that hate is where love begins. On the other hand, we are told that if we fail to love all men then we cannot love at all. How does one reconcile what seems to be a simultaneous acceptance and denial of a function for hatred? The answer would seem to be that men who wish to work for the improvement of all men are, by the nature of their commitment, bound to work against those who would obstruct such progress. Those who hate, because they deny love, must be hated; in hating them, one is hating their hatred and thus emphasizing even further the universal communal nature of love.

The new polarization which emerges, both in *Le Diable et le Bon Dieu* and in Saint Genet, will set up two triads at its extreme points. On the one end there is love, justice, and therefore the good. On the other end, there is hatred, injustice, and therefore evil. The ground between the two extremes is that on which the freedom and honor of all men are displayed as those men move either towards dignity or towards squalor. This redefinition discards the older polarizations of good and evil, God and the devil, right and wrong, and the ethical systems they supported; bath and baby go out together because the bath has deformed the baby beyond recognition.

Such a renunciation—it is actually more of a denunciation—places a great burden on the Sartrean figures who decide to discard the traditional ethical system. They find the necessary courage for the task in their growing skepticism about all systems. A system, as they see it, is any institution or movement whose terms polarize human behavior into the acceptable or the unacceptable, the good or the evil, in defiance of the facts of human experience. Any system whose terms are only applicable to some men rather than to all is defective because of its narrow scope. Such a system is automatically closed to the uninitiated for reasons the uninitiated neither understand nor are meant to understand; in the instances where the system is open to them, it is open only to the extent that they are allowed to possess a passive role within it, a role designed to neutralize their interests and paralyze their capacity to exercise their freedom.

Examples of such systems abound. Society, as Heinrich observes it, is a structure of powerful episcopal princes, intractable barons, and suffering peasants. Though the Church's doctrines should lead it to identify with the peasants, it chooses to barter or do battle with the barons, leaving Heinrich to oscillate ruinously between what the system preaches and what it practices, between love and hate. He cannot accept the passivity of suffering; he hesitates over betraying the poor by entering into his bishop's maneuvers against them. This same society, by making an issue of legitimacy, consigns a bastard like Goetz to a social limbo and expects him to accept its decision; it scorns him even as it demands his allegiance. Social programs are so intimately related with vested interests as to overlook social reality, a situation we have already encountered in the conflict between Hoederer and the Communist party. Systems are especially dangerous when their creators, forgetting that the systems are human constructs, seek divine or metaphysical sanctions for them, appealing either to the will of God or to a privileged understanding of the progress of dialectical materialism. Nasty seems to speak for Sartre and every Sartrean character who has walked into the wall of unbudging systems when he says: "When God remains silent, you can make him say whatever you want" (p. 136).

Goetz makes the same point when he says: "Heaven is a hole" (p. 213). But it is a hole ringed with a divine authority which must be uncompromisingly obeyed. Yet the principles that have customarily been used to fill that hole in order to benefit from the surrounding authority, have almost unfailingly demonstrated two contradictory things. Men make use of God in order to have a sanction for their programs against other men; they do so because they cannot bear, either out of fear of uncertainty or fear of fear, to be on their own. "God," Goetz says, "is the solitude of men" (p. 267). In *Les Mouches* God was just an inconvenience; in this play, while he remains an inconvenience, his existence is seen to provide essential information about men's aspirations and about the defects which endanger those aspirations.

God, as the superior force invoked for approbation, is no more than the human hunger for a *guaranteed* system. The variety of conflicting operations men have assigned to him shows the inadequacy of all presently devised systems. God, as I have said above, is a good idea with an evil history; he is the principle of love which has produced much hate. The Greeks, who allowed their gods to fight among themselves, and who did not hesitate to detail Zeus's troubles in managing his household as well as his libido, probably presented a better image of what God has meant in human history than has any monotheistic system where, as an old woman in *Les Séquestrés d'Altona* says, "God listens to the conquerors because they've won" (p. 175). The further trouble with monotheistic systems is that they are by their nature closed and exclusive. The irony of them is that those they exclude are not those they were supposed to exclude. This, I think, is one of the points Sartre is trying to make in choosing the Peasants' Revolt as the background for his play. To the Christian exhortation to love all men as one loves oneself, the bishops, who sustain the system theoretically, and the barons, who defend it physically, both answer with the same phrase, the young Augustine's "Not yet."

To this answer, Sartre, speaking in the name of the peasants, immediately poses another question: "If not now, *when?*" Because he knows the unspoken answer—"when *you* win"—he replaces the question addressed to them with one addressed to himself: "How?" The same agonized query is more movingly expressed at the end of Ignazio Silone's *Fontamara* by the cry: "WHAT CAN WE DO?" It is not simply a question of what we can do to overturn the system, bring God on our side, and thus have the authority and power to impose a new system. It is more subtly and troublesomely the question of how, once the revolt has been successful, the system can be kept open and prevented from repeating the experience of other systems which, despite open promises, have installed closed practices.

The answer to the question *When?* can be answered neither by Sartre nor by the peasants since both accept the reality of the opposition's unspoken answer; they can win only when they have greater power. Sartre's conviction—which will be elaborated in detail in the *Critique de la raison dialectique*—is that inevitably victory will come since it is dictated by the sweep of history. The speed with which it will arrive depends on the efficacy of the means used to bring it about and, in that sense, depends on the *how*, on the tactics selected. What becomes crucial with regard to the means—and the principal means is, of course, revolution—is that those who pursue them should never lose sight of their purpose. They must assure by their acts that all men will profit from the arrival of the new era; from hatred of the old, they must try to forge love for a new, truly egalitarian social structure.

Sartre realizes that the well-fed are not readily going to believe that a revolution will do them much good, especially since its introduction of violence may very well put an untimely end to their existence. The play, in which the peasants are prodded towards support of their own cause, is partly a polemical warning to the ruling classes. I have said already that Sartre's title indicates the full range of his purpose, which is to deploy the forces of the world in order to show that what men mean by God and the devil has to do with the truth; unfortunately, men have turned that truth upside down. The traditional God is man's devil, the traditional devil, man's friend; good is evil, evil good; hatred of oppression is the first step towards love. Lucifer's *non serviam* becomes the model of man's refusal to negate himself by affirming the rule of the forces which propose to overwhelm him. This reversal must take place because the struggle between good and evil is not the struggle between God and Demiurge in some distant realm; the struggle between good and evil is the stuff of human history. If human history is examined closely, it reveals that the good has been power and its consequence tyranny; evil has been suffering and its concomitant impotence. In *Saint Genet* Sartre writes: ". . . if the just man is not entirely just, the unjust man is not entirely unjust. Good and Evil disappear together" (p. 571).

A number of qualifying remarks must be made here. In talking about good and evil, as the above quotation indicates, Sartre is not talking about general categories, each of which contains an objective list of all the good and bad acts that can be located in the world and catalogued in the textbooks of moral theology. Rather he is talking about the poles around which certain human activities cluster, poles which are opposed and in conflict because those activities are opposed and in conflict. He is talking further about the tendency of one of those poles—the one generally labeled "good"—to create the circumstances which produce the other: his bastardy creates Goetz's opposition to society; the accusation that he is a thief sets Genet in opposition to the society which excludes him. Sartre is also asserting that a society which alienates men from access to what it defines as good can not rightfully express surprise when those men devise stratagems conditioned by their alienation. The degree of their commitment to evil is the measure of the society's distance from good.

What all men must fear and oppose is any group of men which pursues a good that brings about the destruction or the enslavement of other men. They will surely do harm, for they will slaughter Jews and oppress Negroes in order to preserve their idea of value. Where Thomas Aquinas had insisted that evil was the absence of good, Sartre will insist that evil is the resting place of the "good" abandoned by the "good" man; it is the debris he leaves behind in the achievement of his intention, or the detritus he creates in order to justify his intentions. This is the sense of Goetz' discovery; having chosen to do evil, he learns that evil is not what the theologians have made it out to be. In his experience, evil neither does the universal damage it was supposed to do nor does it necessarily have any noticeable consequence on the evildoer; one grows used to it as the world has grown used to the necessity of war. When a man chooses to do good, as defined by the theologians—that is, when he decides to make his acts conform to what is supposed to be the declared will of God, he finds himself accused by other men of contributing to evil. When men confront each other to defend opposed interests, good and evil do indeed disappear.

Goetz's City of the Sun is the most appropriate metaphor for Sartre's estimate of the theologians' idea of good. Localized good, which is only available to some and therefore does not have universal applicability, contributes directly to the development of evil. In the play, that particular evil is the barons' cause. If Goetz keeps his city (where people are undeniably happy in the sense that they are well-off) out of and above the fray, he thereby refuses to do good; for there can be no true good, as there can be no true love, unless it extends to all men. The City of the Sun is beneficial only to its own inhabitants; their satisfaction with their lot keeps them from supporting the peasants' cause and thus aids that of the barons.

At the end of the play, Goetz, Hilda, and Nasty are sadly aware that the good is in someone else's possession. The only way to replace it—their desire to replace it is the mark of their arrival at love—is to adopt its violent techniques. In order to fight for universally applicable justice—the only good—they must pass through evil. Goetz's murder of Heinrich, a ritual act which destroys the ancient distinction between good and evil as categories divinely sanctioned, is where the violence begins. Because it is ritual, it is liberating; this is how the new era starts. But, having been initiated with violence, the new era becomes engaged in violence. Even before he leads the peasants against the barons, Goetz is forced to kill one of his protesting subordinates in order to establish discipline and authority, the essential preliminaries to eventual victory. Kicking the dead man's body,

Goetz mutters: "See how the kingdom of man starts. A great beginning" (p. 282).

There is no other way. The good, who have made violence their companion though they may never have formally declared her their ally, can only be driven away by violence. There are dangers; one of them brings us back to the question of the adventurer's role with which this chapter began. That must now be linked with another danger: the possibility that revolt, once brought to a successful conclusion, will create only another closed system whose chiefs will impose their will on the weak, assuring them that it is the best available good. Goetz, the adventurer enlisted in the service of the militants, may become habituated to the fact of their obedience. Nasty, the restraining influence on Goetz, may be killed or else he may be corrupted by power. The violence, when it has won its goal, may only produce new masters of old situations. Another kind of adventurer is therefore needed, the nature of whose adventure will be to insist relentlessly on what the cause is really about. He is the writer; more particularly, he is Jean-Paul Sartre who here offers himself, discreetly but unmistakably, as a valuable force in the struggle. Since he is not involved in the management of the strategy, he can judge whether it is indeed serving the cause.

There is an even greater danger which menaces militants, adventurers, and loyal writers. Sartre's heroes—Oreste, Hoederer, Goetz, and even Genet—are fundamentally gentle men who have marshalled with difficulty the strength necessary for the ungentle tasks they embrace. They have been willing to go to the limits and even beyond. Some of them have learned an essential and new lesson: that freedom must be used for something, and that the only sensible thing for which it can be used is the human cause. All of them, including Sartre, have been willing to take risks, to leave innocence behind, to see purity as a present impossibility and then to throw themselves totally into the struggle. But gentle men are fragile men. When, if ever, the struggle is done and the dust has settled over the hoped-for new world, they may begin to wonder whether the conflict, with its reciprocal violence and terror, leaves enough of man for them to want to preserve. That possibility is what *Les Séquestrés d'Altona* is about.

RELATED THEMES AND WORKS

There is a serviceable discussion of Sartre's political development in Michel-Antoine Burnier's *Les Existentialistes et la politique* (Paris, 1966). The title of the book is misleading since it is almost exclusively concerned with Sartre and the position of *TM*. The postface to the book, which is a very personal statement on Burnier's part, is a good example of the kind of influence Sartre has had on the attitudes of certain young Frenchmen. As I have shown, Sartre's assessment of his own political growth is best seen in the essay on Merleau-Ponty. Simone de Beauvoir's *FC* gives a good presentation of Sartre's various dilemmas in the postwar years; the portrait one gets is that of a man who learned the power of already existing political structures, the futility of trying to change the world by his own initiatives exclusively, and the need to argue his case from a base more factual than abstract. The political essays of the 1950s also show this; in them Sartre is mainly concerned with proving his case by amassing statistics and examples rather than by arguing in the name of some future good. If he shows nothing else in those essays, he does amply demonstrate that there is a workers' cause and that that cause demands the support of all men of good will and practical reason.

Simone de Beauvoir discusses the ideological background and the general circumstances of the presentation of *Le Diable et le Bon Dieu* in *FC* (pp. 256–62). There she makes reference to *SG* and to the introduction to *Portrait de l'aventurier*. She, too, stresses Sartre's conviction that, because of his intellectual emancipation from his class, he was a bastard and thus knew the bastard's alienation. Jeanson, as I have pointed out, makes this assertion one of the central themes of his *Sartre par lui-même*. It strikes me that such claims are intellectual constructs put together because of the mental excitement they provide. Once created, they become stumbling blocks to other elements in Sartre's thinking, or else are dynamited by those other elements. Sartre cannot, by declaring himself a bastard, escape from his observations elsewhere that, by the sheer fact of being able to see himself voluntarily as a bastard, he makes a choice and decision which other bastards cannot make. Goetz *is* a bastard; Sartre chooses to think of himself as one. What he is seeking to do, of course, is to accept as his own a particular alienation which will make him one with all the other alienated people in the world. One understands why he does this; one does not for that cease to sense that nothing real is effected by such assertions. Burnier suggests that Sartre's lifelong fascination with Flaubert stems from a kind of admiration for the *total* identification between Flaubert and his class which serves as a model for the kind of total identification Sartre would like to have with the proletariat. A similar inspiration may be behind his fascination with Genet and Genet's total identification with his particular project of being at all moments and in every undertaking what, as a child, he had been told he was and would remain. *Le Diable* was revived by Georges Wilson at the *Théâtre National Populaire* in November, 1968, with François Perrier as Goetz.

In *La Nausée* one of Roquentin's most disempowering discoveries and repeated insistences was that there were no "adventures"; any adventure

was a lie organized to hide the essential unpleasantness of existence; the
only justifiable and justifying adventure would be the book he planned
to write which would celebrate the limits of adventure. That project
probably reflected Sartre's own thinking at the time and his conviction that
literature was to be the great adventure of his life. Subsequently, the high
initial estimate placed on a literary career has been severely devalued; concurrently, the sheer process of living and being involved in many causes
and activities has demonstrated that there are, if anything, too many adventures for the attention of one man. The word *adventure*, however, has
ceased to have reference to particular causes and individual activities and
has become the label for a much vaster project: that of determining the
sense of all human life. Thus Sartre talks of the *CRD* and its projected
intention of supplying a global explanation for the direction of human
history, as a singular adventure (*CRD*, p. 140). Literature, which is necessarily partial, clearly has come to have a subservient position to historical
theodicy which, by the nature of the way Sartre conducts the enterprise,
is total.

An early, negative, and rather confused review of Denis de Rougemont's
L'Amour et l'Occident (*Sit. I*, pp. 62–69) contains germs of Sartre's later
discussion of love in *BN*. The review's use of terms like desire, love, and
freedom are especially relevant; this brief essay is also of interest because
it shows the younger Sartre's skepticism about the kind of universal system
which the older Sartre tries to construct in the *CRD*. An even earlier work,
the short "L'Ange du morbide" (in Beigbeder, pp. 149–54), is also of
interest in connection with Sartre's idea of the Other. It tells of a young
professor, Louis Gaillard, who falls in love with a tubercular woman *because*
she is tubercular. His sense of superiority and condescending generosity
is quickly changed once the sick woman coughs up blood; at the end of
the story, he goes to consult a doctor to make sure that he hasn't been
infected.

Other relevant texts are: *SG*, especially the chapter "On the Fine Arts
Considered as Murder" (pp. 483–543); *Les Troyennes*, which presents
a panorama of the different types of women Sartre has depicted in the
body of his works; Sartre's interview with Madeleine Gobeil (published
in the American edition of *Vogue*, July 1965; available in French in Serge-
Julienne Caffie's *Simone de Beauvoir* [Paris, 1966], pp. 38–43) where Sartre
talks about Mme de Beauvoir.

Balint's theory of love is presented in his *Primary Love and Psychoanalytic Technique* (New York, rev. ed. 1965) which is a gathering of
papers written over four decades. Suzanne Lilar's *A propos de Sartre et
de l'amour* (Paris, 1967) is a book-length critique of Sartre's theory of love.
It strikes me as an inadequate treatment primarily because Mlle Lilar

centers her discussion too much around the pages in *BN* and does not pay enough attention to the significance of the later plays, *SG*, and the *CRD*; it also suffers from her stubborn desire to build a theory about Sartre rather than to trace out scrupulously the development of his own theory. Another discussion of love, radically different from that Sartre presents in *BN* but very close to his later ideas, can be found in Gabriel Marcel's "Position et approches concrètes du mystère ontologique" (in *Le Monde cassé* [Paris, 1933], pp. 255–301). Marcel's essay is of particular interest because its description of the function of the Other is quite the opposite of Sartre's pre-*CRD* discussions.

The day after the victory, when

he is in chains, miserable and

trembling, he is a mere man, and, what-

ever the victor may decide to do, there

lurks in his decision a profound dis-

enchantment: to be eager to punish

out of fidelity to oneself is to want

to cling to a dead past, to prefer what

one was to what one has to become;

magniminity, on the other hand, repudiates

past sufferings, rises above years

of struggle and hope.

— Saint Genet

10 *Living Free*—III

The difficulty Sartre now faces can be rapidly seen if we try to gloss a sentence from Trotsky's *Terrorisme et Communisme* ([Paris, 1963 ed.], p. 48): "Who really wishes the end cannot repudiate the means." The statement isolates the terms which condition the decision Goetz makes at the end of *Le Diable et le Bon Dieu*. If one accepts the imperious necessity contained in Trotsky's advice, clearly one does so because of the value attributed to the end sought. But what happens if, the end having been achieved, or at least diligently pursued, you find that the means have repudiated you or caused you to want to repudiate your original end?

The formulas of *Being and Nothingness* had provided an answer. That book began with the assertion that human reality is free because man is continuously aware that, as he is, he is not enough; he is simultaneously aware that he cannot avoid doing something to fill the lack he is. That action may be deliberately outlined and knowingly undertaken or it may be surrender to an external force. The latter choice is where bad faith begins; the former is the recognition of anguish but by no means its destruction, since the decision to live freely is a decision to live with anguish as with a too faithful and nagging companion. The particular nature of that anguish is unpredictable since its expression will depend on obstacles met along the way and on the range of choices available for overturning those obstacles. What this seems to mean is that, even as man acts in the name of a particular goal, he is aware, or becomes aware, that he may be obliged to change his strategy. "In anguish we do not simply apprehend the fact that the possibles which we project are perpetually eaten away by our freedom-to-come; in addition, we apprehend our choice—i.e., ourselves—as *unjustifiable*" (*BN*, p. 464).

The sense of being unjustified is only one element in a wider process of humiliation which comes with the enterprise of living. Though the humiliation is annoying, it is, by the simple fact of its presence, very frequently where men must start. Shame and fear are strong internal springs which exist in all men; what they produce, once their tension makes itself felt, is the variety of reactions this book has been tracing out. At the core of Sartre's thinking is the assertion, contained in the last pages of *Being and Nothingness*, that, no matter how adverse and unbearable a man might find a particular situation:

> He must assume the situation with the proud consciousness of being the author of it, for the very worst disadvantages or the worst threats which can endanger my person have mean-

ing only in and through my project; and it is on the ground
of the engagement which I am that they appear. It is therefore
senseless to think of complaining, since nothing foreign has
decided what we feel, what we live, or what we are. Furthermore, this absolute responsibility is not resignation; it is
simply the logical requirement of the consequences of our
freedom (p. 554).

Existence, which is certainly not foreign to man, may not change the
essential relevance of this statement; it will certainly call for extensive
amplification of it.

Les Séquestrés d'Altona (1959) is a work which catches most suc-
cinctly both the cause of the amplification and the difficulty of conveying
it. It is an immensely dense play which thickens, not so much from the
elaboration of ambiguities, as from the presentation of dilemmas. The
dilemmas are crucial because, while they can be met with the guidelines presented in Being and Nothingness, they do not for that cease being dilemmas
nor do they produce much by way of solutions. They show that man must
act even in the worst circumstances; they show, too, that the worst circumstances yield acts of undetermined moral color. In this book I have
been using terms, derived from Sartre's own vocabulary, to describe the
two basic options that are available to individuals. Individuals either can
live out their lives as circles traced in pursuit of a perfection which is defective because it can only be had by ignoring the internal or external forces
which threaten the circle for all time; or individuals can choose to accept
the thrust of those forces and live with the uncertain future dictated by
honesty. In both cases we have been dealing with single circles and simple
external forces. Even in a play like Le Diable et le Bon Dieu, with all that
it represents in the reformulation of Sartre's ideological positions, the
distinction between what should be fought for and what should be destroyed
was clear and simple, simple in the sense that the structure of argument, if
it were accepted by the spectator, could lead only to Goetz's final decision.

Les Séquestrés d'Altona—it is, I think, Sartre's finest creation and a
major work of this century—does not do away with either circle or external
force. It multiplies both prodigiously until what results is something like
an Op art painting. The straight lines and circles seem now quite distinct
and arranged in a pattern, now chaotically superimposed one upon the
other. One does not live in one circle; one lives somewhere in the midst
of innumerable concentric and interlocking circles; one does not feel the
force of one external influence, one feels the force of many and risks being
impaled by their demands. Added to this multiplication of options and responses is the apparent disappearance of poles from the world. Where, in
former works, a process of polarization not only outlined options but also

suggested which one had to be elected, here there are only reciprocities which solve nothing because they bring everything into question.

Much of the tension in the play comes from the blunt recognition of these ruinous reciprocities. To the observation: "You are working for the Nazis," comes the counterobservation: "Because they are working for me." Frantz, the protagonist, claims that he is the witness at man's trial only to be told that he is the accused. "Which of us," a daughter asks her father, "most needs the other?" He answers: "Which of us most frightens the other?" Frantz says: "Father, you scare me; you don't suffer enough from the suffering of others." And the father quietly answers: "I'll allow myself that luxury when I possess the means of doing away with suffering." [1] The son involves his father in a grim chain of cause and effect—"I am a torturer because you are an informer"—and suggests that even that statement must boomerang, when he says: "My father created me in his image—unless he's become the image of his own creation." It is a world in which, as one of the characters says, there "are two languages, two lives, two truths," a world which provokes the honest individual, which this particular character certainly is, to ask if such a situation isn't too much for one person to cope with. Not only is it too much for a single individual to bear and try to sort out, it is also too much for a single world to bear and sort out in any meaningful way. The reciprocities point to poles of opposition only to show that the poles dissolve each other and leave the individual with nothing. Or with almost nothing. Frantz has worked out an answer: "There's only one person who speaks the truth: the shattered Titan, the ocular, regular, secular, once in a lifetime witness for all time to come. ME!" (p. 79).

That solution closes a circle and brings us back to the point Sartre's philosophy was to carry us away from. From the time of his first important publication, *La Transcendance de l'Ego*, Sartre had denied the ego's validity as a meaningful psychological concept and even denounced its existence as an idea because the idea encouraged men to think primarily about an essential self that needed to be protected against others. The primacy men accorded to the ego was seen more and more as the greatest stumbling block to the creation of meaningful and productive relations with the Other and thus represented an effort to deny an irrefutable fact: there can be no possibility of making any claims for the ego as a valid notion without simultaneously admitting that the ego has been shaped principally as a result of its owner's relations with others.

Sartre has, of course, never denied that there is a self; what he has denied is that it is already totally formed or has some essential unchanging core that must be defended at every instant. What Frantz is asserting in his return

---

1. Heinrich's observations on the same situation in *Le Diable* had less candor and shifted the responsibility for his indifference elsewhere: "The others suffer, not I. God has allowed me to be haunted by the suffering of others without ever feeling it" (p. 57).

tion of man by economic forces man has set loose seems to know no ideology or, more precisely, does not seem to be controlled by either of the great economic forces now at work in the world.

It is probable that the specific example Sartre had in mind was that of the Krupp family which, having cooperated with Hitler—as it had cooperated with both Kaisers Wilhelm—and suffered defeat with him, brought its enterprise back to flourishing life after the war. Alfred Krupp, who was briefly imprisoned as a war criminal, explained his involvement in the war machine in these words: "My life never depended upon me, but on the course of history" (New York Times, 1 August 1967, p. 30). Events were subsequently to catch the family more tightly in Sartre's mesh: in April, 1967, faced with the complexity of modern economic life, Krupp was obliged to renounce family ownership and allow the company to prepare for public ownership; earlier he had had to live with the refusal of his son, Arndt, to have anything to do with the family business other than draw his revenue from it. Arndt explained: "I am not like my father who sacrifices his whole life for something, not knowing whether it is really worth it in our times" (New York Times, 1 August 1967, p. 30).

In the same Livres de France interview, Sartre describes his theater, with great accuracy, as a mixture of ideological drama and bourgeois theater and explains that he effects this fusion deliberately. It is clear that he thereby seeks to appeal to as large an audience as possible. It is less clear, but probably no less right, that the fusion expresses an aspect of Sartre's imagination which sees theater as being involved with the creation of suspense, the development of intrigue, and the excitation of the audience's emotional as well as intellectual responses. These seem reasonable enough goals for a man who told the director of the revival of Les Séquestrés that he resorted to the theater when he was angry. Apparently, the emotions, even though they should be used gingerly, can be made to produce statements and reactions designed to have a very set purpose.

My interpretation of the merit of the play differs rather markedly from that of French critics, who find it less valuable than Sartre's earlier plays, especially Les Mouches. The Atlantic perhaps inverts values and perspectives. The great importance I give to Johanna represents quite a different view from that of other critics, several of whom look upon her as an empty-headed, selfish creature. John Whiting's On Theatre ([London, 1966], pp. 12–20) presents the case for this view. I have made evident my conviction that neither the text of the play nor the context of Sartre's thought supports this kind of interpretation.

Readers of strong imaginative bent might be diverted and even instructed by reflection on the significance of Frantz's name. When one lectures about the play, in either English or French, it is possible to begin pronouncing it as though it were the name of Sartre's homeland. This may be unconscious,

to the ego as the truth is that, if he does not preserve this ravaged truth against a world that seems set on annihilating it, he will be left with no remnant of the self, even in the Sartrean sense of that word. There had been a moment in the evolution of Sartre's thought when the assumption of the ego's danger as a major obstacle to human cooperation seemed indispensable and thus justified. Over the years that assumption has been battered by facts which show that cooperation with other human beings in the great cataclysms of personal and public history destroys the self and with it all sense. If there is two of everything, then the individual who cannot decide which of the two is true, does not *choose* to fall back on himself, he is left with no other option.

This element in the background of *Les Séquestrés d'Altona* reflects the emotional disarray of both Sartre and Simone de Beauvoir in the aftermath of a number of developments in the mid-1950s, the most notable of which was the Algerian war. In her memoirs Mme de Beauvoir gives a striking portrait of her reactions, reactions which she assures us were shared by Sartre. The most significant is clearly the intense hatred she felt for her compatriots, fully aware that some of them returned that hatred with equal intensity. This was a different kind of hatred or repugnance than that experienced towards collaborationists or Nazis, for both she and Sartre were aware that those they hated, and who hated them, were in many cases people who had fought valiantly for France against both collaborationists and Nazis. They had the feeling of being aliens in their homeland, of having no recourse except to manifestos and street demonstrations. Those broadsides and rallies, which indicated they were not alone, also bore witness to their impotence. Sartre saw more disturbing elements in their situation:

> Immersed in stupor, Frenchmen are discovering this terrible piece of evidence: if neither her past, nor her loyalties, nor her own laws protect a nation from herself, and if the passage of fifteen years is enough to make executioners of victims, then the occasion has the upper hand; depending on the occasion, anyone at anytime can become either victim or executioner (*Sit. V*, p. 73).

Faced with the possibility that this might be an inevitable part of the historical process and with the idea that events and not men determined human acts, it seemed futile to demonstrate. They marched and wrote and protested in order to decry colonialism, repression, and especially torture and reprisals in Algeria. But even as they marched, Sartre in his essays was showing a growing awareness that heinous deeds did not necessarily stem from deliberately heinous men; such deeds seemed instead to stem from historical necessity or sheer accident. That did not make them any better nor did it change Sartre's moral values. But it made him more powerfully aware than ever before of how strong the forces of time and tide seem against the individual. Today's colonialist can honestly believe that the colonized are lesser human beings who benefit from being colonized, because today's colonialist is not aware of the process which has brought the exploited native to such a low level of existence.[2]

The more burning issue was that of the tortures; they identified a phenomenon Sartre writes about at length in the *Critique de la raison dialectique*. This is the process of counterfinality, where one human act creates a situation so forceful in its consequences that it henceforth conditions future human acts; the original act rules the men who initiated it in a way they did not predict and perhaps could not have predicted. The tortures, which were perhaps the basest part of the Algerian war, existed on both sides, with each side claiming it was torturing only because the other side was doing so. In such pragmatic systems or conditions, he who desists first proclaims himself to be the situation's chief fool.

Since the torture existed on both sides, both sides had to be condemned. That might be easy enough to do, but the fact that torture existed at all raised a number of questions:

> Can one still have friendship for another who would approve [of torture]? Everyone keeps quiet, looks at his neighbor who is already keeping quiet; each asks: "What does he know? What does he think? What has he decided to forget?" Except among people "of the same leanings" there is fear of talking. What if I were to discover some kind of criminal complicity in the man whose hand I have just shaken; he says nothing, that man; saying nothing means consent. But *I* say nothing either. What if, on the contrary, he reproached me for my listless indifference? Scorn is teaching us a new form of solitude: we are separated from our compatriots out of fear of having to scorn them or of being scorned by them. It's the same thing, in the end, since we are all alike and are all afraid to ask questions of others because their answer risks revealing our own degradation (*Sit. V*, p. 64).

Sartre goes on to point out that this situation has come about in a country which, fifteen years earlier, had been reproaching those Germans who tried to claim they had been unaware either of the concentration camps' existence or the full extent of their programmed horrors. Where in France,

2. Cf. "Portrait du colonisé" (*Sit. V*, p. 54): "The settler can only absolve himself by systematically pursuing the 'dehumanization' of the native, that is, by identifying himself a little more each day with the colonial apparatus. Terror and exploitation dehumanize, and the exploiter uses this dehumanization to justify further exploitation. The machine whirls in circles; it becomes impossible to distinguish the idea of *praxis* from that of objective necessity. . . . Oppression is *above all* the oppressor's hatred of those he oppresses."

he asks, is one to find that collective responsibility which the French had found lacking in the Germans?

He seems to realize, not in this particular essay, but in the whole series of articles written at the time, that collective responsibility may be lost amidst the paradoxes and problems of history. Of paradoxes and perplexities the 1950s had supplied a more than ample number—to his confusion and also to that of the world's powerless citizens. The decade had begun with what seemed to be the factually established invasion of South Korea by North Korea and thus with aggression initiated by a Communist state. Sartre had written ingeniously to show that that act of physical aggression was the answer to economic aggression from the capitalist states; ingenious argumentation was not enough to convince either Merleau-Ponty or others of the validity of Sartre's case.

Stalin's death, Khrushchev's rise to power, and the introduction of de-Stalinization produced other confusions. Sartre had tried to explain, if not defend, the excesses of Stalinism only to discover that the most scathing denunciations of the dictator's habitual treachery were to come from his successor. That might be admirable progress, but it created disturbing images of a man negotiating his way carefully along the corridors of the Kremlin, more interested in his survival than in that of the hordes who were being eliminated or incarcerated; such pictures were much like those created by the Algerians who, in the name of a good cause, were taking savage reprisals against the French whose cause they condemned but whose methods they imitated. Those pictures became starker as the reciprocal reprisals and tortures became worse, and as the man who denounced Stalin turned with equal vigor to crush the rebellious workers of Budapest. The world turned out to have no shortage of external forces trying to break vicious circles; if anything, it had too many.

In those years—and with some major errors already made—it was difficult to sort the world into fixed categories of good and evil, to distinguish Stalin's violence from Khrushchev's and still maintain a theory which was not just a variation on realpolitik. Categories of authenticity and inauthenticity, carried over from *Being and Nothingness*, were simply not adequate as the basis for distinguishing which man's violence was good, which man's evil. The result was that freedom seemed to be a curse so great as to prevent the possibility of its ever becoming, not a blessing, but simply useful. The world, it appeared, was made up of men who were afraid neither of their freedom nor its exercise; it was made up of groups of men who were afraid of other groups of men who were equally ready to use their freedom to protect themselves against those they feared. The significant element in this situation was precisely that absence of any hesitation to use one idea of freedom in order to fight another. Freedom nonetheless remains the good insofar as it must bring men to recognize that it is their common identifying characteristic; evil is the fundamental opposition among those free men. The task, of course, becomes that of unlocking horns without unleashing new violence. The fundamental difficulty of accomplishing such a feat in a world of superpowers, each of which acts in the name of freedom and for the good of all people, is that of deciding which of the superpowers is on the side, not of the angels—for we have abandoned them long since—but of the greatest number of men.

The experience of the 1950s seems to validate all the original bases of Sartre's philosophy and to show that the world, as well as its individuals, is irretrievably given over to conflict. Sartre's patient and sometimes polemical descriptions have not changed that fundamental situation, for his arguments have not convinced men to live by higher reason; as most men go in pursuit of ideal love rather than pragmatic love, so the world's powerful seem to go in pursuit of ideal rather than pragmatic freedom—freedom for themselves but not for the Other if the Other's demands threaten to reduce the amount of freedom they expect to enjoy. Though men do live in groups and manage to get along with one another in particular situations, the Other remains the great threat. Two new dimensions have been added to the problem represented by the Other. The first has to do with the extent to which the Other has been responsible for the conditions under which I live and is therefore responsible for my attitude towards him. The second has to do with the possibility that I may be hostile to the Other simply because I do not like him; that possibility raises the question of how I demonstrate that my hostility to the Other is based on reason and not merely whim. In both dimensions, the inner temptations described in *Being and Nothingness* have been overtaken; what remains is the amassed evidence of my experience of the Other which tells me he is my enemy now and will be my conqueror tomorrow if I do not fight him in the interim. Simone de Beauvoir hates her compatriots because they do not live according to the norms she has taught them; those of her compatriots who hate her are convinced that she would do away, not only with them, but with all values and with France which is their home. What happens if both sides have good reasons, but if neither one has enough reasons to be considered right? And what happens if, against the possibility of stalemate, the only refuge for any kind of truth is the one Frantz has found: the ego?

The situation which gives rise to the action of *Les Séquestrés* is the following. The father of the Gerlach family has learned that he has cancer and has called his son, Werner, and the son's wife, Johanna, back from Hamburg so that Werner can assume the direction of the family's shipbuilding business. Involved in this summons is the additional duty of maintaining the family mansion where the older son, Frantz, lives in seclusion. He locked himself in a first-floor room some thirteen years earlier after an incident with an American officer had made him persona non grata with the occupying authorities. The Gerlach daughter, Léni, who has devoted her life to taking care of him, claims special rights over him—not without some reason, since she supplies him not only with food but also with incidental sexual release. The play's intrigue centers on immediate issues: the father's desire to see his elder son before he dies; Johanna's opposition to assuming the burden the father is imposing on them; Frantz's role in controlling, despite his seclusion, the destiny of other individuals. Frantz rejects this last idea by telling himself that, from his closeted space, he issues no requests to his family.

Frantz's denial is obviously specious; the fact of his existence imposes on the family the burden of sheltering, hiding, and nourishing him. He lives far beyond such concerns, however, because his thoughts are maddeningly centered on the events which have brought him to seclusion. He seeks to defend himself from the "crabs" of his thoughts and to defend his century before the tribunal of history.[3] A major element in his program is his belief that Germany has been brought to her knees as a result of the Allies' victory, that the countryside is filled with orphans, and that abjection is visible everywhere along the Rhine. He must believe this in order to maintain intact the structure of the defense he is elaborating. The defeated must be suffering in order that a key point in his brief may remain valid: they are suffering beyond their guilt or, in another variation, those who are making them suffer are not measurably less innocent.

The first significant incident in his life was his attempt as a very young man to save the life of a rabbi who had taken refuge in the family garden. In so doing, because his education had led him to an instinctive belief in his ability to act freely and sovereignly, he was clearly giving utterance to the implications of that formation; but he was also undoubtedly inspired by a more natural instinct of repulsion against oppression and by sympathy with the rabbi's plight. But in that act, allegedly revealed to the SS by a family servant, he learned that he was not free. The rabbi was killed before his eyes, the elder Gerlach had to use his influence with the Nazis in order to

3. Crustacean imagery has recurred in Sartre's books; it played an especially important thematic role in *La Nausée* where it was used to evoke the experience of the viscous and also that of facticity. Crustacean imagery has also been used by Sartre to describe the hold received or limited ideas can exert on a man's mind (see, for example, *La Nausée*, p. 21, where he portrays an old man who forms lobster-like thoughts). Frantz in *Les Séquestrés* says: "The crabs are men" (p. 167); later he talks of himself as a crab.

Sartre himself had a direct experience of the impression of being pursued if not threatened by crabs and lobsters in the aftermath of a fairly well-controlled experiment with mescaline, administered under medical supervision in a hospital. For a number of years afterwards, he had impressions, of variable duration, that lobsters were following him.

save Frantz from prison and perhaps some worse fate. What the young Frantz learned was that he was not yet meant to be a sovereign but only a crown prince, ceremonially dressed, at the ready, but still waiting in the wings. What he also learned, in less conscious fashion, was that the distribution of penalties in this world follows no code that can be labeled moral.[4]

The second major influence on the formation of his present outlook was his service in the German army. He had tried to be a good officer, instilling discipline, fighting ruthlessly and, when it came to it, torturing prisoners in an effort to obtain information. Since the prisoners died without talking, he lives with a deeply rooted feeling that no argument of obedience to superior authority, no invocation of force majeure and the desperate conditions of war, can excuse his conduct. Against the disturbing inner voices which haunt him about that particular episode, he has chosen, most often, silence and, less frequently, the assertion that he is not guilty because *he* did nothing; force majeure was indeed the culprit. A third significant incident took place in the immediate aftermath of the German rout. In the midst of a ruined town he had stumbled across a mutilated old German woman who accused him of being guilty, not because he tortured, but because he had not tortured enough:

> Each time you spared the life of an enemy, even in his cradle, you took away the life of one of ours; you wanted to fight without hatred and you've infected me with a hatred that eats away at my heart. Where is your virtue, wretched soldier? Where is your honor, soldier of defeat? *You* are the guilty one. God won't judge you on your acts but on what you didn't dare to do: on the crimes that you should have committed and failed to commit. You are the guilty one. You! You! (p. 176).

The question, as it raised itself in Frantz's mind during the war, had a deeper dimension, however, than honor. It had to do with being, with the question of what, in the midst of the extremes of war and the exigencies of command, one *is*. He had not tortured the partisans out of either a sense of honor or a cynicism about honor; he had tortured them in order to be what he was—a soldier in Hitler's army, pushed to the wall because he did not possess the information the partisans alone could provide. He did not torture in order to torture or even because he believed in torture; he tortured because his function demanded that he do so, because there was no other way available, and because discipline had to be maintained in his own

4. Cf. *Litt.*: "Our tasks and duties have just been placed on our backs by society. And one has to believe that society finds us quite redoubtable since it has condemned those from among our number who collaborated with the enemy while letting the industrialists who were guilty of the same crime go free" (*Sit. II*, p. 260).

ranks. The furthest extension of this argument is that he was fighting, not only for Hitler and Germany, but for his own reality, too. It is to that problem that the woman's accusation goes; though she speaks of honor, what she is blaming him for is his failure to live that reality fully enough. What more, he must have asked himself as he listened to her voice, could he have done? To see Germany reduced to ashes and prohibited from rising again would be to have confirmation that the wider reality in which he had existed, *his* reality, also stood condemned; that result—abjection everywhere in his homeland—would have demonstrated that his project had been impossible. Before he can see the German economic miracle, a fourth incident drives him into seclusion.

That final incident was in some way the most banal since it had to do with a living-room brawl with an American officer, provoked by his sister. It escapes banality for two reasons. One is that the incident seems to have been deliberately planned by Léni in an effort to arrive at a special dominion over Frantz; the other is that, as in the incident with the rabbi, he was saved from the ire of the authorities (Americans, this time) by the intervention of his father. The elder Gerlach arranged the affair and made preparations for Frantz to take refuge in Argentina. Frantz rejected the option and instead secluded himself in the family house. In a way the gesture is contradictory; it sketches a refusal of his father's plan on the greater canvas of his father's protection which he now accepts for all time—someone else will have to worry about the practical consequences of his seclusion. But the gesture is also purposeful; it brings time to a stop—he wears no watch—so that he can prepare the dossier of the time he has actively lived. He is preparing for the day when, as the star witness, he can defend his century before the tribunal of history. He freely chooses to live outside of future possibilities in order to evaluate what he has done; the attempt drives him from time to time to the frontiers of folly. The only action in his room is produced by his voice as it conveys to his tape-recorder the evidence for his defense and that of his century.

Neither Frantz's madness nor his seclusion correspond to those of Pierre in "La Chambre." Pierre had chosen his room and his specters in order to escape from an unpleasant and intolerable reality. His seclusion served the single purpose of symbolizing his judgment on a world disdained. But he undertook no effort, similar to Frantz's, to guarantee that his judgment would become spoken or written comment, nor did he make any attempt to effect change in the situation which had produced his madness. Frantz's problematical madness, by contrast, is seen, by Johanna at least, to contain the fullness of the human situation. Life is horror; madness is not radically different from sanity but merely an intensification of it, especially when the world itself is mad. The contradiction visible in Frantz's decision does not imply that he has turned his back on life so much as it underscores the fundamental contradiction of existence.[5]

His project now is to be man's conscious advocate, the witness for the defense, which means that he wants to defend a being who in his very nature is a contradiction. He thus represents a Tintoretto liberated, for if the painter's seclusion was the price he paid in order to have some relationship with his native city, Frantz's seclusion has been elected in order that he may tell the city that the painter stands condemned and knows it. He knows, too, that long before he had dreamt nightmares of condemnation, the city itself stood condemned. What Frantz has learned is that not only is man the being who *is not* because he can never stop being in order to be; he is also the man who can only rarely say—and perhaps only by lying—that he created himself despite the dissuasive pressures of surrounding influences. Contradictorily, Frantz, pleading force majeure as his principal excuse, wishes to be judged; furthermore, he wants that judgment to have general applicability so that, deriving from a universal standard, it will have global significance and serve as a guide for all. But he can find no judge. If the world does indeed contain groupings of powerful circumstances which play a role in the formation of each man, then the world cannot judge negatively those it has formed; such a judgment would only bring into question the value of the formation provided. Under such conditions, any judgment it might pass would have no justification since the world cannot justify itself. If it has formed Frantz to be a soldier who, under a general code of tolerated behavior, must torture, then it cannot condemn Frantz for having done what he had been formed to do.

In such a condemnation, whether or not the world acknowledged the fact, the world would condemn itself and, in the process, despoil itself of any right to establish values. Man, no matter how strong his social instinct may be, no matter how much his life must be lived out in the company of others, is inevitably—and in the worst moment of his existence—thrown back upon himself in the search for a justification the world cannot provide. Goetz, in accepting the command of the peasant army, may have found a function approved by other men; he has not in that bargain found justification for the acts he may be obliged to commit in the exercise of his command.

---

5. I have already pointed out that Sartre in his early career looked upon the emotions—and madness was considered an emotional reaction—as invocations of magical solutions when all other ways out were blocked: "Let it be clearly understood that this is not a game; we are driven against a wall, and we throw ourselves into this new attitude with all the strength we can muster. Let it also be understood that this attempt is not conscious of being such, for it would then be the object of reflection. Before anything else, it is the seizure of new connections and new exigencies" (*Emotions*, p. 59). In *SG*, he was still arguing the same case: "To adopt a mental attitude is to place oneself in a prison without bars. One seems able to escape from it at any moment, and in point of fact no wall or bars can prevent thinking from going as far as it likes" (p. 69).

The role and power of force majeure is shrewdly expressed throughout the play by constant invocation of a phrase which economically catches the whole body of contradictions and boomerangs with which *Les Séquestrés* is concerned: *the loser wins*. It is a phrase which has appeared many times in Sartre's writings; in this play, it receives variations which incorporate and synthesize his earlier reactions to the paradox it catches. He first made major use of it in an essay on Georges Bataille, "Un Nouveau Mystique," published in 1943. (It appears in *Sit. I*, pp. 143–88.) The phrase condenses into three words the New Testament admonition that he who would save his life must lose it and he who loses his life saves it. That statement, on its own terms, either says too little or too much. Too little because, in losing your life, you may only be saving the system which encourages you to that sacrifice by promising to save you through some unexplained alchemical process; the question of the system's value is not raised. It says too much because it outlines a process without giving a clear indication of what the process is for or of what else must be sacrificed in order to sustain it.

As a description, of the life process lifted out of every theological and ideological context, the phrase is, however, exact. We do lose part of our particular allotment of time each day. That fact raises the question of what kind of value the gradual loss will have produced when the allotment is completely exhausted. It is this aspect of the biblical conundrum which most concerned the younger Sartre, who seemed to believe that the phrase was a good measure of men's intentions. Bataille's point of departure, for example, is a complete rejection of the biblical phrase and a resultant assertion of his belief that man must lose himself simply—and alarmingly—because he can't possibly win. To have any kind of project, especially that of winning, is to flee human reality by hiding in projects much as Pascalian man hid in his divertissements.

This, for Sartre, is quite fundamental nonsense trying to transform itself into metaphysical sense. It is also a rejection which really wants to produce an affirmation, since what Bataille is in effect proposing is to take a very bleak view in order to know that he has the right view. If he lives with his drab discoveries and makes them the center of his existence, then, by having elected the sad way, he will have chosen the true way; if man is agony and if Bataille embodies that agony, then Bataille has lost in order to win. We have already seen a similar process in Roquentin's proposal to write a book which would announce to humanity that the game it was playing had been up from the very start and that he alone knew it. Bataille's goal, Sartre claims, is to be able to say "I am the suffering world. Thus I have gained *everything* in losing myself" (p. 178). There is a clearly sought result behind this kind of attempt; it finds expression in Sartre's Clytemnestre who, though she speaks forlornly, indicates that sadness willingly accepted brings its own rewards. "If," she says, "I have won anything by losing myself it's that I now have nothing more to fear" (*Les Mouches*, p. 36).

What Sartre seems to be protesting against are the efforts made by individuals to abstract themselves from the world by claiming to incarnate it. They agree that the world stands condemned only because their agreement places them in harmony with the world-as-cursed and excuses them from having to do anything to redeem it. Sartre rejects such attitudes almost totally. He does allow poets to pursue similar projects because, if in the contemporary era poets play at loser wins, they do so only because they have been forced to. They can be justified because they accept a risk which ends up by having a social function. The crisis of language—the loss of precise meanings for crucial words—has obliged them to risk every imaginative danger in order to clarify language. Though they may live apart and dream strange dreams, they do so as purifiers of the language, a function Bataille is not allowed to claim—he is concerned with ideas, not words—and which Clytemnestre mocks; she uses words like "guilt" and "remorse" easily, because she knows they have nothing essential to do with her reality.[6]

In the ensuing years Sartre discovered two other categories of human endeavor where the reality caught in the paradox seemed to apply and have merit. The first had to do with those individuals, men like Jean Genet, who have been reified by society to a point where their freedom of action is severely restricted by the function that has been ascribed to them. They are allotted very little lebensraum and can react to their small ration in one of two ways. They can accept the reduced portion and lose their right to accede to the fullness of their humanity; or they can take risks and, in so doing, possibly lose even the little space with which they began. Genet's case is of especial interest to Sartre because the two ways, as Genet lives out his life, get thoroughly intertwined; more accurately, the first naturally produces the second when it turns out that Genet, in order to live on the space that has been assigned to him, must take all the risks anyway. He has tried to be the criminal he was told at an early age he was; but the effort to be a criminal has been a long one, demanding resourcefulness and imagination, since what Genet has sought through crime is to be the incarnation of evil.

In other words he, too, has associated a goal with his function. As a result, no matter what he does as he participates in the game of loser-wins, winner-loses, he is bound to win some kind of victory. If he becomes a criminal, then he will be a success; he will have assumed fully the quality he was told was most characteristically his. If he doesn't become a criminal, that is, if he doesn't become a fixed being, then the society is wrong; but he shall

6. Cf. *Litt.*: "Poetry is loser wins. And the authentic poet chooses to lose even unto death in order to win. I repeat that this applies only to contemporary poetry" (*Sit. II*, p. 87).

have discovered that fact as a result of his own endeavors and against the society. Once the society has made such a major error, it has jeopardized its right to assign lebensraum. What the first moves in the game show Genet is the opposite of what he is seeking: he is a free subject and not a fixed object:

> The dazzling emergence of his subjectivity corresponds to the vanishing of his Ego. Thus, for Genet, the general pattern of his projects must remain the generalized *loser wins*. The impossibility of living is precisely the mainspring of his life, the impossibility of Evil is the triumph of the evil principle. The willed failure which is pursued unceasingly in his particular undertakings as in his total destiny becomes his victory (*SG*, pp. 183–84).

In the process Genet shows us how much we are involved in the same game, if only because there would be no game, and he would not have to play, if we hadn't drawn up the rules: "He plays loser wins with his work and you are his partner: thus you will win only by being ready to lose" (p. 585). Sartre is convinced that, as a result of Genet's moves, we have lost so thoroughly as to be bankrupt. The only reason we can go on playing at all is because the world's self-interest has inspired it to abandon debtors' prisons as instruments of effective policy.

The second category of human endeavor referred to above has to do with a reaction similar to Genet's but one which is made under different circumstances; it is the reaction of the man who, not previously limited in negotiating for space, finds himself on one occasion limited to two choices. This is the man who, like Henri Alleg, resists when put to torture; by refusing to yield, he accomplishes two things. First, "the victim liberates us by making us discover, as he himself has discovered, that we have the power and the duty to bear everything" (Introduction to *La Question, Sit. V*, p, 76). The second consequence has to do with his impact on his masters:

> When it's the victim who wins, then it's good-bye to the right of the lord, to mastery. The archangel's wings will fly no more and the guys begin to wonder, a little riled: "And what about me? Would I hold out if I was tortured?" What happens is that in their moment of victory, one system of values has been substituted for another; the slightest nudge would bring the executioners to the edge of giddy folly. Probably not, however; they are empty-headed and harassed with work; and furthermore they hardly believe in what they are doing (p. 88).

Since they hardly believe in what they are doing, they are far different from Frantz von Gerlach. He had desperately believed in his commitment, and, learning from his heroic, resisting victims what all executioners may learn from theirs, he finds himself in a world where the possibility that he will be tortured—and thereby given the chance to know whether he, too, could hold out—has become very remote. Remote, unless he creates it. And that in part is what he is doing by his insistence on living outside time in order endlessly to review the activity in which he was once engaged. Frantz gathers into himself the whole range of Sartre's thinking about the meaning of *loser wins*. He has been Genet, in that he has tried to live fully in the space assigned him; he has become Bataille, in that he now spends his time trying to show that he embodies essential man. But he is not.Alleg. On the contrary, he is the other side of Alleg, and the question now posed is: can the torturer ever come back from his loss and win? Unable to answer that question, Frantz has fallen on a dichotomy first expressed in Genet's life: "there is a time for wickedness: that of praxis, and a time for Saintliness: that of reflection on praxis, of retrospective interpretation of his activity" (*SG*, p. 237). In Sartre's estimation, Genet succeeded because the process of reflection was an action. Thus another question is posed about Frantz. If his present mode of life is his effort at saintliness, will that saintliness reveal itself eventually to be a kind of action or will it serve as the prelude to further action? In other words, can his introspection lead either to new action or to a way of exculpating earlier acts?

Frantz's particular situation within the loser-wins paradox is only one of the many situations that paradox embraces, for the truth it gets at has reference to the whole range of life. Sartre himself, for example, seems ultimately to have become the loser. In *Being and Nothingness* he had argued his way to an exact description of life and its multiple forces. That was a victory, but the victory had led to a defeat since those terms have seemed to be so rigorously true as to describe a situation which cannot be changed. Lived experience justifies the pessimism he was fighting against in his major philosophical works. He had, in the 1950s, added to those works the social dimension that was missing in *Being and Nothingness*. But that dimension had only shown that the kind of interpersonal hostility he had traced out in the earlier work did not disappear because of the larger social organisms; it was translated into intergroup hostility. Every gain, so far, has turned out to be the discovery of an apparently irretrievable loss.

The process seems to be repeated throughout the world. The Communists, having helped the Resistance to win in France, are chased from the government and sit in hostile negativism for over a decade; Stalin rules in the name of the workers and the workers are miserable; Russia is de-Stalinized and becomes more and more capitalistic in its economic policies; the great fraternal bond of communism is loosened, and East and West meet in disastrous imitation of each other as Peking and Moscow hurl at each other accusations which echo, too closely to provide any comfort to anyone, the earlier accusations exchanged by Washington and Moscow. One plays the game of existence in good faith, with great energy and a determination to win, only to find either that the stakes are no longer there or else have lost all their attraction. And one is left to wonder, when all the matches have been played, whether one has been playing the right game. You win and lose the stakes; you lose and win the stakes. France loses in Algeria and France's economy begins to flourish; Algeria, having won its just cause, turns to internecine fighting and, when that is over, begins to rattle sabres on the frontiers of its Arab brothers.

This process, with its multiple mysteries and mutenesses, can be seen at every emotional turn and in every intrigue of *Les Séquestrés d'Altona*. The older Gerlach has organized his whole life around his son's future involvement in the family enterprise with the hope of seeing both son and enterprise flourish; the enterprise grows to a point where it gets away from his control and the son, whose life he has twice saved, lives secluded in his own home, refusing to see him. So great has been his devotion to his older son that he has created a gap between himself and the younger son upon whom he must now rely as the inheritor of the enterprise and the baby-sitter to Frantz.[7] So deep has been his inattention to his daughter's fear of him and her consequent resentment that he does not suspect how guilefully she has plotted to get her own back. She alone of the family communicates with the son around whom the family's existence is centered. All this domestic intrigue takes place against the background of a renascent Germany which, having lost the war, has won the dominant economic position in the Western Europe she had ravaged. The spoils of victory could not have been richer.

On the level of the individual, as on the level of family, state, and hostile superpowers, there is no ultimate control over outcomes and thus apparently no point in trying to make choices. The father claims that he has played out his life on the principle of loser wins. But he must admit at the end that, if the loser wins, once he has won he in turn becomes the loser:

> I am the shadow of a cloud; one shower and the sun will light up the place where I lived. To hell with it: the winner loses. The Enterprise which is crushing us was my creation (p. 218).

---

7. There is adequate reason for believing that Werner's character is inspired by Sartre's study of Flaubert. He finds himself in the same family situation: the second son eclipsed by the family's concern with the first son and haunted by the early promising performance of the older brother. While Werner seems on the surface to have worked out a more successful pattern of compensation than had Flaubert, he still is bothered by the alleged indifference of his father and, more important, he is tempted to answer the father's appeal affirmatively in order to win, late in life and despite what is an apparently successful marriage, his father's esteem and the primary place in the family. He is deluding himself—probably wilfully—because the father is giving nothing and is thinking only of the older son and the older son's welfare to which he unconcernedly sacrifices the independence Werner has won.

At the end, when father and son have decided on suicide—for their existence has neither sense, nor judge, nor solution—Frantz tells Johanna that she has won; her husband is free. But all she seems to have won is the need to ask whether she is winner or loser. She has won her husband, but only at the price of a double suicide, and thus she inherits the worrisome question of whether every victory demands human sacrifice. The two possibilities caught in the win-lose dialectic turn out to be the two sides of a coin endlessly tossed into the air, defying any predictions about which side will turn up. To win or to lose makes only a momentary difference anyway, since the coin is immediately tossed up again.

Despite this grim aspect of the process, there is no sense in trying to opt out of it for the simple reason that it still goes on and, whatever its source, has influence even on those who have tried to escape. Bataille's case is a pertinent example. But so are the cases of all who live in the Gerlach house. They talk about the win-lose dialectic as though it has already exercised its full sway over them. They do autopsies only to find that there is not yet a cadaver; a sequestered Frantz does not stop the dialectic, principally because in his seclusion he is studying it more closely. They are all still playing at loser wins and the winners are losing even as the losers are winning. Frantz, as I have already said, dominates them all; Léni, since she is his amanuensis, seems to dominate them, too. But the elder Gerlach, though he admits to having lost, still yearns for one last interview with his son; when he has it, he and Frantz discover that they have both lost. The outcome is the decision to commit suicide. In that act, jointly undertaken, they perhaps hope to win one last victory over the accumulated loss; if they cannot absorb the losses, they can write them off the book of consciousness by bringing an end to consciousness.

They might never have arrived at the interview and its mortal consequences were it not for Johanna. She enters the atrophied household unwilling to resign herself to losses. By her balkiness, she sets the full lose-win dialectic into renewed motion. Instinct is what seems to drive her. She has won, in a desperate way, too much to be willing to lose by becoming Frantz's guardian. She has acceded to life by acceding to love and knows that her love will be jeopardized if she allows her husband to accept the task his father seeks to impose. As she manipulates, she seems to touch on the principle Sartre had enunciated in *Saint Genet*: that one cannot love one man unless that love implies love for all men. Without ceasing to love Werner, she risks, because of the respect and affection she has for Frantz, losing him and all he represents for her. Yet if she does not fight she loses everything anyway since Werner will be fundamentally changed once he becomes the past's prisoner. Whatever she wins in the end—and we can only have hopes about her future with Werner; we can make no predictions about it—is won only because Frantz is dead.

Chance rules in the world; or, if it does not really rule, it makes such a good case for itself that only the foolish or visionary would spend time making contrary claims. It rules because outcomes cannot be predicted, because categories cannot be securely defended, and because the old distinction between the strong and the weak turns out to be, not a distinction, but the vehicle on which chance makes its way. Strength, which once seemed to be the way to rule the world, turns out to be ruled by the world.

> *Frantz*: You made me a prince, Father. And do you know who made me a king?
> *The Father*: Hitler?
> *Frantz*: Didn't you know it? Oh, I hated him all right. Before. After. But on that day, he possessed me. When there are two leaders, they either kill each other or one becomes the other's woman. I've been Hitler's woman. The rabbi was bleeding and I was discovering, at the heart of powerlessness, some kind of assent. (*He relives the past.*) I have the supreme power. Hitler made me an Other, implacable and sacred: himself . . . power is an abyss whose depths I see . . . sovereign men go to hell, that's their glory; that's where I'll go (p. 206).

Power, though it promises only hell, has become his vocation because, without it, he can effect nothing in the world, just as, without it, he could do nothing to save the rabbi. What possessed him on that day was the conviction that, unless he put himself on the side of power, he would remain nothing and be able to do nothing. He could neither kill Jews nor save them. That has been the horrible fact that the men of his century have had to live with. The only material available to them was evil; the only hope, that they would be able to work with evil so skillfully as to produce good; the result: "the good turned bad" (p. 96).

What had been offered as a justifiable process for Goetz, in Frantz's case has led to failure because Frantz has not had the fortitude to live with the result. Yet prior to the result, he was, if not the perfect Sartrean man, at least man living authentically, aware of the mess he was trying to rearrange into some order. The significant reality he had encountered was the mess as the only arrangement available to him; in a long view it seems no different from other messes which have served as the point of departure for other decisions. The elder Gerlach had reasoned similarly, selling land to Himmler for a concentration camp, keeping his enterprise operating in the name of his family on the principle that, if he did not serve Hitler, others would.

Frantz, of course, can claim that his point of departure was different. He believed in human dignity. He had a conscience to which he tried to listen until he was thwarted in the incident involving the rabbi. But his father will not admit such refined structures of defense. Conscience, he says, is a luxury for a prince. Frantz could well afford to have one; when one isn't doing anything, one believes he is responsible for everything. *I* had my work to do (p. 49).

By which he means that he was plunged, as Frantz was to be, in a world where he, too, had to use the available means to accomplish well-defined ends; this is the world where men like Sartre find themselves compelled to defend violence as a necessary means to good ends, only to discover later that they have not quite become what they intended to be. Frantz's seclusion may be folly's child or folly's father; it is difficult to tell, just as it is difficult to deny that folly may produce the only wisdom.

That wisdom attempts to go beyond the simple assertion, made by Johanna, that madness is the only true reflection of life's horror. In Frantz's mind it goes to the point of affirming that no one is guilty, which is a devious way of saying that everyone is somewhat guilty:

> *The Father*: All right then. Is everyone guilty?
> *Frantz*: Great God, no! No one. No one except the sleeping dogs who accept the judgments of the conquerors. . . . Did Goering drop the bomb on Hiroshima? If they put us on trial, who will try them? (p. 44).

His sister adds to this wisdom and intensifies the difficulty of trying to allocate guilt: "The innocent," she says, "were twenty-year-olds; they were the soldiers. The guilty were the fifty-year-olds—the soldiers' fathers" (p. 45). This is an argument which Frantz picks up and to whose complexity he adds. It is a valuable argument to him because it spreads the responsibility of guilt; it is an even better argument because its ramifications exculpate him slightly by putting the major portion of blame elsewhere. To Johanna's insinuation that everything he did he did freely, he answers:

> Me? But I never make a choice. . . . I am chosen. Nine months before my birth, my name, my character, and my destiny were already chosen. And let me tell you: this cellular regime has also been imposed on me, and you have to understand that I would never have submitted myself to it without a capital reason (p. 107).

In admitting that he has submitted to that regime, he once again contradicts himself, as he contradicts himself in believing in an imposed nationwide abjection which he believes is unjustified. According to his initial premise—that everything is imposed—he should accept the abjection. He must, of course, respond this way because the contradiction which dominates his thinking is that contained in his impossible project: to show that men are not guilty of—by extension, not responsible for—the actions they commit.

Yet his contradiction is a symbol of all the contradictions unveiled by the play. Who is the other who fears and who the other who needs? Who is strong and who weak? Who wins and who loses?

The readiest and probably the most accurate answer is: everyone and at every moment. This is the answer Johanna sees only too clearly and which she finds unacceptable because, as the vehicle for Sartre's longing to find an answer which will be less morally disempowering, she must fight to maintain some grip on a slippery hope. In her we grasp the total reality of the problem, for Johanna is the free being who, having already exercised her freedom to her benefit and that of her husband, finds her freedom confronted with an impossible choice. No matter what option she elects, the outcome will be imperfect and there will be a predictable rub-off of guilt. She can leave her husband and his family and thus undo the love between her and him; but if she does that, she will find herself back in the former existence which had driven her close to suicide and from which she was rescued only by a commitment to love, that is, a binding commitment to the Other. She can accept the situation with Frantz and run the risks I have already mentioned. Even as she stands before the necessity of making a decision, she sees in Frantz an embodiment of the impossibility of making decisions. There can be no pure act because there can be no control over all the consequences of an act. Every act which aims at defending freedom seems to be worked out at the price of another's liberty. Every act is related to a truth or creates a truth; but that truth, or that couple of truths, are so contradictory as to seem to be lies.

What she discovers drives us one step beyond *Le Diable et le Bon Dieu*. Even when you rearrange labels and regroup forces under the right banner, there are no camps. There is only contradiction which produces ruinous reciprocities. Belief in and commitment to different camps stems from a confusion of orientations with realities. Johanna sees only one solution to this, and she cries out to the father:

> Blow up the house! Blow up the planet! Finally we'd have peace. Peace! Peace! Peace! (p. 139).

Despite her outburst, Johanna wants to look steadily at the situation, to act honestly. Yet in order to save her husband, she must lie to him and thus add further particles to the already heavy dust of lies in the house.[8] Even there ambiguity rules, for, in a way, and especially in this house of lies, to lie is to join in the truth of the house, to accept its modus operandi. What appar-

---

8. She seems in several ways to embody Sartre's idea of Camus' program: "I think especially of Camus. For him man's response to the absurdity of his condition is not in any great romantic rebellion but in daily application. To see clearly, to keep one's word, to do one's job—that is where *real* revolt happens. Because there is no reason why I should be faithful, loyal, and brave. And it is *precisely because of that* that I ought to show myself in these colors" ("Aller et retour," *Sit. I*, pp. 242–43).

ently keeps her committed to action, in addition to her love for Werner, is the realization that Frantz is the frozen embodiment of what she will become if she stops. Simultaneously, she is attracted by the temptation he represents. If only she could lie to herself, as he lies to himself, she would . . .

But she does not have the chance to find out what profit she would derive from imitating him, once she discovers, at the critical moment in the play, that Frantz has also been lying to her. When she finds out that he tortured the partisans, she cannot accept him nor can she accord any value to his assertion that *he* did nothing. Instinct comes to the fore again, a strong sense that this is the limit, that this is where camps are clearly distinguishable, that this is the basic situation in which good and evil are clearly separated; if there are two truths, then one has to be false. Though she reacts as though there were a true moral division now to be made, she makes no statements which justify her emotional reactions. Brought to this limit she balks; it is almost as though her experience in the Gerlach house has driven her to the point where the only sanction left is the one she receives from her ego. Yet earlier in her life, reliance on her ego had driven her to the brink of suicide.

The questions Johanna does not ask at this point are the questions Frantz has been asking throughout the play, the questions which serve as the basis for his final conversation with his father. Who will judge when most of the judges need to be judged? The elder Gerlach, at first forbidden by his son to judge him and then exhorted to, refuses; all he can offer is the assurance that *he* still loves his son, an admission that brings little in the way of justification since he has loved his son against the world and the family enterprise against his son. The love he offers is thus a different kind from that offered by Johanna. He proffers his at the end, after Johanna's has been removed; his leads to death, the elimination of the Other, with the major questions unanswered: who most needs the Other? who most fears the Other? [9]

9. There is some answer provided by two of the personal relationships we encounter in the play. Sartre's analysis of love, as I have outlined it in the preceding chapter, is expressed in Johanna's explicit desire to remain faithful to her promise to Werner and her emerging realization that some element in that love is simultaneously justified and put into question by her relations with Frantz. Sartre's description of pragmatic love as a bond of promises which envisages the achievement of common projects is further and more subtly reinforced, though by negative example, in the incestuous union between Frantz and Léni. Sexual need, not unexpectedly, does not abandon Frantz when he elects seclusion. That he satisfies this need incestuously tells us certain things: he has probably been encouraged thereto by Léni; he wants to minimize the importance of sexual relations. They have been held to a minimum which is not clearly defined, and anyway, as Frantz himself points out, in a world where millions of orgasms take place each day, it is exaggerated to attribute much importance to one.

This is the statistical approach to exculpation, and guilt remains strong in Frantz even as he offers it. The guilt has nothing to do with puritanism and everything to do with the self-invalidating error manifest in the incest. For it is an effort to satisfy

It would be depressing to have come as far as Sartre has come, to have written as much as he has written, only to turn up with a maxim as a solution: love one another. It would be depressing, not because there is anything offensive about the maxim, but more realistically because it has never worked and from its failure has come all the evidence Sartre has accumulated. In his essay on Merleau-Ponty he wrote that he had always believed that truth had to be everywhere one, by which he meant that there could be no truth unless it was applicable to all men and visibly expressed in their lives. That truth may indeed have to do with love; but the relationship does not of itself effect a corresponding reality. And Sartre has presented massive evidence to show the absence of that reality. He has also suggested in *Les Séquestrés* a solution, when Frantz says to Johanna: "We must help each other will the truth" (p. 166). The promise of that approach is severely curtailed when Johanna refuses to accept as lovable a Frantz who has been responsible for torture. The will is not enough as long as the Other is able to use his will freely and unpredictably, and we end where we began— with the problem of the Other. At the conclusion of the play, the tape recorder broadcasts—for all time?—Frantz's argument:

> The century would have been fine if man hadn't been spied on by his cruel immemorial enemy, by the carnivorous species which vowed his loss, by the wily and hairless beast, by man. One and one are one, that's our mystery. The beast hid, but we surprised his look all of a sudden in the inner eyes of our neighbors; so we struck out—a case of legitimate self-defense. I surprised the beast, I struck out, a man fell, and in his dying eyes I saw the beast, still alive—myself (p. 222).

---

indestructible need by finding an outlet outside the universal social economy established by exogamy. In disregarding the incest taboo, Frantz is further emphasizing his refusal of all social solutions to his obsessive problems. The refusal, however, solves nothing, in the sense that it creates no bond other than the brief moments of coitus between him and Léni; it thus identifies further the obsession with solitude and with withdrawal as a solution. The incest satisfies a need; it also prevents the use of that need as a means of achieving a better solution. Léni is the Other, but she is the Other used, not to deny the Other, but to refuse to use or cooperate with an Other with whom one would conduct *admissible* common activities.

Because it is taboo the incest is also secret. As a couple Léni and Frantz are precisely what Johanna and Werner, as a couple, are not: they can get nowhere together precisely because incest is the refusal of the social, outgoing aspect of human sexuality. Their relationship is a further example of that "ideal" and impossible love Sartre discussed in *BN*. It is also an important footnote to that earlier discussion which provides a further and transforming explanation: if "ideal" love is impossible and ruinous, that is not because it is either sadistic or masochistic in its expression but because it is incestuous in its inspiration, a refusal of the social commitment which makes life in community possible. One reason for this development of Sartre's analysis—and part of the basis for my own observations—is the impact of Claude Lévi-Strauss's *Les Structures élémentaires de la parenté* (Paris, 1949) must have had on him; he was already familiar with Durkheim's work.

The basic reciprocal process is that of circles looking at each other and seeing the worst of their fears and faculties in each other; the circles multiply, not to infinity, but to the limit of the world's population. This, as Frantz says, has become the problem of his century and it has left a spoiled taste about man. And Frantz becomes the image of that man because he is able to admit that he no longer has any illusions: "My client was the first to know shame: he knows that he is naked" (p. 222). But that is as far as he can go; his voice at the end promises that he will reply on man's behalf, but produces no answer as this play produces no answer.

It probably was not intended to; its concern was with bringing all the world's forces to a dead point where, without a judge, no decision could be possible, no justification found. Frantz, in his effort to articulate personal justification and the defense of his century, had addressed himself to the future, to history, to the judge Sartre will offer in the *Critique de la raison dialectique* as the arbiter who will provide the answers to Johanna's unspoken questions.

RELATED THEMES AND WORKS

Les Séquestrés has received two productions in Paris, the first in 1959 and the second in 1965. In both productions Serge Reggiani played the part of Frantz and received universal praise; a solid, imaginative, and controlled interpretation of this role is essential to the success of the play, for if Frantz is made to be a madman the play then seems to be an overlong anecdote about folly. The second production differed from the first in being scenically a good deal less literal; the effect aimed at in the revival was to create a dislocated, lopsided, allusive decor which reproduced these qualities as found in the Gerlach family. The play has also been staged in London and New York. A very bad film, which Sartre has disowned, was made from the play.

In an interview, given at the time of the play's first production (*L'Express*, 17 September 1959), Sartre described Frantz as a man who speaks nonsense in order to avoid giving an accurate description of the century in which he lives. Sartre understands the reasons for this, but seems to place less emphasis than he should on the kind of comment Frantz makes precisely by refusing to make a rational analysis of the world in which he lives. In a more recent interview (*Livres de France*, January 1966), Sartre makes comments which more fully reflect the broad range of Frantz's complex character and better express the relationship between Frantz and the body of Sartre's thought. In both interviews there is a novel insistence on the Gerlach family as a manifestation of a group of individuals dominated and eventually undone by economic forces they or their ancestors have unleashed. Sartre clearly means this to be read as one of the effects of capitalism. As I shall endeavor to point out in the final chapter, the domina-

it may be intentional; since Sartre makes no distinction between the two, insisting that the unconscious is intentional in its behavior, there is really no issue. However, there is some value to be had from making the slip, or the connection, since the mood in which the play was written was clearly one which sought to establish links between the Germany of Hitler and the France of Algeria. In this sense, France, like Frantz, had become Hitler's woman by saying yes to the same methods the Nazis had used and by seeking to justify such methods in the name of higher (or older) goals. In a more extended interpretation, the process whereby France becomes like Germany (I write, to be sure, only of links made in Sartre's mind), is not unlike the process whereby Frantz becomes Germany's defender. That process is the one whereby Frantz succumbs, not to Nazi Germany, but to his own capacities for doing the worst rather than the best. The polarization which allows a country to behave schizophrenically by claiming imposed paranoia is no different from the oscillating movement characteristic of Frantz's behavior.

Jeanson in his book about Sartre and God (*Sartre* [Paris, 1966]) has some valuable observations on this play, especially in its relationship to the vocabulary of the *CRD*; the Cooper and Laing book is useful for the same reason. Thody discusses the loser wins theme in a different and less lengthy way in his book (p. 129–132); the drama critic of *L'Express*, in his review of the revival of the play (20 September 1965) has some provocative remarks about the subtle but pervasive eroticism of the play.

After the final version of this chapter had been prepared, I read Michel Contat's *Explication des Séquestrés d'Altona de J.-P. S.* (*Archives des Lettres Modernes*, no. 89, 1968) which is an excellent and provocative commentary on the play. Contat—who informs us discreetly that his text has been read by and has elicited the approval of Sartre—is principally concerned with elucidating the drama in terms of the philosopher's more recent thinking, especially the arguments of the *CRD*. Contat also has most helpful observations to make on Johanna's struggles with ethical judgments, Léni's ultimate submission to her imagination, and the reasons which lead Frantz to suicide. Finally, he quotes (pp. 72–73) an important note Sartre wrote for the 1965 production of the play in which the playwright expands significantly on his earlier explications of the play's scope and intent. The bibliography is thorough.

As a result of Contat's monograph, I have also become aware of two other commendable contributions to the understanding of this rich but elusive drama which Contat does not hesitate to call a tragedy: Georges Poulet's "A propos de J.-P. S.: Rupture et création littéraire" (in *Les Chemins actuels de la critique* [Plon, 1967], pp. 393–411); and Philip Thody's Introduction to his edition of the play (University of London Press, 1965).

Our age will be an object

for those future eyes whose gaze haunts us.

And a guilty object. They will reveal

to us our failure and guilt. Our age, which

is already dead, already a thing, *though we*

still have to live it, is alone *in history,*

and this historical solitude determines even

our perceptions; what we see will no longer be;

people will laugh at our ignorance, will be

indignant at our mistakes. What course is

open to us?

— Saint Genet

11 *Free for All*

By the time he comes to write the *Critique de la raison dialectique*, Sartre lives familiarly with two unhappy universes. The misery of the one is not necessarily the cause of any surprise, since it was the multifaceted inadequacy of the observed world which originally inspired his literary and philosophical undertakings. The inadequacy of the other—the universe he had himself created—is a graver source of discontent, for that personal universe, shaped on the basis of analysis, had been created from hope. Its deployment was intended to indicate a way towards improvement by isolating obstacles and presenting a strategy for their removal. We have been watching the process whereby that personal universe fails its own purpose and verifies rather than challenges the observed universe it was meant to correct.

Sartre had very early suggested that recourse to the imagination, though necessary for the establishment of helpful perspectives, was fraught with dangers since too often imagination was used as a haven by consciousnesses that were dissatisfied with available reality. As a result, he has persistently tried to use his own imagination sparingly and prudently. If it has been a probing instrument, it has always been carefully used, by which I mean that Sartre has never allowed it to become its own generator; the materials he has passed through it have always come from the observed world. The universe created by his imagination has always been a close cousin to reality, though cousinship has never implied love. Sartre, in accepting the encumbrance of a misused world, was openly enthusiastic about the chances of lessening its weight by showing that a good portion of its impedimenta was unnecessary; he had only to chip away at stuff and nonsense in order to emerge with an easier yoke and lighter burden. Reflection on the changes that have taken place between *Les Mouches* and the writing of *Les Séquestrés d'Altona* shows that a reverse process has taken place: the burden has become heavier, the yoke intolerable; reality, whether on its own or with the help of generous imaginations, seems unable to save itself from the hideous process in which all victories turn out to be brief preludes to defeat.

Sartre's original social goal seemed easy enough of achievement because the terms of that project had exact value referents: the world's few preyed on the world's many with the result that the many suffered so that the few could be satisfied. The ready formula for a just and efficient solution was to reverse the situation and work for a world in which, by revolution, the few would be displaced by the many. To the extent that this was also an ideal, it risked sharing the history of many ideals: in the fight to impose them they lose all their attractiveness. There were other dangers and problems: the possibility that the fighters in the struggle would lose either their energy or, their particular battle won, any interest in fighting others; the more elusive and more frightening possibility that a just world would be an empty and sterile place. Worst of all, there was accumulated information monotonously indicating that ideals which aimed at the installation of universal justice on this earth overlooked the crucial fact that men possibly do not only *not* love justice but are incapable of working in its behalf. If conflict is where men begin to live out their lives, conflict is where they remain, not because of meanness but because of necessity; a hostile world demands a cagey response. Such a response may not produce gains; it may not even be meant to. It is born from an instinctive realization that if, in this world, one cannot fight for victory, one must fight against loss.

The only information Sartre holds firmly tells what a dismal game humanity has been playing; though the stakes have been high, or perhaps *because* the stakes have been high, the bids have been miscalculated. The game and even the rubber will be won, but the victors, having been set too often, will lose. The strategy they devised, prudent and cautious, was not enough. In a way they achieve what they wanted—for they have won—only to find that the cost of the strategy has robbed the victory of meaning, results, and especially rewards. The game analogy is neither fanciful nor inexact as a way of trying to see what Sartre has accomplished and what is lacking to that accomplishment. In the game, there are partners and therefore there is cooperation between them; but in the game there is also an opposing team, equally skilled in cooperation, equally eager to win, equally cautious and prudent in its bidding, and perhaps equally touched with desperation. Unpredictable forces—a moment's hesitation, an instantaneous failure of nerve, too little ambition or too much—tilt the scales of victory; and hazard indeed seems to rule the world and with such force as to deny that rearrangements of partners, changes in rules, or even the renunciation of all games are intelligent responses. Individual and group maneuvers, despite their dexterity and their visible yield of progress, have ended relentlessly in a bog.

There are, as Emily Dickinson saw and as Sartre has verified, some people who are quite happy to live in a bog so long as the bog is an admiring one. Emily Dickinson's solution, though proposed more cheerfully, was not essentially different from Pierre's in "La Chambre"; to live apart from *them* in the company of another who also wished to live apart from *them*. This, to Sartre, is just another kind of bog whose existence can be explained and even sympathized with but which does not hold any special promise since, rather than resolving conflict, it freezes it. Against those who live in justified or reprehensible bogs, Sartre had proposed those who fight against the bogs—Hoederer and Goetz and Genet—only to turn up with Frantz von Gerlach whose strategy produced results applicable not only to him but conceivably to Hoederer and Goetz. It is not

simply that one bog leads to another or even that one bog seems no different from others; it is more strikingly a question of whether inevitably—
and, if so, *why?*—there have to be bogs at all. The various bogs point to
a phenomenon Sartre identifies as the practico-inert—the bog which spreads
out on all sides of human action to engulf it.

The practico-inert has multiple manifestations, some of which are readily
condemnable, some of which are in themselves neutral, others of which are
understandable. In all its manifestations, it should be fought against for
the very clear reason that it is a bog which man accepts or into which he
falls or which falls on him; it consequently reduces his capacity for further
action and his chance of provoking change. As such it is not much different
from the disempowering obstacles and the resultant temptations which were
outlined in *Being and Nothingness.* What is different are its manifestations
or, more accurately, its power. What is also different is the respect and
understanding Sartre has been showing for that power.

There was a time when he was suggesting that existence could be
managed if only men acknowledged two things: first, that there was no
way on this side of death to cease existing; second, that individuals had
only to recognize their freedom in order to get on with their tasks. Over
the years this advice has demonstrated both its inadequacy and the massiveness of the practico-inert—its inadequacy *because* of that massiveness. The obstacles which had once been readily dismissed have now
come back and are dealt with as true obstacles which can only be set
aside by a cooperative program whose thrust will be greater than that of
the obstacles. What Sartre has discovered is that the practico-inert is not
always an already existing obstacle to be set aside. It is the byproduct of
action and conceivably its entropy. It assumes a life and powerful force
of its own; as a result it can reasonably be said to dominate men because
it conditions their existence from the very outset.[1]

1. In the narrowest sense the practico-inert is the unpredicted consequence of original
initiative. A worker, living in misery, decides to do something to reduce that misery;
he strikes for better wages and eventually receives them, but in order to get them he
makes concessions about the organization and nature of his work which render that
work more tedious. He is better paid and therefore less conscious of his new style of
misery; perhaps he is not conscious of it at all. But his work has become a pure function or begins to manifest itself as totally routine. In a way, he is less well off humanly
than he was when privation made him aware of his humanity as deficient, stunted, or
oppressed. Against the spiritual erosion produced by the monotony of his work, he
cannot form as ready a response or any response at all. The improvement of his
material conditions, and the guarantee of work, have given him better control over the
satisfaction of his material needs; they have not necessarily given him access to fuller
expression of his human potentialities. He is caught in a *process.* He must act through
his work to maintain that process; he may even come to believe that the process is
necessary. At that point he blunts his capacity for praxis—for further enactments
which will produce more fundamental change—and engages his energy in sustaining
the process, in sustaining the monotony of his function.

The implications for collective endeavor are clear; once its original goal has been

This happens because goals, carefully chosen with an eye to improvement either of the individual or the group, turn out to be either unsatisfactory or disempowering once they are achieved. Every Sartrean character we have encountered has had such a goal; most have attained the goal set. Broadly speaking there have been two kinds of result. One has been Lucien's—a goal which, when achieved, produces individual satisfaction bought at a very steep price for others and at a not easily estimable price for the purchaser, since his solution transmogrifies his fear without necessarily taming it. The other kind of goal is that which sports its price tag only too visibly and which, because of that, demands either a capitulation to what has been achieved despite its inadequacy or else the definition and pursuit of a new goal. At the heart of each kind of pursuit, there has been a clear commitment to exist, to act in order to achieve something. In most cases there has been a consequent impasse which has led to withdrawal or suicide or, in the case of the chronicler of all these attempts, a recognition of the need to redefine possibilities in order to respond to the fresh data that new situations have provided.

If individual characters are tempted to give up because of the poverty of their achievement and its high cost, Sartre is not. Yet his personal history is parallel to theirs in that, refusing to manipulate those histories, he has repeatedly had to release them to failure or to death. His literary works are strewn with human sacrifices to the ineffectiveness of his suggested programs. Those sacrifices, rather than disproving the validity of the guiding ideas, confirm them; simultaneously, they show the need for something else—a longer, broader, and, most crucially, a more authoritative view. And that means the location and description of some reality

---

achieved, a collective enterprise may also learn to live both with what has been accomplished *and* with the unexpected accompaniments to that accomplishment. A society which makes use of computers may find, as Norbert Weiner pointed out in some of the more chilling pages of *The Human Use of Human Beings*, that henceforth it *must* make use of computers; a nation that gets involved in the armaments race may come to believe—or learn to its unspoken horror—that it cannot disengage itself from all the consequences of that kind of competition.

The broader significance of the practico-inert is the diversification it introduces into the earlier notion of being-in-itself. Where being-in-itself, despite the temptation it represented for men, was unwaveringly described as the nonhuman or the antihuman—that which man could not be without engaging in ruinously contradictory activity—the practico-inert results from human opposition to being-in-itself. That opposition is the initial moment of praxis; what it amounts to, for a fleeting moment, is man's saying: "I will not be (or cannot be) that." In the subsequent instant, that man must, of course, say what he will be instead and then proceed to direct his life towards that end. But, like the worker, he will find that the end, achieved, produces its particular kind of inertia to which once again he must say no if he wishes to continue controlling his existence or his responses to his situation and others' projects. The practico-inert turns out to have the same kind of relationship to human processes as being-in-itself to nature's processes.

which by its very nature cannot fall into a bog or be a bog. That reality is history.

It is not the solution one would have expected Sartre to come up with since his early attitude towards history was more than slightly skeptical. That attitude has not really changed; what has very much changed is what he means by history. When he first writes about history, he tends to deride it because he sees it as an imaginative construct whose architects have sinister purposes. One of these is to argue for a certain ideology; in so doing ideologists show that history is endlessly malleable and suggest that it is the battleground on which idealism defeats its most persistent enemy, realism. "The history of Egypt," he wrote, "is the history of Egyptology" (*BN*, p. 545), summing up the idealist position which, he goes on to say, is itself historical.

Egyptology may have its value for Egyptologists; what Sartre was doubtful about was what *use* it had for anyone else. Though Egyptology may not be rightfully considered an ideology, it is an idealist activity and remains dangerous because it is part of an effort to suggest that history, as organized in books by men, provides other men with a pattern for life. One recalls his grandfather's insistence that, once the kings had been chased away, everything was just fine and would go on improving. The great danger of history was thus joined to the great danger of all fascination with the past; it turned men's eyes away from the fact that their lot was in the future, or else, as in the case of Anny and Roquentin—who had been inspired by a Michelet text—it encouraged them to organize moments that sought to model present life on past episodes. Written history suffocates men as the task of writing M. de Rollebon's biography suffocated Roquentin. It offers the past as a fixed quantity, and fixed quantities, as Sartre insisted in *Being and Nothingness*, are precisely what men can learn least from. In that work, history was not so much condemned by itself as made irrelevant by the fact of man's flight towards the future.

Though written history might be no more than a way of playing with the meaning of elapsed time, there could be no doubt that time was indeed elapsing and in its passage manifesting some kind of process. Sartre seems always to have been uneasily aware of that process and conscious of the fact that what he said about written history had little relevance to lived history. In *Qu'est-ce que la littérature*, he spoke of it as "this strange reality" which was neither completely subjective nor completely objective and which seemed to have a dialectic of its own.[2] Yet, in the aftermath of the war and especially with the establishment of *Les Temps Modernes*,

2. "One day I shall try to describe that strange reality, history, which is neither objective nor altogether subjective, and where the dialectic is contested, penetrated, and corroded by a kind of antidialectic which is itself dialectical" (*Litt.*, p. 86, n. 4).

such speculation about history had been dismissed as mandarin activity. In "La Nationalisation de la littérature" (1945), he had written, reflecting the attitudes already apparent in *Being and Nothingness*:

> We must be satisfied with *making* our history: gropingly, from one day to the next, choosing from all available sides what presently seems best to us; but we will never be able to hold the kinds of cavalier views about history which made the fortunes of Taine and Michelet (*Sit. II*, p. 42).

Such an attitude, as I have suggested in the first chapter, was increasingly less satisfying. The passage of events showed Sartre that, as a toss of the dice does not abolish hazard, so will-power does not dominate history or even silence its claim for attention. Implicit in his early statements about history was a condemnation of history. The trouble with condemnation is that it may eliminate understanding to a point where the individual, deprived of understanding, may not know what he is doing. Sartre stoutly admitted in the Merleau-Ponty essay that this had been his case; to remedy it, he read extensively in the social sciences while writing the essays which appeared in the 1950s. Through his reading, he discovered the power the past exercises over the present because of the enormous influence the past has in the formation of men and the shaping of events. Henceforth, he will insist that the past cannot stand condemned until it has been understood; more than that, he implies that once it has been understood, condemnation can be left to those who have the time for it. Most significantly, if not too clearly, it is not history one condemns; rather it is history which condemns.

A number of circumstances have produced this shift of emphasis. Perhaps the most interesting and informative is Sartre's study of Jean Genet, which was written at a time when many of Sartre's early emphases were being adjusted; that process is everywhere visible in the rhetorical and dialectical disorders of *Saint Genet*. Genet was bound to transfix Sartre's analytical gaze, if only because his life seems to justify all Sartre's most sweeping statements about human freedom. Genet is an excellent example of the child who has been reified by society, who has been told at an early and therefore impressionable age what he *is*. He is also a fascinating example; he has accepted this reification as forming part of the natural order of things because, like any child, he believes that statements made by adults represent society's authoritative judgment. Yet his acceptance of the reification, while it is objectively an example of bad faith, subjectively turns out to be something quite different because Genet's effort *to be* what he was told he was involves him in a long series of free and radical decisions. He fights hard to be an essence only to find over the years that it is easier to speak of essences than to possess them, easier to pursue them than to find them.

Having been rejected by one part of society, he seeks to be incorporated into another, not simply for comfort, but in order, in that anti-society, to be its most perfect member and therefore the perfect adversary. Sartre calls this an effort to make criminality saintly or sacred, an observation over which we need not linger since its principal ramifications have already been discussed earlier in this book. What is important is that in the nature of his ambition Genet has a project whose realization keeps escaping from him just at the moment when he thinks he has it in his grasp. The project, in Sartrean terms, cannot be achieved since it aims at doing away with projects. The process through which the project passes provides an excellent verification, under striking circumstances, of the sturdiness of one of the cornerstones of Sartre's thought. Even as Genet seeks to escape from his human condition, he gives a stunning example of the multiple possibilities available to him.

Though Genet's obduracy may elicit admiration and even be taken for courage by some, including Sartre, the success of his enterprise depends on cheating. Genet does not really want to accept what the Other has made of him; what he wants to do is escape from the Other by establishing himself voluntarily as the object the Other seeks to make of him. As such an object, he will represent a steady threat. If at first he seeks to be the victim of everyone, he ultimately arrives at a point where he becomes the conscious victim who is aware that his victimization indicated a weakness in the Other: the Other *needs* a victim. Genet's books are the vehicles by which, in proclaiming this special knowledge, he asserts his identity to himself and to the world. He is, according to Sartre, duping himself, but the process whereby he does this reveals at least two truths. First, his reification is a state he accepts freely and, eventually, consciously because of the uses he can make of it. Second, in Genet's situation we see a fully delineated portrait of what the Other really is for us. He is the individual we look at as though he were an object; yet, even as we look, we know that he is a subjectivity who looks at us as the object he cannot be. If he tells us this, then he places us more radically in question than we him.

Genet's attempt thus catches, in its reified form, one of the menacing forces which produces what Hegel called the unhappy consciousness: our object-state for the Other. It is this possibility which explains much of human behavior and which leads men to accept the modes, attitudes, and beliefs of society; as a threat, it is also, as we saw in our discussion of "L'Enfance d'un chef," what leads men to create and then condemn a common enemy who will henceforth bear the brunt of their fear. But the enemy created, isolated, and persecuted as therapy for one part of humanity is nowhere near so menacing as the internal enemy the therapy seeks to pacify. To the extent that, through his books, Genet affects his reader and either shocks or discomforts him, he indicates that his reader's consciousness is unhappy not only because it fears the Other but also because it is fascinated by the possibility of being the Other. The fascination stems from that persistent human desire to retain individuality, a desire which inevitably leads to at least one moment when the individual is strongly tempted to say no to his society's demands.

In most instances, those momentary temptations are quieted by the stronger threat of being excluded from society and thereby turned into a rejected object. Against that risk men choose to live in accord with social norms in order to earn social approval. Either possibility is a form of reification, but the one brings approbation while the other brings condemnation. The recourse to approbation, however, does not significantly reduce the individual's subjectivity; it does not pardon his actions, it does not relieve him of responsibility for those actions, it confers no transcendent authority on his mode of behavior, it does not guarantee that society will *always* approve. Comfort it may bring and company to reinforce the comfort; it cannot stop the processes of consciousness and thus cannot protect the individual from the consequences of Genet's questions.

Genet, of course, had no reason to believe as a child that there was any choice available to him. Imagination and ingenuity led him to experiment with various devices which are not ordinarily available to society's excluded members; those devices made it possible for him, even as he sought to live as one who had been condemned, to raise fundamental questions about the process whereby some are damned so that others may be glorified. In raising such questions, he provides instruction to those who read him. He shows them, first, that exclusion does not eliminate the sensibility of those who have been banished, nor does it spare them the aspirations and the troubles of other men; it may indeed, if they are talented and bright, afford them a better perspective. He also reminds his readers that the excluded have been isolated on the basis of frequently untested norms and judgments.

These are not new ideas in the Sartrean canon; we have already encountered them in *Réflexions sur la question juive*. What is new is the significance Sartre attributes to Genet's endeavors; he finds in them a method of responding to the shrugged replies his earlier announcements risked eliciting. In making them, he had to face the probability that those he was preaching to would not be converted because they would find no advantage in embracing the new faith. If the world really is dog-eat-dog, those who have found a means either of being safe carnivores or else have found a kennel in which to protect themselves are not likely to renounce their solution because Jean-Paul Sartre tells them men should not live that way. In their minds they might agree that it isn't nice; in their hearts they believe it's necessary. If they can escape being reified to their total disadvantage by reifying others to their relative gain, words are not going to discourage them, and Jean-Paul Sartre will not be their judge.[3]

The absence of a judge, as we have seen, has been a growing preoccupation in Sartre's work; if there is no one to judge, then there is no reason why human existence should not be a free-for-all, with the strong ruling and exploiting the weak or disadvantaged and, in the process, producing a kind of order and a system of values to adorn it. Sartre finds this intolerable; as a rationalist, he cannot deny its persuasiveness or disguise the fact that in some of his preceding writings he had been accepting the general principle by hoping that today's weak would become tomorrow's strong. With the realization that Lord Acton's observations about power in human hands were not inaccurate, came the apprehension that the reality they described was inevitable unless there was a tribunal to which men would be accountable.

Sartre thinks he has found one with, first, Genet and, subsequently, with history. If the fear of being objects is what inspires men to make objects of other men, they must be made to realize that eventually they will be turned into objects anyway; eventually they will be judged by history as they have already been judged by Jean Genet. The way in which Genet looks at decent society, Sartre asserts, is the way in which subsequent periods will look at it. Genet judges us as history will judge us because he looks at us as at an object. He raises questions about our right to judge; he provides analyses which show the sham of our assurance and rectitude. Genet is the mirror in which we discover, not the confirming image Estelle sought from mirrors in *Huis-clos*, but the reality we are. That reality indicates how distorted our own mirrors are and encourages us, if we have any capacity for honesty and horror, to look for better images to project into history's mirrors.

This is not very powerful argumentation to be sure; the man who rejects Sartre as a judge can even more comfortably reject Genet and history; what Genet may think of him and the future say about him is not something he cares to hear or needs to heed. Sartre is aware of that, as he is aware, in writing the *Critique de la raison dialectique*, of the need to

---

3. Sartre is of course aware of this; some part of the reasons behind his membership in the Russell tribunal is explained by his sense of the need to create a forum, outside the existing social, legal, and governmental structures, which will permit a factually informed and morally aware humanity to express its indignation at "crimes" which would never be so described by the existing structures. In effect, what Sartre is saying is that certain acts, which may fall within the legal limits or which may be tolerated within the norms of realpolitik, still elicit cries of "shame" from those whose sense of humanity will not tolerate *any* inhumanity. He argues his case in "Le Crime," an interview published in *Le Nouvel Observateur* (30 November 1966, pp. 12–14).

show that history's judgment is important, not because it will condemn bourgeois society, but because it will base the condemnation on inadequacies that all members of bourgeois society are presently subject to. He must convince men that if, in the future, written history will reify them and possibly condemn them, that will be because they are already reified and have in truth condemned themselves. That they do not experience the feeling of condemnation is not in any way proof that they do not stand condemned. On the contrary, it is the proof of their present reification. They have chosen to stand—or have been forced thereto— outside history as praxis, to ignore its lessons, and thus they have chosen or succumbed to the place they will be allotted by the future. History, sweeping over them, will drown them in the futility of their own gestures or the vulnerability of their passivity.

Assigning degrees of individual guilt because of free commitment to the pursuit of futility is no longer an easy task; the equations of *Being and Nothingness* were those of plane geometry, and they do not apply in the three-dimensional reaches Sartre now inhabits. In the *Four Quartets* T. S. Eliot had admitted of the possibility that history might be either servitude or freedom but had put the question aside with the observation that for the moment history was now and England, present time and immediate place. In the *Critique de la raison dialectique*, Sartre is committed to the idea that history is indeed here and now; he is also committed to the task of sorting out which elements in the here and now will bind man to servitude and which will release him into freedom. The latter goal brings him to the task of discerning what in the past has set man to living history as servitude rather than freedom. Since all the categories and terms get mixed up, the task of sorting out becomes immensely difficult and the method whereby the sorting out will be done must be desperately complex. In the most reduced terms, the problem is this: what has been thought free may be no more than servitude and what has been thought servitude turns out to be—probably unwilled and unwanted—freedom.

The works written subsequent to *Saint Genet* provide terms which imply that Genet, precisely because he was excluded from decent society, had escaped from history, considered as the myth of that society, in order to become involved in the real historical process.[4] His life, then, is not just an object lesson or a stern warning; his life is a paradigm of how history must be lived. That this paradigm is writ small makes no difference once its exactness is perceived. Clearly, Genet did not intend to make his life a paradigm, decidedly society's goal was to delimit sharply any

4. Cf. *SG*: "Little Genet cares not a rap about history. Later he will substitute mythologies for it. Nevertheless, his conversion [to wanting to be a thief] involves him in history, for it expresses both his particularity and that of our age, which are indissolubly linked" (p. 51).

intentions at all on his part. One cannot say that he stumbled into history, though one can recognize that nothing in his project was designed to make him an exemplar of the historical process. What explains the result is the paucity of means available to him. In seeking to make a myth of himself, which could be set off in opposition to society's myth of itself, Genet provides the pattern of sorting out which Sartre needs.

For Genet, denied an ideological birthright along with a familial one, was set loose to live history only as unfettered man can live it—freely. Happily or not, Genet could never cease being conscious of the fact that whatever he achieved would be won only by risking the impossible; he had to demonstrate that, when nothing else was available, it had to be possible to hoist himself by his own bootstraps or, more accurately in his case, by his own penis. Genet, wanting to live in the bog to which he was assigned, and subsequently wanting to live there in company with someone else—preferably an attractive *mec*—willy-nilly learned history's most essential and dense lesson. Bogs are where we begin and bogs are where we risk remaining, for history, too, risks being a bog. But it is a bog which, if examined closely, tells us we cannot live in bogs; examined randomly, it tells us insanely that today's bog prepares tomorrow's and allows us to believe, because of the looseness of our examination, that this is how things should be. If we recall the categories of *Being and Nothingness*, we perceive that such a statement may apply to things; it can have no valuable meaning for men.

Ironies and paradoxes abound here. Genet, the man who wanted to live as a thing, full with the consciousness of a total identity between himself and his bog, keeps being defeated. Fettered man becomes free, generally because of the desperation of his situation. Free man becomes fettered and, in Frantz von Gerlach's case, withdraws from the arena into the bog, proclaiming that available truth, if it sets men free, drives them in the process to the fringe of madness.[5] In the case of Flaubert, free man and fettered man get so hopelessly entangled with each other that they cancel everything out and justify one of Sartre's favorite Shakespearian

5. Baudelaire's choice, according to Sartre, showed different nuances: "Throughout his life this man, because of pride and bitterness, attempted to *make himself a thing* both in his own eyes and in those of others. His hope was to place himself on the sidelines of the social feast; like a statue, he would be fully defined, opaque, unassimilable. . . . He would not mind being an object, but he does not wish to be a pure fact of hazard; this thing will really be his and *will be saved* once it can be established that the thing created itself and has sustained its relationship to being on its own. But this forces us back to consideration of the way in which consciousness and freedom are present—the mode we have called *existence*. Baudelaire cannot and will not live out fully either *being* or *existence*. . . . He has chosen instead to have a consciousness which is perpetually torn asunder, a bad consciousness. . . . Because he wanted at once to be and to exist, because he endlessly flees from existence into being and from being into existence, he is nothing but an oozing wound gaping wide. . . . He maintains good in order to do evil" (*Baudelaire*, pp. 97–99).

phrases. "Life," and thus history, "is a tale told by an idiot, full of sound and fury, signifying nothing." The working title of his work-in-progress on Flaubert is, interestingly enough, *The Idiot of the Family*. Why does everything seem to get reduced to sound, fury, and nothingness?

This happens principally because the individual's idea of freedom has been made part of a prescription devised by others before it is presented to him as the medicine which will brace him for life. If the prescription has nothing to do with his needs, it will either kill him, as it does with most of the oppressed, or it will force him to seek other remedies, as it has done with Genet. If it has worked for a time and allowed its taker to grow robust with certainty, as in the case of Frantz, it will have aggravated a condition beyond the prescription's ultimate remedial capacities. In Flaubert's case, the prescription produces and sustains a lifetime's ill-health because Flaubert, seeing that it has worked for others, struggles to make it work for him. The dosage is wrong, that he knows; at times, he acts as though the prescription itself is wrong. But, when everything else fails, he falls back on the prescription because, though it has been ill-prepared, it has the right elements. And anyway it is better to die of known but inadequate cures than of unknown and unpredictably painful ills.

We are here touching on what is probably the most significant and consequential shift of emphasis in Sartre's thought. It is probably best explained by the impact of an observation made by Marx which Sartre cites in the *Critique*: "Men make their history themselves, but they make it within a given milieu which conditions them" (p. 60). The force of that conditioning had been outrightly denied by Sartre in his earlier works; in the *Critique* it is described as being of such great power as to make it impossible for most men to overcome it in order to make their history with the full capacities of their freedom.[6] The reason for this is that too many men have been enslaved at a very early age to a sense of experience and an idea of history which appeared to make perfect sense because it insisted, by its very terms, that they were free to act profitably in the interests of an historical pattern of great value. The fact that a higher view might have revealed different historical patterns is a fact that cannot be used to condemn them since they neither knew that it was available nor did they have any reason to expect any imperfections in the view with which

6. Cf. *CRD*: ". . . everything [that shapes future attitudes] has happened *in child-hood*, that is, under conditions radically different from those of adulthood: it is childhood which shapes unsurpassable prejudices, it is childhood which produces the feeling, amidst the violences of the rearing process and the periodic strayings of the beast being reared, of belonging to a milieu *as a singular event*. Today only psycho-analysis allows us to study thoroughly the way in which a child, in the dark, groping, is going to attempt to play, without understanding it, the social character which adults impose on him; only psychoanalysis will show us whether he is smothered by his role, whether he seeks to escape from it, or whether he assimilates it entirely" (p. 46).

they had been inculcated. When this view of history turns out to be defective or inoperable, they are deprived of the myth which has been the keystone of their thought; with the keystone gone, the whole edifice which provided sense to their experience crumbles, and they must live amidst the rubble.

A crumbled edifice maintains its elements and even in its collapsed state evokes a memory of what it was. The result is that men can frequently set about the task of rebuilding the edifice without wondering either why it collapsed or speculating as to whether it is the kind of edifice they needed. The reasons why they do this are various. If they are not men of strong imagination and broad curiosity, they may have no choice except to fall back on what they have known; if they are proud men, they may want to show that the building did not collapse because of any structural defects but only because it was besieged. Frantz's effort, in *Les Séquestrés*, reflects both these reactions, but from the troubled waters of a mind pushed to the limits of sanity. He wants to rebuild, defend, and accuse, not as part of a simple operation of assigning blame, but because the blame is really there. He says at one point: "It's up to the conquerors to take charge of history. Well, they took charge of it, and they gave us Hitler" (p. 44). Into his tape recorder he pours the muddled arguments by which he seeks to defend himself, and all those who have suffered his disenchantment, against Hilter, against his conquerors, and against the process—history—which has brought them all into confrontation.

He is trying to write history as the myth of his class. He is defending the myth and refusing to examine in depth the process, electing idealism instead of realism. When his sister tells him that plots are being organized against him, he replies: "I am writing history and you come to bother me with anecdotes" (p. 82). The fact that she has invented the plots in no way justifies his reaction, for a true involvement with reality would make further questions about the plots necessary. But his refusal to ask those necessary questions explains much about what his formation has done to him: it has convinced him that the anecdotal—the random events of history randomly considered—should not be allowed to influence the course of history.

I have said that his notion of history has to do with history as the myth of his class, the construct used to supply force to the class's ideals. In much the same way, Sartre's original idea of freedom was mythic because it, too, placed a low value on the anecdotal. Lucien's capitulation to bourgeois values, Hugo's inability to shake off the ideas of his class, Electre's ultimate dependence on Jupiter had all been presented as instances of desultory failure. Their inevitability had not been admitted and therefore was not examined outside the brackets of certain categories. Private and public history was presented as clear and transparent; where there was opacity, the obscurity had been introduced for deliberately planned, ignoble reasons. What we have been seeing in the more recent works, and especially in *Les Séquestrés*, is that this opacity is only intensified by the efforts to dispel it. Frantz does not seek the opaque any more than Sartre does; but the longer he fights and the more deeply he commits himself to transparency—that is, to sense—the more the opaque seems to come about by itself, uninvited and certainly unaided. It comes about because his idea of transparency is wrong, his method for achieving it defective, and his range of choice subjectively limited. Frantz has bravely sought to work in history, to serve history; if, in the end, he is enslaved, that is because the history he has been serving is history as servitude. Insofar as he had originally understood this history, it was perfect because it allowed for his perfection; the only perfection he later allows it is that of being perfectly wrong.

It is also perfectly real in the sense that it provides a comprehensive meaning to a certain mode of experience; because of the nature of its promise, that mode will be defended by those who hold it. They will not be wicked men. If wickedness is one of the offshoots of their behavior, it results from the inadequacy of the modes they have been taught to use and believe in. They are the victims of their past, of a misreading of history, and there is almost nothing they can do about their confusions since their formation has been conveyed with such authority and assurance as to keep them from raising any questions about its value.

In the lives of such men, and in the social force they represent as a group, the past becomes insurmountable because the past lives on in the present. The structures of the present are the results of past undertakings which have either been realized already or are in the process of being realized and which have all been set loose as part of an effort to defend a certain way of life and its accompanying structures of thought. As a result, in order to understand the present and all its structures, it is essential to know why they have been affected by time and how they have affected time. It is also essential to see whether there is any principle which, if it does not hold them together, demonstrates that behind each structure there is a common principle of intention;[7] further, it is essential to determine why structures come about and what happens to them once they begin to operate.

7. Sartre thus remains faithful, in broad lines, to the Husserlian notion of intentionality—that is, to the idea that each act is undertaken with the aim of accomplishing a particular purpose. He has, to be sure, seen deeper complexities in intentions and come to recognize that the individual, because of powerful formational influences, may not understand the full purpose and deepest inspiration of his intentions. This is where a third person, who knows that individual's background in a more detached way than the individual involved, must intervene to explain, as it were, the intention behind the intention.

History thus becomes something more than the establishment of a chronology and the writing of interpretations of that chronology. It is neither the report of the time sequence in which events have taken place— whether randomly or as the result of planning—nor is it the summary, with comparative glosses, of man's presence on the earth. History is to be considered as a force which moves across time and space with a sense of purpose and an intended direction, not because it is an independent force, but because it is the vehicle which tells us, if we look at it in its totality, what men have been seeking.[8] While there is something of Hegel in this idea of history, it amounts to very little since Sartre refuses to accept the cheerfulness with which Hegel strews the path of history's chariot with necessary victims. Sartre's concern is not to show how men serve history as she moves stalwartly on towards the justifying Idea; his concern is to show us what history reveals about man.

He is thus accepting Marx's qualifications about Hegel and adhering to Marx's insistence that men are by their nature opposed to any theory of history which would reify them in the name of an abstraction. By their work, they change the world and thus invalidate any suggestion of a pattern, imposed on them, to which they conform so that an abstraction may emerge justified from their toil and sweat. Sartre and Marx are one in agreeing that if men make history, the history they make is not Hegel's; men would indeed be greatly mistaken if they thought they were making that kind of history. Man works in time, not in order to justify an already proclaimed meaning for that time, but simply and frighteningly because he can do nothing else. To act is his praxis; in acting, he leaves behind a legacy which is his contribution either of shame or glory. He determines history, and he is either a fool or a knave or a victim if he tries to invert the process—a fool, because if he is intelligent he can see that the contrary is true; a knave, because if he argues for determinism he does so out of a wish to determine others; a victim, because he has allowed himself to be reduced to a passivity which serves the ends sought by others.

The notion and uses of history as a determinant provide nonetheless a valuable way of seeing how the world's forces are now deployed. Idealism—and bourgeois life is a form of idealism—may deny a past determinism in history; nevertheless it is committed to a future determinism,

8. Cf. *CRD*: "*The whole historical dialectic rests on the individual* praxis *insofar as it* [the praxis] *is already dialectical*, that is, to the degree that action is in itself a surpassing by negation of a contradiction, the determination of a present totalization in the name of a future totality, a real and efficacious working of matter. We know all that, having learned it a long time ago in subjective and objective experience. This is our problem. What would be *the* dialectic if there are only men and if they are all dialectical. But I have already said that experience furnishes its own intelligibility. We must thus seek at the level of the individual *praxis* (paying little attention, for the moment, to the collective constraints which bring it about, limit it, or remove its effectiveness) what, properly speaking, is the rationality of action" (pp. 165–66).

since idealism is convinced that history must express the realization of its ideals. Idealism seeks to determine the history of those who must be to it what Napoleon was to Hegel's Idea: grist fed into the mill in order to provide meal for others. The true sense of history is not to be found in examination of the meal, but in the process whereby the grist is made to serve. In short, the question of how history as freedom is faring is something that can be evaluated only by examining the place of the oppressed in the world.

Three things must be said here. First, the study of the oppressed as the most meaningful force in history has little concern with arousing sympathy for them. Second, it has everything to do with seeking to find out why they are oppressed. Finally, the study is conducted with an eye to identifying the possibilities they have as free men to break away from their misery. As the slave always represents a danger for his master, because he may one day refuse to accept his servitude, so the idea of a rigid pattern in history is menaced by the unpredictable intervention of man who, in changing history, invalidates the preconceived idea. We have seen a number of examples of this in allusions to racism, and in the bourgeois belief that a class society reflects a natural hierarchy (though the bourgeoisie, in its own past, had to rearrange that hierarchy in order to establish its own). At the basic level history is dialectical because it is made by men who are in conflict—with each other, with an ideology which tries to shape them against their own instincts, or with forces they have themselves unleashed. What the dialectical situation will produce is unpredictable; what it should produce depends very much on what men want it to produce. If you believe that the oppression of one free man by another is internally inconsistent, if you note that there are more oppressed than free men, then, if you are logical, you conclude that what the dialectic should produce is the dictatorship of the proletariat.

If you are Sartre, you find unhappily that the proletariat, before it is allowed to accede to its triumphant position, is enduring rather a lot of intermediary dictatorship. And you discover that if Marxism, with its invocation to the masses to arise and take over the earth which is rightfully theirs, has shown a way out of the bog of bourgeois idealism, it has also managed to slip into a bog of its own. Dialectic loses its dynamism to dogma. Confusion reigns in China where yesterday's revolutionaries are condemned as today's revisionists by those who, conceivably, will tomorrow turn out to be the real revisionists. Out of this emerges one of the cornerstones of the *Critique de la raison dialectique*: every movement which begins as a vehicle of human praxis—that is, of man's commitment to act in order to create a particular open-ended situation in the future —risks becoming a process. Once a movement has become a process it risks defending itself at the expense of individual human praxis. The process thus stifles criticism by invoking its own greater value and by devising propaganda which encourages the individual to serve the process rather than his praxis. It makes a value of the practico-inert, of the bog, and as a result—whether it be expressed in Frantz, in capitalism, or in communism—the process reaches moments when, having no further options, it must resort to repression or oppression. When neither of those works, or when other processes threaten it, it finds itself plunged into conflict either with its enemies or with those who, having been its friends, rebel against the one-sided terms it offers as the basis for continuing the friendship.

This situation raises practical problems. Sartre is convinced that in any given period there is only one philosophy which expresses meaningfully the reality of that period. He is equally convinced that Marxism is that philosophy today because its terms describe the movement towards totalization which is the basic experience of each individual, group, community, and nation. [9] But the truth of Marxism has become compromised in too many countries by the politics of communism. Existentialism, which Sartre no longer considers a philosophy and which therefore is not in the running to be honored as *the* philosophy of the modern world, serves a crucial function; for existentialism, as an approach which raises fundamental questions about individual man, can be used to question, not the fundamental truth of Marxism, but the treatment of that truth by those who supposedly work in its behalf.

Marxism has been faring neither as well as Marx anticipated nor as well as it should, given the world's need of it, because it has been infected with a number of contradictions. The principal contradiction is the one I have already mentioned; it has become a process and has grown fearful of being open-ended. Too often it fights to defend the present process rather than to cultivate the fundamental truth. Though as a system it is based on acceptance of the ineluctably dialectical nature of human experience, it has tended to assert that history is now moving as it should and has closed its eyes to contrary information. This comes not so much from wickedness as from a belief either that all necessary information has been collected or that other information is bad information. It is also

9. There are, to be sure, many processes and many levels of totalization. The word is meant to describe the movement initiated by individuals, groups, and nations to accomplish a fixed project. That fixed project, as conceived of in terms of hoped-for results, is the totality sought. The fascination with a totality as an achieved perfection or the hope that the totality, achieved, will be enough, is the great danger that comes with the pursuit of totalities since, looked on in this light or with these hopes, the pursuit of the totality is the pursuit of the practico-inert. Men must be encouraged to recognize the danger because, if they ignore it, worse harm will come about. No totality can sensibly exist as a process because, as it exists, it is being subjected to other forces, to another more erosive process which Sartre calls detotalization. As a new house does not remain new, so an achieved project does not remain static.

an indication of a fundamental and perennial tendency in all human endeavor: men confuse the process of totalization with the totality sought. In the earlier Sartrean vocabulary of individual experience this would have been described as the temptation of free being to become a fixed quantity on the ground that fixed quantities are the resting places and bastions of value.

Sartre's work has given us numerous examples of this temptation. A man, having met obstacles, sets out to overcome those obstacles by setting his sights on a particular end to be achieved. Once he has arrived at that end, he sets about defending it and pays inadequate or no attention to whether it has become an obstacle either to himself or others. Systems are not much different from individuals in that they, too, seek to defend what they have set up without examining what Sartre calls the process of detotalization. This is related to the winner-loses theme and is clearly delineated in Frantz who, though he wishes to hide it, cannot deny that the end he sought, if it was achieved at all, was achieved only so that it could be immediately eroded. Detotalization, as a concept, is also related to the unrelieved dynamism of all human endeavor. No achieved goal can be preserved in static perfection because no achieved goal exists in isolation; all sorts of forces affect it, some to its benefit, others to its detriment, possibly to its destruction. If, however, the impact of those other forces is denied, the effect they produce will necessarily be at least partially defective.

This is what has happened to communism as a political and economic system. One of the main reasons why it has happened is that the Marxist belief in dialectical materialism has had the effect of reducing man and society to elements which serve the movement of the dialectic rather than enlisting it in their service. Political communism has too often tried to adjust men to the dialectic when, in all honesty, the process should be just the reverse. If the process of totalization is to be maintained in a meaningful way, Marxist theory must never lose sight of the fact that the process, and the totalities towards which it aims, is maintained by men. Having lost sight of this, and having operated on the conviction that dialectical materialism explains all that needs to be known about man and society, communism has tended either to underestimate or to ridicule influences which form a man and furnish him with his attitudes. Like the young Sartre, it has laughed at the contented bourgeois and mocked at the disquieted one; it has not tried to understand either of them and, in its refusal, has deprived itself of essential information. [10]

10. Sartre had been uncomfortable with dialectical *materialism* for a long time. In an early essay, "Matérialisme et révolution" (1946; reprinted in *Sit. III*, 1949), he discussed his uneasiness at length. His basic concern is to demonstrate that materialism, by positing a forceful nonhuman law, contradicts the nature of man and the nature of revolution; for revolution is nothing other than man's attempt, by an act

The result is that communism has not shown proper respect for the freedom of other men nor has it encouraged a saving freedom among its own adherents; it has produced too many parrots and not enough philosophers.[11] Communism has forgotten some essential things about man because it has too often been willing to treat him as an element enlisted in the service of a great nonhuman force. Some of the results of this neglect have been scandalous and not unexpected, for if man is treated as an element it is not surprising that from time to time that element will be carelessly expended in fights against its own interests.[12] That was the most painful lesson of the Hungarian Revolution.

Existentialism's role (that should be translated to read: the purpose of the *Critique*) is to reintroduce man into Marxism by insisting that man makes history by whatever projects he accepts as his own. The sum of individual projects is what human reality is about at any particular moment. This has been the firmest point in all Sartre's work. Existentialism must be introduced into Marxist thinking so that Marxists will recognize that every man's project is essentially dialectical because it is the mode of his response to the challenge of the world. To the extent that Marxism does not persuade him that its project and his have the same end, or to the extent that it appears to ask him to sacrifice his project to an abstract idea, both man and Marxism are lost.

Existentialism, Sartre believes, is peculiarly apt to fill this function be-

---

or an ensemble of acts, to govern nature. If, as Marxist theorists seem to claim, materialism is inscribed in nature, and if nature circumscribes man, then man as a revolutionary being is impossible, and man as the servant of nature's processes is inevitable. In developing his argument, Sartre sought to show that all revolutionary behavior demonstrated the irrelevance of materialism; he tried to show simultaneously that in defending dialectical materialism, theorists were repeating the ruinous earlier errors of human history by seeking to create a myth which would encourage man to believe that there is an organic connection between his processes and natural processes. This, in Sartrean terms, is nonsense since man's process is always conducted apart from nature and frequently against nature.

11. Sartre, whose freedom at crucial times won no respect from the French Communist party, offers a good example of his enraged reaction to Communist parrots in "Opération Kanapa" (*Sit. VII*, pp. 94–103).

12. In "Les Communistes et la paix," Sartre had argued (*Sit. VI*, p. 247) in favor of the need for an authority exercised from above and imposed on the workers as an indispensable element in accomplishing the goals of the proletariat. Indeed, the great value of the party or the union was that it directed the workers towards those goals which, if one were to wait for spontaneous action on the worker's part, might never come. The party, in this sense, understood better than the workers what had to be done; its organization offered effective means for achievement. The presupposition behind this line of thinking was that the party would always be aware of what the workers needed. In "Le Fantôme de Staline" (1956–57) (in *Sit. VII*, pp. 144–307), the essay he wrote after the uprisings in Hungary and the disturbances in Poland, Sartre shows how erroneous those presuppositions were; for, in both countries, the party had become a process, a kind of practico-inert which was more interested in defending and sustaining its functions than in keeping its ear attuned to the workers' needs.

cause, in its insistence on man's perpetual flight towards the future, it has always respected fundamental and inevitable human dynamism. By showing the conditions under which this flight takes place, by identifying the various causes which produce its particular modes, existentialism has shown that man's most persistent project is to move into the future propelled by the hope that he will find there a solution to his present inadequacies. Sartre's concern is thus contiguous with that of Marxism, but it will not be expressed in support of the latter unless he can be convinced that his project will be aided and not annihilated by adherence to the Marxist cause. Marxism can never be allowed to forget the individual, for once it does, its project is rendered senseless.

Where in the past, Sartre's standoffish position with relation to the Communist party had been a source of concern to him, it now becomes the best contribution he can make to the movement, not because it resolves a personal difficulty, but because it provides an essential which otherwise would be lacking: the unfailingly friendly but faithfully critical voice. The wretched of the earth need his orientation as much as, and in some circumstances possibly more than, they need the apparatus of the Communist party. The existentialist outlook will serve as a mediator between Marxism as a political program and human experience as the base in whose interests the program must steadfastly operate.

One of the first things the existentialist outlook will suggest is that, as it mediates between Marxism and men, so other disciplines must mediate between its outlook and social reality. This program—in which the mediator, because he mediates, must pay attention to all other alleged mediating forces—commits Sartre to a greater flexibility and generosity than he has previously shown. In earlier works he had a tendency to dismiss or denigrate whole ranges of human experience and inquiry. Now he reaches out to incorporate all he can, insisting that if men have acted well or ill it is because of the influence of the forces which served as mediators between them and their experience. Since the social sciences—which in French are known more warmly as *les sciences humaines*—have information to provide on these mediational forces and on their influences, and since they attempt to ascertain the reasons why men are influenced and why groups try to influence, their information must be taken into account. Everything that tells something about man must be used in the effort to find out what the truth of man is.

This leads to the formulation of what Sartre calls the progressive-regressive method, a mode of analysis derived from his reading of Henri Lefebvre whose ideas are in turn based on *his* reading of Marx. In simple and not inexact terms, what the method asserts is that no movement can plot a program for the future unless it understands the past in its entirety; otherwise the movement cannot possibly understand what it is about. Sartre holds to his earlier insistence that we cannot know the past; by rigorous application we can, however, try to understand it. In the process of trying to understand why people behaved as they did in the past and what forces were at work influencing them, we enlarge our knowledge of the present because we learn what to look for in its operations. Those influences which worked in the past and produced activity have not disappeared, since that activity has shaped the present in key ways. All analysis of goals must be closely tied to analysis of what goals have been sought in the past as well as to their success or failure. By detailed examination of social groups and individuals, and their reciprocal relations in the past, we can learn a great deal about why individuals have behaved as they have and thus shaped history.

This crucial need to understand, results from a slow evolution in Sartre's thought. In *Les Mains sales* all that had to be understood was the imperative necessity of communism's program and the general advantages of adhering to it. Hugo's hesitations and his ultimate downfall resulted from his fascination with his past, the irresistible urge he felt to get back to it, and his incapacity to strip himself of all its vestiges. The implication was that his project could never be realized unless, like Hoederer, he lived only for the future, furnished with the courage to meet events as they came, to assume whatever dirt was necessary, and to believe firmly that out of all this would come personal and public redemption. Hugo's cry at the end of the play—*non-récupérable!*—was meant to be a comment on him; fifteen years later, it is still a comment on him, but it has also become a comment on the party in which he cannot find a place. Though Hugo may have returned to his past too frequently and for imperfect reasons, neither the Communist party nor Sartre had paid enough attention to *why* he did so. Nor had they paid adequate attention to the fact that adherence to the party too often turned out to be adhesion, with both party and individual becoming stuck.

Frantz von Gerlach represents Sartre's effort to break away from ideology of all kinds. As we have seen, Frantz, up to a certain point in his life, is not haunted by his past; he derives his conviction and therefore his capacity to act from that past. But his past, that is, his formation, has not prepared him for situations in which action will undo him; nor has it made provision for any sort of redemptive therapy whereby he can renounce his formation and still maneuver in the world as a pretender to its power. If his seclusion is absurd, it is also inevitable. Given the sense of experience which is his, he has no choice except to attempt a defense of that sense. His sense of experience has been presented to him as the mode by which value would come into the world, and since he believed in value, he cannot understand how that mode can be done away with and value preserved. To the extent that it joins the voices of his other accusers, the Communist party cannot supply him with an answer.

The final step in Sartre's evolution towards the progressive-regressive method is the definition of the theory in the *Critique de la raison dialectique* and, in his work-in-progress on Flaubert, the application of the theory to an individual. By turns breezy and belligerent, the Flaubert book is fundamentally generous in its attempt to give a concrete example of how one man's childhood produced an adult life full of contradictions. The novelist's memory of that childhood made him hate all its terms; yet he possessed no others. His initial reaction was to withdraw into himself; when that fortress proved inadequate, he had no choice except to arm himself with the ideology of the class he pretended to loathe. The class, in claiming that its ideology was of universal value, had accorded a value to universality; its particular member, Gustave Flaubert, called upon to accept the ideology, rebelled against it because it failed him. What he never lost was the sense that somehow he must pick up the ideology's major promise and become universal. This is, of course, very much like the individual's passion to be God of which Sartre had written in *Being and Nothingness*. But the aspiration must now be seen under two other lights: the place of the totalizing movements in all human actions and the possibility of a true universal which would be no other than that single truth Sartre has been looking for. Finally, it must be recognized that Flaubert's project is a *passion*, an irrational force which, departing from the rational constructs supplied by his class, seeks to rationalize unreason.

Flaubert has been among Sartre's preoccupations for long years; the discussion of Flaubert's psyche begins in *Being and Nothingness*.[13] His presence in the *Critique de la raison dialectique* is the result of what has happened to him at the hands of the Communists, who have made a culture hero of him because of his attack on the bourgeoisie. Sartre sees a cruel two-way irony in this. Flaubert attacked his class because it had not done enough for him; in making him a hero, the Communists have neither understood his particularity nor have they given proper value to the power of his class to shape and frequently to mangle its members to a point where they are powerless. The implication is that the Communists have not understood the menace that such formation represents to their chances of success nor have they properly gone about the main purpose of their mission which is to create a society capable of receiving all men. In the bargain, and worse luck for everyone, they have slipped into a dogmatism no better than that of the

13. See the early pages of the chapter, "Existentialist Psychoanalysis" (pp. 557–75). There Sartre raises the questions which the work-in-progress is attempting to answer; there he also expresses some skepticism over the possibility of doing what, in fact, he is now in the process of doing. The movement from impossible to possible is part of the change produced in Sartre's outlook by his growing recognition of the crucial importance of childhood formative patterns.

bourgeoisie. They have treated their Flauberts as the bourgeoisie treated Gustave; they have asserted a universal that particular individuals are not willing to accept because it is neither useful, universal, nor Marxist. In classical Sartrean terms, they have enclosed too many people in their original hodological space by refusing to open new—and available— Marxist space to them.

These are the principal points of the introduction, entitled "Question de méthode," to the first volume of the *Critique*. The method is to be future-oriented, but it is to take the largest and most detailed view possible, reaching into the past for situations and adopting from the present every method which will illuminate those situations; it is to be Marxist-oriented because of its author's belief in the undeniable relevance of Marxism for the entire human community; it is to be analytic at every point and about everything, and thereby it will show at every point the danger of dogmatism.

The first volume of the *Critique* is devoted to a study of how movement comes about in individuals and groups and, once it has been effected, what happens to the movement itself, as well as to the groups and to the individuals who form the groups. Sartre calls this an outline of the theory of practical ensembles—groups organized to do something. The second volume will apply the discoveries of the first volume to the overall movement of history. The goal of both volumes is to show that, as individuals have been led to realize their projects in larger organisms, so various periods of history have shown a dialectical movement towards the realization of greater and greater totalities such as, in our era, the dictatorship of the proletariat. In terms of the vocabulary I have been using in this book what this means is that, though men seem to move in circles and as individuals may have no other choice, what each seeks in his circle resembles what all the others seek in their circles. But there is an ongoing thrust which pushes all the circles ahead either to be destroyed or absorbed. The thrust is not just that of time, though time makes a contribution; more importantly, it is that delivered by those who, having no circles or having found their circles too confining, resort to the actions or provoke the convulsions which produce change. History incorporates its past and moves forward because of it, just as the individual does. If it has been too often the chronicle of servitude, its overall movement shows that it is also the vehicle of freedom.

The fundamental error communism has made, and the source of its dogmatism, is its consideration of that forward thrust of history as the only significant manifestation of the dialectic. This is to misread the evidence, for while the dialectical movement is incontestable, it is the movement least frequently seen or considered by individual men and groups because they are more proximately immersed in other dialectical situations. The individual, for example, has reciprocal and therefore dialectical relations with the milieu in which he lives, with the others whom he encounters either as individuals or as groups. An inverse pyramid builds up from the individual's situation as groups, communities, states, nations, and power blocs repeat his experience on an augmented scale. The ensemble of all these situations is the totality—always changing—in which he lives. This endlessly shifting, frequently mysterious, annoyingly unpredictable totality is the background of his lived experience—sometimes forgotten, more often challenging. In order to realize his own project, he must come to terms with the pyramid. Since most often what he means by coming to terms with it is that it should come to terms with him, if only to lessen the burden it has placed on his mind, man has a fundamentally revolutionary spirit.

The pattern of this revolt, as it is traced out in individual lives, is the design of *Being and Nothingness* and the literary works. The pattern is made up, first, of man's sense of being unjustified, of constituting surplus being, of living in a hostile world, and, then, of the compromises, capitulations, or withdrawals produced by the initial discoveries. Most often intelligence leads man to recognize the need for personal adjustment to the system. If his intelligence is honest, it also leads him to recognize that the system is a human construct and not a gift of God, however much his leaders seek to convince him of the latter. Having discovered the function that systems serve, man also discovers—though he may do nothing immediately with his discovery—that other systems can be devised to correct that function or to enlarge it. If the system satisfies him, he will defend it in his interests and against others and thereby be rewarded by having his portrait hung in the Bouville Museum or his ashes interred in the Kremlin wall. If he subjects himself to the system in order to work in the interests of others, he wins the right to become Goetz in *Le Diable et la Bon Dieu* and, in so doing, runs the risks I have already discussed. If he knows the inevitability and the dangers of systems, he writes the *Critique de la raison dialectique*.

There he shows that all systems and all reactions to systems result from the fundamental fact of human alienation. The source of this alienation is not exclusively the existence of the Other, nor is it the individual's reaction to the difference between his evanescence and the permanence of things. His reactions are only modes by which he expresses his alienation. The primary source of his alienation is the obstacle he finds standing between his apprehension of his liberty and his free exercise of it: he lives in need. Because of this, he is involved constantly in the effort to satisfy his needs. In a world of scarcity, this effort creates a fundamental tension which can easily become a fundamental hostility. In looking at the world and all its inhabitants, he not only discovers that he has needs, he also discovers that there is not enough for him and everyone else. There is not enough food, not enough power, not enough success, not enough of anything. The greater is his need, the greater is the danger that, when frustrated, it will lead to violence of some sort.

The Other is my enemy, not just because of the psychological designs he may have on me, but because he is my competitor in this world of scarcity where there is not enough to satisfy both of us. When all of us are considered together, there is not enough food available to nourish two-thirds of us. If the first step in alienation came with the feeling that one was surplus being, a second step comes with the realization that, however sufficient unto itself the world may be, it is not enough for its inhabitants. Nor are the explanations and justifications supplied by some of its inhabitants enough for all the others. Men's needs are various, and it is reasonable to say that no man satisfies all his needs. That he learns to live with need does not change the fact that he knows what need is. This provides a common ground of experience accessible to all men because it has been experienced to some degree by all of them.

Certain forms of alienation—religious, intellectual, political, and social—are not necessarily produced as the result of a desire to oppress. They result from elusive issues, ideas, and realities; they must necessarily shift, helping some by their changes, plunging others into despair. But there is one form of alienation—economic—which is rooted in and dependent on oppression. It is also the greatest source of alienation because it affects the greatest number of men—those who are forced to live with an urgent feeling of need so that someone else may derive financial profit from what has been denied to them.

Arguments have been devised to explain the situation; what they explain, either to Sartre or to Marx, is that capitalism creates structures which divide men into two classes—the haves and the have-nots—and then claims that this is the way social arrangements must be. What this suggests is that such a division is the result of a natural process when, in effect, the system has been created by some men and imposed on others. There is a fundamental contradiction in asserting that a system that has changed the face of nature emanates from the nature it has changed. Nature does not change men as much as they change her by creating their human culture whose most noteworthy characteristic is the constant struggle against nature. The fundamental contradiction produces a fundamental conflict, for it obliges man to fight against systems other men have created. This area of conflict extends well beyond the range of the capitalist system to touch at the conflicts we have seen in Flaubert and Frantz. What makes the conflict created by capitalism important is the great number of people who are affected by it.

The basic human conflict as presented in the *Critique* is no longer an interior one between man and his temptations; it is a conflict produced by man's search to satisfy his needs. At its worst, it is a struggle among men;

at its best, it is a struggle of men against nature; at its most puzzling, it is the struggle of men with and sometimes against their own creations.

Sartre's method now becomes that of making a detailed description of the structures which man has created in order to meet the challenge of alienation, of the way in which these structures have operated in history and created new structures, and of what this represents in the way of a global picture. He wishes to show that, while systems are the result of man's efforts to respond to needs, their existence creates new needs. He also wishes to show that any system which becomes frozen and self-defensive, because it asserts that it has satisfied all needs or knows how to satisfy them, assumes such rigidity at its peril. It misunderstands man and it misapprehends the consequences of its own operations.

There is clearly a moral purpose behind this, for Sartre hopes that on the basis of his presentation every man will recognize that his particular situation parallels a universal situation; if he recognizes this, he will recognize that all men must discover the necessity of working cooperatively if every man is to have the assurance of meeting the challenge of his needs. The Other, the toughest problem in Sartre's thought because the most stubborn source of hostility, is now shown to be the only agent of a solution. Only when the individual recognizes himself in the Other and the Other in himself can he fully understand that the unpredictable menaces which possibly threaten him can only be eliminated when he and the Other have a common project which cannot be realized without their constant cooperation.

To the extent that it described any coherent world, *Being and Nothingness* presented the picture of human beings arranged in a random series and responding to challenges on the basis of personal histories. Their relationship with nature or with society was dialectical to the extent that, on the basis of the responses they gave to challenges received, they were not the same as they had been before the challenge was delivered. This was also the situation of the various characters in *Les Chemins de la liberté*, but, as *Le Sursis* showed, vaster forces were going to create another kind of dialectical situation to which these individuals would have to respond as mature persons possessed of some degree of commitment. What results when Mathieu decides to accept the war as a challenge delivered personally to him, rather than as a force which has scooped him up and made him its own, is an alteration of the nature of the dialectical movement. There is a difference between his childish gesture in smashing a vase and his adult gesture in committing himself to shoot at his enemy. The latter response is more than passion flying angrily out at an object; it involves a recognition that the enemy threat, because it has been organized by men, can conceivably be stopped by men. When enemies meet, they meet as men who give sad testimony to the fact that, if war conditions their behavior, it does so only because they, or other men, have created the conditions which have led to war.

Man is unavoidably obliged to constitute himself as a rational being; the process whereby he does this automatically sets loose attitudes which condition the way in which he participates in other situations. The central point, that Sartre is trying to make with these refinements is that the essential dialectical movement of the world is one which is created and controlled by men. They may respond in any one of the ways described in the last volume of *Les Chemins*; whatever their response—whether eager or desultory, whether passive or active—that response contributes to the way in which the dialectical situation will develop.

As men respond to war, so they respond to a host of situations in life. Wherever they find themselves deployed in random fashion (what Sartre calls *sérialité*), they find themselves in a situation which potentially will demand a response by revealing a challenge. The situation may have such a random structure as to make the possibility of common action remote; people waiting for a bus may share nothing until such time as the bus service becomes so bad that, after weeks of frustrated waiting and spontaneous complaints, they decide to form a committee to protest. In another random situation, the possibility of action may be even more remote because, while the individuals in the series have a common activity, they never see each other. This is the case with television viewing and perhaps is one of the reasons why so little is done about the quality of television programming. In both instances, we have an example of what Sartre calls a collective entity. Those who wait for the bus have a direct relationship one to the other; those who watch the television screen have only an indirect relationship. In both cases, there is the potentiality of creating a structure which would be designed to change the nature of the relationship between each individual and the situation; in the bargain, of course, the relationship between him and the other individuals would also be changed.

Modern life creates more complicated collective entities than those which stand and wait for busses or which sit and watch television. These are entities which cut across cities and nations because of their size and because of the numbers of people who are involved in them in more than a random way. They are the places where men work and where consequently they are exposed to each other and to a similar situation in an ongoing relationship. Nothing may come of the relationship. In a saturated labor market where employment is scarce, workers may hesitate about voicing any grievance to fellow workers; they thus offer no structured response to the challenges raised by their condition and live it out as elements in a series. If there is no labor organization, workers in one factory will not have lines of communication with workers in another factory, and thus they can have no influence over what wages are paid to all members of, say, the steel industry. In such circumstances, they may feel that they have no control over their destiny and, as long as they are given over to such beliefs, they can rightly be looked upon as being shaped by, rather than as shaping, the dialectical forces which govern the management of industry.

The owners, at a similar point in industrial history, can also be said to live in a pure serial arrangement. Initially, their response—that is, the way they run their businesses—is formed by two challenges: the conditions of the market with its law of supply and demand and the competitive practices of other owners. They exercise a great degree of control since, in answer to a sudden change in either challenge, they can raise or lower prices, increase or decrease production, hire or fire men. But there comes a time when need changes the situation of each group: an entrepreneur like Rockefeller may begin to take capitalism a bit too seriously and decide to eliminate the competition; a Socialist like Marx may begin to make the workers aware of their misery as *shared* misery and point the way to remedies. Other structures begin to form which change the nature of the original relationships: if the workers unite, they represent a challenge to which the owners will respond; the American Federation of Labor will produce the National Association of Manufacturers in what is surely a most striking example of the past being reborn as an answer to the movement of the future. When the guns of the owners' goons have managed neither to kill all the strikers nor to end the strike, the owners must reckon with a new structure, the union. The owners also are made aware of the fact that in addition to competition they have common interests; since they are ingenious and discreet, they manage to preserve the reality of the latter and a fiction about the former in a shrewd operation known as price-fixing. The socialism of the many serves as the model for the socialism of the few; if the workers can cooperate to get the same wages, the executives can cooperate to get the same prices. They can even cheat, sure in the knowledge that the courts will be kinder to upper-class wrongdoers than to a Jimmy Hoffa.

An equipoise—or simply patience with the periodic bargaining sessions— eventually develops between the two groups as the processes of their relationship are worked out. The structures are known; the attitudes of the leaders of each side can be anticipated; maneuvers for negotiations can be worked out in the time between sessions. A form of the practico-inert sets in, hidden from the leaders by their belief that the give and take of their bargaining is something more than habit. They thus may not be aware of other forces which have been set loose. The owner of a small factory finds he can no longer make the same profits because of increased labor costs, or the need to replace outworn machinery, or cheaper competition from abroad. He must react by merging, automating, or going out of business. If he merges, he risks losing his top position; if he automates, he introduces a sophistication which eventually will replace managers with the latest computer; if he goes out of business his portrait may not only never hang in a museum, it may never be painted at all. In each of these cases, the worker's security is also once again threatened, and he faces anew the risk of unemployment. There has been progress for a time: the worker's lot was improved, the owner learned the value of cooperation with other owners. But the common phenomenon about which all negotiations were centered—industrial society—appears to have got away from both its managers and its workers. This is what Sartre calls counterfinality; what man has wrought begins to determine the conditions of his existence and therefore creates a new challenge to which he must respond, if not by the creation of fresh structures, certainly by shaking off the lethargy of the practico-inert into which he has sunk.

The above is a perilously condensed summary of the structures discussed in Book I of the *Critique*'s first volume. I hope it has caught the principles Sartre discusses there. The most basic is that of scarcity as a phenomenon which has manifested itself at every level of life and at each moment when individuals are confronted with need and the possibility that there will be no way of satisfying that need. In specific circumstances, especially when those circumstances have to do with the most fundamental needs of his life, he cooperates to create groups which are initially based on common interest. The group has an organic function only for the time that it pursues that common interest, as the organized Resistance under the German occupation showed. Those who formed the Resistance managed to forge a kind of supergroup out of a number of subgroups because each subgroup could agree on an immediate common goal: opposition to the occupying forces. Beyond that immediate common goal each subgroup had an ulterior goal which meant, once the Liberation had come to pass, that the Resistance dissolved and those who had cooperated in it opposed each other once again. Other groups—for example, The Citizens' Committee to Protest Late Busses—also cease to function once their goal has been accomplished; more often, they find other goals, for committees are not given to death wishes. The citizens' group, once the busses run on time, might find that the vehicles are crowded, or dirty, or old, or inadequately scheduled. As long as either group functions in terms of its goal it reduces the freedom of its members: internecine political struggle ceases when confronted with the greater menace; one gives up a night's television to attend a committee meeting. The members, of course, trim their freedom voluntarily. When the Germans are driven out, the old political struggles can resume; when the busses run on schedule, one will have even more time to look at television.

The example dealing with busses is a fairly trivial one; a good deal less trivial example is one dealing with civil rights.[14] What is of interest in the civil rights movement in this country, as in the Resistance in France, is that the group's function does not guarantee either the group's permanence or its health; it certainly does not guarantee that all members will be faithful to the group until its function has been accomplished. This is partly because, even within the group, the tension between freedom and necessity continues; it is also because once my needs have been satisfied I may wish to withdraw or may fail to see the connections between Martin Luther King's position on civil rights and his position on American involvement in Vietnam. The question of the functioning of the group in time, as well as the question of its effectiveness and relevance over a period of time, is what Sartre discusses in Book II of the *Critique*.

What Sartre wants to show is that the group is the place, or the collectivity, where liberty and necessity meet in an equilibrium of forces rather than under the stresses of tension; for, in the collectivity, liberty as necessity is balanced off by necessity as liberty, which is perhaps a complicated way of saying that one enjoys as much freedom as one is willing to work for. The underpaid worker, for example, can, out of fear of associating himself with others, maintain possession of his full freedom and elect to remain underpaid. He will have preserved his total freedom of choice, but he will not have satisfied either his needs or those of others who are dependent upon him; in so choosing, he may also have reduced the chances of other workers to exercise their freedom and reduce their misery. If, exercising another option, he decides to join the union, his freedom is reduced; he must accept union discipline, leave decisions up to others, undergo the possibly prolonged misery brought on by strikes. His freedom is reduced in the name of goods to be won: discipline will give force to the group; his leaders will have the skill and knowledge he does not possess; if the strike is successful, his condition will be improved. With higher wages, he will have greater freedom or, in less abstract terms, he will be less victimized by unsatisfied needs.

In less extreme circumstances, the athlete, because he likes exercise or derives pleasure from competition, joins a football team where the coach will decide what his position will be. If the team is to have any chance of success, there must be a single individual who makes such decisions. This is a limitation on the player's freedom since he may be assigned to a position he does not like or may not be allowed to play as often as he wants. If the coach possesses the proper acumen, there will be rewards: the team will win, and the individual player will experience the pleasures of team victory.

Worker and player can always withdraw from the union and the team

14. Wilfrid Desan in his *The Marxism of Jean-Paul Sartre* saw the illuminating pertinence of the American civil rights situation in explaining the terms of the *CRD*, and I am taking this lead from him.

in order to become what Sartre calls the nongroup. This is a nonstructured mass until such time as the worker organizes a counterunion or the player another team. We have seen many examples of this: Hugo's refusal to accept party discipline, Heinrich's almost constitutional inability to associate with any group, Frantz's dissociation of himself from all active forces, and, in a more comic vein, the Bolchevik-Bolchevik party in *Nekrassov* which has only one member who is wary about admitting others because of the tension which may result. But if the nongroup is to work, it must follow the pattern of the group it has been set up to oppose; it must make the same demands on its members and run the same risks. The nongroup thus represents the preservation of radical freedom; it also flirts dangerously with chaos for when it proliferates and reforms into new groups one is faced with the sort of splintered political situation which brought France to her knees in 1957.

Compromise thus becomes a necessity of the dialectic, but the compromise is across the board; it exists between the individual and the terms of the challenge to which he responds, between all individuals and the goals of the group to which they belong. Together these individuals form a unity, seeking to achieve a common cause through the group they constitute. The group can only function properly as long as its members continue to constitute it by free association and support. The group thus neutralizes the problem of the Other by directing all its members to a common goal; it could not exist without a continuous recognition by all members of their total interdependence. The group, of course, because it has a function which seeks to satisfy a need, and because it seeks to bring force and power to that function, becomes the Other for whoever or whatever is responsible for the existence of the need it seeks to dispel. The Resistance is no longer a motley of Catholics, Communists, Socialists, and Gaullists; it is Frenchmen united to oppose the Nazis. The agreement to compromise has provided the individuals who have formed the group with a power they would never have possessed singly; it allows them to meet the threatening Other in a radically new way. The important thing for the grouped members of the Resistance, as for the members of the labor union, is that so long as the group pursues its program the members are the Other only to that force which seeks to frustrate their needs or to reduce them to servitude. In the group the disempowering results of Otherness—which were traced out in *Being and Nothingness*—are dissolved.

The groups which have been discussed so far are those which are knowingly constituted; the individual enters into them because he has decided to make their goals his. He knows that, in instances where those goals dissatisfy him, he can work to reformulate them, and he also knows that he can withdraw if reformulation is impossible. In the last instance he would, like Frantz, become unstructured, a member of a nongroup with the choice of remaining in that condition, or of moving to another group as Goetz does, or of forming his own group as the isolated Russian in *Nekrassov* does. These associations can be dissolved when their function has been fulfilled, or they can fall into lethargy. They can also be picked up by the great tides of history which destroy them or carry them away.

History, which had earlier been said to have worn Merleau-Ponty out by riding him too hard, seems to have done the same to Frantz; he has been cast aside and left with no group. We know, however, that this is not the case; he has elected to withdraw while the group he was associated with—in the largest sense, the German state—remained involved with its destiny and has flourished. By a somewhat different process, the dissolution of the Resistance has removed a grouping from the historical scene, but not the groups which formed it. The constituent groups have returned to earlier ways and older ambitions. There are laws of process, if not of conservation, which apply to groups. If they can be created quickly, they cannot easily be destroyed.

History, the chronicle of man's response to challenge, is made by groups; history also conditions groups—that is what the dialectic is about. It is also what surrounds man. History's reaches appear to be so vast and its power so great as to make its dialectic appear an independent process in which man's part is to do and die, to do and be destroyed: the athlete finds that amateur sport is for future professionals, that its concern is with success and not the good health of his body, that both he and the coach are expendable; Frantz finds, against a background of greater cosmic consequence, that he, too, is expendable. The goal of the group, when it becomes involved in the combat of nations, gets away from it in order to be absorbed into vaster enterprises; a monster is born and endowed with insatiable appetites and inscrutable purposes. If men impetuously cry out "Stop the world, I want to get off!" what they may really be trying to say is "Stop the world, I want to see what's going on." That surely is what Frantz is attempting to say just as surely as it is the truth behind the restlessness of many American university students today. Everything is too big, too complex, too inhuman. If the world has any purpose it must be Hegel's: history progresses by burning human sacrifice on the altar of an Idea the victim will never see and therefore cannot be expected to appreciate or serve.

Given these conditions, the group experience is nothing but a fling permitted to the multitude because the multitude, like the individual, has wild oats to sow and excess energy to expend before it returns resignedly and perhaps in despair to the paternal home there to devote itself to a cult it cannot control. The group, both as initiating force and as solution to the problem of Otherness, is an illusion. Sartre must deny this for a number of reasons. If it is true, then history *is* a force independent of man; the only meaning left for human action is that it can affect nothing and therefore can effect nothing. If that is true, then dialectical materialism, or something like it, is an accurate description of the historical process and men are victims at its service. If, in turn, that is true, then the evidence of history is either bizarrely false or else caprice reigns. Since, for Sartre, the evidence is all we have and since it has meaning, the task is not to enthrone caprice but to show that all surrender to caprice is an expression of bad faith. The group, the agent of individuals and their bond with time and events, is also the device by which they seek to break the back of bondage. When the young, who are sometimes as brave as they are restless, decide to say no to adult stupidity masked as wisdom or inevitability or prudence or national destiny, they, too, form groups.

If there is not a flagrant contradiction in such a decision, there is cause for uneasiness. The life history of groups seems to lead to the graveyard of initiative where the only attitude left is acceptance. But when the group reaches that point what it proves is that the supposed power and mystery of history can be evoked as an excuse only when the group has become inert. Persuasive reasons may explain the inertia; more frequently, however, the inertia occurs because it satisfies a class within the group which, rather than being disturbed by the sweep of events, is convinced that the tide is running in its favor. The uneasy consciousness is not ordinarily that of those in control, which is perhaps why—we *must* hope this—they ultimately exert so little real control. A belief in the divine right of kings, in America's or Egypt's special relationship with God, in China's privileged intimacy with the future—these are beliefs which beg all the basic questions; they do not answer them. Because of this, the graveyard is the destiny not of initiative but of ideology; ideology, bolstering satisfaction and prolonging smugness, not only reduces spontaneity but also makes it suspect. And yet spontaneity is what creates the group originally and brings it into history. The group remains as the most effective and perhaps the only instrument with which individuals can influence events in order to form their own history.

Sartre's description of the movement of the individual into the group and of the group from its initial organization into involvement with history centers about the events of the French Revolution. He is concerned with showing what might be called the anatomy and physical history of the group from the moment when the individuals who comprise it recognize its instrumental worth to the moment when it encounters various crises. As an instrument the group supplies a tool for individual ambitions. The individual, having already had the experience of tyranny and now wanting to do something to rid himself of it, joins with others because he recognizes that he shares their ambition; he fights along with them, and finds, at the end of the afternoon, that together they have destroyed the Bastille. At any moment in the movement which led to the destruction he might have fled, inspired by fear or caution. Even after the destruction he might withdraw quietly in order to avoid the unpredictable consequences of and punishment for his act.

But participation has revealed a number of things to him not the least of which is his accession to a position in which he can act meaningfully and with some promise of directing events. The group permits him to exist as he has not previously existed; simultaneously, his membership makes him aware that, by cooperating with others, he has made a contribution to their new-found freedom of action. Each member of the group mediates the other members and is mediated by them; the value of the group is expressed in the process by which it is formed. Because it is value, it has the power to overcome earlier fears and indifference and to elicit an adherence to the group *after* the event. Instead of slipping off, the individual remains to prolong the life of the group, to make it into a structure through which he will seek to influence the world.

His enthusiasm for the group is, of course, not enough. Demands other than participation in heady events will be made on the members; dangers hedge their action, one of the greatest being the problem of keeping the group intact. This is effected by what Sartre calls the oath: the agreement of each individual to cooperate with the group, to shape his will to its. This in turn produces overlays of hesitation and menace which Sartre groups together under the label of terror. There is the individual terror of having enlisted one's freedom in the service of a cause that may not succeed; there is also the terror induced by the process of violence and struggle by which the group will seek to impose itself on the other groups it seeks to replace.

Once organized the group gives a sense of purpose to humans who otherwise would have remained in a serial arrangement; it has set itself up in dialectical relationship to other forces; its members live significantly in history because they have a goal they seek to achieve—the destruction of the ancien régime. What happens to the group is that, under the Convention, it is transformed into an institution which operates through subgroups. The institution seeks to influence other groups, it is compelled to respond to conditions created by other institutions, and it must deal with opposition groups in its own midst. Its goal is no longer as clear as it was originally; opposition to its purposes has led to the formation of other groups. At home, opposition threatens an essential stability; abroad, the *émigrés* seek to influence the policies of other states in order to overthrow the new domestic regime. The group's functions have multiplied with the assumption of power to a point where its original goal seems to be buried under present pressures. Because so much of its attention must be taken up with the immediate, it risks losing the support of those who originally made its accession to power possible.

The institution may not in fact have lost sight of the ideal which created it; but it sees more clearly the immediate obstacles to its very existence. In desperation or out of cynicism, it may resort to a terror of its own, designed to preserve its existence: riots are savagely suppressed, censorship imposed, diversity of opinion discouraged, the guillotine employed as the new altar for human sacrifice. In the process, the institution has got so far away from the original hope of the group as to have become another version of the state against which the group had rebelled; it is now a state which has elaborated a strategy that it defends at all costs; its police force seems no different to its victims than the police force of the ancien régime. Between the new violence and the old violence there seems to be no distinction, since the mind is paralyzed by the substantive before it falls victim to whatever differences the qualifying adjectives are meant to describe. When one is its victim, violence is violence, and it makes little difference whether it be old or new.

What has happened is that in its totalizing movement—its effort to achieve the goal which inspired it—the group has fallen into a process of totalization quite different from what it originally sought, because events elsewhere, like the issues and problems originally undiscerned, have had to be met. In the process of meeting them, those members of the original group who have assumed positions of leadership have also yielded to the needs of the new totalization. They defend their actions, they defend the necessity of the changes which have taken place, they even defend the failure to make promised changes. But even as the leadership defends itself and its programs, those members who feel they have been deceived or betrayed discover in their deception and betrayal a phenomenon that the new leaders have either not recognized or paid enough attention to: detotalization. The phenomenon is associated with dynamism and change and thus expresses the impossibility of maintaining any human activity or accomplishment in a static condition. Two reactions to the phenomenon are possible. The first is the realization by the disappointed members of the original group that they have been deceived because they have not accomplished what they sought; their lot has not been essentially changed. The other reaction points out the possibility of their regrouping in order to detotalize the institution which has resulted from their earlier commitment.

For those of the original group who have not assumed power, the state still represents "the unity of all the impossibilities which define negatively the exploited individual." This is not gibberish, though it does read very much like German. What it means is that, if I am a worker, I consider the bourgeois state to be the unifying force which brings together and defends all the forces which assure my misery. The state exists to defend the interests of the class from which I am excluded and by which I am exploited. The state wishes to maintain the status quo, which means that the state wishes to keep me in powerless seriality, for random beings are more easily manipulated than grouped beings. The fall of the Bastille in the long run has verified nothing more important than the old French slogan: *plus ça change plus c'est la même chose.* Yet I have had the experience—or if I have not had it, history will provide me with the examples of those who have—of detotalization and therefore I still have recourse to other Bastilles. I also have information about what happens in the aftermath of fallen bastions.

The observer who has made this discovery can thus begin to attack the state which, committed blindly to a belief in the possibility of being a totality, has slippped into totalitarianism. And totalitarianism is simply and scandalously another bog. When it exists in Communist countries, it shows a wretched cynicism about the meaning of the dialectic which it uses to justify itself; when it exists in bourgeois societies it provides further evidence of why such societies should be destroyed. Wherever it exists—that is, wherever states are happy with what they are doing because they believe that what they are doing is in some way annexed to truth—it is based on a contradiction, since the practico-inert, to the extent that it defends itself and makes a mystique of itself, denies the very praxis which first unleashed the force the practico-inert now seeks to petrify. In some recess of its discomfort, the state is aware of this. Under the worst circumstances, it produces what Sartre calls—in one of the many examples which shows that he speaks excellent Franglais—*extéro-conditionnement,* a phrase borrowed and transformed from David Reisman's vocabulary. The state devotes much of its energy to creating the outer-directed man.

The state thereby becomes the most intense expression of Sartrean man as we discovered him in *Being and Nothingness.* Through a multifaceted process of conditioning, the state and its subordinate institutions try to fascinate the Other, who is the individual citizen, in order that he will accept the Other, who is embodied in the state, without protesting too much. The state tolerates only as much protest as will be ineffective. To produce fascination, the state must persuade the individual that the political situation has been created with his advantage in mind; when this fails, the citizen can be assured that under other circumstances he would be even worse off.

When states are not seeking comparisons favorable to their own interests, they offer promises, telling the poor boy that he may one day be president and the rich boy that poor boys may one day be allowed to join him if only they work hard .The rich boy is simultaneously told that only a few poor lads will enter into competition with him and is assured that those who do will have accepted all the values he cherishes. The aim is to create a situation which has all the appearance of an open society. If the citizens feel they are free, and if they are convinced that the government is doing its best, then they and the government live in an easy relationship with one another. The government is then free to do what it wants because it can always fall back on the claim that what it wants is what the people want.

Behind the method there is usually a mythology—a hieratic order which is used to justify hoaxes by presenting them in slogans as noble as "the civilizing mission of France," or as irrelevant as "we've never lost a war," or as perplexing as "the dictatorship of the proletariat" (at some future date.) For Sartre these are the most distressing of all mythologies because through them governments, and those who run them, seek to impose their interests on everyone. It is quite possible and even probable that the governing class has been fascinated by its own myths; this does not change the fact that the continued imposition of those myths is effected in order to defend the material and ideological interests of the rulers. The tactic which emerges is that of organizing the Other—and this may seem paradoxical—not as the Other who is free but as the Other who is fascinated and therefore not free. Instead of encouraging him to discover the world as the space in which he must work out his destiny, states bombard him with encouragements to take as his destiny that which has already been elaborated. They are supported or reinforced in this effort by the various propaganda machines of contemporary society which encourage citizens to drink a certain beverage in order to be in the Pepsi generation, to apply Eterna Cream in order to stay young, and to admire books because *le Tout Paris* admires them.

What gives the situation an ironic hue is that all these messages are sent out by cheap, uncritical intellects who do not mind living with lies. What gives the situation its most tragic color is that the government uses its praxis not only to preserve the practico-inert situation which is its vested interest, but also to discourage all manifestations of praxis among its citizens, and especially those kinds of praxis which would change the nature of the state. Or else, at the highest level of sophistication, it seeks to control that praxis by making it ineffective: the boys in Vietnam are dying so that dissenters can enjoy the right to dissent. The implications of that sort of concession are clear. The dissenters will not be allowed to produce change; the boys will keep dying in Vietnam to defend what an objective eye can only evaluate as colossal stupidity; that such colossal stupidity should be disguised under claims that democracy is being defended is a ghastly commentary on the state of our times and our minds.

We have come a long way from *Being and Nothingness* only to discover that another circle has been drawn, enclosing a reality which may be more frightening than that which served as the basis for the earlier work. Where in that book the individual confronted another individual in fear and with growing awareness of risks to be encountered, in the *Critique de la raison dialectique* he confronts a vast apparatus designed to elicit his assent or, that failing, equipped to cow him. The journey around the outer edge of the circle is a defeat only if the individual accepts the circle as perfect or, since all circles are perfect, believes that circles are the best imaginable kind of perfection. What the individual can learn is the value of the group as the agency which, intervening in history, saves the individual and, in so doing, is faithful to the dialectical thrust of human experience. These are not lessons fancifully taught, and the *Critique* is not meant to be a fictional escape from despair into ideology. Though the movement it traces seems destined to defeat, the impetus behind the movement is the source of optimism. In the group, the individual can redeem himself on the gamble of redeeming the times. Against the static group, another group can be formed.

The book, then, despite all its analytical equipment, is essentially a long effort at persuasion and a further example of the descriptive method Sartre has constantly used in his effort to convince his readers and, through them, a vaster body of men, to work in such a way as to enlist individual human dynamism in the service of all humanity. Since that dynamism is unavoidable—it is what human nature is and explains why human nature cannot ever be adequately defined—the dialectical movement of history is unavoidable. It reflects the periodic glory and the more frequent shame of man.

What the dialectic shows is that both man and history are intelligible and reflect each other's purpose. Man has a place in history and in the world because it is through him that the world has a history. The not inconsiderable task of getting the message through and having it accepted remains. It is one thing to elaborate a system designed to show men that the great catastrophes of history are images, projected on the screen of space and time, of the comparatively smaller irritations of individual existence and thereby to indicate that men have more reason to cooperate than to compete. It is quite another thing, and a more thankless task, to convince men that this is the sort of wisdom with which they should inform their lives. The problem is not simply that men who ignore history are condemned, as Santayana memorably pointed out, to repeat it. The problem more pertinently is that men who shape events may never have heard either Santayana or Sartre, or having heard them, may have decided that there is no connection between philosophical wisdom and immediate ambitions or imperious necessity.

Hindsight may indicate that history is intelligible; men may indeed always be responsible for their destiny and always capable of initiating the acts which will shape it. But time is relentless in refusing to stop, intelligence is limited, knowledge is restricted, and men do not always agree about what their collective destiny should be. Their disagreements are not always based, as Sartre has too frequently insisted, on deliberate malice but on the fear that miscalculation will set humanity to preying on itself again, on the uneasy awareness that the adversary's intentions are never fully known, on the conviction that what may be lost may never be replaced. Men frequently go to war to prey on each other; but, as Sartre learned in World War II and as he sees in his commitment to revolution, some men go to war in order to defend themselves and what they believe are their ideals. The greatest weakness in the *Critique* may be that, in trying to be everything, it, like Sartrean man, is not enough. This deficiency is related at least partially to a dilemma

Sartre has known recently: a man can understand in great detail all the reasons which push Israel and the Arab countries to reciprocal violence and still be incapable of doing anything to forestall the arrival of war. History may be intelligible; tragically, it is not always enacted by intelligent men.

RELATED THEMES AND WORKS

Sartre's involvement with Marxism has passed through three different phases. As a young man, his reading of Marx was a purely intellectual exercise which elicited none of the enthusiasm, the sense of epiphany, which was to emerge later; in the second phase, Marx is recognized as presenting a coherent analysis and program for the liberation of the proletariat and thus serves as the basis from which Sartre works out his own commentaries and theories. The essays in *Sit. VI* (1964) and *Sit. VII* (1965), most of which were originally published in *TM*, show the development of his thought. *TM* was not meant to be an instrument of Communist party programs and policies, though some of its editors have always had a particular affinity with Marxist methodology and have always accepted the fundamental accuracy of Marx's analysis of human society. In the "Présentation" of the first issue (reprinted in *Sit. II*, pp. 9–30), Sartre was already distinguishing between the analytic cast of mind which tended towards an idealistic description of man and another cast of mind which refused to forget that man could not be understood outside the situation in which he was plunged. Sartre proposed to study man as a biological constitution which, in its processes, produced change; he never meant to study man as a biological phenomenon but rather was concerned with the biology of man's interventions in the world.

Other essays which should be consulted in order to understand his position vis-à-vis communism and Marxism are "Matérialisme et révolution" (1946) which I have already discussed; "Réponse à Albert Camus" (1952; in *Sit. IV*, pp. 90–125), and, in conjunction with this, Camus' original letter to *TM*, "Révolte et servitude" (in *Actuelles II* [Paris 1953], pp. 82–124); Sartre's comment on Camus defines a fundamental difference between those who, because they have freedom of choice, are radically alienated from the working class, and the members of that class; it also distinguishes between those who, like Camus, wish to soar above history because they fear being soiled by history and those who recognize that only in history can any redemption be found for man. In 1961 Sartre defended *TM*'s friendly feelings towards Russia by pointing out two things: (1) any opposition to Russia, in the climate of the postwar period, immediately was translated into a defense of bourgeois society and capitalist interests—there was no choice save to be indulgent towards the one society which at least partially embodied the hopes of the working class; (2) *TM* did not hesitate to condemn excess in the internal and external policies of the Soviet Union.

Sartre's hesitations about Hegel—because Hegel makes man history's victim—were expressed in "Qu'est-ce qu'un collaborateur?" (*Sit. III*, p. 53). A more recent expression of his thinking about Marxism and existentialism can be found in *Marxisme et existentialisme: controverse sur la dialectique* (Paris, 1962). This is the report of the *Semaine de la pensée marxiste*. It is important to note that in this second phase of friendly hostility—the third phase is that of the *CRD* where Sartre is convinced he has found his role—Sartre seemed to find particular sustenance from the example of Yugoslavia and the earlier example, which he often recalls, of Rosa Luxemburg, whose ill-treatment at the hands of Marxists who had neither her intellectual acumen nor her commitment seemed to parallel his.

Several quite reliable books discuss Sartre's political thought and involvements. I have already cited Michel-Antoine Burnier's *Les Existentialistes et la politique* (Paris, 1966). An earlier book, David Caute's *Communism and the French Intellectuals 1914–1960* (New York, 1964), discusses the question against a broader background than that of Burnier's book. An even broader background is supplied in Roy Pierce's *Contemporary French Political Thought* (New York and London, 1966; see esp. pp. 148–84). Also relevant is *Entretiens sur la politique* (Paris, 1949; conversations among Sartre, David Rousset, and Gérard Rosenthal).

The *CRD* is a book which runs perilously close to canceling itself out because its many excitements are counterbalanced on an almost one-for-one scale by its annoyances. It was written in an atmosphere of compulsion and anxiety—compulsion that it had to be done, anxiety that the task was impossible; it shows an absence of discipline that is more than the result of impatience and fatigue. No effort has been made, either by Sartre or his publisher, to facilitate the reader's task. The proofreading is frequently fanciful; there is no index; the table of contents is so unhelpful as to be nothing more than a foolish expense of paper if not of print. Surely a man of Sartre's reputation and a publishing house of Gallimard's affluence could have come up with something that would do greater honor to their reputations and rendered better service to the public. Mary Warnock is being something other than petulant when she asserts that it is wrong to write and publish books like this. The major error, I think, is the disservice done to an important work.

The *CRD* is divided into two distinct parts. The first, originally published in a Polish review, is the "Question de méthode." (An English translation, *Search for a Method*, has been made by Hazel Barnes [New York, 1963]). It is divided into three parts: "Marxism and Existentialism" (pp. 15–32); "The Problem of Mediations and the Auxiliary Disciplines" (pp. 35–39); "The Progressive-Regressive Method" (pp. 60–

103). There is a "Conclusion" (pp. 103–111) which is more a survey of implications than a summary of statements already made.

The second part is the *CRD* itself, and it is divided in the following way.

Introduction
A. Dogmatic Dialectic and Critical Dialectic, pp. 115–35.
B. Critique of Critical Experience, pp. 135–62.

Book I: From Individual "Praxis" to the Practico-Inert
A. Concerning Individual "Praxis" as Totalization, pp. 165–77.
B. Concerning Human Relations as Mediations between the Different Sectors of Materiality, pp. 178–99.
C. Concerning Matter as Totalized Totality and the First Experience of Necessity.
    1. Scarcity and the Means of Production, pp. 200–224.
    2. Worked Matter as the Alienated Objectivation of the Individual and Collective "Praxis," pp. 225–61.
       Interest, pp. 261–79.
    3. Concerning Necessity as the New Structure of Dialectical Experience, pp. 279–305.
D. The Collectivities, pp. 306–377.

Book II: From the Group to History
A. Concerning the Group. The Equation between Liberty as Necessity and Necessity as Liberty. The Limits and Significance of all Realistic Dialectic, pp. 381–552.
A. (sic) The Being-One of the Group Is Imposed on It from Outside by Others. And in this First Form the Being-One of the Group Exists as Other, pp. 553–61.
B. In the Interiority of the Group, the Movement of Mediated Reciprocity Constitutes the Being-One of the Practical Community as a Perpetual Detotalization Engendered by the Totalizing Movement, pp. 562–631.
C. Concerning Dialectical Experience as Totalization: The Level of the Concrete, the Locus of History, pp. 632–755.

A number of important questions which are discussed at length in the *CRD* have not been adequately treated in my chapter. Among the most significant are: the question of the third man who not only mediates the experience of other parties by informing them of the relationship he sees between their experiences but who is also mediated—that is, who finds *his* function by being able to serve as the mediator; the complex reciprocity that is involved in man's dual role as subject and object, shifting back and forth endlessly from one to the other; the process of interiorization which is proposed as the effective means of living with the subject-object dualism; the role of fascination in the installation and defense of public "morality"; the question of counterfinality which is partially conveyed in my discussion of *Le Diable* and *Les Séquestrés* where Goetz (for part of his life) and Frantz (in the last phase of his life) find themselves living with consequences they had not anticipated but which are the results of their own actions; the issue of violence and terror which very much reflects the thought of Trotsky and other Marxists; and the discussion of man's role as the antinatural force in the world, which in the *CRD* receives its culminating treatment.

The preoccupations of the *CRD*, as well as its vocabulary, turn up in other Sartrean writings; that is no surprise since Sartre has always insisted that reality must be all of a piece or, more precisely, that all the pieces of reality must form a coherent whole. Readers will derive value from reading his critical appreciation of Lapoujade ("Le Peintre sans privilèges," *Sit. IV*, pp. 364–86) and the essay "Doigts et non-doigts" (*Sit. IV*, pp. 408–34) which is devoted to Paul Klee and Wols. In the former essay he is concerned with showing how Lapoujade's depiction of crowds supports Sartre's ideas of what a group is and how it comes into being; in the latter essay, Sartre makes some perceptive remarks in relation to the detotalizing effects of Klee's paintings. In an interview in the *Revue d'Esthétique* (new series, 3–4, 1965), entitled "L'Ecrivain et sa langue," and again in another interview, "Jean-Paul Sartre répond" (*L.'Arc*, 30, 1966), he discusses language as an example of the practico-inert with which the writer must tirelessly wrestle, and also alludes to literature as a project which is falsified once the writer slips into the erroneous belief that an individual work can be a totality. He also, in the later interview, makes reference to the relationship between psychoanalysis and the phenomena of the practico-inert and the totalizing process. Finally, in a more creative vein, *Les Troyennes* can be usefully studied as a description on a global scale of the forces described in the *CRD*; in that play, two nations meet in a senseless conflict and achieve nothing because their force is not as great as the forces which they have set loose unawares. The play, in this sense, is clearly not an effort to set up perspectives; rather it seeks to impose the perspective of the *CRD* in a more available way.

If Sartre's doggedness has done nothing else it has imposed new directions on Marxist theory in France. As faithful a stalwart as Roger Garaudy, who in the past could be relied upon to toe, however awkwardly, the party line, has recently shown greater flexibility—a flexibility partially provoked by Sartre's prodding. His *De l'anathème au dialogue* (Paris, 1966) and *Peut-on être communiste aujourd'hui?* (Paris, 1968) were the result both of the greater freedom of intellectual movement within world communism and of Sartre's provocative and persistent challenges. Garaudy has fared less well with the French Communist party since the invasion of Czechoslovakia; early in 1970, he was expelled from the Central Committee. Louis Althusser's *Pour Marx* (Paris, 1966) is also an example, not of direct Sartrean influence, but of the kind of discussion Sartre has been urging: free, open, unhampered by allegiances to an ideological purity put forth by others.

There has been much comment on the *CRD*. Among the most useful general works are: Colette Audry's *Sartre et la réalité humaine* (Paris, 1966) which is a general review of Sartre's philosophy and which is especially lucid about this, his least lucid work; the book admirably and economically shows the *CRD*'s relationship to the body of Sartre's thought. Wilfred Desan's *The Marxism of Jean-Paul Sartre* (New York, 1965) is a book-length study which concentrates principally on the *CRD* and which is at all times fair and sympathetic and which, most importantly, is an eminently clear exposé of a text which does not share that particular eminence. Laing and Cooper's *Reason and Violence* (New York, 1964) discusses, using perhaps too much of Sartre's vocabulary, the decade of work preceding the *CRD*; the last chapter is devoted to that work. The *Revue française de Sociologie* (2:1961) is an issue devoted to the *CRD*. George Lichtheim's *Marxism in Modern France* (New York, 1966) provides a highly reliable discussion of the background against which Sartre's attitudes, rebellions, and hesitations developed. In a more general way, Leonard Beaton's *The Struggle for Peace* (London, 1966) offers the evidence of another writer's evaluations of the political and military situation in postwar Russia to show that Sartre is not alone in believing that the USSR's position was principally defensive rather than offensive.

Dissenting or reserved appraisals of Sartre's writings on Marxism can be found in: Merleau-Ponty's *Les Aventures de la dialectique* (Paris, 1955; see esp. pp. 131–271), written before the publication of the *CRD*; Simone de Beauvoir's counterattack on Merleau-Ponty can be found in her book *Privilèges* (Paris, 1955, pp. 201–72). Claude Lévi-Strauss, admiring and even adopting much of Sartre's general thought and a good bit of his vocabulary, outlines his dissent in some detail in *La Pensée sauvage* (Paris, 1962, pp. 324–57). Georges Gurvitch's *Dialectique et sociologie* (Paris, 1962) takes up Sartre's criticisms of Gurvitch and answers them in an argument which stresses what Gurvitch considers Sartre's arbitrary limitations of the meaning, range, and presence of dialectic in human existence ("La Dialectique chez Jean-Paul Sartre," pp. 157–76). Serge Doubrovsky's *Corneille ou la dialectique du héros* (Paris, 1963) has some extremely illuminating things to say on the ultimate goal of Sartre's book ("Corneille et Sartre," pp. 504–10). Professor Doubrovsky was one of the first commentators to discuss the

CRD ("J.-P. Sartre et le mythe de la raison dialectique," *Nouvelle Revue Française* 9:105–106–107, 1961). There is a very good article on the methodology and purpose of the *CRD* by Robert Castel ("Un Beau Risque," *L'Arc* 30 [1966]: 20–26). Jacques Houbart's *Un Père dénaturé* (Paris, 1964) is an almost thoroughly negative commentary on Sartre which derives its dissenting energy from an equally vast passion to defend Hegel. An examination of Sartre's and Merleau-Ponty's interest in Marxism can be found in Raymond Aron's *Marxism and the Existentialists* (New York, 1969). Raymond Aron, in *D'une Sainte Famille à l'autre* (Paris, 1969), analyzes the Marxism of both Sartre and Althusser and finds it wanting mainly because of what Aron believes are internal contradictions. In the case of each commentator, Aron claims, we see the example of a philosopher who is seeking to provide Marxist thought with a basis acceptable to him. Aron concludes that while such an undertaking may help both Sartre and Althusser it does not do much that is useful either for or with Marx's actual thought.

Pertinent chapters from *SG* are "The Eternal Couple of the Criminal and the Saint" (pp. 73–137) and "Please Use Genet Properly" (pp. 584–99). The former chapter is related, as is much existentialist discussion of interpersonal relations, to Hegel's treatment of "Lordship and Bondage" in *The Phenomenology of the Mind* (tr. by J. B. Baillie, London, 1931, pp. 229–40). A similar discussion of one man's experience as exemplary for others is Sartre's introduction to Andre Gorz's *Le Traître* (*Sit. IV*, pp. 38–81). In that essay Sartre establishes direct connections between Gorz's experience and Genet's.

Almost simultaneously with the outbreak of the hostilities between the Arab countries and Israel, *TM* published an immense special issue (253 *bis* [June 1967]) which is a compilation of the grievances of each side written by representatives of each camp. Sartre provides an introductory essay, written with a sorrow so great that it excludes conclusions or even the taking of sides. In that essay, he promises to publish fuller observations at a later date when time will have permitted the establishment of some perspective.

Art is the presentation of the world as it would be

were it recaptured by human freedom.

— Interview with Clarté

12 All for Freedom

If we agree that the definition and elaboration of the basic terms of revolution—its natural necessity, its essential continuity—demand the work of a lifetime, we begin to appreciate the number and the magnitude of the obstacles Sartre encounters. The most considerable is time, which offers two immediate troubles: there is not enough of it and there is too much. There is not enough in the sense that no single life is sufficiently long to allow a man to read all the books, make all the studies, pursue all the inquiries which would serve as the basis for or the certification of his own theories. There is too much time in the sense that, even as one man works, devotedly and diligently, other men are working, acting, misbehaving—in sum, adding to the material to be studied by raising new questions that need answers. The philosopher or social theorist can abstract a system from these conditions only by risking the worst outcome: that of being wrong, of being undone in his theories and proposed therapies by a movement of events which demonstrates, even when it does not necessarily verify, the precise opposite of what he has foreseen. Once the possibility of being wrong has been admitted, a man may feel encouraged to remain silent, to abstain from further and conceivably more dangerous abstractions.

The other great obstacle is man himself in his multiplicity and unpredictability. Like time, he is, because of his numbers, too much; because of his unpredictability, he is too little. We cannot easily get hold of him; less easily can we manage him. We cannot make him see what he should see; we cannot control him for good or ill and, painfully, we know that this inability is the indication precisely of the fact that he is free to do fine deeds and to enact abject crimes, to live on the basis of love as well as of hate, to turn a deaf ear to disturbing truths or even to deny that there can be such a thing as truth.

A man who is not a philosopher, but who is not a fool either, might very well agree that he must be responsible for the consequences of his acts. He may simultaneously recognize that the number of acts available to him is limited by his physical situation and his most essential responsibilities. He may feel genuine compassion for the world's suffering peoples but have immediate tasks which compel him to be here, supporting his family, rather than there, in the midst of the latest social upheaval. He may feel the temptation to join street protests and demonstrations and yet stumble on the fact that such gestures take him away from the other gestures he should perform and thereby lower the quality of participation he should bring to more immediate responsibilities. As the man of decent sentiment cannot be everywhere to see that good is done, so the philosopher of universal social reform cannot take *everything* into consideration; such a desire would involve him in so much preparatory activity as to delay for all time the establishment of any reforms.

If the man of decent sentiment cannot serve all his causes, he must decide which causes are good and orient his life and possibly his checkbook around those causes. If the philosopher realizes that time and other men condition negatively the ambitions of his project, he can elect an idea of time and a definition of man which, by the nature of their presentation, will at least raise questions and stir doubts in the minds of all men. The philosopher who seeks reform must be willing to banish certain niceties and neglect certain kinds of finesse—what is today referred to as elegance—in the elaboration of his argument. He must convince his readers that he is right, not by presenting them with statistics patiently assembled and aptly applied, or with transcriptions of psychoanalytic sessions perseveringly taped and imaginatively interpreted, but with descriptions of such power that from them will emerge the conviction that, despite the revulsion they may engender, the true image of man is indeed to be found in them.

Sartre's method is always descriptive. Even when the philosophical vocabulary is at its weightiest and the argument at its most convoluted point, the elements of anecdote and the will to shock are not far off. Though the sum total of his work amounts to a vast theory, particular moments are most often and most powerfully expressed in terms of real people facing real situations in the commonplace contexts of life: a child looks at a tree and shudders at the difference between it and him; an adolescent breaks a vase because its serenity frustrates him; a man stops climbing a steep mountain, claiming he is too tired, but knowing that he is lying to himself; a woman pretends she is not cooperating in a petting session; a priest hates humanity because, afraid of himself, he is afraid of other men; a woman cheats because that is the only method she possesses for managing her life. At no point is the reader far from exposure to some ordinary experience; at no point is he allowed to believe that the experience is quite as ordinary as he had thought. A sophisticated goal uses a technique of apparent unsophistication to show the reader that there are motives in his everyday behavior which reveal more about him than he has ever wanted to have disclosed.[1]

1. These gestures, which seek to hide the true goal they seek, reveal it all the better to the objective eye; they clearly resemble those discussed by Freud in *The Psychopathology of Everyday Life*. The essential difference between Freud and Sartre is that Freud discounted the degree of conscious awareness on the part of the performer; Sartre, especially in his first works, insists that the performer is fully conscious of the meaning of his act and has, on the basis of that awareness, deliberately chosen one tactic over another.

If the attentive reader's periodic reaction is, like Professor Ayer's, "What a lot of gibberish it all is," his more frequent reaction is: "I'd never quite seen it like this before." The more frequent reaction influences the periodic impatience and often brings the reader back to a reconsideration of the "gibberish" and to the discovery that it is not quite so senseless as it had originally appeared. No matter how complicated the sentences and eccentric the vocabulary, the whole enterprise never escapes the shadow of reality and thus never has the chilly detachment of classical philosophy or the mannered deportment of linguistic philosophy, both of whose practitioners are among Sartre's harshest critics.

What the descriptions seek is to accumulate data to a point where what they describe seems undeniable; once that has been accomplished, the way may have been prepared for the presentation of even more radical assertions. If Descartes' experience can be described in terms designed to show that it is an experience most men have had, then the ensuing comment on the widest meaning of that experience will not seem outlandishly exaggerated:

> A man cannot be more of a man than others because freedom is similarly infinite in each. . . . It matters little how quickly or slowly we have understood, since understanding, however it comes to us, must be total in everyone or not be at all (*Sit. I*, p. 319).

At other times the radical statement is presented initially as though to condition the reader to the unfamiliar intellectual climates through which he will be subsequently traveling; it prepares him for later descriptions which will show that the radical statement, when subsumed in a theory, is not as odd as it seemed at first blush:

> Destruction is an essentially human thing . . . *it is man* who destroys his cities through the agency of earthquakes or directly, who destroys his ships through the agency of cyclones or directly . . . destruction, although coming into being through man, is an *objective fact* and not a thought (*BN*, p. 9).

The method is clear. The startling assertion is made abruptly; the essential qualifying remark which justifies the abrupt statement is not written until the maximum astonishment has been elicited, the reader stirred to protest, his pencil lowered to inscribe hostile evaluations in the margin. When works written over the years have built up a dossier and exhibited the value of a technique designed to show the fundamental insufficiencies of human existence as we know it, and most particularly of the class which is most responsible for those insufficiencies, then enabling theory can also be set apart and moral condemnations enunciated as though they, too, were *objective facts*:

> Today bourgeois ideology is that of a class on the decline, wavering because it has lost its own principles; tomorrow it will be engulfed by the proletariat. It has already begun to slip, its positions are purely defensive; the proletariat, the rising class, will incorporate it and bring about the classless society, that is, the society with a single ideology. Thus proletarian ideology, although it is subjective since it expresses the point of view of the working class, passes over to absolute objectivity since later it will become man's point of view; for, in the end, it is this class which will write history (*Sit. VI*, p. 27).

The early Sartrean phrase is meant to provoke thought; later it is meant to jolt or shock; finally, it is meant to exhort readers to follow the right path, the *only* way which will offer a promise that, in the future, it may become possible to write better descriptions. This is the rhetoric, not of phrases, but of purpose and progress. In this scheme, theory, based on revolution carried on in the name of a single universal truth to be established, need not be overly concerned with inadequate time and unpredictable man. What it needs to be concerned with is the task of convincing the reader that the human situation is so dreadful now that only revolution and commitment to a specific ideology can change it. The reader must assume Sartre's experience and with it Sartre's wisdom, the key point of which is that, over the years of patient describing, he has discovered where evil dwells and has learned how good is to be found.[2]

Sartre has frequently referred to his Manicheism and described it as an outlook produced by the confluence of his personal background and the historical events of his time. He has made great efforts to renounce this Manicheism. More precisely, such renunciation is the condition which leads to his project. One also has the impression that Manicheism best expresses the most characteristic mood of the author's mind and produces the polarizations which are found throughout his work. Because poles

2. Beigbeder early saw and aptly described some of the characteristic operations of Sartre's thought: "The movement of its variations has set loose one image: we are not dealing, despite its ready reasoning processes, with a deductive and abstract mind whose system was already fully prefabricated and brought forth without any contact with the earth except that made necessary at the moment when it was set up. This man lives with his ear to the ground, proceeds by trials and errors, by experiments. He is an artisan who constructs in fits and starts, uncovering one piece, then another, each time melting down the ensemble, but always hooked to his object, using as his fresh starting point the feeling he has for it in his fingers. He does not think without matter, and one could even say that his ideas are engendered on the basis of matter" (*L'Homme Sartre*, p. 112).

seem inevitable—even praxis and the practico-inert are poles—and because language cannot do away with them but only suggest a different
meaning for them, language must be used to effect changes which, in
the face of all the evidence, have little chance of coming about otherwise.
If all the blame is placed on man, perhaps he will begin taking some of the
responsibility. If the bourgeoisie is faced with total destruction, perhaps
it will initiate redemptive programs. If life is depicted as universally
miserable, perhaps those who are not haunted by their misery will become
haunted by that of others. If existence is everywhere fragile, perhaps men
will tread cautiously and not knock up too abruptly against others.

Perhaps, too, the reverse will happen. That possibility—that all the
above "if" causes will produce the opposite response—only intensifies
the Manichean mood; that in turn reinforces the commitment to language
and description and widens the area of human affairs to which they must
be applied. Language, for Sartre, is, both in the beginning and at the end
(despite modifications along the way), the only recourse against the
random initiatives and stray results of other human actions. It must keep
up with the world in order to continue being accepted as pertinent comment rather than bracketed as a construct, like any other, to be embraced
by those it pleases and spurned by those it hinders. If men create destruction because they apprehend it with their consciousness, then they create
evil, too, and by the same process. It is all words, and if reality exists only
in the aftermath of words, then words must also deal with the aftermath of
reality. It is chicken and egg with this variation: for Sartre the egg is more
important than the chicken because the egg tells us something about what
chickens do; it may not tell us enough about what chickens are, but that is
not an issue Sartre has been greatly bothered by. Words and acts may
be the only remedies we have. They come from a certain stock or soil,
and stock and soil need to be given important consideration: first, in selecting one remedy rather than another; second, in evaluating particular remedies; and, third, in knowing why in certain circumstances particular remedies
have been chosen.

We can say, without simplifying too much, that Sartre's lifetime project
has evolved through two interconnected hopes. The first has been to show
the inevitability of human freedom despite the anguish caused by its discovery; the second has been to show that universal justice can only come
about through the cooperation of all men working together in the interests of everyone. That latter project has been inspired by a personal ambition. Sartre had always hoped that the statements and the system used to
describe the project, would be all-inclusive, *le Tout. All* of human reality
would fall within the system's terms and *all* of human reality would
therein be explained and its inner tensions resolved in the realization of
the project.

I am convinced that two difficulties haunt Sartre as he pursues his effort. One is objective: all human reality has not yet provided much evidence that it wants to be or is capable of being One, united in its goals and methods. The other is subjective: all human reality, in order to become One, would have to heed Jean-Paul Sartre. Against the challenge raised by the first difficulty, the way proposed by the second loses any tint of crassness or egotism with which critics might seek to color it; if the solution is right, the circumstances surrounding its proposal are unimportant. Sartre's project can only be carried out if it is driven by the force of passion, and only the cynical can be unimpressed by a project so deeply committed to justice. Against the cynical, Sartre has sought support designed to remove his project from the realm of the visionary and to place it squarely in psychological and historical reality.

In the process, the first goal—individual human liberty—and the first difficulty—impediments to that liberty—are subjected to the Cartesian *cogito* and the consequent theory of consciousness; the second goal—universal human freedom—and the second difficulty—finding a unifying orientation for all human reality—is tied to the Marxist dialectic and the consequent assertion that human history is intelligible and the threats to its progress discernible. These fusions clearly solve some methodological problems, but they do not, in that particular bargain, justify the resulting method; while each fusion supplies a vocabulary for individual and group experience, the vocabularies are verified as exact only because they support the Sartrean project. What happens to them when they confront other vocabularies or, more critically, when they confront each other, is not always examined; frequently, when such a confrontation is examined, the consequence is either dismissed out of hand or else condemned as bad faith. Those other vocabularies cannot be allowed to jeopardize the only vocabularies which allow for the coexistence of reason and romance in a union so intimate as to defy efforts that aim at trying to determine which inspires which.[3] Romance wants existence to make sense, to have a purpose; reason wills the categories which permit this to happen. Yet it is quite possible that romance is born out of fright over what reason has initially seen and comes back, like Roquentin at the end of *La Nausée*, to invite reason to make music together with it in the hope that the harmony of their combination will be persuasive or sweet enough to tame savage instincts by driving them into disabling shame.

Since Sartre's project seeks a universal good and corresponds to what we think men mean when they speak of human welfare, it is perhaps wrong to carp over the methods chosen for its pursuit. The trouble is that

3. Iris Murdoch was probably the first to note this uneasy fusion of reason and romance in her brief and perceptive book, *Sartre, Romantic Rationalist* (New Haven, 1953).

the method carps with itself, producing contradictions which set loose both the internal and external tensions that attack Sartre's system. The most visible internal tension is the one that keeps forcing the system to collapse; the evidence against it is so strong that almost everyone ends in defeat—Oreste *and* Electre, Hoederer *and* Hugo, the Trojans *and* the Greeks, *all* the von Gerlachs. Each collapse, it is true, produces lessons, and the lessons produce a new impetus for the system to try again; but the tensions are still there. Despite them, the system tries again in the *Critique de la raison dialectique* where, if it cannot be said to collapse in the totalization-detotalization movement or the phenomenon of counter-finality—Sartre does of course try to show how it can be made to spring back—it does find itself under siege from other systems, that is, from the other vocabularies it has been seeking to destroy or at least hold at bay. A less visible internal tension (which points to another recuperative technique which may yet be brought into use) is the limited scope of the progressive-regressive method.[4] Though a late discovery on Sartre's part, it is applied neither across the board nor in full depth; rather its use seems to be limited to reinforcing once again the exactness of the system's two main props: Cartesianism and Marxism. The *cogito* remains authoritative because it asserts the kind of information Sartre needs to have about individual man; Marxism is *the* philosophy of our times because, as far as Sartre can see, Marxism is the only philosophy which resolves the dilemma of the individual—he is a free being who discovers his freedom in the midst of need. Were the method to be applied as exhaustively either to Descartes or to Marx it might come up with other results because it would have to ask *why* they arrived at their systems. This in turn might lead to the more basic question of why there have to be patterns, and the implication that what is more important than any one system is the existence of systems as a recurrent human phenomenon.

A man of Sartre's brilliance is not altogether unaware of such tensions. Yet, even as he glimpses them, he is involved in a rescue operation: the ego is destroyed and then replaced with the circuit of ipseity which does not appear to be essentially different from what others have meant by the ego. The ego against which he argues, like the bourgeoisie against which he fights, is not quite a figment of his imagination; yet ego and bourgeoisie are not quite the "realities" he asserts they are either, since, before they can be what he needs to have them be, they must be stripped of their density and made transparently contradictory or evil. The imagination and its world are anatomized and atomized for several hundred pages in his

4. In his critique of Sartre's use of the method, Lévi-Strauss makes a similar point; he stresses the value of using the method when such application is completely open and suggests that, for Sartre, the method is valuable principally because it supports and therefore seems to validate observations Sartre is determined to make even before he employs the method.

early works, sacrificed on the altar of consciousness, and then saved at
the end because they provide a perspective consciousness needs. The
implication is that one must use the imagination carefully or else it will
make one its victim. A reader, however, may feel that in discussing the
imagination Sartre is somewhat like Abraham's God who, if he saves
Isaac in the end, provides no consoling explanation of why he endangered
him in the first place. The emotions are subjected to an even more complete dissection; yet in later works love seems to be the only solution—
love arrived at reasonably or through an oath implicitly sworn in the
emotional heat and constraint of a crucial moment.

Man is presented as living in essential isolation in *Being and Nothingness* because of the Other and then encouraged in the *Critique de la
raison dialectique* to recognize that he can effect nothing truly beneficial
unless he works with the Other. A tentative conclusion suggests that
the glimpses have been taken and the tensions risked only because the
rescue operation was always part of the original purpose. What allows
for the risk is the conviction that reason will always be able to effect the
rescue; this leaves unanswered the question of whether reason can *justify*
the rescue.

Two forces in Sartre's make-up explain this kind of risk-rescue operation. One is a conviction that reason is a reliable tool; as it allowed Descartes to face nothingness and come up with consciousness, so it allows
Sartre to face the inconvenience of Descartes' God, to recognize that even
without God the system does not fall apart but produces anguish, and
then to reason about what to do with agnostic Cartesian man.[5] This is
where the second force plays an indispensable role. Sartre has acknowledged in *Les Mots* the deep hold that optimism has on him and has suggested that it is the one part of his bourgeois heritage he has never been
able to shake off. One might say that faith was the one element from his
background Descartes never shook off. The slate is never completely blank
nor can it be wiped completely clean. If God comes to support the Cartesian system because of a lasting affinity between Descartes and his
society's faith, it is not outlandish to say that Marx comes to support an
enduring affinity between Sartre's and his family's faith in progress. Once
again romance and reason revolve about each other, and it is difficult to
say which is the planet, which the satellite.

Since Sartre's reason is bound in optimism, it is not surprising that
optimism and reason should get involved in a relationship much like that
existing between reason and romance; optimism leads reason to believe

5. See "La Liberté cartésienne," (*Sit. I*, pp. 314–55). Sartre considers Descartes' God
to be the freest ever created by human thought, primarily because, in supporting the
total freedom of the *cogito*, he is an aid rather than a hindrance to man's recognition
of his inevitable liberty of choice.

that other men will accept reason's constructs because of the good results they promise. Cartesian man, despite what might have been more convincingly predicted about him, will agree to live in the Marxist world because that is the more reasonable thing to do. He will tailor his individuality, not merely to the point of accepting the rules and customs of his country, but also to the point of serving them and periodically revolting against them. In radical terms, the argument is not convincing, if only because Cartesian man might decide to go into exile; in reasonable terms, there may be no other argument available. Reason is what Sartre increasingly and almost poignantly invokes.

Once again he is aware of troubles, for some of his characters have reasoned well indeed and brought themselves and others to naught. If reason is everywhere equally valid, then justice is everywhere going to be unequally distributed—an unacceptable situation since the characteristic of reason in the Sartrean system is to produce progress rather than additional hurdles. Reason, as a result, is polarized into analytic reason, which is enlisted in the service of the practico-inert and history as servitude, and dialectical reason which marches in the company of praxis and history as freedom. The trouble with this, as Lévi-Strauss has pointed out in his lucid critique, is that, if analytic reason is dethroned, there is no faculty left to evaluate what dialectical reason is up to. We can understand what Sartre is fighting against here—the movement of analytic reason towards dogmatism and immobility; but we can also imagine, and perhaps may even be experiencing, the clash of two systems each of which claims to be dialectical and reasonable. Some norm must decide which of the two is really the open system; there again one stumbles, for we have seen presumably honest men opting for one against the other. Sartre opts for Marxism because Marxism is the tide of history and what is the tide of history is the philosophy of our period and what is the philosophy of our period is the genuine vehicle of dialectical reason. This, as I have pointed out, is reasoning on the basis of an a priori commitment. Sartre believes that the commitment is to a forward-moving pattern. What this means is that the forward movement must be described in such a way as to justify the reasoning process; to accomplish this justification becomes his special task. In the end, as in the beginning, the method is all and everything hinges on it. Does it work?

It is at least partially impeded by certain of Sartre's own hedgings. At various points in his career, and most notably in *Qu'est-ce que la littérature?*, Sartre has dealt with the question of what literary engagement means, in other words with the question of what writing is for. While in *Les Mots* he reduces considerably the importance formerly accorded to the writer by making his labors no more than part of the common task, he appears to have remained committed to his original belief that one cannot write without a public and without a myth—without a *certain* public which historical circumstances have formed, without a *certain* myth of literature which depends, in very large measure, on the demands of that public. In a word, the author is situated like every other man (p. 188).

Sartre's public, the bourgeoisie, is a public he will write against in the *interests* of another public, the proletariat, by which he does not expect to be read.[6] The myth he will serve is that of literature as a dialectical experience which involves the freedom of the writer as well as that of the reader but which has been too often basely used by writers who have written in order to confirm the readers' preconceived notions or else to give readers the kind of titillation that does not undermine the status quo so much as it enhances the author's sales and thus bolsters his ego. What Sartre's books seek is to elicit the reader's freedom by providing situations the reader can recognize as clearly akin to his own. This was his expressed hope with Hugo.[7] Involved with this design, however, was a certain number of beliefs—the decline of the bourgeoisie and the rise of the proletariat; the end of capitalism and the triumph of Marxism—which encouraged the defense of his myth against all others and which therefore risked isolating it from the kind of density other observers were to find in reality. In the beginning, when reform was his goal, loaded or prejudiced descriptions could be said to serve a tactical purpose. When, however, reform is subsumed in the desire to elaborate a global system, there can be some hesitation on the part of other honest men as to whether the system is an outgrowth of the myth and the tactical compromises that have gone into its establishment or whether all the tactical devices have really been done away with in the interests of making a genuinely fresh start. In short, the question is whether the method is based on observation or whether all observation has been sifted through the commitment and its special structures of belief.

The kinds of effort which are involved in fighting for a cause and in establishing a key to universal human history are conceivably quite dif-

6. In *Litt.* Sartre had written with enthusiasm about the promise mass media held for the intellectual in his efforts to contact and influence a broad, nonbourgeois public. In the years immediately after the war he did allow several films to be made of his works and wrote scenarios himself. In 1967 he returned to this activity, writing the scenario for a filmed version of "Le Mur."

7. He told Jeanson: "First of all, I was hoping that a certain number of young people of bourgeois background who had been my students or my friends, and who had just turned twenty-five, might find something of themselves in Hugo's hesitations. Hugo was never an especially sympathetic character for me and I never thought that he was right and Hoederer wrong. But I wanted to depict in him the torments of certain youths who, despite an indignation very much like that of the Communists, could not manage to join the party because of the liberal culture they had received" (*Sartre par lui-même*, p. 49).

ferent. If, as an essential part of his orientation, the writer has put himself squarely on one side, a reader may feel he must in turn do some sifting of his own. It is true that in the *Critique de la raison dialectique* Sartre adopts ideas and incorporates material that he has formerly discounted or paid little attention to; but there is the possibility that this material is more shaped by the practico-inert of his already formulated attitudes than that his mind is shaped by the new material. Actually, it seems to be a draw.

Belief in the conclusions produced by the method is further impeded by internal information provided by the method; structurally, the information is not different from that inherent in the dialectic itself where synthesis, whatever its accomplishments, produces dissolution of some former synthesis, and simultaneously threatens to slip into the practico-inert. The phenomenon of dissolution has been the steadiest gauge of the vitality of Sartre's thought where proposed solutions turn out to be only momentary responses; they are inadequate either in themselves or else when they are measured against the demands of new situations. Oreste yields to Hugo-Hoederer, Hugo-Hoederer yields to Goetz, Goetz yields to Frantz, and, in a way, Frantz and the rest are absorbed into the conflict of massed forces described in *Les Troyennes* where the individual's role is to protest as he awaits the next cataclysm. The dialectic rationalizes this process by making it the substance of history; when it becomes the Marxist dialectic it surrounds the process with hope by promising, if not Utopia, at least something better than the present circumstances. At the point when he embraces Marxism, Sartre's honesty and impatience involve him in what appears to be a contradictory program: the acceptance, despite some discouraging information, of Marxism as the dialectical force which will not dissolve and which can avoid the practico-inert. Marxism's escape is not miraculous; it is willed.

It must be willed because otherwise it could not happen. Yet one is not quite sure what this Marxism is or where it is to be found. It is not an independent force in history so much as it is a sense derived from the study of several forces in history; paradoxically, it is a sense which survives the present actions of men. Though it is said to be stalled at the present moment, to be at rest, and as a result must be got moving again by the mediation of existentialism, the presumption is that it has lost neither its privileged position nor its force as a result of being absent from history awhile. A number of questions can be raised here. If it is stalled, why? During the period it has been stalled, what else has happened? What is the influence of "what else has happened" on Marxism? Can Marxism pretend to be coincident with the movement of history and yet be in the curious position of being stalled? Can it be allowed its special claims if it periodically goes away or is put on holiday by others and then comes back pretending that nothing of essential importance has transpired during its absence?

The answers provided by the *Critique de la raison dialectique* are not convincing because they are based on an unresolved paradox: there is a force, Marxism, which mysteriously guards itself against certain historical developments that seem to be undoing it from two sides—that of its friends and that of its foes. It holds this impregnable position because it expresses the deepest sense of history. What this appears to demonstrate is that Marxism is not history, but a way of looking at history. If it is to triumph, it must be fought for by those who wish to look at history in this way. The presupposition is that it will win, and that may explain much about the motivation of its faithful. Yet the fact of the fight indicates more than a struggle; it indicates the possibility of defeat.

Marxism becomes the ethical system Sartre has so long been looking for and which he expected to construct as the second panel of *Being and Nothingness*. He was discouraged from that project by two principal considerations. One had to do with doubts about the value of what ethical systems seek to establish:

> The ethical moment aims at eliminating itself on behalf of a calm plenitude. The contradiction of ethics is that it requires its own disappearance: ultimately, the prescriptions of the ethical will become social reflexes; the identity of Being and Good, which existed at the starting point and which one finds again at the finish, will entail the disappearance of values. Virtue is the death of conscience because it is the habit of good, and yet the ethic of the honest man infinitely prefers virtue to the noblest agonies of conscience (*Saint Genet*, p. 371).

The other has to do with the impossibility of living an ethical *moment* in the continuum of time where events are unpredictable:

> Any ethic which does not explicitly profess that it is *impossible today* contributes to the bamboozling and alienation of man. The ethical "problem" arises from the fact that Ethics is *for us* inevitable and at the same time impossible. Action must give itself ethical norms in this climate of nontranscendable impossibility. It is from this outlook that, for example, we must view the problem of violence or that of the relationship between ends and means. To a mind that experienced this agony and that was at the same time forced to will and decide, all high-minded rebellions, all outcries of refusal, all virtuous indignation would seem a kind of outworn rhetoric (*Saint Genet*, p. 186).[8]

8. Simone de Beauvoir writes that, at the time he was working on *SG*, Sartre was

Marxism seems to resolve these hesitations because, posited as a force which is the dynamism of history, it avoids being static; yet, because it provides a way of commenting on events and because it sets a goal—which will be achieved—it answers man's need for ethical guidelines. Furthermore, it seems to provide an answer to the dilemma which earlier perplexed both Sartre and Simone de Beauvoir and which inspired her book on ethics: any program undertaken to help man will hurt, rightly or wrongly, some men.[9] Since Marxism proposes to hurt only those who are opposed to other men's enjoyment of their rightful freedom, the reason for its acceptability as an ethic is clear. But if today its practitioners have made it into a political dogma, what guarantee is there that Marxism is any different from any other ethical system? Sartre had condemned Christian ethics because they had unrealizable ambitions and because the difference between the proclaimed ethical standard and the lived reality was the home of scandal. Yet he acknowledges that the practitioners of communism have also dwelt too much in scandal's home. What this infers is that they have strayed from Marxism, pure and undefiled, and must be brought back. Christian reformers also spoke of a Christianity pure and undefiled to which they wished to lure back the sheep who had gone astray. Christian reformers also provided the same kind of spectacle, in their mutual accusations about where Babylon's whore dwelt, as the Russians and Chinese offer in their assertions of where Lenin's spirit most purely breathes. The trouble is that Marxism offers no greater promise than Christianity did; it changes the vocabulary of the promise by offering heaven on earth—but not yet!—and then falls into the hands of men who have never needed God's angry judgment in order to make their existence hell.

A reader understands what Sartre is doing; what he finds initially perplexing is that a mind capable of such rigor and possessing such rare and fine intelligence falls into a system which looks so much like other systems and then defends the system instead of examining its resemblances with others and seeking whatever wisdom can be derived from such an

---

consciously abandoning all his personal thinking on ethics. She quotes an unpublished note of his which explains that this renuciation was brought about because "the moral attitude appears when technical and social conditions render positive conduct impossible. Morality is an ensemble of idealistic tricks which allows you to live through the condition imposed on you by the penury of resources and the gap in techniques" (*FC*, p. 218).

In an interview with Frédéric de Towarnicki (*L'Express*, 20 October, 1969), Martin Heidegger made similar comments: "Who today," he asked, "can allow himself to impose—and in the name of what authority—an ethic on the world? As soon as you get involved with that, philosophy gets sidetracked. I know whereof I speak. Philosophy resists being organized and thought is always partially solitude."

9. *Pour une morale de l'ambiguïté* (Paris, 1947). In her memoirs Mme de Beauvoir discusses this essay and calls it the worst of her books, the only one she wishes she had not written.

examination. The perplexity is at once reduced and intensified by the realization that Sartre has never completely lost his deep belief in something akin to the *tabula rasa*. As man comes into the world in order to negate the world, so the present comes out of the past in order to negate the past. What we learn from history—generally too late—are negative lessons, what *not* to do. The process of totalization, because it cannot achieve the totality sought, demands the manual for getting away from the resultant collapse and possible catastrophe, a guide to survival in a hostile and frustrating world. There are two intertwined implications in this: even as the history of the past generally provides bad information, the study of history yields a method by which we can escape.

That raises the fundamental question of whether escape is the answer, and brings us to consideration of the external tensions which pull at Sartre's system. These are the other vocabularies whose existence menaces the integrity of his vocabulary. The first to be rejected, long before he was evolving a system of his own, was idealism in all its manifestations. It was rejected because its tidy systems and consequent assurance of sense were looked upon as frauds designed to make men live a hoax as though it were reality. The second to be cast off was the heritage of empiricism; its methods, and especially its assertion of a core-self developing across a lifetime and serving as the reservoir of personal motivation, hindered the assertion of the radical freedom Sartre was offering as the definition of man. What Sartre would instinctively resist in neopositivism and other methodological or metalogical systems is the suggestion, radically contrary to his own way of seeing things, that man is a spectator in the world, concerned with observing, along with other men, what the world as a physical or social process is already doing; such philosophers are capable only of describing what has already happened. The other philosophical schools are, of course, aware of a broader reality, of other actions and of human involvement in them. But they seem to foment an atmosphere in which thought is concerned with how to describe and analyze what may happen and not with organizing and directing those future happenings. In terms of modern economics they seem most concerned with what to do with what they already have rather than with how to do away with it in order to install a more promising situation.

The third vocabulary to be thrown off, Freudianism, is probably the one from which Sartre has escaped least successfully. Initially, his objections to it were the same as his objections to empiricism; but his fear of it was much greater since it posited a core-self, the unconscious, not only in the individual but also in the race, whose existence severely curtailed the range of choice available to free men. Yet Freudianism has dogged all Sartre's intellectual footsteps; its terms have slipped into his vocabulary; its reality has seemed to be strongly buttressed by his own works. Hugo, for example, is a perfect Freudian prototype in whom id, ego, and super-ego wage constant war on a terrain between the life wish and the death wish. Finally, the Freudian technique and certain elements in the pro-gressive-regressive method could no longer be said to be distinct. The past, however condemnable it was, could no longer be overlooked in its role as a force so great as to seem to justify living according to its dictates.[10]

It remains, of course, a question of *seeming*, and Sartre continues to insist that under other circumstances, and even in therapy, what really happens is that the individual is awakened to his freedom, to his ability to break away from the hold the past has on him. What Sartre does not pay adequate attention to is the fact that in therapy the aim is to bring the patient to the point where he realizes that the past need not disempower him. The question of how the past has *empowered* him remains un-examined beyond Sartre's assertion that any power he has derived from it has been freely accepted, though sometimes under apparently irresistible pressures, with an eye to serving specific interests. That leaves open the issue of how much control the individual has over *choosing* what his interests are, and it also isolates the fundamental issue which separates Sartre from psychoanalytic theory and practice. Is man free in a deter-mined situation whose elements manipulate him before he can ever think of manipulating them, or is he potentially free to determine his essence by responding to his own actions and conceivably ridding himself of all manipulative influences and their heritage? [11]

10. The work-in-progress on Flaubert is an excellent example of the Sartrean failure to escape from Freud. It is full of terminology which, if it is not a pure reproduction of the Freudian vocabulary, is a perfect representation of Freudian thought. Sartre writes, for example: "In truth Gustave's pessimism is not the product of his history but of his *proto-history*: he appears, about the time he is eight, as a totalization, not of the cosmos, but of his family life and the consequences it has had on his charac-ter. . . . Thus Gustave is *made* but he is not made by a conscious experience; rather he is made by an ensemble of processes which preceded his experience and condi-tioned it" ("Flaubert: du poète à l'Artiste," *TM* 22 [1966]: 238).

11. In the introduction to her critical edition of *La Transcendance de l'Ego* (Paris, 1966), Sylvie Le Bon claims that Sartre has thoroughly revised his hesitations about the role of the unconscious (p. 8). I think this exaggerates the reduction in his re-sistance, for it strikes me that fundamentally he still refuses to accept the notion that men can be in any way determined—even if only by the limited range of possi-bilities available to them. Simone de Beauvoir gives a good example of the same kind of reluctance in her conversation with Francis Jeanson (*Simone de Beauvoir ou l'en-treprise de vivre*, see esp. pp. 257–62) when, accepting the reality of certain Freudian categories, she refuses "absolutely" to believe that particular psychic facts or tenden-cies or conditions are already implanted in the human being at the moment when con-sciousness begins to operate.

Sartre has been consistently upset by the apparent, and possibly abject, passivity of the patient undergoing psychoanalysis and has suggested that the process, as a process, demeans the patient by stripping him of his subjectivity and by making him an object for himself and the analyst. He elaborates this idea in the April, 1969, issue of *TM*; in the same issue J. B. Pontalis and Bernard Pingaud register strong dissents

As he rejects Freud because of Freud's steady postulate of a determinism which cannot easily be shaken off, so Sartre—and with even greater vigor and less argument—rejects arguments from evolution or biology which locate the source of human behavior in either men's genes or the marrow of their bones. While he accepts evolution as a description of physical development in prehistory, he does not admit that the evolutionary process has produced or still provokes any psychological carry-over. In a similar vein he has rejected the vocabularies of all structuralists who talk of man as operating in response to a system of potentialities and needs which set the limits of man's action. Sartre is under pressure here; in certain French intellectual circles today he is discussed as one who made a brave and admirable and unsuccessful try. Not only is he unwilling to admit defeat, he is also continuing to fight, and the second volume of the *Critique de la raison dialectique*, if it ever appears, will surely reflect his responses and perhaps indicate further concessions. In the interim, he has been basing his reaction on three tactics. One is to attack by suggesting that undertakings like Claude Lévi-Strauss's and Michel Foucault's are the last gasp of bourgeois idealism, a final effort to reach into science in order to come up with consoling systems which excuse man from responsibility. The second is to insist ever more strongly that man has reason and energy, that he can be made to see the problems which confront him and the dangers which threaten him, and that, as a result, he can be brought to use his reason to meet the tasks which still await him. The third is to suggest that structuralism's systems are irrelevant to today's problems.[12]

What Sartre fears is that structuralism's investigations, with their strong suggestion that man is determined within strict limits, will tie man unbreakably to despair. What the structuralists claim is that Sartre's system is simply another expression of the reality they are describing; it is, however, a defective expression since it insists on denying the existence of an important element in that reality; it is a myth which, refusing to admit its mythic nature, claims it has brought an end to myths. What has not emerged clearly in this controversy is the structuralists' belief that man, as they describe him, is a good bit more capable of solving his problems than is Sartrean man. The human reality they describe is not one into

about Sartre's views, Pontalis insisting that Sartre misunderstands and has always misunderstood everything about psychoanalysis.

12. As they were irrelevant to Flaubert who, according to Sartre, thought erroneously that language organized itself within him according to its own rules; it thus was accused of stealing his thought and subjecting him to the empire of commonplace ideas: "Flaubert does not believe that *one speaks; one is spoken*" ("La Conscience de classe chez Flaubert," *TM* 21 [1966]: 2125). Later in the same essay, Sartre comments: "The truth is that he 'has no ideas' and that he is aware of it. In other terms, he has not the means of distinguishing between thought, as a synthetic and constructive activity, and language . . ." (p. 2140).

which man comes forlorn, unequipped, and puzzled; it is a system which endows him with the functions by which he can manage both his life and the system. Some structuralists insist that man need not live by a metaphysic of either/or when naturally he is capable of living with both/and. Finally, the structuralists claim that any applicable system must explain *why* polarizations occur and seek to demonstrate that man need not try to eliminate them but learn to live with them as with instrumental values.

Sartre's resistance to the vocabularies of other systems amounts in the long run to a resistance to the vocabulary of reality. In an early, not altogether reliable essay, "Sartre ou la duplicité de l'Etre" (in *Les Sandales d'Empédocle*), Claude-Edmonde Magny suggested that Sartre's description of the world allowed for a single response—one had to cheat. The cheating, however, could be expressed in two modes; if the world was discovered as too fearful and overpowering in its insistences, one could retreat from it; if it was seen as a challenge to be met endlessly with all the resourcefulness at one's disposal, then one cheated honestly because one was trying to impose sense on something that made no sense. Mme Magny's distinction is a succinct way of explaining Sartre's notion of man as one who intervenes in the world in such a way as to create a radical separation between himself and nature. Human culture is man's answer to and defiance of nature; its existence places man in an endlessly hostile relationship to nature. He cheats it by refusing to be like it. Once man is consciously part of human culture, he comes across those other oppositions we have seen in this book and, if he is a philosopher, finds that what may have been an adequate answer in nature is not an answer to other voices and other philosophies produced within human culture.

Sartre's reaction to these other voices has been to ignore them or oppose them; where he has paid attention to them, he has incorporated them because of the uses they can serve in the management of his system. Since that system wants to be concerned with *all* of human reality, it is not unreasonable to expect that all of human reality should be heard, if not out of respect for what is being said, at least with attention to the possible ramifications of statements made by other voices. While there is something admirable and a little frightening in seeing an individual taking on the whole world with the ambition of delivering it up whole and redeemed, there is something unsettling about the operation. One wants to know a little more about who the individual is; one feels the need to examine very closely the process by which redemption is taking place; and one wonders, with some regret, whether in the end it is the kind of operation which can be performed by one individual. One wonders about the last because other similar efforts in the past have produced results which explained a good deal more about why they had been produced than about the world. What we must now examine is the encounter between Sartre and reality.

In the first years of Sartre's fame, his critics liked to attack his fondness for cafés; the implications of the attack were meant to evoke bistros darkened to hide darker doings. The suggestion was that if only Sartre would get out of cafés he would surely cheer up and issue brighter utterances. Cafés abandoned for households do not, I think, lead to instant remedies for pessimism, and many a café exists as a remedy against pessimism caught in households. The significant thing is that the café, whether in Saint Germain-des-Prés or in the northern slums of Paris, is not a very good place for seeking remedies to the problems of reality or even for seeing reality clearly. There is too much of the café about Sartre's work. For all its generous intentions and its willingness to correct itself under pressure, for all its deep commitment to man and his feckless world, Sartre's work is strangely devoid of the key elements of life. It deals with an adult world in which children appear rarely and then generally only to indicate how their childhood has produced ruined adults.[13] In both the philosophical and literary works, it is a world of adults who have no intimate commitment to each other and who are not tied down by family responsibilities; the family as a unit is ignored, and when it appears it is in the background as that which has been abandoned either by young men in rebellion or by men who have gone off to fight for causes. Most of its inhabitants have been set loose without cause or explanation to roam over the reader's mind and imagination much as Sartrean man wandered, without cause and in search of inauthentic explanations, across the dry wastes of *Being and Nothingness*. Their experience is of a world where neither blood nor friendship creates a bond strong enough to resist or explain intellectual disquietude.

Simone de Beauvoir, answering criticism that she had had no children, makes a strange confusion. She has every right to reply that the reason why she has no children is no one's business. When she replies that her books are her children—or what she has chosen to produce instead of children— she expresses the confusion of this Sartrean world and, interestingly enough, its defensiveness. There is no relationship at all between bearing children and writing books, except perhaps a negative one: people who have a lot

---

13. In the *CRD* Sartre addresses this very criticism to the Communist apparatus, which he accuses of dealing with men as if they had only an adulthood and no childhood. One of the principal purposes of the progressive-regressive method, and thus the contribution existentialism will make to universal human improvement, is to remind Communists as well as others of the need for total understanding of all the forces which go into the formation of an individual, orient his understanding of the future, and indicate both his problems and potentialities. Childhood, of course, must receive detailed attention; but, as I shall point out, even in this scheme, it is generally considered as the period when bad things happened.

of children may not write many books, and may not have many causes; they may be too deeply involved in a reality others' books will help them to illumine. I am not trying to suggest that what we need is a literature about jolly families; nor am I saying that Sartre's or Beauvoir's books are bad books because they are on the whole devoid of family life as part of human experience.[14] What I am saying is that their books, which seek to make global statements about reality, make those statements on the basis of a reality which is partial in both senses of the word. These books show only a part of human reality and illuminate that part under a very partisan light; they then presume that the part revealed is either reality itself or its only worthwhile sample.

Behind this view is the not uncommon human attitude which asserts that the world only makes sense in terms of my experience of it. Such an outlook can produce a number of reactions. A man can decide that, the world being a large and complex place, his experience of it may need to be broadened; or he can decide, as Roquentin did at the end of *La Nausée*, that the world needs to learn that his interpretation is the true one, even if the world, as a result of the lesson, must accept living in shame. The latter has been Sartre's attitude, and the only significant change it seems to have undergone was his decision, which Simone de Beauvoir writes about, to accept the age of reason and to communicate with the world. There is a peculiar kind of arrogance in such an attitude, the arrogance of café disputes, or of *The Magic Mountain*, where individuals heatedly and mercilessly discuss the meaning and the inadequacy of others' actions while the world heads towards cataclysm and while the young Hans Castorp looks on and listens and has the right to believe that there is no point in wishing further curses on houses already abundantly plagued. This was the attitude of Sartre and Beauvoir in the 1930s; they had the right thoughts and wrong convictions, wrong because they presupposed that the world either would not listen to their thoughts or else could not be redeemed. They cherished and developed their thoughts and let the world go its way; Mathieu in *Les Chemins de la liberté* is their portrait. He does not vote, he does not act, he exerts no leverage on the world; like Martial, his thoughts are pure despite his deeds.

When these two are born late, not into reason, but into reality, they already have the habits reason has inculcated in them. Once they agree to

14. In *Les Belles Images* (1966), Mme de Beauvoir has turned away from her usual kind of café society in order to deal with society's *cafard*. Her book tries to present a cross section of bourgeois society and specifically deals with the question of raising children in a society whose plenty is still not enough for those who benefit from it. Mme de Beauvoir's bourgeois do not escape, however, from her a priori ire with their very existence, with the result that the book is full of her categories. Those categories yield a very dim portrait indeed. All is dismal, dull, and desultory; there is no hope, and the book's heroine at the end is fighting she knows not whom in order to achieve she knows not what.

influence their times, their agreement is based on an attitude which is rather
schoolmarmish: they will teach the truth, and their students, wanting to be
free, will listen and obey. Rebels will be treated as renegades. The world,
which had earlier stood condemned because it was beyond their ken or
control, later stands condemned to the extent that it does not listen to them.
Any world which refuses to listen to voices proposing change is deaf to its
own peril, and questions like "Where were you when. . . ?" express an
understandable petulance and frustration without producing reform. But
a world interested in change or, more pertinently, a world which cannot
avoid change, can reasonably ask that change which seeks to be global
in scope should also be global in understanding. The world has its habits,
too.

And the meeting of its habits and theirs—Sartre's and Beauvoir's—
can produce only two possible results: compromise or conflict. If the world
announces that it is glad to have them aboard, Sartre and Mme de Beauvoir
reply that the world is lucky they have decided to come on ship. And then
they immediately set about showing how the ship should be run. The new
reality continues to astonish and anger them. It astonishes them because
it has held onto so many of the attitudes they know are wrong; it angers
them because it is slow to take the tack they have outlined. It wants
compromise when they want conflict. Condemnations and astonishment
proliferate because those who seek to reform reality cannot tolerate any
recalcitrance on reality's part. Nor can they conceive of any reason why
the recalcitrance should be examined, until the obduracy of this recalcitrance forces them to try to understand the basis of its resistance.

I have already written about Sartre's and Mme de Beauvoir's troubles in
understanding what they have not experienced or of seeing benefits to be
derived from experience different from theirs. When in her memoirs or
in her novels, Mme de Beauvoir writes about the emotionally troubled,
there is a chilling tone in her approach which is not distinguishable from
impatience, a conviction on her part that such people need only to pull
themselves together; yet in *Les Mandarins* and in her memoirs she gives
a vivid portrait of the emotional disarray of the woman abandoned by her
lover. The field of *her* experiences must be ploughed over and over again;
the field of others' experience is declared fallow and not ploughed at all
until it somehow slips into her possession.

Similarly Sartre, writing about those he admires—Merleau-Ponty and
Nizan—expresses wonder about the importance they accord to certain
values they experienced in childhood. He does not quite approve, yet he
certainly does not disapprove; he seems to be astonished. Underpinning his
astonishment is his incredulity that anything good might come out of a
class, the bourgeoisie, which he has condemned in all its manifestations.
There is a very strange confusion here which suggests that human reality

somehow has no common bond but only common anguish, and that the experience of the bourgeois youth reflects no value whatsoever. These are all attitudes which subsequently have to be adjusted because reality offers neither sense nor hope unless adjustment is made. But where there is change—as in his description of love or his acceptance of the truth of certain psychological categories—it is announced more as a new invention than as a late discovery.

Other realities enter Sartre's thought only by the side door; the main door is most often kept closed. It is opened only when the time has come to expel someone in one of those depressing operations where certitude feels compelled to drive complexity away. The exclusions are doubly depressing. Intellectually, they are full of risk in their presumption that certitude always knows it is right. On a personal level, they are gloomy in their vitriolic condemnations of those to whom hospitality is being denied. Sartre and Mme de Beauvoir, when they cease to agree with people, also begin to dislike them and place the blame for the eventual rupture on those others. Camus, whose growing commitment to extracting some sense and a little truth from *all* human experience perhaps best revealed the troubles of this era, is denigrated and insulted and denied his own reality in a curious formula devised, not because it yields sense, but because it produces insult. He is told that he cannot, despite his origins, understand the worker because he has become a bourgeois. There are no two-way streets. Hugo could not sympathize with the worker in any continuous way because Hugo was born into the bourgeoisie; Camus cannot identify with the worker because Camus has been assigned to the bourgeoisie by Sartre. Throughout the process, the unique pertinence of Sartre's thought to the world's realities is asserted. The procession of the banished is long, and its banner—which is carried involuntarily—is always bad faith as determined by Sartre. This leads to personal and intellectual contradictions. Communist journalists and ideologists are condemned because they do not think freely; Aron and Merleau-Ponty are castigated or excluded because they do not think correctly. Retribution comes later, so that when Merleau-Ponty and Camus are dead, they are found to have rendered services which can now be incorporated into the evolving system.

What this means is that all other marketplaces stand condemned because they are *other* marketplaces. At the least, that is an ironic counterpoint to a philosophy which is firmly rooted in investigation of the phenomenon of the Other; at the most, it means that the phenomenon of Otherness is so essentially a part of Sartre's apprehension of experience as to have bound him to a habit of thought which cannot be open-ended. In seeking to affirm constantly an ontological contiguity between his way of seeing the world and the way the world is and must be, he is possibly and unconsciously seeking to neutralize the Other either by incorporating him or else by

excluding him and then immediately insisting that his exclusion demands
that he be destroyed. Ultimately violence is tolerated because the ex-
clusivity of the system demands it, the habits brought to maintaining
the system require it, and the development of the system has come to make
the system seem the way of the world. Love may evolve to a point where,
in its acceptance of compromise, it becomes possible; need can evolve
out of hostility and into the oath; but both bonds—that of love and that
of the oath—are forged with the intention of destroying the Other whose
existence has led to their enunciation. The end of Otherness comes only
when the recalcitrant Other has been destroyed by violence.

Nothing in human history or in Sartre's system justifies entertaining this
hope. Violence in history, as Raymond Aron has pointed out, comes about
precisely because states meet as individuals who look hostilely at each
other and depend upon the possibility of violence as one of the options
available to them; the destruction of the Other state is an instrument of
policy and not the spontaneous offshoot of despair. Nothing in Sartre's
system allows us to believe, purely within the terms of the system, that the
proletariat's triumph will tranquilize all the psychological disquietudes
described in *Being and Nothingness;* nor is there much consolation to be
drawn from a system which, maintaining itself through vitriolic condemnations of other systems, must presuppose that, with the proletariat's
triumph, will come an end to all other systems and that no voice will be
raised, no Sartre will emerge, to suggest that things might perhaps be better
if they were done in another way.

Trotsky was aware of this problem, but he was aware of it in a somewhat
different way. He knew quite as much about fundamental human psychology as Sartre and realized that a uniform system would not necessarily
respond appropriately to the human desire for individual enterprise and
initiative. He spoke of the need to create incentives and rewards for those
who served the state or the community well.[15] While that answers one part
of the difficulty, it avoids the other, more serious part: the attitude of those
who do not receive rewards and are not the object of emulation for their
peers. The range of human need is so vast and its manifestations so unpredictable that we cannot yet be confident that a system, like the one outlined in the *Critique de la raison dialectique,* represents a full answer.

The scarcity and corresponding need which Sartre discusses in that book

15. In *Terrorisme et Communisme* Trotsky writes: "Emulation rests on a vital instinct—the struggle for existence—which, under a bourgeois regime, is covered over with
a competitive character. . . . [In a socialist society] it will be translated by a tendency to render the greatest possible service to the village, the district, the city, and
the whole society in order to be rewarded by popularity, public recognition, understanding . . . by the inner satisfaction which comes from the feeling of a task well
done. But in the difficult period of transition . . . emulation must fatally be attached
in some measure to the desire to acquire objects for personal use" (pp. 225–26).

are powerful intellectual concepts identifying real and fundamental human situations. Whether ideology is the answer to the poverties scarcity creates is quite another question since ideology can play on needs without satisfying them; frequently the extent to which it plays on them is the measure of its incapacity to do much about them. Sartre in certain of his analyses—of religious belief, for example—has recognized this incapacity and condemned it. In his anatomy of the bourgeois mentality he has seen that some classes have satisfied the needs of their members but he has immediately condemned them, too, by writing an equation which reads: satisfaction here = sacrifice there. In his works this translates to read: no middle class without pariahs. In the reader's mind it also translates into: no victory anywhere without corresponding defeat somewhere else.

This implies that the struggle is endless, with violence necessarily breeding more violence because it is the only instrument by which absolutism can be established on this earth. And Sartre's system seeks an absolute in the sense that it denies the possibility of incorporation without destruction. The bourgeoisie, as the quotation at the beginning of this chapter shows, must die; capitalism must be done away with. Mediation, the idea which is the key to redemption in Sartre's system, because it aims at preserving the possibility of individual intervention and therefore initiative, does not produce the ultimate synthesis through compromise but through violence. Workers *must* learn to compromise in order to cooperate with each other. Marxism can *never* compromise if such compromise were to defile its purity or demean its goal. In the end one question remains to haunt the whole system. To what extent does the method by which it has been created contain, organically, its future difficulties?

Individually inspired, individually maintained, the system is full of quirks which, even as they fight against determinism, allow the individual who has initiated the system to determine who are the good men and who are the bad, which are the promising forces and which the despicable, what rides the tide of the future and what does not. The system wants to be firmly rooted in reality and yet keeps having to adjust reality to the goal the system has set for itself. Individuals are told that their finest function is in contributing their individuality to the service of the group even as they are being warned of what happens to individuals within groups and what happens to groups because of what they do to individuals. This is what mankind is and yet it isn't what mankind is because the individual is always able to break out of the group. How much of the habits and techniques of the group remains when he severs his relationship to it is not explored in depth which means, in terms of the present argument, that not enough attention is paid to how one does away with violence when violence not only is allowed to breed violence but made responsible for the violence it breeds. One can admit this; one can see, for example, all the justifying reasons behind the belief that only violence will produce the reforms demanded by logic, reason, and justice. One does not for that lose the hope that somewhere and somehow the vicious circle of violence must be broken. Nor does one lose the belief that when the earth's pariahs engage in violence they are not so much resorting to it as an acceptable tactic as giving way to despair.

Programmed violence, it strikes me, is a phenomenon of the bourgeois or educated mind; it fascinates the intellectual for reasons which are not altogether discernible but which may have to do with its purity, its suggestion of ideals bought at the price of blood and therefore marked as being of great value, its expression of impatience with law and order because law and order are unexciting and because at times they are a shibboleth used by those who want to keep the disadvantaged in their places. Finally, one hopes that intelligent men will recognize that law and order must exist, not to keep the disadvantaged in their places, but to punish and exclude those who are responsible for their disadvantages and the ensuing despair.

What the violent carry away with victory in Sartre's work is the sure promise that a heritage of violence has been left behind if only because, in a world divided into frozen categories, violence is the only tactic left. The world, as I have tried to show at various points in this book, does not operate in such tidy ways; Sartre's efforts to insist that it does, help nothing, least of all his system. In a paradoxical way, the complexity of his system emerges from a refusal of complexity; war does not allow for fine distinctions and Sartre is at war; yet war, to be maintained, demands some complex strategy and maneuvers. But if we believe that war is failure, then we must assert that reasonable men who elect war as a tactic are bound both to befog reason and assure the continued use of war as an acceptable option. They are also likely, despite the idealism behind their motivation, to do rather a lot of damage.[16]

16. One of the less menacing dangers is the risk of being accused of not having done enough in the way of terror and violence. In a marvelously insane article in *L'Arc* (30, 1966), Pierre Trotignon accuses Sartre of just that and writes: "That unity of literature and philosophy which Sartre maintained with a flourish is something we must destroy. On the one hand, philosophy, abandoning its flirtation with novelists and poets, will find once more its pure theoretical intention; and, on the other hand, political involvement will no longer rise out of the art of words because the society in which we live is condemned to refuse more and more savagely to listen to reason, thereby driving us slowly but surely to the necessity of pure violence because nothing besides terror will force the bourgeoisie to withdraw. This will doubtless be political violence, but it will be intellectual violence, too, for the ideal of pure philosophical theory—make no mistake about it—is not a humanistic and delicate love but the will to know, the will to understand, the will to oppose the nothingness of the poets with the inflexible rigor of the true which is, as Plato clearly saw, a form of violence. . . . if we are taking another path than [Sartre's], it will be in order to go and kill our tyrants who are his, too" (p. 32).

Though refused, or perhaps because refused, reality's complexity keeps coming back to box Sartre in. We have already seen one example in his uneasiness with Freudianism. Other examples are not lacking to indicate that the method he falls into in the *Critique*—his insistence on the need to understand before condemning—may result from a growing awareness that such understanding has not only been lacking in the Communists but also in himself. The slowness to understand and the haste to condemn (or, in some cases, to defend what others are condemning) have placed Sartre too frequently in a situation where the outcome in no way corresponded to his predictions or where his conditions seemed to allow for no outcome at all.[17] His anticolonialism has been frequently invoked, because of its steadiness and its universal application, as one of the finest and most justified of his causes; it has also been a buttress to his own theory of freedom since he has seen in the colonial uprisings examples of men taking a liberty which, because it is theirs as men, cannot be given to them. Yet the aftermath of independence, with all its forlorn histories of military coups and re-emerged tribal hostilities, raises questions which are not answered by the monotonous insistence that these, too, are the fault of the colonizers. His opposition to the Marshall Plan, based on his conviction that it was a cover device for an American takeover of Europe, raises the question of whether any promise of human betterment is to be repudiated if it comes with the slightest hint of being proposed for ulterior reasons or if it affects only one part of humanity.

The past may explain the present and the future may salvage it, but in our time and in our space the present has its own complexities which cannot be dealt with simply by invoking the past as the source of all blame and the future as the distant time and remote place in which everything will be set aright. The blight of contradictions which falls on Sartre's position because of the Arab-Israeli conflict is an example of what happens when complexity has been shunned, for he finds himself in a position where all the wires he would like to have straightened out and clearly labeled according to the dangers of their voltage are crossed; the system, paralyzed, risks being obliterated by a massive short-circuit. Each gain burns away and the losses multiply.

An American commentator touches only gingerly on the most striking

17. I have already written about his attitude towards DeGaulle's handling of the Algerian situation, an attitude which was couched in the prediction that certain nefarious results were bound to come to pass; they did not. His rejection of the Nobel Prize, with his derogatory remarks about the earlier award of the prize to Boris Pasternak, is another important example of Sartre's making a serious mistake by trying to do just the opposite. Russian intellectuals, who had been seeking the kind of freedom to criticize that Sartre has always valued so highly in his personal life, were appalled to see Pasternak, who had become an ideal for them, so casually treated and their own cause so badly understood by one they had counted on for greater and more perceptive support.

example of Sartre's refusal to take the world as it is. This is his insistence that the United States is irrelevant to the direction in which the world is moving, primarily, I gather, because what it is is not what the world will be. What stands out in Sartre's references to the United States is not the vitriol of his remarks or the generally offhand way in which he treats the country; what stands out is how little he understands about it or has ever understood about it. To say that he does not understand it, is not an academician's way of regretting that Sartre doesn't love the United States enough or appreciate it properly, nor is it the chauvinist's method of re- pulsing critics by condescending to them. Rather it is to suggest that, to his peril and that of the world, Sartre has refused to consider the possibility that the messages being written on the wall of the future may be in the language of "Americanization" rather than in that of Marxism.

One could assent to every one of Sartre's criticisms about the United States—though some inner voice might insist on pointing out that New York's skyscrapers may be more the result of land shortage than of hu- bris—and still feel that condemnation will neither alter the course the United States is taking nor advance Sartre's cause. Here is Sartre's anti- natural force at its acme which may only mean here is human culture run cancerously rampant: a country rich beyond the expectations and imagin- ings and perhaps the understanding of men; bound, because of its wealth and all the by-products of that wealth, to mold the destiny of the world no matter what it does, because such wealth brings power. No matter how that power is displayed, it is bound to create competition and fear. As com- petition decreases because of American technological power, the fear of becoming economic colonies increases in the other nations of the industrial world. The vision one gets of the United States from abroad is indeed awe- some and frightening—a great spastic octopus stretching its tentacles relentlessly, indefatigibly, and almost instinctively in every direction, clawing at what it cannot control, destroying what it cannot devour.

To say that this mammoth—or monster, if one prefers—has come about by exploiting the poor is to simplify history; to say that it will choke and die on its own social paroxysms is to overestimate its vulnerabilities, underestimate the resilience of its institutions, and misestimate the relation- ship between social challenge and national energies. To say it will not pro- duce the kind of life we may want men to have is to begin raising the essential questions. Such questions need detached discussion rather than polemics. That discussion needs to pay serious attention to the fact that, as America becomes bigger and bigger, individual liberty receives greater and greater protection from the courts—those courts which may be America's most magnificent institution and whose functioning as social forces receives little attention in Europe. Still, one can assert, dreading the prospect, that life as it is lived in America is life as it is going to be lived increasingly in the future and conclude, not that the world must fall in line, but only that American reality must be dealt with rather than dismissed. It is not likely that Russia can follow a different path and, as a result, we verge on living in an era whose rich will sacrifice ideologies for economic realities—as both Russians and Americans have partially done already—and whose poor will seek hope in ideologies they cannot afford to defend.

As the gap between the rich and the poor grows, and as wealth produces military and economic arsenals with which to control or annihilate the unruly, the era of dialectics enters a new period where the rich and the poor are so frighteningly far apart as to make it doubtful that any "natural" or historical movement will of itself produce a synthesis. The task then becomes one of seeing how one develops a conscience in the rich about their responsibilities to the poor rather than that of plotting a collision course for them. Whatever god is served by the collision is not one who will do much for the poor. Sartre, of course, does not urge conflagration, but he is unhappy with coexistence and anticipates collision. From that unhappiness one can only infer that coexistence must in some way imperil Marxism's triumph and therefore delay the moment when the bourgeoisie will become the holocaust it merits being. Against the risks involved in the pursuit of this triumph and that sacrifice one can only hope that compromise will intervene.

Compromise, as he asserted in his essay on Merleau-Ponty, has long ceased to be an indispensable part of Sartre's strategy. It is too often a hoax word by which the advantaged cheat the disadvantaged, all the while telling them that it is better that things be not so good relatively than that they be absolutely bad. It is one of the methods whereby outer-direction is achieved and the status quo maintained; it is therefore the practico-inert transformed into a virtue, and we have seen what Sartre thinks of virtue. Compromise, when the Communists begin to use it, also smacks of promises unmet. Sartre expects such failure from bourgeois society because it has a long history of promises broken in the name of higher and vague ideals. Compromise risks being the rationale of exploitation and, if Communists and capitalists sit down together, some third party will be deprived of the rights Marxism should guarantee to him. The Cuban missile situation and the compromise arising out of it is an example of this; when one is eyeball to eyeball, peripheral vision, which should be concerned with the interests of other parties, is severely curtailed.

Others, to be sure, might point out that there is a profit column in the ledger of compromise. In the long run it seems to do less harm, produce less violence, and cause less unhappiness. Men do not as a result get all they want immediately; but they seem to get it faster and at less human cost than when they resort to intransigent demands. It is also possible that the process works because man is essentially a compromise; as long as he can make judgments and decisions he is able to follow a comparatively peaceful existence. It is when this equipment fails him in his personal life, as when it fails nations in their dealings with each other, that negotiations become impossible and men and nations are plunged into the wars which they keep insisting are uncharacteristic of them. Sartre has recognized, in his analysis of the individual's affiliation with the group, that some forms of action cannot take place unless there is compromise, unless the individual, quieting his own individualism, enlists in the service of the group. But, as I have said earlier, the group in the *Critique* seems always to be formed *against* something; not enough attention is paid either to the coexistence of groups or to what they work for.

The passenger committee which seeks better bus service does not consider the destruction of the bus company as a desirable goal since it instinctively senses that such a goal would destroy the problem of bad service by destroying the possibility of any service. The structure and discipline of the football team does more than explain how the individual player operates freely within the organization. There would be no team if there were not other teams; and the teams are not set on each other's destruction but on keen competition with, hopefully, a bearable distribution of victories and defeats. It seems imperative to hope that East and West can be made to see that the world cannot live by destroying tensions in the name of ideology; both sides must, as Konrad Lorenz has movingly pointed out, seek the means for resolving tensions by allowing them to be worked out in nondestructive ways. The Other can be a source of challenge rather than fear. What humanity needs are structures which preserve the challenge and allow it outlets which are not ruinously destructive.

Reform, when it replaces compromise with ardor, begins to use a vocabulary which distorts further the already unseemly face of reality. This happens, I imagine, because reform tends to be undertaken in the name of abstractions which have little to do with recognizable reality. The traditional Christian approach to marriage, based on Pauline neuroses, invoked nature in order to urge men to live as nature had not created them. Those of the church's theologians who are diabetics do not hesitate to take insulin even as they condemn contraceptive devices as interruptions of natural processes; Paul Goodman urges educational reforms based on the model of a medieval university whose realities have very little to do with his images; the yippies urge an anarchy which, if it were realized, would change the essential nature of their habitual activities; the hippies preach a program of psychological release which displays every psychological distemper Freud has discussed in his essays on the unsophisticate's reaction to the pressures of maintaining human civilization.

The Sartrean description of man offers some of the same vagueness and confusion. There is a refrain in Sartre's polemical writings, readily adopted by some of his followers, which talks about the urgent task of making man possible. One understands what this wants to mean without being quite sure that what it says makes any sense or that the sense it makes alludes to anything desirable. Man already is. That the conditions of his material existence should be equalized and therefore, in the great majority of cases, improved, is a goal to which all sane men will ascribe. But that there is an object-goal "man" which we should set about creating, firm in the knowledge, first, that we know what we are doing and, second, that what we are doing will sensibly change the face of man is a mystical statement that is not readily evaluable unless what we are seeking is the brave new world which Sartre is the first to fear because of its sterility.

On this side of the brave new world man, as we know him, is a compromise; on the other side of the brave new world, he is compromised. In the conversation of cafés, he is an abstraction. As a compromise he is many things; as an abstraction he is expectably bloodless, possibly because Sartre's dedication to preserving individualism leads to the definition of a man who is curiously a-social. Even when he participates in group activity he lacks the social characteristics most men experience naturally. He does not have to do quite as much self-convincing as Sartre believes before joining a group, possibly because he finds himself already in a group, probably because he does not feel fully human outside the group. For man as man is many men and not an idea on a page or a cog in the machinery of history or a cause whose destiny is determined by intellectuals in the *Café des Deux Magots*.

He is the worker whose economic lot may be miserable; yet he may also be—though one recognizes that economic conditions do affect this gravely—a happy husband and father; he may enjoy a glass of beer; he may exercise and experience kindness. Man is also the relatively well-paid government executive who believes he is working in the interest of other men and who, in that interest, sacrifices the pleasures of family and leisure. He is also the Jewish parent in the concentration camp who does what he can to save his children and, when that fails, to console them in the face of the approaching horror. Men are brutalized and victimized by other men; precisely because, in such moments, they may be more human than their persecutors, they are not necessarily reduced to the serial impotence and insignificance that Sartre so often speaks about.

Man has survived and kept a rough hold on some fairly impressive ideals precisely because he is *already* possible. To the extent that what we mean by man is connected to those ideals man has affirmed across history, one of the major questions that confronts us is not whether Marxism will make man possible but whether in a technological society being created by both Marxism and capitalism those ideals will have any relevance. Neither

Marxism, nor capitalism, nor Sartre has paid enough attention to the possibility that the economic development which is supposed to liberate man may deliver him up to a world which is boring, ugly, and dull—a world where free men cannot breathe clean air or drink pure water or find spaces where they can be alone. In a world whose citizens live under common menaces, the defense and prolongation of ideology ultimately seems irrelevant to human needs.

The particular position in which Sartre has found himself as an intellectual explains a great deal about the ways in which he has expressed himself, the kinds of issues he has discussed, and the method he has evolved over the years for the examination of issues and events. That career expresses a dilemma that most intellectuals have had to face at some point in their lives. If they choose to remain on the sidelines of events, looking at them and commenting on them but not actively involved in working with them, they risk slipping into an essential indifference or else having no effect on the direction events take. If they become actively involved in the management and direction of events, they may cease to be intellectuals. The question comes down to what ivory towers are for. Are they impregnable fortresses into which one retreats? Or are they towers one mounts, with some difficulty, in order to see better?

In Sartre's case the dilemma has produced something which looks like a compromise. His own absence from events in the 1930s was given a very significant meaning when he, along with the rest of his countrymen, was caught up automatically in the events of Munich and after. Once he had escaped from the prisoner of war camp, he returned to Paris firmly determined that he would not again avoid commitment; over the years that determination has known shifts and minor retreats, but it has remained fairly firm and evolved to a point where he asserts that the intellectual or writer, since he is no different from other men, has no right to stay away from the struggles in which those other men are involved. The intellectual's project is the same as humanity's; it is expressed in a particular form of endeavor.

That form, however, seems to be somewhat more than a little different since it can only be carried on at some distance from the struggle. The intellectual is associated with the struggle in a way which allows him to evaluate it; the worker is associated with the struggle in order to obey the orders of the leaders in whom he has placed his confidence. He cannot disobey them without breaking the solid front his cause demands. The intellectual cannot blindly obey anyone without risking the possibility of betraying the workers' interests; he is their spokesman against the possible malfunctioning of their leaders' initiatives. The hope is that the intellectual's association with the

Communist movement will be something like Tito's relations with the Kremlin: friendly but independent, in the same camp but not in the same tent. The further hope is that this association will gradually be recognized as so beneficial in keeping vision clear and purpose sharp that it will become part and parcel of the movement's inner struggle.[18] In the interim what proves the intellectual's commitment and loyalty is his total and unyielding opposition to the other camp.

Others, who at some point had sought to maintain a similar position vis-à-vis Marxism, abandoned it. Aron, Merleau-Ponty and Camus each decided that there was too much confusion and too much vagueness in trying to associate one's analytic powers with the need to make constant allowances for one of the camps while persistently blaming the other. In such exercises, humanity seemed to lose. Humanity, which was so strong a concept for Camus, has been a much less strong one for Sartre. The evil must know who they are lest, if they are left alone, they think they are making some contribution to the good; the good will not emerge when all men recognize—this had been Camus's hope—that their humanity is more important than their camp allegiance. The good will emerge and humanity will enter its first moment as humanity when the right camp wins.

There is more to it than that. On the one hand, Sartre does not believe in objectivity except as the refuge to which the bourgeois mind retreats when it becomes uncomfortable with reality. There it cultivates, not reality, but its own purity, its own need not to be involved with and possibly soiled by history. There, too, it cultivates its ego, making use of whatever is at its disposal to perform the appropriate rites of purification. But when the chips are down, the dice tossed, and ivory towers under siege, the "objective" mind will declare its allegiance and, like Flaubert, retreat into the bourgeois camp because that camp promises to respect the cherished "objectivity." The "objective" intellectual is suspect because he does not really want to serve. He wants to use his supposed objectivity as the excuse for not serving; he wants to preserve a privileged position, which means he wants to be distinguishable from other men. He thereby exercises a freedom of choice which separates him essentially from the workers; he can withdraw, the worker cannot. Were Sartre to abandon the broader meaning of the Communist cause, he would demolish the foundation

18. In his essay on Yugoslavia, Sartre wrote: " 'You must explain', Tito says, 'you must explain without stopping'. That is true on the condition that you don't paste the explanation onto consciousness like a plaster, but rather seek to have the explanations discovered by the consciousnesses themselves, on the condition that the interest elucidated, with a conscious understanding of its implications, is not a means whereby the leaders seek to stabilize their control but rather is a springboard for future exigencies; on the condition that the dogma of bureaucratic infallibility is replaced by a perpetual self-criticism which the leaders will exercise on themselves" (*Sit. VII*, p. 64). All of the *CRD* is an effort to show the advantages of such a program; one cannot say that it or Tito's "explanations" have met with unqualified success in Yugoslavia.

on which his mature life has been erected. Involvement, too, it turns out, has its forms of purity.

Ultimately, Sartre seems to look upon himself as an artisan whose purpose is to create a coherent image of man. In the end what he presents, though he abhors Platonism, is something like Plato's probable story: a whole truth, constructed as much as possible out of the whole cloth of reality, whose purpose is to provoke. In an interview with Madeleine Chapsal, he showed that the original terms of his interest in Dos Passos had never completely disappeared from his vocabulary; what has happened to the original Dos Passos is another issue. Describing what the aim of literature should be, Sartre said:

> Man lives surrounded by his images. Literature gives him a critical image of himself. . . . It is a critical mirror. Show, demonstrate, represent. That's what commitment is. After that has been done, people look at themselves and do what they want (*Les Ecrivains en personne,* p. 225).

The intention, of course, is that, having looked at themselves in the particular critical mirror he holds up before them, people will shudder and want to change. The further intention is to keep producing mirrors so that readers will never be able to do what they want *comfortably.* The hope is that the artisan, by the very nature and constancy of his activity, will have a singularly open and pertinent attitude to the reality he contemplates. What he conveys will not simply be something he imposes on reality but something reality imposes on him. In his essay on Wols, Sartre wrote, summing up this process: "Whatever models he may have chosen, the painter will never make them say what they are without learning in the same stroke what he is" ("Doigts et non-doigts," *Sit. IV,* p. 414). The world must be seen as it is; a direction must be found for it; the possibility of following that direction depends very much on the capacity of the individual. Seeing it and the world, he must discover whether he has the energy to pursue the direction proposed. If his response is affirmative, he must decide whether and how he will expend that energy, knowing that he will never be able to declare firmly, as he encounters the world, whether there will be gain or loss.

No one of the criticisms or hesitations I have expressed, nor indeed the ensemble of them, can destroy the *power* of Sartre's work. That is, I find, its most striking characteristic. From the relentless argument of *La Transcendance de l'Ego,* through the forceful integrity of the stories, novels, and plays, to the vast and sometimes infuriating reaches and depths of the *Critique de la raison dialectique,* the reader is in the presence of a passion that is usually at the height of its commitment, of a vision that rarely underestimates the strength of the opposition, and of an honesty which, though it wanders, never loses sight of its proposed goal: the liberation of man. Sartre may exasperate the reader and wear him down; he never bores him. This is not because he seeks to be urbane and render his argument glib and palatable, but because he has an uncanny ability for anticipating objections and a distressing gift for stimulating uneasiness. The distress and the uneasiness are the readers'. Some argue with Sartre and some insult him. But argument and insult demonstrate just what his power is: the casual reader does not emerge unscathed from the world he depicts; a serious reader emerges changed. The world can never again look so comfortable, the old intellectual assurances can never be allotted the same truth, the ways of the known world can never again he accepted at their face value. It is not surprising that many a younger reader, finishing "L'Enfance d'un chef," has put away, as Burnier tells us, the idea of growing a moustache. What is surprising and unsettling is that some have not.

For what Sartre represents is humanity's impatience in one of its most splendid expressions, its fatigue with moderate voices and calm solutions, its frustration with virtues which disguise vice, its belief that the nonsense has gone on too long and that the time for radical change is thus grievously overdue. In the *Critique de la raison dialectique* Sartre has defined man as the sum of all the impossibilities that define him negatively, which means that man is the creature whose unattained goals tell us more about what he is and why he must be impatient than do the sum of all humanity's accomplishments. The same definition can be applied to Sartre's work. As a whole it is defined by what has not been achieved. If such a judgment contains any suggestion of failure, the reasons for the failure cannot be found in Sartre. They are in the world—in its steady temptation to let go, in its persistent refusal to live reasonably, in its ugly habit of justifying misery. There is little letting go and less deliberate unreason in Sartre.

Only in making a comparison between how he has operated and how the world has gone can we see the immensity of the task he has set for himself and can we understand how crucially important it is that such tasks be undertaken. He is, as he affirmed in *Les Mots*, a man among men; but he is also, contrary to his further affirmation, worth a good deal more than many men. His particular value can be seen in his understanding—it has been the chief guideline of his life—that if he is free, humanity is not.

New Haven-Paris-Haines Falls-Middletown
1966–1970

Bibliography

There is a character in Boris Vian's novel, *L'Ecume des jours*, who finds himself driven to frustration and then to despair as he tries to keep track of the speeches and writings of his idol, Jean-Sol Patre. This character's difficulties begin in the first years of his intellectual hero's activity; had the disciple not died an untimely death, he might have abandoned Patre and sought to record the utterances of a less prolific author.

The critic who seeks to make a comprehensive listing of the works of Jean-Paul Sartre can understand the frustration of Vian's enthusiast. He can also appreciate the recent herculean efforts of Michel Contat and Michel Rybalka whose bibliography, *Les Ecrits de Sartre* (Paris: Gallimard, 1970), appeared shortly after my text had gone to the printer. Their work is thorough and indispensable; it also has Sartre's endorsement as a listing which contains all the works known to him as well as a few he had forgotten. The authors—for *Les Ecrits de Sartre* is indeed a book and not merely a compilation—have elected a format which makes a biography of a bibliography. They have listed texts in chronological order, have given full bibliographical details, and have supplied succinct summaries for each work. Their publication clearly supersedes previous bibliographies, the most notable of which are:

Douglas, Kenneth. *A Critical Bibliography of Existentialism: The Paris School. YFS* special monograph (1950).
"Sartre's Work in French and English" (*YFS*, no. 30 [1963]).
"Essai de Bibliographie (*Livres de France* 17, no. 1 [January 1966]).

Les Ecrits de Sartre also supersedes the bibliography I had originally prepared for this book. As a result of the work of Contat and Rybalka, I have simplified mine since it was neither possible nor necessary to attempt what would have been an inadequate duplication of their labors. The following lists all the published texts of Sartre, exclusive of interviews and of some other materials I have judged to be of marginal interest. Readers wishing more detailed bibliographical information will wish to consult *Les Ecrits de Sartre* where their research will be very much aided by the excellent indexes Contat and Rybalka have prepared. The book also contains in appendixes some texts of Sartre which are not otherwise available.

My bibliography of secondary sources is *selected* and not necessarily select. It reflects my own readings and also aims at presenting a cross section of materials which still seem to have a high degree of relevance to Sartre's overall thought. Many essays, once useful, have been excluded because the range of their conclusions is no longer pertinent to the evolution of Sartre's thought. A few titles have been included for "historical" reasons.

They have been chosen because they mirror the polemical opposition Sartre has met at various points in his career. I have listed them not only to suggest ways of finding out how the other side has seen Sartre but also to indicate how many other sides there have been. They range from orthodox Christian to orthodox Communist; the language, if not the specific ideas, is remarkably similar.

I am grateful to Barbara Hall Christen for her vigilance in helping me correct the galleys of this bibliography.

An asterisk indicates an edition which is quoted in my own text.

1. WORKS BY SARTRE, INCLUDING ESSAYS WHICH HAVE APPEARED IN BOOK FORM (*arranged alphabetically by title of work*)

L'Affaire Henri Martin. Commentary by Sartre; texts by Hervé Bazin. Paris: Gallimard, 1953.

L'Age de raison. Paris: Gallimard, 1945.* Vol. 1 of *Les Chemins de la liberté.*
    Age of Reason. Translated by Eric Sutton. New York: Knopf, 1947.

Bariona. Privately multigraphed, 1962, 1967. Reprinted in *Les Ecrits de Sartre*, pp. 565–633. Play written while Sartre was a prisoner of war.

Baudelaire. Précédé d'une note de Michel Leiris. Paris: Gallimard, 1947. Collection Idées, 1963.*
    Baudelaire. Translated by Martin Turnell. Norfolk, Conn.: New Directions, 1950.

"La Chambre." *Mesures* 3, no. 1 (1938): 119–49. Also in *Le Mur.*

Les Chemins de la liberté. Paris: Gallimard, 1945–49. See: *L'Age de raison, Le Sursis, La Mort dans l'âme,* and "Drôle d'amitié."

Critique de la raison dialectique. Précédé de *Question de méthode.* Paris: Gallimard, 1960.*
    Search for a Method. The Sartrean Approach to the Sociology and Philosophy of History. Translation by Hazel Barnes of *Question de méthode.* New York: Knopf, 1963.
    The Philosophy of Jean-Paul Sartre. Edited and with an introduction by Robert Denoon Cummings. New York: Random House, 1965. An anthology which contains passages from the *CRD* not otherwise available in English.

Descartes 1596–1650. Introduction et choix de textes par Sartre. Geneva-Paris: Traits, 1946. Introduction included in *Situations I.*

Le Diable et le Bon Dieu. Paris: Gallimard, 1951.*
    Lucifer and the Lord. Translated by Kitty Black. London: H. Hamilton, 1952.

The Devil and the Good Lord. Translated by Sylvia and George Leeson. New York: Knopf, 1960.

"Drôle d'amitié." *TM*, 49–50 (1949).* A fragment from *La Dernière Chance*, the unfinished fourth volume of *Les Chemins de la liberté.*

L'Engrenage. Paris: Nagel, 1948. A scenario.

In the Mesh. Translated by Marvyn Sabill. London: Dakers, 1954.

Entretiens sur la politique. With David Rousset and Gérard Rosenthal. Paris: Gallimard, 1949.

Esquisse d'une théorie des émotions. Paris: Hermann, 1939. 2d ed., 1948.

The Emotions, Outline of a Theory. Translated by Bernard Frechtman. New York: Philosophical Library, 1948.*

L'Etre et le Néant. Paris: Gallimard, 1943.

Being and Nothingness. Translated and with an introduction by Hazel Barnes. New York: Philosophical Library, 1956.*

L'Existentialisme est un humanisme. Paris: Nagel, 1946.

Existentialism. Translated by Bernard Frechtman. New York: Philosophical Library, 1947.

Explication de "L'Etranger." Paris: Palimugre, 1946.

L'Homme et les choses. Paris: Seghers, 1947. Also in *Situations I.* About the poet Francis Ponge.

Huis-clos. Paris: Gallimard, 1945. Also in *Théâtre.* Paris: Gallimard, 1947.*

Huis-clos. A film directed by Jacqueline Audry, 1954.

No Exit. A film directed by Pedro Escudero and Tad Danielewski. Argentina, 1962.

Huis-clos. A recording produced by Moshe Naim. Deutsche Grammophon Gesellschaft, no. 43.902/3, 1966.

In Camera. Translated by Stuart Gilbert. London: H. Hamilton, 1946.

No Exit. Translated by Stuart Gilbert. New York: Knopf, 1947.

L'Imaginaire, psychologie phénoménologique de l'imagination. Paris: Gallimard, 1940, 1960. Collection Idées, 1966.*

The Psychology of Imagination. Translated by Bernard Frechtman. London: Rider, 1949.

L'Imagination. Paris: Librairie Félix Alcan, 1936.*

The Imagination. Translated by Forrest Williams. Ann Arbor: University of Michigan Press, 1962.

"Intimité." *NRF* 299 (1938): 187–200. Also in *Le Mur.*

Les Jeux sont faits. Paris: Nagel, 1947. A scenario.

Les Jeux sont faits. A film directed by Jean Delannoy, 1947.

The Chips Are Down. Translated by Louise Varèse. New York: Lear, 1948.

Kean. Adaptation by Sartre of the play by Alexandre Dumas. With the Dumas text. Paris: Gallimard, 1954.*

   Kean. Translated by Kitty Black. London: H. Hamilton, 1954.

   Kean. Translated by Sylvia and George Leeson. New York: Knopf, 1960.

   Kean. A film directed by Vittorio Gassman, 1957.

Literary and Philosophical Essays. Translated by Annette Michel. New York: Criterion Books, 1955. A gathering of essays selected from *Situations I, II, III*.

Les Mains sales. Paris: Gallimard, 1948.*

   Les Mains sales. A film directed by Fernand Rivers, 1952.

   Dirty Hands. Translated by Lionel Abel. New York: Knopf, 1949.

   Crime Passionnel. Translated by Kitty Black. London: H. Hamilton, 1950.

Marxisme et Existentialisme: Controverse sur la dialectique. With Roger Garaudy, Jean-Pierre Vigier, J. Orcel. Paris: Plon, 1962.

La Mort dans l'âme. Paris: Gallimard, 1949.* Vol. 2 of *Les Chemins de la liberté*.

   Troubled Sleep. Translated by Gerard Hopkins. New York: Knopf, 1951.

Morts sans sépulture. Geneva: Parguerat, 1956. Also published in *Théâtre*. Paris: Gallimard, 1947.*

   Victors. Translated by Lionel Abel. New York: Knopf, 1949.

   Men Without Shadows. Translated by Kitty Black. London: H. Hamilton, 1950.

Les Mots. Paris: Gallimard, 1963.*

   The Words. Translated by Bernard Frechtman. New York: George Braziller, 1964.

"Le Mur." *NRF* 286 (1937): 38–62.

Le Mur. Gallimard, 1939.* Contains: "La Chambre," "L'Enfance d'un chef," "Erostrate," "Intimité," and "Le Mur."

   Le Mur. A film directed by Serge Roullet, 1967.

   The Wall and Other Stories. Translated by Lloyd Alexander. Norfolk, Conn.: New Directions, 1948.

La Nausée. Paris: Gallimard, 1938.*

   The Diary of Antoine Roquentin. Translated by Lloyd Alexander. London: J. Lehmann, 1949.

   Nausea. Translated by Lloyd Alexander. Norfolk, Conn.: New Directions, 1950.

Nekrassov. Paris: Gallimard, 1955. A hitherto unpublished scene appears in *Les Ecrits de Sartre*, pp. 714–19.

   Nekrassov. Translated by Sylvia and George Leeson. London: H. Hamilton, 1956. New York: Knopf, 1960.

Nourritures. Suivis d'extraits de *La Nausée*. Pointes-sèches de Wols. Paris: J. Damase, 1949. Also in *Les Ecrits de Sartre*, pp. 553–56.

La Putain respectueuse. Paris: Nagel, 1946. Also published in *Theâtre.* Paris: Gallimard, 1947.*

    The Respectful Prostitute. Translated by Lionel Abel. New York: Knopf, 1949.

    The Respectful Prostitute. Translated by Kitty Black. London: H. Hamilton, 1950.

    La Putain respectueuse. A film directed by Charles Brabant and Marcello Pagliera, 1952.

Réflexions sur la question juive. Paris: P. Morihien, 1947. Paris: Gallimard, Collection Idées, 1962.*

    Anti-Semite and Jew. Translated by George J. Becker. New York: Shocken Books, 1948.

    Portrait of the Anti-Semite. Translated by Eric de Mauny. London: Secker and Warburg, 1948.

Saint-Genet, comédien et martyr. Vol. 1 of the *Oeuvres complètes* of Jean Genet. Paris: Gallimard, 1952.

    Saint Genet. Translated by Bernard Frechtman. New York: George Braziller, 1963.*

Sartre on Cuba. New York: Ballantine Books, 1961. A collection of articles which appeared in *France-Soir* from 28 June to 15 July 1960. No French book edition.

Jean-Paul Sartre répond à ses détracteurs. Grand débat avec J.-B. Pontalis et al. Présentation de Colette Audry. Paris: Editions Atlas, 1948.

Les Séquestrés d'Altona. Paris: Gallimard, 1960.*

    The Condemned of Altona. A film directed by Vittoria De Sica, screenplay by Abby Mann, 1962.

    Loser Wins. Translated by Sylvia and George Leeson. London: H. Hamilton, 1960.

    The Condemned of Altona. Translated by Sylvia and George Leeson. New York: Knopf, 1961.

Situations I. Paris: Gallimard, 1947.* Contains:

    "Aller et retour" (1944). About Brice Parain.

    "Aminadab ou du fantastique considéré comme un langage" (1943). About a novel by Maurice Blanchot.

    "A propos de *Le Bruit et la fureur.* La Temporalité chez Faulkner" (1939).

    "A propos de John Dos Passos et de *1919*" (1938).

    "M. Jean Giraudoux et la philosophie d'Aristote. A propos de *Choix des élues*" (1940).

    "L'Homme ligoté" (1944). About Jules Renard.

    "Une Idée fondamentale de *Phénoménologie* de Husserl" (1939).

    "M. François Mauriac et la liberté" (1939).

"Un Nouveau Mystique" (1943). About Georges Bataille.

"*Sartoris*" (1938). Review of Faulkner's novel.

Situations II. Paris: Gallimard, 1948.* Contains:

"La Nationalisation de la littérature" (1945).

"Présentation" (1945). Introduction to *TM* issues devoted to the USA.

"Qu'est-ce que la littérature?" (1947). Translated by Bernard Frechtman.
What Is Literature? New York: Philosophical Library, 1949.

Situations III. Paris: Gallimard, 1949.* Contains:

"La Fin de la guerre" (1945).

"Individualisme et conformisme aux Etats-Unis" (1945).

"Manhattan" (1946).

"Matérialisme et révolution" (1946).

"Orphée noir" (1948). Introduction to *Anthologie de la nouvelle poésie nègre*. Paris: Presses Universitaires.

"Paris sous l'occupation" (1944).

"Présentation" (1946). Introduction to *TM* issue devoted to the U.S.A.

"Qu'est-ce qu'un collaborateur?" (1945).

"La Recherche de l'absolu" (1948). About Giacometti's sculptures.

"La République du silence" (1946). About France under the Occupation.

"Villes d'Amérique" (1945).

Situations IV, Portraits. Paris: Gallimard, 1964.* Contains:

"L'Artiste et sa conscience" (1950). Preface to René Leibowitz' book of the same title.

"Albert Camus" (1960).

"Doigts et non-doigts" (1963). About the painter Wols.

"Gide vivant" (1951).

"Masson" (1961).

"Merleau-Ponty" (1961).

"Paul Nizan" (1960).

"Un Parterre de Capucines" (1952).

"Le Peintre sans privilèges" (1961). About Lapoujade.

"Les Peintures de Giacometti" (1954).

"Portrait d'un Inconnu" (1948). Preface to Nathalie Sarraute's novel of the same title.

"Des Rats et des hommes" (1958). Introduction to André Gorz's *Le Traître*.

"Réponse à Albert Camus" (1952).

"Le Séquestré de Venise" (1957). About Tintoretto.

"Venise de ma fenêtre" (1953).

Situations V, Colonialisme et néo-colonialisme. Paris: Gallimard, 1964.* Contains:

"L'Analyse du référendum" (1961).

"Le Colonialisme est un système" (1956).

"La Constitution du mépris" (1958).

"Les Damnés de la terre" (1961). Preface to Frantz Fanon's book of the same title.

"D'une Chine à l'autre" (1954). Preface to Henri Cartier-Bresson's book of the same title.

"Les Grenouilles qui demandent un roi" (1958). About De Gaulle's return to power.

"Nous sommes tous des assassins" (1958). About the execution of Jacqueline and Abdelkader Guerroudj.

"La Pensée politique de Patrice Lumumba" (1963).

"Portraits du Colonisé, Portrait du Colonisateur" (1957). Reviews of books by Albert Memmi.

"Le Prétendant" (1958). About De Gaulle.

"Les Somnambules" (1962). About the Fifth Republic.

"Une Victoire" (1958). About Henri Alleg's *La Question*.

"Vous êtes formidables" (1957). About torture in Algeria.

Situations VI, Problèmes du Marxisme 1. Paris: Gallimard, 1964.* Contains:

"Les Communistes et la paix" (1952–1954). Translated by Irene Clephane. *The Communists and Peace*. London: H. Hamilton, 1969.

"Faux-savants ou faux lièvres" (1950). Preface to Louis Dalmas's *Le Communisme yougoslave depuis la rupture avec Moscou*.

"La Fin de l'espoir" (1950). Preface to Juan Hermanos's book of the same title.

"Portrait de l'aventurier" (1950). Preface to Roger Stéphane's book of the same title.

"Sommes-nous en démocratie?" (1952).

Situations VII, Problèmes du Marxisme 2. Paris: Gallimard, 1965.* Contains:

"A propos de l'*Enfance d'Ivan*" (1963).

"La Démilitarisation de la culture" (1962).

"Le Fantôme de Staline" (1956–1957).

"Opération Kanapa" (1954). About Communist ideological lackeys.

"Quand la police frappe les trois coups" (1957). About the alleged suppression of Jean Genet's play *Le Balcon*.

"Le Réformisme et les fétiches" (1956).

"Réponse à Claude Lefort" (1953). Reply to an article by Lefort in *TM* 89 (1953): 1541–70. Translated by Irene Clephane. "Reply to Claude Lefort." In *The Communists and Peace*. London: H. Hamilton, 1969.

"Réponse à Pierre Naville" (1956). Reply to an article by Naville in *France-Observateur* (8 March 1956).

Le Sursis. Paris: Gallimard, 1945.* Vol. 2 of *Les Chemins de la Liberté*.
Reprieve. Translated by Eric Sutton. New York: Knopf, 1947.

Textes choisis. Edited and presented by Marc Beigbeder and Gérard Dele-
dalle. Paris: Bordas, 1968.

Théâtre. Paris: Gallimard, 1947.* Contains: *Les Mouches, Huis-clos, Morts
sans sépulture, La Putain respectueuse.*

"La Transcendance de l'Ego: Esquisse d'une description phénoménolo-
gique." *Recherches Philosophiques* 6 (1936–37). Also published as *La
Transcendance de l'Ego.* Introduction, notes, and appendixes by Sylvie
Le Bon. Paris: Vrin, 1966.
    The Transcendence of the Ego. Translated, annotated, and with an intro-
duction by Forrest Williams and Robert Kirkpatrick. New York: Farrar,
Straus, 1957.*

Les Troyennes. Adaptation and preface by Sartre. Paris: Gallimard, 1965.

Visages, Précédé de *Portraits officiels.* Avec 4 pointes-sèches de Wols. Paris:
Seghers, 1948. Also in *Les Ecrits de Sartre,* pp. 557–64.

2. Works by Sartre Published in Book Form
A Chronological Listing

"La Transcendance de l'Ego," 1936–37.
L'Imagination, 1937.
"Le Mur," 1937.
"La Chambre," 1938.
"Intimité," 1938.
La Nausée, 1938.
Le Mur, 1939. Contains, in addition to "Le Mur," "La Chambre," "Inti-
mité," "L'Enfance d'un chef," and "Erostrate."
Esquisse d'une théorie des émotions, 1939.
L'Imaginaire, 1940.
L'Etre et le Néant, 1943.
Huis-clos, 1945.
L'Age de raison, 1945.
Le Sursis, 1945.
Descartes 1596–1650, 1946.
La Putain respectueuse, 1946.
L'Existentialisme est un humanisme, 1946.
Explication de "l'Etranger," 1946.
Morts sans sépulture, 1947.
Réflexions sur la question juive, 1947.
Baudelaire, 1947.
Les Jeux sont faits, 1947.
Situations I, 1947.
Jean-Paul Sartre répond à ses détracteurs, 1948.
Visages, 1948.

Les Mains sales, 1948.
L'Engrenage, 1948.
Situations II, 1948.
La Mort dans l'âme, 1949.
Entretiens sur la politique, 1949.
Situations III, 1949.
Le Diable et le Bon Dieu, 1951.
Saint-Genet, 1952.
L'Affaire Henri Martin, 1953.
Kean, 1954.
Nekrassov, 1955.
Les Séquestrés d'Altona, 1960.
Critique de la raison dialectique, 1960.
Sartre on Cuba, 1961.
Bariona, 1962.
Controverse sur la dialectique, 1962.
Les Mots, 1963.
Situations IV, 1964.
Situations V, 1964.
Situations VI, 1965.
Situations VII, 1965.
Les Troyennes, 1965.
Textes choisis, 1968.

3. OTHER WRITINGS BY SARTRE (*arranged alphabetically*)

"L'Affaire Thorez." *TM* 63 (1951): 1343–44.

"American Novelists in French Eyes." *Atlantic Monthly* 178, no. 2 (1946): 114–18.

"L'Ange du morbide." *La Revue sans titre* (January 1923). Also in *Les Ecrits de Sartre*, pp. 501–5.

"A nos lecteurs." *TM* 102 (1954): 1923–24.

"A propos de l'Existentialisme: mise au point." *Lettres* (Geneva) 3, no. 1 (1945): 82–85. Also in *Les Ecrits de Sartre*, pp. 653–58.

"L'Art cinématographique." Originally published as a brochure by the Lycée du Havre (1931). Also in *Les Ecrits de Sartre*, pp. 546–52.

"Avoir faim, c'est déjà vouloir être libre." *Caliban* (October 1948).

"Brecht as a Classic." *World Theatre* 7, no. 1 (1958): 11–19. French text reprinted in *Les Ecrits de Sartre*, pp. 720–29.

"C'est pour nous qui sonne le glas." *Caliban* (April 1948).

"La Chronique de Jean-Paul Sartre." *Europe* 198 (1939): 240–49. On Nabokov, de Rougemont, and Charles Morgan.

"Un Collège spirituel." *Confluences* 1 (1945): 9–18. About Baudelaire.

"La Conscience de classe chez Flaubert." *TM* 240 (1966): 1921–51; 241 (1966): 2114–53.

"Conscience de soi et connaissance de soi." *Bulletin de la Société Française de Philosophie* 42, no. 3 (1948): 49–91.

"La Conspiration." *NRF* 302 (1938): 842–45. Review of Nizan's book.

"Débat chez M. Moré." *Dieu Vivant*, 4 (1945). About Georges Bataille.

"De la vocation de l'écrivain." *Neuf*, Revue de la Maison de Médicine, 2 (1950): 35–36. Also in *Les Ecrits de Sartre*, pp. 694–98. Pages from the manuscript of *Saint-Genet* which were not included in the published book.

"De partout on veut nous mystifier." *La Gauche* 4 (1948).

"Détermination et liberté." Conference delivered at Rome in 1964. Also in *Les Ecrits de Sartre*, pp. 735–45.

"Drieu la Rochelle ou la haine de soi." *Les Lettres Françaises* (clandestine mimeographed edition) (6 April 1943). Also in *Les Ecrits de Sartre*, pp. 650–52.

"Ecrire pour son époque." *TM* 33 (1948): 2113–21. Also in *Les Ecrits de Sartre*, pp. 670–6.

"L'Ecrivain et sa langue." *Revue d'Esthétique* 3–4 (1965): 306–34.

"La Faim au ventre, la liberté au coeur." *La Gauche* 1 (1948): 15–30.

"Flaubert: du poète à l'Artiste." *TM* 243 (1966): 198–253; 244 (1966): 423–81; 245 (1966): 599–674.

"Forgers of Myth: The Young Playwrights of France." *Theatre Arts* 30, no. 6 (1946): 324–35. Also in *Playwrights on Playwriting*. Edited by Toby Cole. New York: Hill and Wang, 1960. A rudimentary French version, "Pour un théâtre de situations," appears in *Les Ecrits de Sartre*, pp. 683–84.

"Julius Fucik." *Les Lettres françaises* (17 June 1954). Also in *Les Ecrits de Sartre*, pp. 709–13. On torture.

"L'Homme au magnétophone." *TM* 274 (1969): 1813–19. Commentary on a psychoanalytic session.

"Introduction." *TM* 253 *bis* (1967): 5–11. On Arab-Israeli problems.

Introduction to *Les Fleurs du mal* by Charles Baudelaire. Paris: Le Livre de Poche, 1961.

Introduction to *L'Inachevé* by André Puig. Paris: Gallimard, 1970.

Introduction to *Liberty Ship* by Suzanne Normand. Paris: Nagel, 1945.

Introduction to *Poésies* by Stéphane Mallarmé. Paris: Gallimard, 1966.

Introduction to *Le Problème moral et la pensée de Sartre* by Francis Jeanson. Paris: Editions du Myrte, 1947.

Introduction to *La Promenade du dimanche* by Georges Michel. Paris: Gallimard, 1967.

Introduction to *Trois générations* by Antonin Liehm. Paris: Gallimard, 1970.

"Jeunes d'Europe, unissez-vous." *La Gauche* 3 (1948): 16–30.

"Jésus la Chouette, professeur de province." Fragments from a novel. Published under the pseudonym Jacques Guillemin. *La Revue sans titre* 2 (1923); 3 (1923); 4 (1923). Unpaginated. Also in *Les Ecrits de Sartre*, pp. 506–16.

"Les Jours de notre vie." *TM* 51 (1950): 1153–68. With Merleau-Ponty.

"Légende de la Vérité." *Bifur* (8 June 1931). Also in *Les Ecrits de Sartre*, pp. 531–45.

"Une Lettre de Jean-Paul Sartre." *Marxisme et philosophie de l'existence* by Roger Garaudy, pp. 110–13. Paris: Presses Universitaires, 1960.

"La Libération de Paris: Une semaine d'apocalypse." *Clartés* 9 (1945): 1. Also in *Les Ecrits de Sartre*, pp. 659–62.

"Manifeste." *Combat* (31 December 1947).

"Les Mobiles de Calder." *Alexander Calder.* Paris, Galerie Maeght, 1946. Also in *Situations III.*
  English translation and abridgement in *Art News* 46, no. 10 (1947): 22, 55.

"*Moby Dick* d'Herman Melville." *Comoedia* 1 (1941). Also in *Les Ecrits de Sartre*, pp. 634–37.

"La Mort dans l'âme, pages de Journal." *Exercice du silence.* Brussels: Librairie du Centre, 1942. Unpaginated. Also in *Les Ecrits de Sartre*, pp. 638–49. Deals on an autobiographical level with some of the situations which also appear in *La Mort dans l'âme.*

"New Writing in France." *Vogue* (May 1945): 84–86.

"Nick's Bar, New York City." *Caliban* (July 1948). Also in *Les Ecrits de Sartre*, pp. 680–82.
  "I Discovered Jazz in America." *Saturday Review of Literature* 30, no. 48 (1947): 48–49.

"Notes sur le théâtre." *Paris-Théâtre* 166 (1961): 2–5.
  "Beyond Bourgeois Theatre." *Tulane Drama Review* 5, no. 3 (1961): 3–11.

Les Orgueilleux. A film directed by Yves Allégret. Scenario by Sartre (1953).

"Père et fils." *Livres de France*, 17, no. 1 (1966): 19–23. About Flaubert.

"Présence noire." *Présence africaine* 1 (1947): 28–9. Also in *Les Ecrits de Sartre*, pp. 684–87.

"Présentation." *TM* 276 *bis* (1969): 5–6. About Greece.

"Le Processus historique." *Gazette de Lausanne* (8 February 1947). Also in *Les Ecrits de Sartre*, pp. 676–79.

Que peut la littérature? Paris: Collection 10/18, 1965. Sartre's untitled contribution appears on pp. 107–27.

"Réponse à François Mauriac." *Le Figaro Littéraire* (7 May 1949). Reply to Mauriac's "La Politique de M. Sartre." *Le Figaro Littéraire* (25 April 1949).

"Réponse à M. Mauriac." *L'Observateur* (19 March 1953). Anti-Semitism in Russia.

"Réponse à Marcel Péju. *TM* 194 (1962): 181–89. About Péju's exclusion from the editorial board of *TM*.

"La Responsabilité de l'écrivain." *Conférences de l'UNESCO*. Paris: Fontaine, 1947, pp. 57–73.

"Saint-Georges et le dragon." *L'Arc* 30 (1966): 35–52. About Tintoretto.

"Jean-Paul Sartre on the Nobel Prize." *New York Review of Book*s (17 December 1964).

"Sculptures à *n* dimensions." Introduction to the *Catalogue* of an exhibit of works by David Hare. Paris: Galerie Maeght, 1947. Also in *Les Ecrits de Sartre*, pp. 663–69.

Les Sorcières de Salem. A film directed by Raymond Rouleau. Scenario and dialogue by Sartre (1957). Based on Arthur Miller's *The Crucible*.

"The Theory of the State in Modern French Thought." *The New Ambassador* (Paris) 1 (1927): 29–41.

"La Théorie de l'Etat dans la pensée française moderne." Translated from the English translation by Maya Rybalka. *Les Ecrits de Sartre*, pp. 517–30.

Tribunal Russell. Paris: Gallimard, 1967–68. 2 vols.

Vol. 1; *Le Jugement de Stockholm*. Texts by Sartre: "Discours Inaugural," pp. 25–34; "Réponse à M. Dean Rusk," pp. 184–85.

Vol. 2; *Le Jugement final*. Text by Sartre: "Motivation du Jugement sur le génocide," pp. 349–68. Also appears as "Le Génocide." *TM* 259 (1967): 953–71.

On Genocide. Boston: Beacon Press, 1968.

"L'Universel singulier." *Kierkegaard vivant, Colloque organisé par UNESCO* (April 1964). Paris: Gallimard, 1966, pp. 20–63.

4. ARTICLES AND BOOKS ABOUT SARTRE (*listed alphabetically by author*)

Albérès, René Marill. *Jean-Paul Sartre*. Paris: Editions Universitaires, 1953, 1960.

Philosopher without Faith. Translated by Wade Baskin. New York: Philosophical Library, 1961.

Anders-Stern, Guenther. "Emotion and Reality." *Philosophy and Phenomenological Research* 10 (1950): 553–62.

L'Arc 30 (1966). *Jean-Paul Sartre.*

Arnold, A. James. "*La Nausée* Revisited." *French Review* 39, no. 2 (1965): 199–213.

Aron, Raymond. "La Lecture existentialiste de Marx. A propos de la *Critique de la raison dialectique.*" In *D'une Sainte Famille à l'autre*, pp. 32–67. Paris: Gallimard, 1969.

———. "Sartre's Marxism." Translated by John Weightman. In *Marxism and the Existentialists*, pp. 164–76. New York: Harper and Row, 1969. See also pp. 19–41: "Sartre and the Marxist-Leninists." Translated by Helen Weaver.

Audry, Colette. "Connaissance de Sartre." *Cahiers* de la Compagnie Madeleine Renaud—Jean-Louis Barrault 3, no. 13 (1955): 5–111.

———. *Sartre et la réalité humaine.* Paris: Seghers, 1966.

Ayer, A. J. "Novelists-Philosophers: V—Jean-Paul Sartre." *Horizon* 12 (1945): 12–21; 101–10.

Barnes, Hazel E. *The Literature of Possibility: A Study in Humanistic Existentialism.* Lincoln (Nebraska): University of Nebraska Press, 1959.

———. *An Existentialist Ethics.* New York: Knopf, 1968.

Bataille, Georges. "Jean-Paul Sartre et l'impossible révolte de Jean Genet." *Critique* 65 (1952): 819–32; 66 (1952): 946–61.

Bauer, George Howard. *Sartre and the Artist.* Chicago: The University of Chicago Press, 1969.

Beaujour, Michel. "Sartre and Surrealism." *YFS* 30 (1963): 86–95.

Beauvoir, Simone de. *Privilèges.* Paris: Gallimard, 1955. See "Merleau-Ponty et le pseudo-sartrisme," pp. 201–72.

———. *Mémoires d'une jeune fille rangée.* Paris: Gallimard, 1958.
Memoirs of a Dutiful Daughter. Translated by James Kirkup. Cleveland: World, 1959.

———. *La Force de l'âge.* Paris: Gallimard, 1960.
The Prime of Life. Translated by Peter Green. Cleveland: World, 1962.

———. *La Force des choses.* Paris: Gallimard, 1963.
Force of Circumstance. Translated by Richard Howard. Cleveland: World, 1965.

Beigbeder, Marc. *L'Homme Sartre, essai de dévoilement préexistentiel.* Paris: Bordas, 1947.

Blanchet, André. *La Littérature et le spirituel.* Paris: Aubier, 1959. See "Comment Jean-Paul Sartre se représente *Le Diable et le Bon Dieu*," pp. 253–66, and "La Querelle Sartre-Camus," pp. 269–79.

Blin, Georges. "Jean-Paul Sartre et Baudelaire." *Fontaine* 59 (1947): 3–17;
60 (1947): 200–16.

Brochier, Jean-Jacques. "Le Dossier Sartre." *Magazine Littéraire* 5 (1967):
6–20.

Brombert, Victor. *The Intellectual Hero; Studies in the French Novel,
1880–1955*. Philadelphia: Lippincott, 1961. See "Sartre and the Existentialist Novel: The Intellectual as Impossible Hero," pp. 181–203.

———. "Sartre et la biographie impossible." *Cahiers de l'Association In-
ternationale des Etudes Françaises* 19 (1967): 155–66.

Brun, Jean. "Un Prophète sublime à la recherche d'un message: Jean-Paul
Sartre." *Cahiers du Sud* 364 (1961–62): 287–95.

Burnier, Michel-Antoine. *Les Existentialistes et la politique*. Paris: Gallimard, 1966.

Campbell, Robert. *Jean-Paul Sartre ou une littérature philosophique*. 2d ed.
Paris: P. Ardent, 1956.

Catesson, Jean. "Théorie des ensembles pratiques et philosophie." *Critique*
167 (1961): 343–46.

Caute, David. *Communism and the French Intellectuals, 1914–1960*. New
York: Macmillan, 1964.

Champigny, Robert. *Stages on Sartre's Way, 1938–1952*. Bloomington, Ind.:
Indiana University Press, 1959.

———. *Pour une esthétique de l'essai*. Paris: Collection Situations, 1968.

———. "Langage et littérature selon Sartre." *Revue d' Esthétique* 19
(1966): 123–29.

Collins, James. *The Existentialists, A Critical Study*. Chicago: Regnery,
1952. See "Sartre's Postulary Atheism," pp. 38–79.

Contat, Michel. *Explication des "Séquestrés d'Altona" de Jean-Paul Sartre*.
Paris: Archives des Lettres Modernes, 1968.

Contat, Michel, and Rybalka, Michel. *Les Ecrits de Sartre*. Paris: Gallimard,
1970.

Cranston, Maurice. *Jean-Paul Sartre*. New York: Grove Press, 1962.

Desan, Wilfrid. *The Tragic Finale: An Essay on the Philosophy of Jean-Paul
Sartre*. Cambridge, Mass.: Harvard University Press, 1954.

———. *The Marxism of Jean-Paul Sartre*. New York: Doubleday, 1965.

Doubrovsky, Serge. "Sartre and Camus: A Study in Incarceration." *YFS* 25
(1960): 85–92.

———."Jean-Paul Sartre et le mythe de la raison dialectique." *NRF* 105
(1961); 106 (1961); 107 (1961).

Dreyfus, Dina. "Jean-Paul Sartre et le Mal radical: De *L'Etre et le Néant* à la *Critique de la raison dialectique.*" *Mercure de France* 1169 (1961): 154–67.

Earle, William, et al. *Christianity and Existentialism.* Evanston, Ill.: Northwestern University Press, 1963. See "Man as the Impossibility of God," pp. 82–112.

Falk, Eugene H. *Types of Thematic Structure. The Nature and Function of Motifs in Gide, Camus, and Sartre.* Chicago: University of Chicago Press, 1967.

Faye, J.-P. "Sartre entend-il Sartre?" *Tel Quel* 27 (1966): 9–16.

Fell, Joseph P. III. *Emotion in the Thought of Sartre.* New York: Columbia University Press, 1965.

Fergnani, Franco. "Marxismo ed esistenzialismo nell'ultimo Sartre." *Il Pensiero Critico* 1 (1959): 48–78.

Fitch, B. T. *Le Sentiment d'étrangeté chez Malraux, Sartre, Camus, Simone de Beauvoir.* Paris: M. J. Minard, 1964. See "Le Mirage du moi idéal— *La Nausée* de Jean-Paul Sartre," pp. 95–139.

Foucault, Michel. "Foucault répond à Sartre." *La Quinzaine Littéraire* 46 (1968): 20–22. See also "Une Mise au point de Michel Foucault." *Ibid.* 47 (1968): 21.

Gorz, André. "De la conscience à la praxis." *Livres de France* 17, no. 1 (1966): 3–7.

Greene, Norman N. *Jean-Paul Sartre: The Existentialist Ethic.* Ann Arbor: University of Michigan Press, 1960.

Grene, Marjorie. *Dreadful Freedom. A Critique of Existentialism.* Chicago: University of Chicago Press, 1948.

Grubbs, Henry A. "Sartre's Recapturing of Lost Time." *Modern Language Notes* 7 (November 1958): 512–22.

Hardré, Jacques. "Jean-Paul Sartre, Literary Critic." *Studies in Philology* 40, no. 1 (1958): 98–106.

Hervé, Pierre. *Lettre à Sartre et quelques autres par la même occasion.* Paris: Table Ronde, 1956.

Houbart, Jacques. *Un Père dénaturé, essai critique sur la philosophie de Jean-Paul Sartre.* Paris: Julliard, 1964.

Jameson, Frederic. *Sartre: The Origins of a Style.* New Haven: Yale University Press, 1961.

Jarrett-Kerr, Martin. "The Dramatic Philosophy of Jean-Paul Sartre." *Tulane Drama Review* 1, no. 3 (1957): 41–48.

Jeanson, Francis. *Le Problème moral et la pensée de Sartre.* Prefatory letter by Sartre. Paris: Seuil, 1947. 2d ed. with new chapter, "Un Quidam nommé Sartre," 1965.

———. *Sartre par lui-même.* Paris: Seuil, 1955. Revised edition. 1961.

———. *Sartre.* Paris: Desclée de Brouwer, 1966.

———. "Le Théâtre de Sartre ou les hommes en proie à l'homme." *Livres de France* 17, no. 1 (1966): 8–13.

Jolivet, Régis. *Les Doctrines existentialistes de Kierkegaard à Jean-Paul Sartre.* Paris: Editions de Fontenelle, 1948.

———. *Le Problème de la mort chez M. Heidegger et Jean-Paul Sartre.* Paris: Editions de Fontenelle, 1950.

———. *Sartre ou la théologie de l'absurde.* Paris: Fayard, 1965.

Kanapa, J. *L'Existentialisme n'est pas un humanisme.* Paris: Editions Sociales, 1947.

Laing, R. D., and Cooper, D. G. *Reason and Violence. A Decade of Sartre's Philosophy, 1950–60.* New York: Humanities Press, 1964.

Laurent, Jacques. *Paul [Bourget] et Jean-Paul [Sartre].* Paris: Grasset, 1951.

Lévi-Strauss, Claude. *La Pensée sauvage.* Paris: Plon, 1962. See "Histoire et dialectique," pp. 324–38.

Lichtheim, George. *Marxism in Modern France.* New York: Columbia University Press, 1966.

Lilar, Suzanne. *A propos de Sartre et de l'amour.* Paris: Grasset, 1967.

Magny, Claude-Edmonde. *Les Sandales d'Empédocle.* Neufchâtel: La Baconnière, 1945. See "Sartre ou la duplicité de l'Etre," pp. 105–73.

Manser, Anthony. *Sartre, A Philosophic Study.* London: The Athlone Press, 1966.

Maulnier, Thierry. "Jean-Paul Sartre et le suicide de la littérature." *La Table Ronde* (1948): 195–210.

———. "L'Ironie de Jean-Paul Sartre." *La Table Ronde* 73 (1954): 37–48.

Merleau-Ponty, Maurice. *Les Aventures de la dialectique.* Paris: Gallimard. See "Sartre et l'ultra-bolchevisme," pp. 131–271.

Morot-Sir, Edouard. "Sartre's Critique of Dialectical Reason." *Journal of the History of Ideas* 22, no. 4 (1961): 573–81.

Murdoch, Iris. *Sartre, Romantic Rationalist.* New Haven: Yale University Press, 1953.

Naville, Pierre. *L'Intellectuel communiste, à propos de Jean-Paul Sartre.* Paris: M. Rivière, 1956.

La Nouvelle Critique 173–74 (1966): 96–198. "Sartre, est-il Marxiste?"

Nelson, Robert J. *The Play within a Play. The Dramatist's Conception of His Art.* New Haven: Yale University Press, 1958. See "The Play as Lie," pp. 100–114.

Paissac, Henry. *Le Dieu de Sartre.* Paris: Arthaud, 1950.

Pierce, Roy. *Contemporary French Political Thought.* London, Oxford University Press, 1966. See "Jean-Paul Sartre: Existentialist Marxist," pp. 148–84.

Peyre, Henri. *The Contemporary French Novel.* New York: Oxford University Press, 1955. Rev. ed. 1967.

———. *Jean-Paul Sartre.* New York: Columbia University Press, 1968.

Plantinga, Alvin. "An Existentialist's Ethics." *Review of Metaphysics* 12, no. 2 (1958): 235–56.

Poulet, Georges. *Le Point de départ.* Paris: Plon, 1964. See "*La Nausée* de Sartre," pp. 216–36.

Prince, G. J. *Métaphysique et technique dans l'oeuvre romanesque de Sartre.* Geneva: Droz, 1968.

Rau, Catherine. "Aesthetic Views of Sartre." *Journal of Aesthetics and Art Criticism* 10 (1950): 139–47.

Reinhardt, Kurt F. *The Existentialist Revolt.* New York: Ungar, 1952, 1960. See "The Ape of Lucifer: Jean-Paul Sartre," pp. 156–76.

Richter, Liselotte. *Jean-Paul Sartre.* Berlin: Colloquium Verlag, 1961.

Roy, Claude. *Descriptions critiques.* Paris: Gallimard, 1949. See pp. 161–89.

Salvan, Jacques Léon. *To Be or not to Be. An Analysis of Jean-Paul Sartre's Ontology.* Detroit: Wayne State University Press, 1962.

Simon, Pierre Henri. *L'Homme en procès.* Neufchâtel: La Baconnière, 1949. See "Sartre ou la navigation sans étoiles," pp. 53–92.

Spielgelberg, Herbert. *The Phenomenological Movement, A Historical Introduction.* 2 vols. The Hague: Martinus Nijhoff. See "The Phenomenology of Jean-Paul Sartre," 2, pp. 445–515.

Thody, Philip. *Jean-Paul Sartre: A Literary and Political Study.* New York: Macmillan, 1961.

Troisfontaines, Roger. *Le Choix de Jean-Paul Sartre, exposé de "L'Etre et le Néant."* Paris: Aubier, 1945.

Tulane Drama Review 5, no. 3 (1961): 3–57. "Theatre of Jean-Paul Sartre."

Varet, Gilbert. *L'Ontologie de Sartre.* Paris: Presses Universitaires, 1948.

Warnock, Mary. *The Philosophy of Sartre.* London: Hutchinson, 1965.

Yale French Studies nos. 1, 10, 16, 30.

Index